৭৮১

New Directions in Faulkner Studies
FAULKNER AND YOKNAPATAWPHA
1983

New Directions
in Faulkner Studies

FAULKNER AND YOKNAPATAWPHA, 1983

EDITED BY
DOREEN FOWLER
AND
ANN J. ABADIE

UNIVERSITY PRESS OF MISSISSIPPI
JACKSON

1985

NOV

*This book has been sponsored by
The University of Mississippi*

Library of Congress Catalog Number 84-40306
ISBN 0-87805-220-8
ISBN 0-87805-221-6 (pbk.)

Contents

Introduction

With Faulkner scholarship burgeoning all over the country and all over the world and with articles on Faulkner multiplying seemingly exponentially, the 1983 Faulkner and Yoknapatawpha Conference tried to respond to this explosion of scholarship with its conference topic—the assessment of the current status of Faulkner criticism. In the heat of a Mississippi August, the leading names in Faulkner scholarship converged on Oxford, Mississippi, home of William Faulkner and the University of Mississippi, to participate in the tenth of a series of annual conferences honoring the Mississippi author. Throughout the conference, both formally in the papers contained in this volume and informally in discussion, the recognized authorities in Faulkner scholarship addressed these questions: what has Faulkner criticism so far accomplished? what directions should meaningful scholarship take? and, finally, where do we seem to be getting off track?

The French critic André Bleikasten, author of two major critical works on Faulkner, leads off the discussion with a critique of past critical methods and a recommendation for future scholarship. Too often, in the past, Bleikasten opines, critics have approached Faulkner with standards appropriate for judging realists, as if Faulkner were a traditional old-fashioned novelist. For this reason, there has been too much critical concern with what the text is presumed to say, with its "moral message," rather than with what it is, how it functions, what it does. To date, for example, little has been written on the aesthetic dimensions of

Faulkner's text, and few critics have addressed such key questions as—what happens to us when we read Faulkner? how can
Faulkner be read? how should he be read? Such paths, Bleikasten notes, may be more fruitful than more traditional critical
methods which attempt to explain and interpret Faulkner.

Another scholar who, like Bleikasten, voices misgivings about
certain kinds of critical treatments of Faulkner is Thomas L.
McHaney. In "Faulkner and Modernism: Why Does It Matter?"
McHaney takes issue with those critics who seem to read Faulkner as they would a Southern traditionalist, a romantic realist, or
a primitive writer. By reason of his background, biography, and
the conventions of his art, McHaney argues, Faulkner is a modernist, and those who do not treat him as such may misunder-
stand his work.

While Bleikasten and McHaney identify lines of critical inquiry which they see as unproductive, other scholars suggest
approaches to Faulkner that have not yet been often tried and
might lead to fresh insights. For example, Michael Millgate,
author of the seminal critical work *The Achievement of William
Faulkner*, notes that while much has been said about individual
Faulkner works, little is known about the meaning of Faulkner's
literary career as a whole. For instance, is there, Millgate asks, a
consistent design to Faulkner's career? Attempting to answer his
own question, Millgate poses a thought-provoking hypothesis:
perhaps in the mid-1920s Faulkner had a visionary experience,
and in that single moment of vision all of the novels in his
Yoknapatawpha sequence were born. According to Millgate,
Soldiers' Pay and *Mosquitoes* predate the moment of vision,
while the non-Yoknapatawpha fiction was born of a different,
experimental, creative surge, a surge more urgent but less reliable than that which spawned the Yoknapatawpha tales.

Another approach to Faulkner which, like the broad perspective recommended by Millgate, might provide fresh insights
into Faulkner's complex fictional world is the application of
Freudian principles to Faulkner's novels. Taking for the title of
his essay Quentin Compson's revealing phrase, " 'The Dungeon

Was Mother Herself,'" Noel Polk sketches the rich possibilities which Freudian interpretations of Faulkner might yield. Many of Faulkner's characters, Polk shows, seem almost to have stepped out of the pages of Freud's case histories; given such startling similarities, the application of Freudian psychology may well enrich our understanding of these characters.

Yet another direction for Faulkner scholarship is endorsed by Berndt Ostendorf, Professor of American Cultural History at the University of Munich. In "An Anthropological Approach to Yoknapatawpha," Ostendorf shows that Faulkner's methods, concerns, and goals are essentially those of an anthropologist. What an anthropologist proposes to do in the field, Faulkner achieves with words; and a knowledge of anthropology can enhance our understanding of this accomplishment.

Several papers read at the conference pick up where Ostendorf leaves off by considering issues of interest to an anthropologist as they relate to Faulkner. For example, in her study, "Faulkner's Relationship to Jews," Ilse Dusoir Lind first ascertains the social and historical reality of Faulkner's relationships with Jews during his life and then examines Faulkner's attitude towards Jews as it appears in the fiction. Interestingly, Lind finds that Faulkner's later fiction, fiction written during and after the Holocaust, shows evidence of philo-Semitism. While Lind takes up the subject of Jews, Arthur F. Kinney focuses on another culture-related issue—families in Faulkner's fictional world. Dubbing Faulkner "the premier novelist of family," Kinney finds that, in a sense, all of Faulkner's novels are about the need for family and, ultimately, about the one family to which all human beings belong. Another speaker, James Hinkle, also undertakes a kind of anthropological study. Setting off on a long field trip that takes him from San Diego to New York and, finally, to Charlottesville, Hinkle searches for and finds authentic pronunciations of Yoknapatawphan names. In his quest for authenticity, Hinkle goes to the source—the University of Virginia's tapes of Faulkner reading from his work and answering students' questions. From these tapes of the author's own voice, Hinkle prepares a sometimes surprising list of forty-nine indisputably authentic Yoknapatawphan pronunciations.

Many of those who spoke at the conference—among them James B. Carothers, James G. Watson, P. V. Palievsky, and Panthea Reid Broughton—called for more studies in areas of Faulkner scholarship that have so far failed to attract much scholarly interest. Carothers, for example, a short story writer himself, pointed out that now (with the recent publication of *Uncollected Stories of William Faulkner*) more of Faulkner's stories are available for study than ever before and that, while certain stories ("A Rose for Emily" and "The Bear") have received an inordinate amount of scholarly attention, other stories of merit have been largely overlooked by the scholarly community. Also overlooked, according to James Watson, are Faulkner's letters, which are of special interest because of their confluence with the fiction. Often, Watson maintains, Faulkner's real-life letters (or versions of them) would find their way into the author's fiction. Another as yet untapped area of investigation is Faulkner's nonfiction prose. Two conference speakers— P. V. Palievsky, the well-known Russian specialist in American literature, and Panthea Reid Broughton—address this topic. According to Palievsky, Faulkner's remarks, in essays, speeches, and interviews, about the art of writing are "an integral part of the author's oeuvre" and sometimes the most successful way Faulkner achieved the main goal of his career; and Panthea Broughton, who surveys Faulkner's reviews from 1920 to 1925, shows that during these years the author seemed to absorb and assess various critical principles, gradually formulating his own artistic creed.

In a sense, the conference ended where it began: André Bleikasten had led the discussion with a call for more studies about Faulkner's technique, and the three concluding speakers all focus, as Bleikasten had urged, on not what but how Faulkner writes. Sonja Bašić, Professor of English at Zagreb University in Yugoslavia, compares and contrasts Faulkner's modes of discourse in *The Sound and the Fury* and *Absalom, Absalom!*;

Sergei Chakovsky, Research Fellow at the A. M. Gorky Institute
of World Literature in Moscow, explores the textual implications
of Faulkner's use of characters as narrators; and Judith Bryant
Wittenberg closes appropriately with a study of Faulkner's endings.

While the papers contained in this volume constitute the major endeavor of the conference, a word should be said about the
numerous special events which also formed an important part of
the 1983 Faulkner and Yoknapatawpha Conference. These
events included guided tours of Lafayette County and North
Mississippi; exhibits of the University's Faulkner holdings and a
special exhibit of L. D. Brodsky's collection, with Brodsky himself on hand to describe his most recent acquisitions; discussion
sessions for conference participants, including a special session
led by Oxford residents who knew William Faulkner; black
music sung by Sister Thea Bowman and the Christian Unity
Community Choir; a symphony performance celebrating Faulknerian themes written by Kenneth Haxton, conducted by
Ronald F. Vernon, and sung, in part, by Sister Thea Bowman; a
multiarts program performed by Elaine Fruchter and the University Dancers; a dramatic reading of passages from Faulkner's
novels; a book exhibit sponsored by the University Press of
Mississippi; a picnic on the grounds of Rowan Oak, Faulkner's
antebellum home; the dedication, by the Yoknapatawpha Arts
Council, of a Faulkner plaque for the Lafayette County Courthouse; a buffet supper held at St. Peter's Episcopal Church;
numerous parties sponsored variously by the Friends of the Performing Arts, the Yoknapatawpha Arts Council, and Square
Books; an art exhibition entitled *Yoknapatawpha Through
Other Eyes;* a series of Faulkner films presented by the University's Communication and Resource Center; and, finally, four
slide presentations—"Knowing William Faulkner," narrated by
the author's nephew, Jimmy Faulkner, and Jo Marshall; "The
Architecture of Yoknapatawpha: The Built Environment of William Faulkner's World," narrated by Thomas S. Hines; "The
Architecture of a Yoknapatawpha Town," narrated by Hubert H.

McAlexander; and "Viewing Faulkner's South," narrated by Eva Miller.

With each successive year, more names are added to the list of those who contribute their time and energy to help make the University of Mississippi's Faulkner and Yoknapatawpha Conference a significant and successful enterprise. Limitations of space make it impossible to identify here all those involved in the manifold conference-related activities. But to all the individuals who, each year, contribute to the conference in an attempt to make the life work of William Faulkner more widely known and more deeply appreciated, the editors wish to express their gratitude. One individual in particular, however, must be singled out for special thanks—Evans Harrington, Chairman of the Department of English, who, with unfailing good will and Faulknerian endurance, has directed the conference each year from its inception, ten years ago, to the present day.

Doreen Fowler
University of Mississippi
Oxford, Mississippi

Presentation of Faulkner Plaque

Lafayette County Courthouse
Sunday, July 31, 1983

CHESTER MCLARTY

Mr. Chairman, Honored Guests, Ladies and Gentlemen:
What would Bill Faulkner think about being the center of all this commotion here this afternoon?
This was the question that would not go away earlier this month when I began thinking about what I might say here today. It finally occurred to me that this might provide a point of departure for a few observations on Bill's perception of himself and his work.
Throughout his life he remained a very private person. As his fame spread, this desire for privacy brought him into repeated conflict with the national and international press—though his relations with the local paper were generally good. In the process of shielding himself from encroachment he appeared to be eccentric, antisocial, and downright contemptuous of the opinion of others.
These public perceptions were reinforced by several highly publicized episodes. We have only to recall that he at first declined to go to Stockholm to receive the Nobel Prize. It was only in response to much pressure by his government, his family, and his friends that he agreed to go to Stockholm, accompanied by Jill, to receive the award.
Twenty years later he would decline with a flippant remark a dinner invitation to the Kennedy White House.
Whatever our public perceptions may be, his letters often present a much different picture: the year was 1931. Bill was not yet famous, but in that year he did become a bona fide celebrity.

The occasion, of course, was the publication in February of that year of *Sanctuary*. Whatever its artistic merit, it was literally a sensational success. Bill left Oxford in late October to attend a writers' conference at the University of Virginia. After the meeting he went on to New York. On November 13th he wrote to Miss Estelle describing his reception there. The eagerness with which he welcomed his new status is apparent.

> I have created quite a sensation. I have had luncheons in my honor by magazine editors every day for a week now, besides evening parties, or people who want to see what I look like. In fact, I have learned with astonishment that I am now the most important figure in American letters. That is, I have the best future. Even Sinclair Lewis and Dreiser make engagements to see me, and Mencken is coming all the way up from Baltimore to see me on Wednesday. I'm glad I'm level-headed, not very vain. But I don't think it has gone to my head.

We must pause to remind ourselves that his outburst of youthful exuberance was written by a mature man in his mid-thirties. Who among us, I ask, would have responded any differently?

As the years passed, Bill continued his cat-and-mouse game with the press. He always viewed his work with great detachment and seemed baffled when others insisted on focusing their attention on him rather than on his writing. It may appear a contradiction to point out that Bill could, even in the early years, insist that his writing was worthy of high praise, while maintaining that he himself was unworthy of public notice. This seeming inconsistency is resolved to some degree by a truly remarkable letter written to Joan Williams in April 1953:

> And now I realise for the first time what an amazing gift I had: uneducated in every formal sense, without even very literate, let alone literary, companions, yet to have made the things I made. I dont know where it came from. I dont know why God or gods or whatever it was, selected me to be the vessel. Believe me, this is not humility, false modesty: it is simply amazement. I wonder if you have ever had that thought about the work and the country man whom you know as Bill Faulkner—what little connection there seems to be between them. . . .

In this passage Bill is, of course, trying to explain the inexplicable. He knew the word that would have made a long explanation unnecessary, but he could not bring himself to use the word "genius." His personal modesty would not permit it.

In 1953 Bill had another of his disagreements with the press—this time it was *Life* magazine. For many years Bill had trusted local newspaperman Phil Mullen. Phil, or "Moon," as he was usually called, acted as a sort of unofficial press secretary. To vent his frustration with the influential national magazine, Bill wrote to his friend: "What a commentary. Sweden gave me the Nobel Prize. France gave me the Legion d'Honneur. All my native land did for me was to invade my privacy over my protest and my plea."

Of course Bill has been honored in his native land. In the more than two decades since his death, Bill's work has continued to attract readers and scholars alike. The fascination is undiminished. In other words, Bill's stories are doing quite well on their own. But then—Bill always knew they would!

And so we gather today to honor Bill in the personal way that is appropriate among friends. We may do so secure in the knowledge that Bill would indeed like to be recognized by the people who are so much in his debt.

And finally, with this plaque we honor ourselves. We take this means of recording for posterity our recognition of our good fortune to have had such a man among us. A man who looked at us with great compassion and wrote: "about honor, truth, pity, consideration, the capacity to endure well grief and misfortune and injustice and then endure again, in terms of individuals who observed and adhered to them not for reward but for virtue's own sake, not even merely because they are admirable in themselves, but in order to live with oneself and die peacefully with oneself when the time comes. . . ."

I count it a great honor to present at this time this plaque on behalf of the Yoknapatawpha Arts Council and the Mississippi Arts Commission to the citizens of Oxford and Lafayette County and to Yoknapatawphans everywhere.

"But above all, the courthouse: the center, the focus, the hub;
sitting looming in the center of the county's
circumference like a single cloud in its
ring of horizon, laying its vast shadow to the
uttermost rim of horizon;
musing, brooding, symbolic and ponderable,
tall as cloud, solid as rock, dominating all:
protector of the weak,
judiciate and curb of the passions
and lusts, repository and guardian
of the aspirations and the hopes . . ."

WILLIAM FAULKNER

Requiem for a Nun, 1951

YOKNAPATAWPHA ARTS COUNCIL
MISSISSIPPI ARTS COMMISSION
1983

Reading Faulkner

ANDRÉ BLEIKASTEN

"Today the essential question is no longer that of the *writer* and the *work*," wrote Philippe Sollers in 1968, "but that of *writing* and *reading*."[1] Fifteen years later his statement has lost none of its relevance. Not only has the Author been bereft of the godlike attributes which had been his ever since the Romantics (in France vanguard critics periodically announce his death), but even the Text, a later fetish launched by the New Critics in the forties, has now ceased to inspire unanimous reverence. Critical attention has been increasingly diverted from these two relatively stable entities, and focused instead on the elusive processes of writing and reading. Indeed, the rapid and massive growth, on either side of the Atlantic, of audience-oriented theory and criticism may well be the most significant and appears at the very least to be the most spectacular event among recent developments of critical inquiry. Not so long ago the reader was still considered by most critics a nonentity, a blank figure at the receiving end of literary communication. No one cared about his status, nor was his activity felt to be worthy of serious investigation. Then, almost overnight, he was promoted from his half-forgotten peripheral position to a starring role. Benign neglect suddenly gave way to fevered concern. For some time now the reader has been subjected to zealous theoretical speculation from a wide variety of angles (rhetorical, semiotic, structuralist, phenomenological, psychoanalytical, sociological, historical, etc.), and studies devoted to the topic have been multiplying over the past years at an almost inflationary rate.

1. *Logiques* (Paris: Editions du Seuil, 1968), 237–38.

1

The current vogue of reader and reading-oriented criticism should not blind us, however, to its essential pertinence. After all, literary critics are also readers, and are readers to begin with. Reading is the precondition for any kind of critical activity and the starting point of any attempt at aesthetic evaluation. So much, of course, is taken for granted by everybody; yet this is no valid reason to leave it unexamined, and, if it is right and proper that critics should reflect on the premises and procedures of their enterprise and perform their duties with a modicum of epistemological awareness, one can only wonder how the question of reading could ever be evaded.

It remains to be seen, though, how the various theories of reading now available can be used for purposes of practical criticism. The theorist is not concerned with individual works as such, he only refers to them to illustrate his arguments. What he aims at is by definition the general, not the particular. The critic, on the other hand, must confront a unique object in its irreducible singularity. Yet he is also expected to account for it, to make it accessible to the language of common reason. His is therefore a paradoxical task, one he can only hope to accomplish by moving back and forth between the particular qualities of a specific text and the general categories afforded by poetics.

How, then, to address a topic like the one I have chosen with proper tact and rigor? One possible approach would be to take Faulkner's fiction as a test case, to try to see to what extent it validates—or invalidates—the working hypotheses and basic presuppositions of a given theory. But this is not the direction I wish to follow. My intention is rather to proceed from my scanty knowledge of theory and from my experience as reader and critic to ask a few questions: What happens to us when we are reading Faulkner? How can he be read? How should he be read? These questions will be raised and considered, yet I shall not presume to answer them. All I have attempted to do is to map out the contours of a still virgin territory of Faulkner criticism for future critics to explore; all I have to offer is a handful of observations and speculations, with the timid hope that they will prompt more sharply focused and more closely argued analysis.

Readings all have their beginnings, however often they may be rebegun. So let me begin at the beginning: What is it like to read one of Faulkner's novels *for the first time?* This is admittedly an embarrassing question, perhaps even one impossible to answer, for the cultural and individual variables involved are so many that any general statement must at once come under suspicion. If we ask individual readers, their answers will vary according to which novel was read first, and it seems safe to assume that the reader who started with *The Sound and the Fury* or *Absalom, Absalom!* and the one who started with *The Unvanquished* or *Intruder in the Dust* will have gone through very different experiences. And even if everyone were to start with the same book, there would still be a wide range of responses, for the obvious reason that every reader is bound to respond in terms of his own personality. Any extrapolation about first readings may therefore seem hazardous. Their idiosyncratic character, however, should not be overemphasized: in many significant ways first readings are also very much alike, and as it is always with the excitement of a first encounter that our engagement with a writer's work begins, their common properties deserve careful consideration. Surprisingly enough, none of the theories of reading elaborated over the past years, not even those based on the premises of phenomenology, properly acknowledges the qualitative difference between first and second readings. Yet it might be argued that the first reading of a literary text is in a sense the only true one. What comes after are *re*readings, ever farther removed from the stab of wonder we experienced in reading it for the first time. Later readings will be deeper, keener, richer, and put us in fuller possession of the text. What differentiates the initial reading from its successors is precisely the impossibility of any appropriation. When someone reads a poem or a novel for the first time, he does not possess it nor is he possessed by it; he simply lets it be. As Maurice Blanchot notes:

> The act of reading does not produce anything, nor does it add anything; it lets be that which is; it is a form of freedom, not the freedom that grants being or takes it away, but a freedom that welcomes and

consents, that says yes, that can say nothing but yes, and, in the
space opened up by this acquiescence, it allows the unsettling decision of the work to assert itself, it lets the work affirm its existence—
and nothing more.[2]

I am well aware that most contemporary theorists, whatever
their persuasion, would probably object to Blanchot's non-
dialetic, nontransactional reading concept and denounce the extreme idealism of its underlying assumptions. Those with Freudian leanings would deny the possibility of free acquiescence and
recall that all readings, especially all readings of fiction, are
processed through fantasy, while those more culturally oriented
would insist on the primacy of codes and conventions and of the
prestructured expectations of the reader. Indeed, one could easily take a stand diametrically opposed to Blanchot's and contend
that there is no such thing as pure, spontaneous reading, that no
one ever reads alone nor even ever reads anything for the first
time, since whatever we read is perceived in terms of what we
already know and tested against the background of all the books
we have read before. So Blanchot's description of the act of
reading may well be the evocation of a utopia; it points to what
reading might be under ideal conditions: a state of dynamic
passivity, of alert stillness, as when we listen to music, which
would allow us to open ourselves to what a text *is* and experience
it in pure immediacy. Such readings are perhaps approximated
in rare moments of grace, but few readers will ever be capable of
the ego-free readiness it would take to turn reading into a
smooth, unbroken gesture of mute assent. More often than not
the actual reading of fiction is an innocuous form of embezzle-
ment, and there is just no way of preventing people from reading *Sanctuary* as a pornographic novel or *As I Lay Dying* as a
sociological document.

Misappropriations such as these reduce reading to vulgar consumption or gross manipulation; they cheapen what they prey
upon, foreclosing the aesthetic experience which literature is

2. *L'Espace littéraire* (Paris: Gallimard, "Idées," 1968), 257–58.

supposed to induce. For a worthwhile aesthetic experience to occur, one's reading must at the very least partake in some measure of Blanchot's "light and innocent Yes" *(le Oui léger, innocent, de la lecture).*[3] Only if it develops into an open, sensitive, and generous response to the text, to the delicate miracle of its being there, and becomes a true welcoming of its strangeness, of its otherness, is reading reading in the fullest and finest sense: a brush with the unknown or a refreshing of the familiar, a dark or dazzling adventure through the mystery of words, an experience, in short, that can be as unsettling as the accidents of a journey or the hazards of love. Such reading, whatever the time of its occurrence, will always be a *first* reading, true to the spirit of wonder of all beginnings. For it is with wonder that it always begins. When we read a great novel for the first time, something happens to us, and we feel both uncomfortable and excited because we don't know what it is. Swept along on a tide of words, we are not yet in a position to gain mastery over the text and to fit it into our prior reading experience, and it is this very helplessness that guarantees our sustained exposure to the troubling impact of an unfamiliar presence. Thus, on reading *The Sound and the Fury* for the first time, we shall feel baffled and betrayed insofar as our desire to make sense of what we read is thwarted. Yet, unless we are at once turned off (a hypothesis not to be excluded), we shall also be drawn into a text, respond to its pulse and power, to the dynamics of its unfolding and to the raw intensities of sensation and emotion it conveys. To read *The Sound and the Fury* is first and foremost to participate in an ongoing process, not to consume a finished product. Later, rereading the novel in a cooler, more distanced mood, we can attempt to discover the law of its turbulence, but before trying to understand it, we must have gone through it, experienced it in all its phases—from the inarticulate urgency of Benjy's section through the brooding inwardness of Quentin's and the fumbling fury of Jason's to the shrill

3. Ibid., 261.

dissonances of the novel's close. And chances are that our brains, hearts, and nerves will never register it as sharply as in the bewilderment of the first reading, and that we shall never feel as close to the sense of loss and chaos from which the whole novel springs as at the time when Benjy's pathetic "trying to say" is replicated by our own "trying to read."

All novelists, of course, seek to surprise their audience, and surprise within reasonable limits is what most fiction readers expect. With Faulkner, however, there is more than surprise or even puzzlement. Disorientation, for his readers, is not a provisional condition, but a permanent state resulting from the deliberate shattering of nearly all fictional codes, and so calls for different adjustments. As Leon Edel observed twenty years ago, a novel like *The Sound and the Fury* requires in fact "a new way of reading fiction."[4]

Whether this requirement has been met remains an open question. As new reading habits are slow to form, innovative writers always run the risk of being misread by their contemporaries, and the fact that Faulkner, though never a popular novelist in the way Fitzgerald and Hemingway were, won worldwide recognition before his death is no proof at all that his work was read with proper respect for its newness. Nor should it be taken for granted that the new readers postulated by his fiction have acquired existence twenty years after his death.

At this point it may be useful to refer to the distinction made by nearly all contemporary theorists between the actual reader and the potential, hypothetical reader encoded in a writer's text.[5] If applied to conventional fiction, the distinction would be

4. "How to Read *The Sound and the Fury*," in Stanley Burnshaw, ed., *Varieties of Literary Experience: Eighteen Essays in World Literature* (New York: New York University Press, 1962), 242.

5. Over the past years the concept of the reader-in-the text has become increasingly popular. However, what is meant by the concept varies significantly from one theorist to another: there is Wolfgang Iser's "implied reader," Stanley Fish's "informed reader," Michael Riffaterre's "superreader," and Jonathan Culler's "qualified reader," to name only a few. In my own use of the "encoded" or "implied" reader, which I find preferable to the other terms because of their lack of ambiguity, I refer to the reader programmatically inscribed in the textual structure, not to be confused with the ideal reader intended by the real or "implied" author, though the distinction is not always easily made.

of little use, as such fiction, tailored to meet the common reader's culture-bound demands, is precisely meant to cancel it. In innovative fiction, on the other hand, the gap between the actual reader and the encoded one will be perceptible from the outset, and the more daring a writer's inventiveness, the wider the gap. Now Faulkner was beyond doubt an innovative novelist, and he clearly belongs with the small group of American and European writers who, during the first half of the twentieth century, radically altered the means and ends of fiction and opened up possibilities which other novelists have been exploring ever since. It should be remembered, though, that Faulkner's experimentalism was much less of a *parti pris* than that of some of his peers, and was not pursued consistently throughout his career. While Joyce departed ever farther from established literary models and ended up dismantling language itself, Faulkner would change methods according to occasion and need, and traditional procedures were to him as valid as modern ones if they happened to suit some specific purpose he had in mind. If considered in its development, his oeuvre therefore fails to offer the kind of gradual radicalization we find in Joyce or, to take an earlier example, in Henry James. His novels are not only remarkable for their variety; they differ so strongly in their aesthetic conception and effects that one may be tempted to call them heterogeneous: *The Sound and the Fury, As I Lay Dying*, and *Absalom, Absalom!* were received at the time of their appearance as aggressively modern books, and are indeed unique experiments, which have lost little of their subversive potential over the years. Not so Faulkner's later novels: many of them still attest to his passionate concern for formal innovation, and some of them, like *The Hamlet* and *Go Down, Moses*, may be counted among his finest and most original achievements, yet the demands they make upon their readers are not quite of the same order as those made by his early masterpieces.

Another matter worth considering in this connection is Faulkner's ambivalent and variable relationship to the actual audience of his day. In his most fiercely idiosyncratic books, which in my view are also his most fascinating ones, Faulkner may be said to have written *against* his audience rather than *for* it, and if his own testimony is to be believed, there was at least one time in his career when he did not care about his readers at all, the intended addressee of his writing being no one but himself: this was the time when, after the rejection of *Flags in the Dust*, he "shut a door between [himself] and all publishers' addresses and book lists," and said to himself, "Now I can write. Now I can make myself a vase like that which the old Roman kept at his bedside and wore the rim slowly away with kissing."[6] This is how Faulkner came to write *The Sound and the Fury*, a book not even thought of as a book when it was started.[7] Its writing was an experience of almost absolute creative freedom, merging the writer with his reading double in narcissistic self-embrace, a borderline experience never to be repeated. For once Faulkner had decided not only to become a writer but to make his living by his pen, he could not afford to ignore his audience altogether. If he was to win public recognition and to achieve commercial success, he had to make some allowance for the expectations of the ordinary reader. And this is what he did in the novel he began only a few months after completing the typescript of *The Sound and the Fury*. He now "began to think of books in terms of possible money,"[8] and, revealingly enough, in trying to find out what might sell, his first move was to conjecture his potential reader: "I took a little time out, and speculated what a person in Mississippi would believe to be current trends, chose what I thought was the right answer and invented the most horrific tale I could imagine and wrote it in about three weeks."[9] Admittedly Faulkner's notorious introduction to the Modern Library reissue of *Sanctuary* must be read with due caution, and we all know how seriously the novel's first version was revised "to make out of it something which would not shame *The Sound and the Fury*

6. "William Faulkner: An Introduction for *The Sound and the Fury*," James B. Meriwether, ed., *The Southern Review*, N.S., 8 (October 1972), 710.
7. See "An Introduction for *The Sound and the Fury*," 710: "When I began it I had no plan at all. I wasn't even writing a book."
8. "Introduction" to *Sanctuary* (New York: Modern Library, 1932), v.
9. Ibid.

and *As I Lay Dying* too much."[10] *Sanctuary* is by no means the lurid potboiler it was once pretended to be. Still, it does rely, albeit with a fair amount of irony, on the melodramatic stock-in-trade of Gothic fiction and on the repertoire of the thriller, and so does build on familiar generic expectations, even though it frustrates them in the end. All in all, *Sanctuary* is assuredly more of a popular novel than *The Sound and the Fury* and did in fact sell much better than its immediate precursor.

The *Sound and the Fury* and *Sanctuary* point in almost emblematic fashion to the conflicting claims of Faulkner's writing: the imperious demands arising out of his innermost creative self and the no less stringent ones of the reading public upon whom he depended for economic survival. It could be argued that Faulkner's writing was at its purest and freshest when he listened to his inner voices (to what he called his "demons") and to them alone, and that it was at its weakest when he attempted to conform to current standards and to cater to popular taste, as he did, reluctantly but repeatedly, in particular when manufacturing short stories for the national magazines. There is some truth, obviously, to this view, and Faulkner himself, to judge by some of his private statements, would probably have subscribed to it. It is only a half-truth, though, since for Faulkner it was not simply a matter of choosing between mutually exclusive possibilities. What he actually needed was a strategy that would allow him to have it both ways, to engage his reader and hold his interest without forfeiting his integrity and his originality as a writer. If the reader in the text could be made to reach out toward the actual reader, and if the latter could be maneuvered into sharing the former's assumptions, then the conflict would be solved to the benefit of both parties.

Faulkner was thus led to evolve a dual strategy of *aggression* and *seduction,* designed both to shake the reader out of his complacencies and to win him over to different, more demanding but also more rewarding ways of reading fiction. There is

10. Ibid., vii.

unfortunately no way of measuring its effects with preciseness, yet the mere existence of a Faulkner audience, in America and all over the world, is, I think, evidence enough of its efficiency. Not that it works with everybody: Faulkner will probably never be a novelist for the masses. Yet, if I may for once generalize from my own observations, first responses to his fiction, whether positive or negative, are in most cases remarkably strong, and more often than not they will be typically Faulknerian mixtures of amazement and outrage, which is hardly surprising, as even in the late twentieth century most readers approach fiction with the criteria of the nineteenth-century novel. Their "horizon of expectations" is that of realism: if they agree to enter a text of fiction, they do so to be carried immediately beyond it into a pseudoreality; all they care about is the gratifying experience of an *illusory* world, in which they can recognize "lifelike" characters and "lifelike" events. This, incidentally, is also the approach to Faulkner taken by a number of critics ever since Malcolm Cowley, to whom the creation of Yoknapatawpha County is the writer's supreme achievement. They are in good company, since it was Faulkner's proclaimed ambition to create "a cosmos of [his] own."[11] And as a world of and for the imagination, his "cosmos" undeniably exists. But Faulkner's is not Balzac's world; it lacks the monumental solidity and deceptively self-evident autonomy of the *Comédie humaine*. With Faulkner as with Joyce or Virginia Woolf, the world is broken up into its manifold representations, so as to leave the reader puzzling about the degree of reality and relevance of what lies behind. Moreover, the mimetic illusion is undermined time and again by the indiscretion—or by what might be called the foregrounding—of Faulkner's language. His world, if it is still a world, is unmistakably a world within the word, a world so visibly conjured up by the magic tricks of its maker that it can hardly fail to draw the reader's attention to its fictional status. Small wonder, then, that

11. "Interview with Jean Stein vanden Heuvel" (1955), in James B. Meriwether and Michael Millgate, eds., *Lion in the Garden: Interviews with William Faulkner 1926–1962* (New York: Random House, 1968), 255.

he who approaches Faulkner's work with conventionally
referent-oriented expectations should feel assaulted. It almost
looks as if the novelist's most characteristic devices had been
perversely calculated to antagonize his audience in every possible way. Instead of supplying his readers with orderly narratives, in which chronology and causality are given their customary due, Faulkner prods and pushes them into thorny thickets,
compels them to grope their way through tangles of narrating
voices and temporal strands, and in some cases—*Absalom, Absalom!* at once comes to mind—the story will not even be told,
its matter remaining conjectural and its significance elusive to
the very end. Textual perspectives multiply, intersect or inter-
weave, yet fail to cohere into unified patterns. Unstable, shifting
configurations of meaning, endless circlings around an absent
center, are most of the time all we get, and in its baroque exfolia-
tions, even Faulkner's style is often little more than an eloquent
gesturing on an empty stage.

These peculiarities of Faulkner's technique and language—
the dismantling of traditional narrative, the fluid and open structures, the cultivation of semantic ambiguity and syntactic suspense—have been intriguing to readers from the beginning.
The justification usually offered by the critics is that they are
intended to make fiction-reading a more active process. To "ac-
tualize" Faulkner's fictions, it does indeed take more than "a
willing suspension of disbelief." What is requested, rather, is a
willing suspension of our reading habits and a readiness to play
the game according to new rules yet to be defined. Reading
Faulkner is not a matter of acquired skills, but of skills to be
acquired. To read his work in conformity to its own law, we must
be able both to learn and to unlearn, as we do whenever we are
summoned to adjust to new, unforeseen circumstances. Alert-
ness and flexibility are the primary prerequisites. Without them
there can be no meeting of the many challenges awaiting us on
our way. For ours is the task to dispel the obscurities, to remove
the ambiguities, to fill in the gaps, to reassemble the fragments,
and so to restore the textual web to consistency and wholeness.

Like all modern texts, Faulkner's call for the reader's diligent participation. More than that: inasmuch as they are open, un-completed structures, they invite him to avail himself of his freedom to become in turn a "producer." Yet to say that Faulk-ner's work stimulates "productive" or "creative" reading is clearly not enough, for as much could be said of the works of many others, and our concern here is not what reading Faulkner may share with the reading of other modernist (or postmoder-nist) authors, but rather what makes it unique. Besides, one has only to think of Joyce, Nabokov, Borges, or Robbe-Grillet to become at once aware of the difference. What these writers provide is aesthetic excitement of the highest order; their ap-peal, however, is first and foremost to the intellect, and the readers they are most likely to attract are sophisticates with a marked taste for recondite riddles. Such readers will of course also enjoy the playfulness of Faulkner's fictions, yet reading *The Sound and the Fury, Absalom, Absalom!*, or *Go Down, Moses* is surely more than playing games with words.

What Faulkner's strategy is intended to touch off is a reading experience that includes intense emotional involvement as well as intellectual participation. As the reader must first be jolted out of his inertia and urged to fight back, aggression is one of its modes or at least one of its moments. Seduction, however, is always at its heels. Seduction: a leading away *(se-ducere)*, a winning over, a drawing in. The sense of fascination which so many people have experienced in reading Faulkner is perhaps the most immediate effect of this unique combination of brutal-ity and bewitchment.[12] To read Faulkner is not primarily to struggle through a difficult text; it is to come under a spell, to yield to a magic flow of words and let oneself be carried away. As Conrad Aiken pointed out in his amazingly perceptive essay of 1939, Faulkner works "by a process of *immersion*, of hypnotizing

---

12. The first to comment upon this sense of fascination was André Malraux in his famous 1933 preface to the French translation of *Sanctuary*. That fascination also plays a major role in Faulkner's imaginary world is persuasively demonstrated by Michel Gres-set in *Faulkner ou la fascination* (Paris: Klincksieck, 1982).

his reader into *remaining* immersed in his stream."[13] And, as Aiken also notes, Faulkner's mesmerizing is most often successful: "the reader *does* remain immersed, *wants* to remain immersed."[14] About ten years later, Claude-Edmonde Magny, another brilliant representative of early Faulkner criticism, made similar comments on the novelist's relationship to his readers, with even greater emphasis on their complicity:

> His spell is not cast directly, he merely leaves at our disposal the tools necessary for producing the desired effects—as one discreetly leaves a revolver within the reach of a condemned man so that he may conveniently do justice to himself. We ourselves come to wish the anguish expected from us. We lend ourselves to the novel to the point where we find in it only what we deposited. In short, we accept entire responsibility for the witchcraft practised upon us.[15]

That the effects of Faulkner's fiction have been described so often in terms of magic and witchcraft or in terms of hypnosis and hallucination is certainly not fortuitous. Indeed, as these metaphors suggest, there seems to be something almost eerie about the compelling force of his art, something that again sets him apart from all other writers of his time. Among the major novelists of the twentieth century, there are quite a few who, in range of thought or depth of insight, in formal ingenuity or stylistic brilliance, are his equals, perhaps even his betters, but the sheer power that Faulkner's language achieves in its most inspired moments is unsurpassed. There is probably none of his readers that has not at some time felt its mysterious grip. Only think of the admirable openings of so many of his novels: the confusingly simple start of Benjy's monologue in *The Sound and the Fury*, the abrupt tension in the opening scene of *Sanctuary*, the suspended, dreamlike quality of the first pages of *Light in August*, or the brooding evocation of a "long still hot weary dead

13. "Faulkner: The Novel as Form," in Robert Penn Warren, ed., *Faulkner: A Collection of Critical Essays* (Englewood Cliffs, N.J.: Prentice Hall, Inc., 1966), 48. Aiken's essay first appeared in the November 1939 issue of the *Atlantic Monthly* and was also reprinted in *A Reviewer's ABC* (New York: Meridian Books, 1958).
14. Ibid.
15. "Faulkner or Theological Inversion," in *Faulkner: A Collection of Critical Essays*, 74. Translated from *L'Age du Roman américain* (Paris: Editions du Seuil, 1948).

September afternoon" at the beginning of *Absalom, Absalom!*
Openings serve to set the rules of the game to be played, and
this is precisely what Faulkner's do: not all of them push us *in
medias res,* but each time we are thrust into the middle of a text
which bears the imperious signature of its author. Faulkner's
novels take hold of us even as we resist them (and even as they
resist us), and before long we shall have given up all resistance
and turned into the consenting victims of their enchantments.
Now such a reading experience is hardly compatible with the
productivist reader models promoted by recent criticism. For
insofar as he becomes affectively involved and allows himself to
be possessed by a fiction, Faulkner's reader is clearly also a
passive reader, although his passivity is anything but inertia.

To read Faulkner, then, is to be "paradoxically rapt and alert at
the same time."[16] It is to find oneself in a state of spellbound
attention and eager expectancy—a disposition in many ways
reminiscent of that of an entranced listener. Telling and listening
are, as we know, essential activities in Faulkner's fiction, and
just as oral telling overshadows his writing, listening overshadows our reading. As many critics have already pointed out,
there is scarcely a novel of Faulkner's in which one does not get
an unmistakable sense of the spoken word, of its onrush, of its
immediacy and fluidity, of its cadences and intonations.[17]
Throughout his fiction we are listening to voices, whether they
are the secret, solitary voices overheard in the interior monologues of *The Sound and the Fury* and *As I Lay Dying* or the
persuasive public voices of his many storytellers. They are
pseudovoices, of course, voices on paper, voices in print, and so
we can only be pseudolisteners, readers under the illusion of
listening. Yet the illusion is pervasive and strong; Faulkner's
language does indeed affect us many times as if it were living
speech. Not all literary language affects us in that way, nor is it

16. *Light in August* (New York: Modern Library, 1968), 349.

17. On Faulkner's indebtedness to the Southern oral tradition, see Helen Swink,
"William Faulkner: The Novelist As Oral Narrator," *Georgia Review,* 26 (Summer 1972),
183–209.

always desirable that it should. And it would be mistaken to assume that Faulkner's achievement as a novelist rests solely on the prodigious mastery with which he used the Southern tradition of oral storytelling to his own purposes. What gives the actual measure of his genius is rather the capacity he had to incorporate at once a rich local tradition and the cosmopolitan "tradition of the new," to use the well-seasoned rhetorical wiles of the communal storyteller as well as the disruptive stratagems of the modernist, and to fuse them in a creation triumphantly his own.[18] It is to this densely textured, many-faceted creation that the reader must respond, and to respond well and fully, he will have to play the role, or rather the roles, Faulkner's texts have prepared for him, and to be both a deft decoder and a sensitive "listener."

Whether Faulkner has been read in this manner by those who are assumed to be his most competent readers—i.e., by the critics—is, it seems to me, very doubtful. Although criticism is an outgrowth of reading, it is also its antithesis, its negation. The true reader, as we have seen, is a gentle host, taking in the text in a spirit of generous welcome; the critic, on the other hand, steps back, considers it from a cool distance (a distance he takes care to argue if he is an honest critic), transforms it into an object for investigation, and while reading is a silent and solitary adventure, criticism breeds discourse and generally ends in public performance. Its very function is a public one: as a cultural institution, its major task is to accommodate and assimilate, to classify and categorize, and to filter out whatever is incompatible with accepted value systems and established patterns of intelligibility. Faulkner is, I fear, a case in point. Once it had become evident that he could no longer be ignored, everything was attempted to defuse the newness of his work, to neutralize its strangeness, to drain it of its power to disturb. Not surprisingly,

18. On Faulkner's singular relationship to modernism, see Hugh Kenner's brilliant essay "Faulkner and the Avant-Garde," in Evans Harrington and Ann J. Abadie, eds., *Faulkner, Modernism, and Film: Faulkner and Yoknapatawpha, 1978* (Jackson: University Press of Mississippi, 1979), 182–96.

Faulkner critics over the past decades have been above all *explicators* and/or *interpreters,* the former attending to particulars and doing their best to smooth things down for the reader, the latter treating Faulkner's fiction like a palimpsest and taking great pains to decipher the *ur*-text presumed to be beneath the text and from which they expect the ultimate revelation of the work's meaning. Now explanation and interpretation are surely useful and respectable activities; they have been central to literary criticism ever since its beginnings and are most likely to remain so in the future. There is no valid reason, however, to make meaning the critic's exclusive concern. Meaning is all-important as long as language is used as a mere medium of communication; it no longer is when language is diverted from its everyday pragmatic uses to be reshaped in a work of art, i.e., when it becomes *literature.* Not that writers are indifferent to the meanings of words, far from it; but more than other people they are aware of the arbitrariness of signs, and so do not take their meanings for granted. Literature, at its truest, is no bid for truth, or, rather, the only truth it conveys is that there is none upon which we might all agree. It makes us feel that our discourses on reality are only random patternings, and never stops reminding us that all meanings are fabricated, that they are nothing but the precarious fictions of our desires and the erratic impositions of our wills. The greatest novelists are not those who improve our understanding of the world; they are those who shatter it, those who make the world darker for us. Faulkner is one of them.

Yet it is from the assumption that his work radiates with positive meaning and that the determination of that meaning should be given priority that most past and present Faulkner criticism proceeds. There has been much more interest in what his fiction is presumed to *say* (its social or psychological significance, its moral "message," etc.) than in what it *is,* how it *functions,* and what it *does,* and whatever the approach, there has been throughout the same impulse to unify, to totalize, to see each of Faulkner's novels, if not the entire "saga," as an "organic whole," in which form and meaning are miraculously one. Until recently very few critics have been willing to meet Faulkner's work on its own ground, to heed its uncertainties and indeterminacies, its disjunctions and dissonances, and to acknowledge them as distinctive and vital features of his art. If Faulkner was both a restless experimenter and a skillful adapter of tradition, the former has been granted far less critical attention than the latter.

All too often Faulkner is still discussed as if he were a comfortable old-fashioned novelist à la Balzac or à la Dickens. Like so many of his readers, a substantial number of his critics still approach his fiction with the standards and prejudices inherited from the realists, and admire him above all for being a master illusionist. They give him credit for having created a "world" both colorful and true to life, teeming with memorable characters and full of exciting events, and then go on to speculate about them as if they were real people and real events: What happened in the courtroom during Goodwin's trial? What happened during Quentin's visit to Sutpen's Hundred? Who was Miss Quentin's father? How good is Dilsey? How bad is Popeye? How stupid Lena? How guilty Mink? I am not suggesting that all concern for the referential aspects of Faulkner's work is misplaced, or that all character evaluation is idle chatter. But I do think that there are other questions to be asked, other areas to be explored, and perhaps also other methods to be applied. True, over the years Faulkner has been examined from many angles; there is no shortage of thematic inquiries, no lack of psychological and sociological studies, and even his narrative strategies have come to be thoroughly scrutinized. But little has been written on the specifically aesthetic dimensions of his texts, and the quality of our experience as readers is seldom honored. In the discussion of works of fiction, more perhaps than with poetry and other literary forms, it is hard for the critic to recapture the immediate resonance of a text. Yet, if he does not recover something of the freshness of his first response, he will not be able to restore it to its exact mystery. The better critics never forget that before becoming an object of knowledge literature is an occasion for experience, and the best read not only *for* us but also *with* us.

William Faulkner:
The Shape of a Career

MICHAEL MILLGATE

You will all of you have assumed, quite correctly, that the "career" of my title refers to what dictionaries customarily define as "a person's course or progress through life," "a profession affording opportunities for advancement"—as once upon a time one used to be able to speak of "an academic career." But that usage of the word apparently doesn't date back beyond the beginning of the nineteenth century. Earlier, and still available, meanings of the word include "a race-course," "a short gallop at full speed," "a (swift) running course, as of the sun or a star through the heavens," and, more abstractly, "full speed, impetus." (I quote from the *Shorter Oxford English Dictionary*, but Webster reads almost exactly the same.) Accustomed as we are to think of an author's career as something finished and finite, as the posthumous listing of completed works, it does no harm to be reminded that the bibliographical record is simply the frozen retrospect—collected and re-collected in academic tranquillity—of what was created by the author in and through profound emotion and excitement. At the time when it was in progress that career may indeed have been a gallop at full speed, its impetus little short of headlong. That is spectacularly true, I suggest, of Faulkner's career, particularly during those extraordinarily productive years of the late 1920s and the 1930s, and I want in this paper to raise the question of whether he was, at that time and throughout his writing life, directing his energies with some deliberateness towards preconceived goals—or simply giving those energies their head, running not so much a race along a marked course as a hunt after an always elusive experience of final and absolute creative achievement, taking each unanticipated hedge as it came, looking back only at a later stage over the route he had taken, the career through which he had, so to speak, careered. "Carcassonne," often read as an early statement of creative aspiration, points in one direction: *"me on a buckskin pony with eyes like blue electricity and a mane like tangled fire, galloping up the hill and right off into the high heaven of the world."*[1] Many of the statements Faulkner made towards the end of his life point in quite another direction: after writing *Soldiers' Pay,* he told Jean Stein in 1955, he found out "that not only each book had to have a design but the whole output or sum of an artist's work had to have a design."[2]

Gary Lee Stonum[3] would have us think of a literary career as a sequence of prospective and retrospective decisions more or less consciously taken, of texts played off against one another in almost dialectical fashion, each book responding in some degree to its predecessor and predetermining in some degree the shape of its successor. He offers analogies which serve to suggest that such processes occur in conformity with general laws and may therefore be expected to manifest themselves within any career of reasonable length. But attractive and suggestive as this approach may be in many ways, the multiplicity of Faulkner's work, the sheer density of his career, renders its application to his case peculiarly resistant to effective demonstration. And by declining to consider the role of Yoknapatawpha County or indeed of any overall directive principles that might conceivably be operative, Stonum effectively sidesteps the question of whether or not there was any larger framework within which the interplay between one book and another was being conducted— any larger strategies to which such tactical maneuverings could be seen as ultimately contributive.

For those of us who do not plan our work on a long-term basis,

1. William Faulkner, *These 13* (New York: Jonathan Cape and Harrison Smith, 1931), 358.
2. *Lion in the Garden: Interviews with William Faulkner 1926–1962,* ed. James B. Meriwether and Michael Millgate (New York: Random House, 1968), 255.
3. Gary Lee Stonum, *Faulkner's Career: An Internal Literary History* (Ithaca: Cornell University Press, 1979), esp. 13–40.

who gaze around us in pleased surprise at the discovery that we
have finished something and might yet live to tackle something
else, it is not hard to think of a career as a series of events either
unrelated one to another or as related merely through contrast—in the sense that having done one sort of thing one tends
to do a different sort of thing, for variety's or self-education's or
promotion's or simply occupation's sake. Contrapuntal without
integration. And yet nothing is more obvious than that historians
and scholars are perpetually embarking upon Declines and Falls
and Oxford English Dictionaries and editions of Rousseau and
Boswell that they have no right to expect that they will see the
end of. E. H. Carr (I read in a recent review) began the writing
of his massive *History of Soviet Russia* when he was three years
older than Gibbon had been at the publication of the final
volume of his great work. And so with those writers—Balzac,
Zola, Proust—who embark upon sequences of novels whose
hoped-for completion must lie years and decades in the future.
It is true that it seems to be mostly the French who are capable
of handling such Napoleonic ambitions in Napoleonic fashion
and that the English and American examples one might cite are
altogether less impressive. Even so, it would clearly not have
been unprecedented for Faulkner to have projected a patterned
series of novels early in his career and devoted himself thereafter to its progressive realization.

There is much ground to be cleared, however, before we can
address ourselves at all usefully to the question of whether or
not, or to what extent, Faulkner does seem to have set himself
such a goal. And some ground that will perhaps never be satis-
factorily cleared. When we speak, loosely, of an author's career,
we do so in terms of publication dates. Faulkner's career, we say,
began with *The Marble Faun* (1924) and ended with *The Reivers*
(1962). Even those of us who have explored that career in detail,
however, have rarely incorporated into our sense of its main-
stream any adequate recognition of the completion of short
stories, poems, essays, and film scripts during the intervals between the publication dates of novels. By hiving such items off

into a separate category or categories we are implicitly acknowledging our own limitations, finding a way of maintaining some
sort of intellectual grasp of what must for Faulkner have been an
integral whole, a dense, teeming reality of every day.

But even a bibliographical listing which included in a single
sequence the publication dates of all of Faulkner's works, large
and small, would still be sadly inadequate as a reflection of that
reality. For it would be a record of public events only, events all
too often conditioned by the accidents of history and biography,
the exigencies of the marketplace, or the whims of editors. It
would tell us very little about the actual time devoted to the
composition and revision of particular works—about the long
gestation of A Fable, for example, the shifting complexities of the
writing and publication of the Snopes trilogy—and provide no
clear sense of how any particular work was related, in point of
time, to this or that other work. Moreover, Faulkner's tendency
to work in holograph and on the typewriter almost in tandem—
often typing up his manuscripts as he went along instead of
waiting until any single form of the work had been completed in
its entirety—makes it extremely difficult, sometimes impossible, to make statements about the detailed history of a particular text that are at once reasonably simple and reasonably accurate. And since he generally destroyed his rejected drafts, those
manuscripts and typescripts that do survive may represent only
a tiny proportion of those that were actually written. Who is to
tell, now, how far the published Requiem for a Nun of 1951 harks
back to the abortive Requiem that was projected and started in
1933? Of what kind and what length were the "three manuscripts" of which Faulkner said in 1957 that they "never did
quite please me and I burned them up"?[4] All we know about
them is that they did not refer to the period between 1870 and
1912–14.[5] And as for the impact of outside influences: Would The
Wild Palms have been differently perceived, at the time of its

4. Faulkner in the University: Class Conferences at the University of Virginia 1957–
1958 (Charlottesville: University of Virginia Press, 1959), 85.
    5. Ibid., 251–52.

publication and since, if Faulkner had been permitted to retain his preferred title, *If I Forget Thee, Jerusalem*,[6] or if Random House had accepted in 1946 his suggestion[7] that the "Wild Palms" segment be included, rather than *As I Lay Dying*, with that Modern Library reprint of *The Sound and the Fury* which for so long served as a college text? What other novels and stories would we have had if Faulkner had not felt obliged to work in Hollywood for extended periods? Was the fiction he did complete significantly affected by his Hollywood experience? Would the gap between *Go Down, Moses* (1942) and *Intruder in the Dust* (1948, but projected in 1940) have been as great if World War II had not occurred? Had there been no war, how would *The Mansion* have been narratively worked out? Would *A Fable* have been written at all?

I am not at all suggesting, of course, that Faulkner's career was the only one to have been affected by accidents and other external events that had little or nothing to do with the works themselves or with their composition—although some other novelists have had greater control over their circumstances and even (though this is more rare) over their publishers. Sir Frederick Macmillan always took the position that he could not afford to disoblige an author of Thomas Hardy's standing—for which read, at least in part, of Thomas Hardy's profitability. My point is simply—very simply—that Faulkner's career may have very imperfectly embodied his own ambitions for it and that, in any case, the standard forms of recording such a career give us very little impression of what it was like in process. A comprehensive date-book—a *Faulkner Log*, a *Days and Hours of William Faulkner*—might prove a somewhat more sensitive indicator of what Faulkner was writing when, but I suspect that what is really needed (and what I cannot, alas, offer to provide) is some elaborate graphic representation of the sequence and overlapping of

6. Thomas L. McHaney, *William Faulkner's "The Wild Palms": A Study* (Jackson: University Press of Mississippi, 1975), xiii.
7. *Selected Letters of William Faulkner*, ed. Joseph Blotner (New York: Random House, 1977), 228.

his multifarious undertakings—done in different colored inks, perhaps, or on a computer.

To accept the difficulties of comprehending Faulkner's career in anything like its full complexity need not, however, mean abandoning entirely the question of whether, and to what extent, he had from early on a strong sense of the directions he wished his work to take. Can one tell, despite the inadequacy of the evidence, whether there was a consistent design running through that intricate mesh of creative threads? Did he carry with him a conceptual map of what the completed oeuvre should ideally look like? Was he able—would he have been able—to look back after the publication of *The Reivers* and cry "It is good!" Or even, since Faulkner always had a secure sense of his own creative standing, "It is God!" To what extent, specifically, had he realized the promise of that visionary moment when, back in the middle 1920s, he "thought of the whole story at once like a bolt of lightning lights up a landscape and you see everything."?[8]

The difficulty here, of course, is that we do not know what exactly it was that Faulkner saw. The "whole story" of what? And what did he mean by "story"? Not, I think, the plots of *Light in August, Absalom, Absalom!, The Wild Palms*, or even *The Sound and the Fury*. He made the statement at the University of Virginia while responding to a question about the origins of *The Hamlet*, and we need not doubt, I think, that in the mid-1920s he foresaw "Father Abraham" and the broad pattern of events that might potentially fall into place around the career of Flem Snopes—as that career is summarized in the pages of *Sartoris*.[9] He saw the ways in which the central idea of the Snopes' progress—their spreading like a mould over cheese, as he said in a 1939 interview[10]—could provide the vehicle for an expansive sociohistorical presentation of an imaginary world based upon— by which I of course mean distorted by symbolism, fable, fan-

8. *Faulkner in the University*, 90.
9. William Faulkner, *Sartoris* (New York: Harcourt Brace, 1929), 172–73.
10. *Lion in the Garden*, 39.

tasy, satire, and humor from—the familiar actualities of his own native region. Remember that the landscape of his vision was a landscape seen not by the light of day but in the altogether less normative illumination of a nighttime lightning flash. Doubtless he saw too, in a general way, how the kinds of stories he had been hearing all his life could find a hospitable location within the loose narrative structures by which that imaginative world would be constituted, given realization and substance.

What, indeed, he seems chiefly to have glimpsed and grasped in that seminal moment was not so much a specific "story" as the possibility and promise of narrative acts on a scale commensurate with the reach of his literary ambition. He saw (even if he could not yet name) Yoknapatawpha County not simply as a region, a distinctive, personalized body of material that he could exploit in Hardyan or Andersonian fashion, but as a rich source of narrative strategies. Yoknapatawpha offered, in fact, a framework that answered superbly to his purposes as he then understood them, providing at one and the same time a device for giving coherence to a mass of perceived but as yet unabsorbed material and for providing access to an infinite range of tales and tellers. The regional definition validated the exploitation of the tale-telling convention, and that convention offered a basic situation of fictional narrator and dramatically present fictional narratee that could be exploited in many different ways and to many different ends—above all as a means of bringing the experience and emotions of the past immediately to bear upon the consciousness of the present. (It remained available, of course, throughout his career, up to and including the "Grandfather said" of The Reivers.)[11] Meanwhile the fundamental conception of a region developing and changing through time made it possible to think of narrative material from different social strata and from different dates as being at least minimally linked together through the direct experience of socially mobile central

11. William Faulkner, The Reivers (New York: Random House, 1962), [3].

characters (salesmen, lawyers, doctors, children) or through structural devices of contrastive juxtaposition.

Seized with such possibilities, Faulkner appears to have launched upon several different projects almost simultaneously—upon what eventually became the Snopes trilogy, upon a Sartoris/Benbow narrative that achieved at least fragmentary publication as *Sartoris* and *Sanctuary* (perhaps also in parts of *The Unvanquished*), and upon a series of regional short stories for which Quentin Compson was at one stage to have been the central narrator and which found partial realization in *These 13* and *Go Down, Moses*. In each instance the structural control was loose, what we have become accustomed to call episodic, and the narrative was built up in blocks that were related one to another by contrast, by regional affinity, and by the interweaving paths of the pivotal characters—Bayard Sartoris and Horace Benbow, for instance—who were themselves linked by contrast and by locality even though they might rarely or never meet. If it is easy, and familiar, enough to think of *Sartoris* in such terms—easier still when it is read in that earlier form which is now approximately available to us as *Flags in the Dust*—it is not difficult, either, to see the same terms as broadly applicable to *Sanctuary, The Hamlet, The Town*, and *The Mansion*, or even to *These 13* and *Go Down, Moses*.

The last time I was in Oxford I talked about the connections I saw between *Flags in the Dust, Sanctuary*, and *Requiem for a Nun*, and also about the role of Quentin Compson as a framework device once apparently intended by Faulkner to bring together a wide range of otherwise separate narratives whose human and regional significance would be drawn out by Quentin's intelligent and sensitive—sometimes oversensitive—responsiveness to them.[12] I don't intend to go back over that ground today—copies of *Fifty Years of Yoknapatawpha* are still

12. Doreen Fowler and Ann J. Abadie, eds., *Fifty Years of Yoknapatawpha: Faulkner and Yoknapatawpha 1979* (Jackson: University Press of Mississippi, 1980), 23–43, 90–109.

available and since I don't get a royalty I can be accused only of vanity and not of venality in bringing the volume to your attention—nor do I wish to pretend that what I said then is any the less speculative for having achieved the dubious distinction of print. But I would like, if I may, to invoke those earlier remarks as well as this evening's comments in support of my contention, undramatic as it is, that persisting throughout Faulkner's career was a major strand whose origins could, had we the documentary evidence, be traced directly back to that visionary moment of the mid-1920s.

I profoundly suspect, for example—criticism believes before scholarship demonstrates, or even, in this instance, without scholarly demonstration—that the origins of *Sanctuary* date from before the conception and completion of *The Sound and the Fury*, that it derived from an inchoate mass of partly written, partly conceptualized, narrative that also included not just "Father Abraham" and other Snopes episodes but the Sartoris material of *Flags in the Dust, The Unvanquished,* and such war stories as "All the Dead Pilots," "Ad Astra," and "With Caution and Dispatch." Horace Benbow himself may indeed have been central to much of this material, partly as a first sketch for the kind of sensitive, neurotic character, fit vehicle for streams or at least trickles of Joycean consciousness, whom Faulkner's evolving genius was shortly to transform into the Quentin Compson of *The Sound and the Fury,* more substantially as a naively crusading lawyer moving through different strata of the regional society, allied to the established power structure yet liable through choice or chance to become involved with the likes of Popeye and Miss Reba—or of Nancy Mannigoe. This, of course, was the role which Faulkner was later to assign to Gavin Stevens; and since in taking over much of Horace's background and personality Stevens seems also to have taken over some of the narratives with which he was associated, it seems feasible to think not just of *The Town* and *The Mansion* but also of *Knight's Gambit, Requiem for a Nun,* and even *Intruder in the Dust* as ultimately, if not directly, referable back to Faulkner's original 1920s conception.

By the time they eventually appeared even such works as *The Town* and *The Mansion* had of course grown to be very different from Faulkner's first idea of them. As he and the world grew older, as the Faulknerian oeuvre itself grew larger, generating its own patterns and its own dynamic, Yoknapatawpha could scarcely remain unaffected and unchanged. We are all familiar with that Author's Note to *The Mansion* in which Faulkner ingeniously but not, I think, too disingenuously justifies on grounds of long cohabitation with his characters the narrative discrepancies between that book and its predecessors in the trilogy. There is indeed an astonishing difference between *The Mansion* as published and the outline of that same novel which Faulkner supplied to Robert Haas of Random House in December 1938, when *The Hamlet* was still *The Peasants*, *The Town*, *Rus in Urbe*, and *The Mansion* itself *Ilium Falling*.[13] By the time he had completed *The Hamlet* the following fall, however, he had settled on the final titles of all three novels[14] and on a plan for the defeat of Senator Clarence Snopes.[15] That plan, or part of it, was in fact used to get Montgomery Ward Snopes into jail in *The Town*—the actual disposal of the Senator in *The Mansion* occurring within the context of historical events which Faulkner in 1939 could scarely have foreseen (and of tall tale, not to say lifted leg, contrivances that he might have done well to forget)— but such shifts in the narrative content of the books seem altogether less remarkable than the sheer fact of their projection over the long term.

What I've thus far suggested, or implied, then, is that *Soldiers' Pay* and *Mosquitoes* predated Faulkner's moment of vision (they may, of course, have contributed, positively or negatively, to its occurrence) but that several subsequent works seem to

13. *Selected Letters*, 107–9.
14. Ibid., 115.
15. *Lion in the Garden*, 40.

have derived quite identifiably from it: *Sartoris (Flags in the Dust), Sanctuary, These 13, The Unvanquished, The Hamlet, Go Down, Moses, The Town,* and *The Mansion.* Four other books, *Intruder in the Dust, Knight's Gambit, Requiem for a Nun,* and *The Reivers,* seem to fall into a secondary category as having been generated by texts that themselves figure in the primary list I have just given. And perhaps one could add *Big Woods* and *Collected Stories* as well. For all these texts I believe that one could draw a convincing stemma or family tree, showing clearly their direct descent from that moment when Faulkner saw "the whole story at once." They are, by and large, the works in which the elaboration of Yoknapatawpha County for its own sake—its geography, economy, history, demography, class-structure—is most specifically, centrally, and extensively conducted. As I suggested earlier, they also display a considerable degree of technical consistency, carrying through to the end of Faulkner's career those narrative methods and structures that had first been adopted in *Flags in the Dust.* That is not, of course, to say that they are necessarily lacking in technical finish or even in technical innovation—*The Hamlet* is one of the most brilliant of Faulkner's novels—but it is, I think, to imply that they represent, collectively, a relatively conventional strand within Faulkner's achievement as a whole, *textes de plaisir* rather than *textes de jouissance.* Dare I also venture the suggestion that they tend to embody a generally conservative set of moral positions? They comprise, for example, with the addition of a brief reference to *Light in August,* the texts upon which Noel Polk depended when speaking on "Faulkner and Respectability" at the conference held in Oxford in 1979.[16]

It is, I think, notable that most of the books on the list fall within the latter part of Faulkner's career. It has always been clear that as the years passed he became increasingly concerned to elaborate on paper his matured conception of his fictional world, to fill it out in both historical and social terms, to give it

16. *Fifty Years of Yoknapatawpha,* 110–33.

greater solidity, to strengthen (so to speak) its defenses. The Compson Appendix, his cooperation with Malcolm Cowley in the preparation of *The Portable Faulkner*, the Prologues to *Requiem for a Nun*, the projected Golden Book of Yoknapatawpha County—these were only the most obvious signals of an intention everywhere apparent. One's suspicion that this intention may have represented a resumption rather than an uninterrupted continuation of that initial Yoknapatawphan undertaking is sometimes intensified—fine as most of the later books are—by the possibility that Faulkner may from time to time (during his difficulties with *A Fable*, for example) have turned back to these long-familiar and long-pondered conceptions, and perhaps to already existing manuscripts, with a certain sense of relief or release, with the expectation of undertaking tasks that could be depended upon to be relatively straightforward, creatively manageable.

It was certainly not so in those years between *The Sound and the Fury* and *The Wild Palms* when, as I remarked earlier, Faulkner's career was indeed a gallop at full speed. If in writing *Flags in the Dust* Faulkner established his claim to a region and a setting, it was in writing *The Sound and the Fury* that he discovered the challenge and excitement, the all-absorbing passion, of the struggle with form. With *The Sound and the Fury* another Faulknerian voice—that of the modernist, the radical experimentalist and untrammelled moralist—for the first time makes itself clearly audible, and for a period of a dozen years following the completion of *Flags* it is possible to perceive the outline of a fairly regular alternation between what might be called aboriginal, essentially conservative, works on the one hand and what might be called opportunistically conceived, essentially experimental, works on the other. By "opportunistically" I simply mean seizing upon what is creatively available, *en disponibilité*—as when Faulkner speaks of having begun such novels as *The Sound and the Fury* or *Light in August* with little sense of the course they would eventually follow. Thus *Flags in the Dust* is followed by *The Sound and the Fury, The Sound and the Fury* by *Sanctuary* I, *Sanctuary* I by *As I Lay Dying, As I Lay Dying* by *Sanctuary* II, *Sanctuary* II by *Light in August.* So far so good, but (if short stories and poems are set aside) the sequence then runs *Light in August/Pylon, Pylon/Absalom, Absalom!* before returning more neatly (for argumentative purposes) to *Absalom, Absalom!/The Unvanquished, The Unvanquished/The Wild Palms,* and *The Wild Palms/The Hamlet.* Whether any significant, discussible pattern does in fact exist I'm not at all sure. After all, the short stories of these years (which cover the publication of *These 13* and *Doctor Martino*) are so important and so numerous that they cannot properly be ignored; it is also possible that Faulkner devoted more time than we now realize to the working out of his first conception of *Requiem for a Nun.* And of course there are doubts to be raised, qualifications to be registered: *As I Lay Dying,* for all the self-consciousness of its technique, may well have been organized about an aboriginal Yoknapatawphan anecdote (Faulkner always insisted that he "knew from the first"[17] where the book was going), and there can be no doubt of the profound moral intensity of *Go Down, Moses* or, as I suggested earlier, of the stylistic sophistication of *The Hamlet.* But the pattern to which I have tentatively pointed does at least suggest that Faulkner felt a tension—a counterpoint, if you like—between these two strands in his work, and that at this particular period, at least, he was being driven headlong forward not so much by the desire to stake and develop his claim to Yoknapatawpha County as by what Yeats called the "fascination of what's difficult."[18] To such an extent, indeed, that during the great culminating act of his experimentalism, the writing of *Absalom, Absalom!,* Faulkner sought resolution and release not in the completion of one of his initial Yoknapatawphan conceptions but in the rapid, straight-from-scratch composition of *Pylon,* a specifically non-Yoknapatawphan exercise based on recent events in his own personal

17. *Faulkner in the University,* 87.
18. *The Collected Poems of W. B. Yeats* (London: Macmillan, 1955), 104.

experience and possessing technical and intellectual affinities to
Absalom, Absalom! itself.

Perhaps I'm not saying more than that Faulkner seems to have
had, following *The Sound and the Fury*, two creative agendas:
the original Yoknapatawphan agenda, which called for the progressive literary colonization of his imagined world, and another,
less predictable because altogether more peremptory, which required him to realize to the fullest possible extent his personal
potential as an artist. I have alluded only in passing thus far to
the imperiousness of Faulkner's ambitions, to his need and determination to match himself against the greatest of novelists
and the most intractable of technical problems—but perhaps
such propositions scarcely need to be demonstrated and justified
to an audience such as this. My present concern, after all, is
simply to suggest that this second, self-testing, experimentalist
agenda, increasingly set aside during Faulkner's later years, was
at periods of the greatest creative urgency liable to take precedence over everything else. Asked at the University of Virginia
why *The Town* had taken him so long to finish, Faulkner in his
reply characterized the book as a chronicle rather than as a novel
and explained:

> There were so many other things that got in the way of it. I would
> write a little on it and then I would think of something else that
> seemed more urgent, that did fit into the more or less rigid pattern
> which a novel has got to conform to and this was too loose to fit into
> that form to give the pleasure which doing a complete job within the
> rules of the craft demand. That it's more fun doing a single piece
> which has the unity and coherence, the proper emphasis and inte-
> gration, which a long chronicle doesn't have. That was the reason.
> Though it had to be done before I did stop writing.[19]

The job had to be done because it was an integral part of that
expansive Yoknapatawphan project with which his career proper
had begun. But because it offered only a relatively minor technical challenge, hence only relatively minor creative rewards, it
was a job that had again and again been pushed to one side.

19. *Faulkner in the University,* 108.

Echoes of the other side of this process can clearly be heard in those remarkable prefaces to *The Sound and the Fury* which Faulkner drafted in the early 1930s. The most famous of the constitutional documents of the Faulknerian kingdom is of course the interview with Jean Stein, concluding with that richly stuffed final paragraph (how should we academics ever have found a title for anything without it?) about the "little postage stamp of native soil," the "cosmos of my own," and so forth.[20] I quoted a sentence from it at the beginning of this paper, and I'm sure we could all stand here together and recite it like a creed. But let us not forget that it is a document dating from long after the creative episode to which it refers—that those words were not spoken (or written) until 1955, and that it was still two years more before Faulkner made that remark about seeing every-thing at once, as if in a lightning flash. Those unused prefaces to *The Sound and the Fury*, on the other hand, were written much sooner after the event, much closer to the front line, and they record with extraordinary sharpness what was clearly nothing short of a second epiphanic experience, no less powerful or important than the first:

> I wrote this book [*The Sound and the Fury*] and learned to read. I had learned a little about writing from Soldiers' Pay—how to ap-proach language, words: not with seriousness so much, as an essayist does, but with a kind of alert respect, as you approach dynamite; even with joy, as you approach women: perhaps with the same secretly unscrupulous intentions. But when I finished The Sound and The Fury I discovered that there is actually something to which the shabby term Art not only can, but must, be applied. I dis-covered then that I had gone through all that I had ever read, from Henry James through Henty to newspaper murders, without mak-ing any distinction or digesting any of it, as a moth or a goat might. After The Sound and The Fury and without heeding to open another book and in a series of delayed repercussions like summer thunder, I discovered the Flauberts and Dostoievskys and Conrads whose books I had read ten years ago. With The Sound and The Fury I learned to read and quit reading, since I have read nothing since.[21]

20. *Lion in the Garden*, 255.
21. William Faulkner, "An Introduction for *The Sound and the Fury*," ed. James B. Meriwether, *Southern Review*, n.s. 8 (October 1972), 708.

Those allusions to the "delayed repercussions like summer thunder" nicely (for my purposes) suggest that it was only with the writing of *The Sound and the Fury* that Faulkner realized the full implications of that earlier lightning flash. He had had the experience all right, but missed, as *Flags in the Dust* in its relative crudeness shows, a good deal of the meaning. And Faulkner in the same piece acknowledges, somewhat obliquely, that the writing of *Sanctuary* was a throwback to that earlier period and manner: "that part of me which learned as I wrote, [he says] which perhaps is the very force which drives a writer to the travail of invention and the drudgery of putting seventy-five or a hundred thousand words on paper, was absent [during the composition of *Sanctuary*] because I was still reading by repercussion the books which I had swallowed whole ten years and more ago."[22] It is of course true that Faulkner goes on to lament that the "ecstasy" he had experienced in writing *The Sound and the Fury* had not recurred even with *As I Lay Dying* and *Light in August,* and never would do so.[23] But that was said before the writing of *Absalom, Absalom!,* when perhaps the ecstasy did return for him—as something at least remotely comparable miraculously recurs for the reader at each new reading—and it needs in any case to be set alongside a passage from the other, evidently earlier, draft preface (dated 19 August 1933) in which Faulkner declares that, even if that ecstasy has gone forever, "the unreluctance to begin, the cold satisfaction in work well and arduously done, is there and will continue to be there as long as I can do it well."[24] In that phrase about work not just "well" but "arduously done" Faulkner puts into his own words that fascination with what's difficult, that need of the artist to meet the self-posed challenge, that is fundamental to the distinction I have been trying to draw. And in "cold satisfaction" he identifies the kind of unyielding determination that was later to enable—and to oblige—him to bring *A Fable* finally to the point of publica-

22. Ibid., 709.
23. Ibid.
24. William Faulkner, "An Introduction to *The Sound and the Fury,*" *Mississippi Quarterly,* 26 (Summer 1973), 414–15.

tion, an effort that figures as but one text in the bibliographical record but that needs to be reckoned, in terms of sheer expenditure of creative energy, as equivalent to several of those less demanding (which is not in the least to say unserious or irresponsible) Yoknapatawphan completions and reworkings that otherwise dominated the latter part of his career.

It would of course be highly artificial to attempt to draw a clear dividing line between Faulkner as artist and Faulkner as regionalist. All his major works were written within a regional context, even the deliberately non-Yoknapatawphan fiction— *Pylon, The Wild Palms,* and *A Fable*—being in some sense defined and "placed" by his and our awareness of that context, much as they contribute, by their very difference, to the definition of Yoknapatawpha. The community of the novels as regional works lends them a distinctive group identity that is crucial to their quasi-pastoral function, provides a powerful inducement to the reader to move on from one text to another (as Scott and Hardy had earlier realized), and insists that they be read not just individually but also in terms of their interrelationships. And nothing Faulkner wrote—nothing, at least, that he offered within the covers of a book—was allowed, as he put it in the introduction to *Sanctuary,* to "shame" his best work. At the same time there remains, I think, some validity to that notion of the two distinct moments of vision and the two consequent agendas. I would certainly argue that there was a period of ten or twelve years from the late 1920s to the late 1930s when Faulkner's passionate need for self-development and self-challenge as an artist took precedence over his specifically regionalist and world-creating ambitions—conceivably because the demon that then drove him, the gadfly of this most impetuous phase of his whole impetuous career, derived much of its coercive power (as Professor Wittenberg has shown)[25] from personal, from psychological sources.

Six of the eight novels of those years were set in Yok-

25. Judith Bryant Wittenberg, *William Faulkner: The Transfiguration of Biography* (Lincoln: University of Nebraska Press, 1979).

napatawpha and so made contributive to the process of regional elaboration—or at least rendered capable of drawing upon elements of the settings established in earlier novels, Faulkner having already allowed himself to assume that the reader of each novel would be, at any rate should be, familiar with all of its predecessors. But this is clearly not the main thrust of at least the major works of the period, and their localizing features cannot always be readily accommodated to pre-existing Yoknapatawphan patterns: the Jefferson of *Light in August,* for example, seems less like the Jefferson of *Sartoris* (and later of *Requiem* and the Snopes novels) than does the Charlestown, Georgia, of *Soldiers' Pay.* And it is possible to suspect that the insertion of the first Yoknapatawpha map into the first edition of *Absalom, Absalom!* constituted not so much an act of regionalist assertion as an attempt to add yet one more to that series of enigmatic appendices that begins with a grossly inaccurate chronology and continues with an excessively informative genealogy.

To think of Faulkner's entire oeuvre as laid out as on a map, as existing on a single plane, is of course one way of solving or at any rate circumventing the problems I have been trying to consider. Since the career is, after all, finished, no longer in motion, what harm can there be in arranging its individual components like features on a map, pieces on a board, figures in a design? No harm at all, obviously, in purely critical terms, though it soon begins to seem necessary to turn the map into a relief map, supply its contours with a third dimension, in order to give adequate expression to one's sense of the relative stature of the various works as well as to the nature of their intertextuality, the narrative, structural, fabular, or symbolic play between one work and another, or several others. Ultimately, of course, the critic, the reader, can impose upon, read into, Faulkner's career any shape his knowledge, intelligence, or urge for singularity may dictate. He may, indeed, take the view that Faulkner himself is irrelevant to the entire discussion, that the works essentially wrote themselves.

Coming to Faulkner's work with my own biographical,

genetic, and chronological biases, however, I cannot help thinking of his career, as he lived and worked it through—pursuing
that swift-running course as of the sun or a star through the
heavens—as having a dynamic of its own, one that may not
always have been consistent either in its operation or in its
direction but that it seems interesting, and important, and even
necessary to come to terms with in some way. At present the
principles of its operation remain mysterious. Doubtless we
shall gain more insight into the matter as we come to understand
more, critically, about the intricate relationships that seem to
exist between so many of Faulkner's texts, early and late, major
and minor, finished and unfinished. Perhaps, when the surviving Faulkner manuscripts and letters have been more fully explored, we shall learn more about the genetic interdependence
of certain texts and hence about the factors which determined
the particular timing of their completion and publication. Just
how did *Sanctuary* relate to *The Sound and the Fury*? Or *Light
in August* to *Absalom, Absalom!*, both at one stage entitled *Dark
House*, both owing a debt to "Evangeline"—much as "The Big
Shot" was drawn upon both for *Light in August* and for *Sanctuary*? How did the composition of other texts during the evolution of *A Fable* affect, negatively or positively, the progress of
the latter? Was *The Reivers*, that charmingly appropriate act of
closure, in any sense intended to be Faulkner's final word? For
the time being, however, we must continue to ponder with
speculative sympathy the riches left behind in the wake of his
tumultuous, unresting career—certain only that, to quote from
Go Down, Moses, it was "a fine race while it lasted, but the tree
was too quick."[26]

26. William Faulkner, *Go Down, Moses and Other Stories* (New York: Random
House, 1942), 30.

Faulkner and Modernism:
Why Does It Matter?

THOMAS L. MCHANEY

By way of beginning, I offer the work of two critics whom everyone acknowledges for their accomplishments, their acumen, and
their erudition, and who appear to represent two major cultural,
literary-historical, and critical points of view. Cleanth Brooks is
the best of those Southern-born critics who have been successful
in discussing Faulkner's works in terms of how they satisfy a
traditional Southern view. Giving Faulkner full marks for control
of his structures and styles, Brooks has argued persuasively that
Faulkner's greatness proceeds from his deep appreciation of the
power of community—present or absent—in defining the moral
life of humankind; from his accurate treatment of race and class
in the traditional Southern community; and from his successful
adaptation of a folk style and a romantic viewpoint to the exigencies of twentieth-century fiction. Brooks does discuss Faulkner's
debt to other writers, including Eliot and Joyce, whose coun-
terarguments to the "old-fashioned romanticism" on which
Faulkner had been nourished, Brooks writes, proved the
"proper alloy wherewith to give tensile strength and a cutting
edge" to Faulkner's point of view.[1] Yet Brooks's discussions of
Joyce, Eliot, and other authors (Conrad, Housman, Swinburne)
from whom Faulkner learned or borrowed remain source- or
influence-study in his hands, and never become part of a discussion of Faulkner's own modernism. Brooks in fact appears reluctant to admit that Faulkner's work is as much or as importantly

1. Cleanth Brooks, *William Faulkner: Toward Yoknapatawpha and Beyond* (New
Haven: Yale University Press, 1978), x.

37

modernist as Eliot's or Joyce's. Many of the trapping of modernism he in fact ignores or resists, including Faulkner's application of Freud, Bergson, and, with witty disdain, James G. Frazer's *The Golden Bough.* Doubtless, having read lame or padded speculations on Faulkner's sources, there is something we can all agree with in spirit when we hear Brooks's remark: "Shall there be no more innocent consumption of pork chops and spareribs in Yoknapatawpha County because someone has read *The Golden Bough?*"[2] But, like many of his other remarks on what we might call the symbols and emblemata of modernism, this sentence begs what is a very important question.

A critic with an apparently very different background and interest from Brooks's is Hugh Kenner, chronicler of the Pound Era, as he calls it, and vigorous Joycean. Kenner appears to have embraced and studied the modernist movement with as much seriousness as Brooks has applied himself to the traditional perspective. For Kenner, Faulkner "is clearly part of something modern," as he said at Ole Miss five years ago in a lecture entitled "Faulkner and the Avant-Garde."[3] But he goes on to argue that Faulkner, nonetheless, is still not really part of the post-Imagist Revolution of the Word that emphasized the literary characteristics of creation and the look of writing on the page. The basis of Faulkner's storytelling, Kenner says, is oral. In addition, because Faulkner wrote no manifestoes, frequented no literary cafés, and "wanted no part of pedagogy, nor of literary politics," he cannot be considered avant-garde, a term reserved for those active on the barricades of art revolutions.[4] All that might be well enough; Faulkner undisputably came along in the wake of Pound, Eliot, Joyce, and other writers and artists who make up the vanguard of the modern movement. But Kenner goes on to assert that Faulkner is a far cry from Joyce in other

2. Brooks, *William Faulkner: The Yoknapatawpha Country* (New Haven: Yale University Press, 1963), 8.
3. Hugh Kenner, "Faulkner and the Avant-Garde," *Faulkner, Modernism, and Film: Faulkner and Yoknapatawpha 1978,* ed. Evans Harrington and Ann J. Abadie (Jackson: University Press of Mississippi, 1979), 182.
4. Ibid., 183.

ways, too—that, for instance, the reader of Faulkner's works is not the "ideal reader suffering from an ideal insomnia" whom Joyce demands, but instead a kind of stranger *listening* in a strange land who must make such adjustments and pretenses that allow him or her to become "what he cannot be, a sympathetic member of a vanished community."[5] Thus Kenner and Brooks seem not really so far apart. Kenner even comes up with a bit of West Coast mysticism, shades of Castenada's Don Juan, that is an ironically amusing corollary to the romantic traditionalism we have often heard from Southern critics: Faulkner in a classroom, he says, would be "like a shaman who has wandered into a conference of brain surgeons, knowing that he commands skills of incantation incompatible with their discourse of subtle instruments." Faulkner, he also says unequivocally, could not have written *The Sound and the Fury* in Paris![6]

Couldn't he have? Odd that in "Elmer," written in Paris,[7] Faulkner created what amount to sketches for the Compson novel. Odd that while there he also penned material that wound up in the brutally modernist *Sanctuary*.[8] And odd too that in his recent introduction to *Helen: A Courtship* Carvel Collins says that Faulkner told the plot of *The Sound and the Fury* to a Paris friend while sojourning in the City of Lights.[9] But couldn't he have written it there? What about the fact that he typed it in New York City? That ought to count for something, and without inviting a shouting match between Faulknerians and Joyceans or for that matter without taking anything away from Joyce, I would nevertheless like to know why Joyce, whose work may be stretched to thirteen volumes by including juvenilia and abandoned projects and whose literary criticism amounts to one

5. Ibid., 195–96.
6. Ibid., 186, 194.
7. *Uncollected Stories of William Faulkner*, ed. Joseph Blotner (New York: Random House, 1979), 710.
8. *Selected Letters of William Faulkner*, ed. Joseph Blotner (New York: Random House, 1977), 17.
9. Carvel Collins, "Biographical Background for Faulkner's *Helen*," *Helen: A Courtship and Mississippi Poems* (New Orleans and Oxford: Tulane University Press and Yoknapatawpha Press, 1981), 26.

volume of mostly youthful work, is in Kenner's words "the greatest man of letters of the twentieth century,"[10] while Faulkner, whose canon runs to three times thirteen volumes in startling variety, including mature essays, is a folk-talking shaman.

Certainly, a number of scholars have contributed to our understanding of aspects of Faulkner's modernism, especially insofar as various single or related forms of notation are concerned. Darrell Abel, Robert Slabey, Carvel Collins, Richard P. Adams, Ilse Lind, Panthea Broughton, Noel Polk, Michael Millgate, Margaret Yonce, Arthur Kinney, Donald Kartiganer, Gary Stonum, Victor Strandberg, Gail Morrison, and others have documented or discussed relationships between Faulkner's work and some of the literary, musical, artistic, and intellectual phenomena that lead into or express modernism, including the influence of or affinities with Frazer, Freud, Bergson, Eliot, Joyce, Pound, Stein, Anderson, Aiken, William James, Schopenhauer, Nietzsche, Marx, impressionism, postimpressionism, and cubism. Martin Kreiswirth, one of Michael Millgate's students who has published several articles on Faulkner's borrowings and adaptations, will publish a book soon that traces the development of images, characters, and allusions through Faulkner's early work into *The Sound and the Fury*, and Lothar Hönnighausen of the University of Bonn, West Germany, a specialist in fin de siècle literature and art who spoke at the Ole Miss Faulkner Conference in 1982, is completing an astounding work on Faulkner's poetry, drawings, and early prose in relation to the pan-European arts movements of the late nineteenth century that are generally recognized as the precursors of high modernism.

If all this has been or is being done, you may ask, why worry about Kenner and Brooks? Well with all respect to the previous contributions to this discussion, including my own, one has a right to be concerned because the subject of Faulkner and modernism has been approached heretofore so often only piecemeal

10. Kenner, "Faulkner and the Avant-Garde," 191.

or with the kind of wariness or mysticism exhibited by Brooks and Kenner. Though they are both appreciative of Faulkner's remarkable genius, when Brooks and Kenner ignore or diminish Faulkner's relationship to the modernists, they appear to be no more sympathetic to Faulkner's artistic self-consciousness, intellect, and ambition than the anonymous scholar whom Carvel Collins cited thirty years ago as claiming that Faulkner could not possibly have based an episode of one of his novels on "The Inferno" because Faulkner, being a Mississippian, "would never have read *The Divine Comedy* or any other large and difficult work."[11] Today most critics would not make that kind of statement, of course, certainly not Brooks or Kenner, but many critics would still write that Faulkner's use of Dante, which we can now document in several novels, is merely a standard allusion, representing a source or a literary influence in the nineteenth-century sense, not a modernist notation, peculiar in meaning to the early twentieth century, commensurate with Eliot's citation of Dante in "The Waste Land" or Joyce's use of Homer. The annual lists of "new scholarship" are full of articles and notes that at best do no more than this. But even critics who, like Kenner, recognize Faulkner's affinity with his times, often seem unable to acknowledge the nature of Faulkner's literary achievement. For example, Donald Kartiganer in his recent book on Faulkner discusses Faulkner's modernist connections, yet seems almost apologetic for discovering Nietzschean power in *Light in August* and *Absalom, Absalom!*, though his discussion is illuminating, and finds that myth "becomes in [Faulkner's] hands a heavy and sterile form," not an effective structuring agent,[12] especially in *The Sound and the Fury*. Kartiganer must be allowed an opinion, but one can only guess that he has missed much of the mythic structure (which is not limited to the Easter story) and all of the irony (though he perceives

11. Collins, "The Interior Monologues of *The Sound and the Fury*," *English Institute Essays 1952* (New York: Columbia University Press, 1954), 29–56.
12. Donald Kartiganer, *The Fragile Thread: The Meaning of Form in Faulkner's Novels* (Amherst: University of Massachusetts Press, 1979), 174, 185.

some irony in *As I Lay Dying*). Faulkner's use of myth in the Compson novel, Kartiganer writes, does not "unify" the novel, at any level, as *The Odyssey* unifies *Ulysses*.[13] What he means by "unify"—a vague enough critical term at any time—might, I suppose, also be brought into question, but the main point here is that another supposedly sympathetic and reasonably well-informed critic seems predisposed to measure Faulkner by Joyce, not altogether fairly, and as a result to miss the unique quality of Faulkner's achievement as a modernist writer.

The grudging acceptance of Faulkner as a modernist deserves an explanation which this essay will not attempt, except to suggest that it has resulted in part from what has been perceived as Faulkner's anomalous literary life—the creation of startlingly innovative work from an apparently provincial base. Despite evidence that Faulkner's alleged provinciality is a fiction created by his own self-protective posing and fed by a certain amount of condescension on the part of outsiders, including Southerners, toward his native place, critics continue to regard him as a primitive or mystical writer rather than a self-conscious artist. The view that Faulkner is a magical practitioner of mid-nineteenth-century storytelling techniques who occasionally and almost unwittingly slips twentieth-century allusions into his work—a position one perceives in the influential viewpoints of Brooks and Kenner—supports the naiveté that lurks within us all and the commonsensical aesthetic that equates successful fiction with narrow verisimilitude rather than with the orches-tration of complex harmonies of representation. Brooks uses the term "universality" to identify what in Faulkner's art resolved the conflict between romanticism and realism. Yet how much of the "universality" Brooks perceives could be explained in terms of Faulkner's relationship to that pan-European—and thus, in the limited Western sense, "universal"—arts movement we know as modernism? Kenner's belief apparently is that it was Faulkner's adaptation of the devices of oral storytelling, an un-

13. Ibid., 180.

conscious primitivism, that served him so well. Both views seem cut from the same cloth; both leave us with Faulkner the shaman. It is my view, however, that Faulkner's "universality" and his magic are subject to rational, if not perfect, explanation. This will be done best when we have acknowledged and dealt with the fact that Faulkner was not just a simple Mississippi boy occasionally copying the "important" writers up East or abroad, but an artist whose work, rather than derivative, is an important and revealing reflection of the impact of modernity on his country and region and their art.

Kenner says that Faulkner's prose creates its effect by forcing the reader to become "what he cannot be, a sympathetic member of a vanished community." Kenner seems to believe that this effect is not in accord with high modernism, yet to me it appears to be in perfect accord with what Stravinsky was doing in "Rites of Spring" or Picasso in his use of African masks, an effect achieved by Faulkner not because he was a shaman or a communal agrarian, not even because he read a manifesto, but because like Stravinsky, Picasso, Eliot, Pound, Joyce, Williams, Stevens, Aiken, Cummings, Hemingway, and the rest of their generation, his was a prepared mind, fed with similar abstractions and cultural experiences and charged with sufficient ambition and discipline to accomplish tasks he deliberately undertook. We should also realize about modernism and its artifacts that it was not the invention of Pound, Eliot, or Joyce nor restricted to English-speaking writers, and, two, that neither the movement nor its results were in a way something the young artists who created them had much choice about, but what the age (not Ezra Pound) demanded. It is true that modernism was not the only thing that the "age demanded," but it was one of them, and a young artist could bring back to Oxford, Mississippi, some of the same demands that were being felt in Vienna, Munich, Berlin, Prague, Paris, and London, if, in fact, they had not already reached him at home. The quality of his response doubtless should be unique, especially if he remains, as we know Faulkner did, a doggedly uncompromising artist and person. Faulkner once said that there are no "mute inglorious Miltons." Probably there are no mute inglorious modernists, either—the movement is filled out only by those who define it. And how can anyone read, or even look at, novels like *Soldiers' Pay, Mosquitoes, Flags in the Dust, The Sound and the Fury, Sanctuary, As I Lay Dying,* and *Light in August*—to name only those works that specifically fall within the generally accepted dates of the modern movement in the arts—and deny that Faulkner is one of those who help define the work of that period? How can anyone, seriously studying these works, deny that Faulkner is part of the Revolution of the Word or assert that he is an oral storyteller immune to "subtle discourses"? I should think that anyone who has looked into those books whether as common reader or as student knows the importance of an "ideal insomnia." At the simplest level, not a one of them fails to call attention to itself as a modernist artifact. Each announces that here are words configured on a page: from the obvious application of italics, eccentric punctuation, rubrics, and unusual chapter structures to the more subtle presentation of modern notions about time, memory, and the nature of personality as they were being redefined during the first decades of the twentieth century.

To his credit, Cleanth Brooks has in the past been quick to castigate journalistic critics of Faulkner who in a single breath noted that Faulkner's books had incredible impact but that Faulkner did not know how to write, as if, Brooks says, it were not the style that caused all the excitement.[14] But Brooks has never spent much time with what we might call Faulkner's non-representational style, preferring to dwell on his "nature poetry" and upon the ambiguities created by that nonrepresentational style for someone who expects conventional storytelling. In that regard, he has not left us much better off than Hugh Kenner.

14. Brooks, "The British Reception of Faulkner's Work," *William Faulkner: Prevailing Verities and World Literature,* ed. Wolodymyr T. Zyla and Wendell M. Aycock (Lubbock: Interdepartmental Committee on Comparative Literature, Texas Tech University, 1973), 53.

Both Brooks and Kenner, it seems to me, feed the prejudices or laziness of the weary undergraduate or the common reader who only wants fiction to reflect "life." Let me say that I do not want to deny either the undergraduate or the common reader, nor even to forego my own pleasures, as someone raised in north Mississippi, seeing a familiar landscape and culture revealed in Faulkner's work. But we have established Faulkner's credentials as an acute observer of the local scene. Let us now establish his credentials not simply as a great provincial artist but—to use the phrase bestowed on him by the French novelist Claude Simon— as the "Picasso of Literature."[15]

The point I wish to make here is that there are indeed allusions in Faulkner, and perhaps many of them are just that, no more or less significant that any figures of speech or devices of rhetoric; but there are also citations that carry special functions and meanings for the time in which Faulkner wrote, and we will not understand them well until we accept the challenge of studying him as in very many ways a typical (and typically innovative) member of the modernist writing community. As Michael Millgate has pointed out, among the writers whom he cites, either in his fiction or in his interviews and public statements, Faulkner had both sources and masters, materials for his literary carpentry and images to measure himself by.[16] If we spend enough time studying his relationship to modernism, we may come up with another list of writers whom we might refer to as his elective affinities, which, taken together, could help us to explain both how and why Faulkner transcended literary regionalism and a narrowly defined romanticism, realism, or naturalism in his writing.

To illustrate the appropriateness of such a quest—one that would have been ridiculed no more than thirty years ago—let us apply to Faulkner a little of that irony that Henry James applied

15. Claude Simon, quoted by Vivien Mercier, in *The New Novel from Queneau to Pinget* (New York: Farrar, Straus & Giroux, 1971), 27.
16. Michael Millgate, "Faulkner's Masters," *Tulane Studies in English*, 23 (1978), 143–55.

to the situation of young Nathaniel Hawthorne leaving college in 1825. In his English Men of Letters biography of Hawthorne, James, you recall, enumerated all the things lacking in American life at that time that were necessary to produce an artist and art. In Faulkner's case, however, let us reverse the situation and consider what must be omitted from his life for Faulkner to remain a primitive writer (if there are such), a Southern traditionalist, a great romantic realist, or only a powerful naturalist. We must let him be born, of course, and we cannot take away his family; in general we will not start taking things away from him until about the time of adolescence, so it is given that he is from a small town, Oxford—not the country—and of the literate middle-class. We can allow him to keep his famous great-grandfather, who wrote in various nineteenth-century styles and forms, and perhaps even his artist-mother, who painted portraits and magnolias, and his great-aunt 'Bama, although the contents and tone of his letters to both of them from Paris suggest that each was a bit too receptive to new ideas to be the perfect mother or great-aunt to a provincial realist (but then we aren't going to let him go to Paris, are we? He won't be writing letters or anything else there!). His cousin Vannye and her daughter are even a risk, because they will go to Paris in 1925, but "they are very nice, of the purest Babbitt ray serene,"[17] Faulkner *might* write his mother, if we let him, and so they constitute less a threat to the young Mississippian's provincial status than a reading of Sinclair Lewis's novel (never you mind that Vannye's sister Natalie, about whom Faulkner seems to have some childhood memories latent with eroticism, sends a son to the University of Virginia and then to Harvard; we can't stop everything).

Like most young men with the background we must grant him, Faulkner would have received through his home and education the two major literary traditions of the nineteenth century, romanticism and realism. His first exposure to both is apt to have been of the sort prepared for children and young people

17. *Selected Letters of William Faulkner,* 22.

of the nineteenth century—children's editions of mythological and chivalric tales, adventure writing, perhaps some sentimentalized religious educational material; Dumas and Scott and Dickens in the home library; the school interpretation of the British and American romantics. He seems naturally to have leaned toward the romantic—he was, after all, more like Tom Sawyer as a boy than he was like Huck Finn—and appears to have been late discovering or at least late recognizing the literary value of such American realist writing as the best of Twain and the small-town antebellum Southerners or the naturalism of Dreiser. To this one must add the great nineteenth-century Europeans whom he read, apparently reading them before he read or at least before he appreciated the classic American writers. Always in the background is Shakespeare, plain, filtered, and king size, as one might say to describe the way one receives him in this culture: first from the school master; then from the romantics; and finally, when and if one has struggled with words and structures and life itself, through the enormity of the raw confrontation with colossal competent genius. Milton is there, also through the romantics, and the lyricists of the Oxford Book of English Verse, or some such collection, from the time of Elizabeth to the fin de siècle.

Read and reread, this is a considerable and powerfully useful heritage—and I do not suggest that it is by any means all, but only the vivid minimum one can expect for Faulkner's class, place, and time. And one sees that if Faulkner is to remain a great primitive, he is already in trouble. He had better drop his books, forget what he has read, and hide out somewhere in the hills or the tropics. Perhaps he could still give the false impression of being a primitive, a character like the Melville or Poe of legend. But he is already doomed to self-consciousness, and the best we can do for him is to see to it that he remains a traditionalist, a provincial, a realist or naturalist who cannot write a major book in Paris. (Since Oxford was and is not just a small town but a university town, Faulkner could become a card-carrying member of the Agrarian literati—even an academic:

after all, he owned a tweed jacket with elbow patches, a pipe, and a set of courtly manners.) What will we have to do to insure that this comes about?

It is all right if Faulkner really serves in the war—after all, more young men returned to take up ordinary lives than to write esoteric novels and poems; he can be like Sergeant York, and best trained in a Southern encampment. We will keep him away from Toronto, and especially not let him travel there by way of New Haven and New York. After the war we keep him away from Ole Miss even more strenuously than we would have tried to keep him away from it prior to 1918. Under prewar conditions it might have been all right for him to hang around the campus, painting buildings (but not pictures), even palling around with young folks like the Somerville girls and Ben Wasson and Louis Cochran and George Healy, as long as it was only for laughs, but in the postwar period one fears that even these young Mississippians have eaten some of the forbidden fruit of the late nineteenth and early twentieth centuries. Any relationship to the University is a difficulty.

He might keep his friendship with Phil Stone only if Stone remains nothing but a Civil War buff and the scion of an old family; we can even let them read Balzac together and listen to music, so long as they don't talk about it. But Stone disqualifies himself as friend to the primitive by virtue of his tenure at Yale, his friendship with the young Yale poets, and especially his charge account at the Brick Row Bookshop. (We can't keep a man who orders *The Dial* and *Ulysses*.) Faulkner must also not know Stark Young and certainly he must never come to New York at his suggestion, stay at his apartment, or take a job at the Doubleday Bookstore managed by Elizabeth Prall, future wife of Sherwood Anderson and sister to Young's former teaching colleague David Prall, a philosophy professor and the granddaddy of aesthetics in America.

We are having to interfere more and more now. We scratch his sojourns in New Orleans, his friendships there, especially those with Anderson and Spratling, and if we send him to Europe at all it is alone and to do a walking tour of the Faroes and the Shetlands or, at most, a genealogical retreat into Scotland itself. No Paris, no intelligible glimpses of recent painting or bohemian life, no Berlioz in the Luxembourg Gardens, no shy looks through the cafe smoke at Joyce, no letters to the folks back home about Cézanne or Picasso, no bragging about having penned work so modern he cannot understand it himself. No writing *The Sound and the Fury.*

Riding herd on Faulkner like this is hard work demanding constant vigilance. It would be nice, after we have sent Faulkner to the colder reaches of the British Isles instead of to Paris, hoping to preserve his traditionalism, if we could let him warm up by visiting southern France—surely an old place like Carcassonne couldn't hurt a traditionalist nor give him dangerously modern ideas for, say, fiction—but the danger is that to travel there he might pass through the landscapes of Cézane, Monet, Van Gogh, and, innocent as it may seem, the sight of them could damage him: it is well established by art history that red poppies, yellow sunflowers, and pale hills that appear to resolve themselves in the blue air into planes bestriding planes are dangerously modern.

And now we must also start to restrict his reading: Housman in the pocket may be all right, but Swinburne and the French symbolists might be used for more than philandering. The Russian realists, perhaps even Thomas Hardy are acceptable, but Conrad may be read only for the adventures. Faulkner may read some of Anderson's stories, but not *Winesburg, Ohio,* and if necessary we will send the police to confiscate that 1924 *Ulysses* Phil Stone orders, before Faulkner can open it. He won't be going to New Orleans, so Anderson's copy of Frazer's *The Golden Bough* is not going to be a threat to the meaning of pork production in Lafayette, not to mention Yoknapatawpha, County. He may not read Eliot, Conrad Aiken, or Cummings, and it's best he be ignorant of Ernest Hemingway. The words impressionist, cubist, and vorticist must not enter his vocabulary, not even as terms of contempt. No slipping up on Bergson,

Freud, or Einstein in the encyclopedias or popular magazines, either, much less in their standard editions. This becomes comical—I hope—but my serious purpose is to remind us how hard it would have been for someone of Faulkner's genius, passion, energy, curiosity, ambition, and need, living in a small university town in Mississippi, to avoid being touched by the modern movement not merely in literature but also in art, music, and general areas of thought. Granted that some people have touched all the phenomena we have denied Faulkner and remained either mediocre or not demonstrably modernist or both. Still in order to believe that Faulkner was a primitive, a provincial, even only a traditionalist, we would have to leave out of his life the little that we know he saw and read. And it is still true that we know relatively little about the reading, study, and crucial experiences of his formative years. We will eventually know much more about his early self-conscious imitation and his painstaking practice of symbolist and modernist forms. What we do know with some assurance from letters, early reviews and essays, drafts and rejected passages, drawings and handmade books as well as from the reminiscences of friends like Wasson, Stone, and Spratling is that, long before he completed his first published novel *Soldiers' Pay*, he had worked very hard to become a self-conscious contemporary artist. If we compare his apprentice work to that of other recognized modernists in America, we will find that it is done very much in the same manner and concerned with the same things as their work, using similar strategies of voice and structure. We have hardly begun the discussion of Faulkner's early imitations, however, because not enough of us have had a chance to look at them closely—some of the work, like *Vision in Spring*, is still partly sequestered, while other parts have only recently been made available by the energy and generosity of L. D. Brodsky. Nor have we really begun discussion of the ways in which Faulkner arrived at unique conceptual as well as technical contributions to his contemporary scene.

A problem already touched on is the relationship to Joyce. For years one has been hearing, from both coasts, that there is no novel after Joyce, but that is either wrong or the word *novel*, as Eliot suggested in 1922, is not the word we should be using anyway. Joyce, like Eliot, clearly synthesized much of importance between 1909 and 1922; but it is time we tried to understand what it is that Faulkner synthesized between 1929 and 1932, a crucial time in the world. As for his later work, after the end of what has been called high modernism, Faulkner did not create anything like *Finnegans Wake;* instead he gave us *Absalom, Absalom!, The Wild Palms, The Hamlet, Go Down, Moses, Requiem for a Nun,* and *A Fable,* among others—books which produce all told more voltage than *Finnegans Wake* without the danger of a meltdown! This is not to belittle Joyce's enormous experiment, but simply to say that as Faulkner's early work deserves recognition for breaking new ground for the modernists, so his later work deserves serious study not simply to understand it perceptually and conceptually but also in order to see clearly the place of that work in its time and what it reveals about that time. Novels like *The Hamlet, Go Down, Moses, Requiem for a Nun,* and *A Fable* all exhibit to some degree what has been interpreted as a retreat to the forms of the nineteenth-century novel; yet a critic fully appreciative of Faulkner's mastery of modernist techniques in the earlier work may find that the later works represent a synthesis rather than something epigonic or reactionary in art.

It cannot be denied that what has happened to us when we come reeling from a concentrated reading and rereading of a Faulkner novel is decidedly that "shock of the new" which Robert Hughes wittily chronicles in his series of television programs and essays on twentieth-century art. With what have our senses been assaulted? With raw life? Or with words? With the chronological patterns of human living? Or with complex, nonrepresentational but harmonious structures? How were these books achieved? First, by virtue of a great imagination, to be sure: by which we mean not something primitive, provincial, or in touch with traditional verities or magic, but a ready mind trained in English lyricism from Shakespeare to the 1920s and in most of the styles and structures of Western fiction since the eighteenth century, including sentimental, gothic, and historical romance, picaresque and documentary realism, the parodistic, naturalistic, impressionistic, expressionistic, musical, and mythical methods. A mind forged in the crucible of its time: in the social, political, economic, military, scientific, aesthetic, and other changing forces operative from about 1910 to 1925. And also by virtue of acutely deployed manipulations of words, syntax, punctuation, format, and typestyles to insist that these works are "made"—words on paper, just as painting from impressionism onward emphasizes that it is paint or other material on canvas.

The modernist yawp is different from Whitman's "who touches this book touches a man." It cries, Who touches this book touches a mind, touches mind with mind, a contact seething with ambiguities perhaps known well enough by the British, German, and American romantics but renamed by Freud, Frazer, Jung, Bergson, Einstein, Picasso, Eliot, Stravinsky, Schoenberg, and others. Sometimes there is more in this encounter than one can easily bear. Perhaps that is why we have shied away from Faulkner the modernist: he is strong enough medicine when we pretend that he is a shaman or a shaken Southern realist, a man who has more in common with Henry Adams and George Moore than with Henry Moore and George Seurat. Or could it be that we are more comfortable with Faulkner's messages for us if they are felt to be irrational or primitive, and not well-orchestrated presentations of twentieth-century life? If we do not find that Faulkner's career provides material to define and explain the modern and the post-modern novel, it will be because the terms themselves have to be changed.

So far I have only asserted that, given his biography, Faulkner's modernism is a kind of foregone conclusion and that, given his body of work between 1926 and 1939, its defining qualities should be obvious to the initiated. The degree to which Faulkner's work is not only deliberate and self-conscious but also in perfect accord with a nearly worldwide aesthestic perspective dominant in his time may be more convincingly illustrated by reference to one of the better treatments of literary modernism, a book edited and in part written by British scholar and novelist Malcolm Bradbury and his colleague at East Anglia, James McFarlane, entitled *Modernism 1890–1930*. This book ranges Western literature and art in the period, tracing the development of various characteristic or defining ideas, styles, forms, and works. As good as the work seems to be, even here— shades of Hugh Kenner—Faulkner is mentioned only thirteen times in a book of over 600 pages, with one six-page discussion of *As I Lay Dying* in conjunction with Virginia Woolf's *The Waves* and André Malraux's *La condition humaine* in terms of their similar symbolist inheritances and common "unease" about language.[18]

Traditionalists and even their antagonists have often maintained that Faulkner's work is a microcosm of the South, and more than one recent Southern writer has lamented that it is also a microcosm of all Southern fiction, containing nearly all that can be said about the levels and intensities and ambiguities of Southern living. On the basis of reading Bradbury and McFarlane's *Modernism 1890–1930*, one is tempted to make a similarly extravagant statement about Faulkner's relationship to modernism: that his fiction is a microcosm of the literary experiments which belong to the period we know by that name. To be sure, modernism is a slippery term, and despite efforts to limit its application to twentieth-century phenomenon, it keeps drawing nineteenth-century writers, artists, musicians, and philosophers under its banner. Whether it is all to the good to be a modernist—as most of us seem to have assumed up to now—is another question that will have to be faced one of these days, one that may have an important bearing, for instance, upon how we regard Faulkner's work after 1939. But the reception of Faulkner

18. *Modernism 1890–1930*, ed. Malcolm Bradbury and James McFarlane (Middlesex, England: Penguin Books, 1976), 459–65.

by writers throughout the world appears to validate his contemporaneity, at least, and, as I have said, if the broad term modernism does not apply easily to that work, perhaps we need another term and perhaps Faulkner's career will help us discover it. But I have set out to say why it is important that we regard Faulkner under the aspect of modernism, and since the term is what we have, I will proceed to that matter now.

First and simplest, it seems to me that if we don't perceive the ways in which Faulkner's fiction is characteristic of the times, we risk attributing to Faulkner the man idiosyncracies that are symptoms of an era: what the age demanded. Second, it also seems to me that we have used Faulkner long enough to explain the nineteenth century. Let us use him now to explain our own. There may be surprises for us if we do this, especially if we accept the novels beginning with *The Hamlet* as reflecting not modernism but yet another era.

One might begin a discussion of Faulkner and modernism by taking up the question of his traditionalism. Literary history has long recognized that the traditionalist movements of the early twentieth century, such as Eliot's or that of the Nashville Fugitives, are in effect part of the modern movement, too, conservative rather than radical reactions to modernity. This traditionalism—embraced by university men and litterateurs more than by village or farm dwellers, interestingly enough—is an intellectual and artistic response, as well as an emotional one, to modern cultural alienation, as it is called, or to the "dissociation of sensibility" remarked by Eliot and Allen Tate, which amounts to the same thing. As J. P. Stern points out in *Modernism 1890–1930*, the traditionalism of writers like T. S. Eliot or Thomas Mann, however, was part of their literary strategy and not an unself-conscious expression of their lives.[19] The same might be said of Faulkner. A look at his biography will remind us that his

19. J. P. Stern, "The Theme of Consciousness: Thomas Mann," *Modernism 1890–1930*, 418.

THOMAS L. MCHANEY 55

famous great-grandfather was not an aristocrat but one of the "new men" in Mississippi, self-made and minus refinements (he did not live on a plantation but in a gaudy but not grand house near the square in Ripley); his grandfather was a successful lawyer, apparently, but essentially small-town bourgeois; his father failed in several kinds of trade; Faulkner's household at Rowan Oak, as revealed by the testimony of his late stepson, was solipsistic, eclectic, including Bastille Day in its calendar of festivals,[20] and Faulkner's roles as the squire of Oxford or the huntsman of Charlottesville reveal themselves, even without the context of his earlier poses, as amusing postures and mysterious strategies. Faulkner is doubtless also in some respects like D. H. Lawrence who, Bradbury observes, "was both a rooted native intelligence and an eclectic cosmopolitan, with slightly unusual sources."[21] Or perhaps we could say of Faulkner, as has been said of Yeats, that the "slow organic evolution of his poetic life is in part the reward of his own energy and tenacity, and in part a gift of fortune—the fortune that cast his lot in with that of a small country, comprehensible by individual intelligence and will."[22]

What of Faulkner's tortured characters and equally tortured— as some would have it—style? Even with reference to those patently fabricated books *The Sound and the Fury, As I Lay Dying, Sanctuary,* and *Light in August,* the style was once—and the characters are still—pointed out as based in Faulkner's tortured region or twisted personal psychology. Richard Sheppard, however, observes in his chapter on "The Crisis of Language" in *Modernism 1890–1930* that the "overwhelming sense of the imminence of linguistic aridity and imaginative death" in modernist writing—and here he cites Rilke, Eliot, von Hofmannstahl, and Yeats—"is an aspect of a much wider socio-cultural problem:

20. Malcolm Franklin, *Bitterweeds: Life With William Faulkner at Rowan Oak* (Irving, Texas: The Society for the Study of Traditional Culture, 1977).
21. Malcolm Bradbury, "London 1890–1920," *Modernism 1890–1930,* 176.
22. Graham Hough, "The Modernist Lyric," *Modernism 1890–1930,* 321.

the supercession of an aristocratic, semi-feudal, humanistic and agrarian order by one middle-class, democratic, mechanistic and urban."[23] He doesn't mention the American South even once. As for Faulkner's structures—that poetics of absence he often uses to tell stories about characters who are no longer present— the authors of *Modernism 1890–1930* point out that as early as Mallarmé—he who gave or at least didn't miss the title of Faulkner's first published poem—there was a manifesto of symbolism with a capital "S" in which it was said that the nature of the new poem was to "conjure up, in a specially created penumbra, the negated object, with the help of allusive and always indirect words, which constantly efface themselves in a complementary silence."[24] Faulkner's emphasis upon consciousness, though done in his own way, is perfectly in keeping with the concerns of the age, when the joining of impressionism and expressionism projected "a consciousness into the environment, making phenomena into the images and instruments of consciousness rather than some objective reality."[25] Likewise, his manipulation of conventional punctuation, however he decided upon using it, has deeper precedent than, say, Joyce. In *Les lauriers sont coupes,* Dujardin used nothing but semicolons for punctuation, Clive Scott points out, "isolating phenomena while not hindering the flow of the consciousnesses on which they register. 'Stream of consciousness' technique is as much a result of Impressionism as of advances in psychology."[26]

The modern novel reflects the new realities of physics, psychology, biology, philosophy as well as the fragmented culture of alienation, and the result for the novel may be expressed in the following quotation: "Since logical development is ruled out, and traditional narrative composition discarded, an architectonic of concatenation, sometimes described as *collage,* is rational-

23. Richard Sheppard, "The Crisis of Language," *Modernism 1890–1930*, 324–25.
24. Clive Scott, "Symbolism, Decadence and Impressionism," *Modernism 1890–1930*, 209.
25. Ibid., 221.
26. Ibid., 222.

ized, and the 'logic of the imagination' upheld against the 'logic of concepts.'"[27]

Do Faulkner's novels employ this architectonics of concatenation? Even a hasty survey of the structures used from *Soldiers' Pay* through, say, *The Wild Palms*, indicates that they do. Did he obey some "logic of the imagination"? Most of his statements about how he wrote his works affirm that he very much did. In fact, Faulkner's preoccupations seem to have been exactly those that Malcolm Bradbury summarizes as those of the modernist novel: "with the complexities of its own form, with the representation of inward states of consciousness, with a sense of the nihilistic disorder behind the ordered surface of life and reality, and with the freeing of narrative art from the determination of an onerous plot."[28] The novelists most often mentioned in the discussions of this new novel are the same three that Faulkner identified as the three great ones of his time: Proust, Mann, and Joyce, a pantheon that providentially leaves room for an American name. In Proust, Mann, and Joyce, according to John Fletcher and Bradbury, the modernist introversion of the realistic novel produced the desire for pure form, the pattern of wholeness that makes art into an order standing outside and beyond the human muddle[29]—we might here recall Faulkner's "Carcassonne" or the image of the Tyrhennian vase in the essay on *The Sound and the Fury*. Yet this desire for the transcendent object, the luminous whole, was not to be satisfied and was regarded and practiced by the writers of the early twentieth century with "an abiding irony." Thus, Mann's heroes are given

27. Natan Zach, "Imagism and Vorticism," *Modernism 1890–1930*, 236. On the same page, he quotes Eliot's introduction to St. John Perse's *Anabase*: "The reader has to allow the images to fall into his memory successively without questioning the reasonableness of each at the moment; so that, at the end, a total effect is produced. Such selection of a sequence of images and ideas has nothing chaotic about it."

28. John Fletcher and Malcolm Bradbury, *Modernism 1890–1930*, 393. Or, as they put it on page 406, "central to Modernism" is that "it sets form over life, pattern and myth over the contingencies of history; the power of the fictive presides."

29. Ibid., 406–7.

in their "historical location" and his artists struggle, finding always the "chaos and the abyss that underlie and condition" the sought-for perfection."[30] In this regard, we might study such artistic or artistically-inclined characters as Quentin, Horace, Darl, Hightower, or Gavin Stevens. Mann dramatizes this condition most fully, Bradbury and John Fletcher argue, in his character Felix Krull, the confidence man, subject of an early story and a late novel, the artist as confidence-trickster who expresses the tensions between creation and deception.[31] This observation gives us a hint to reconsider "The Liar," where the tall tale turns out to be true, or to study the evolution of V. K. Ratliff, one of whose late pronouncements is revelatory: if it ain't complicated up enough, it ain't right.

The conventions of the modernist novel that the writers in *Modernism 1890–1930* identify are all alive in *Soldiers' Pay, Mosquitoes,* and *Flags in the Dust,* as well as in the work beginning with *The Sound and the Fury,* and it would be possible to go on citing additional material from this and other historical, cultural, and literary studies of the period that might apply convincingly to the study of Faulkner. Faulkner of course did not choose to develop his genius in the role of systematic thinker, a fact for which we are all richer, but it is a little much to call him a shaman when we have a reasonably filled-out portrait of the artist as a young man in the currently available materials and sufficient evidence that Faulkner developed his "modernism" in much the same way as others of his generation. As for his adoption of the folk voice or the illusion of oral storytelling, we can see that he merely had the good sense to adopt something that Joyce first rejected and then had to readopt when he came to *Finnegans Wake.* In his early review of O'Neill, Faulkner stated boldly that no great literature could come out of folklore, just as Joyce japed at the folk collections of Lady Gregory.[32] (Faulkner,

30. Ibid., 407.
31. Ibid.
32. Faulkner, "American Drama: Eugene O'Neill," reprinted in *William Faulkner: Early Prose and Poetry,* ed. Carvel Collins (London: Jonathan Cape, 1962), 89. Cf. Joyce, "The Soul of Ireland," a review of Lady Gregory's *Poets and Dreamers,* reprinted

it might be noted, produced a novel out of his return to folk materials before Joyce did.)

Faulkner served a long apprenticeship to literary craft. He was lucky enough to feel truly the things in human existence that moved him most deeply and he was courageous enough to speak them. He stumbled upon a resourceful literary short-hand—Yoknapatawpha—that was rich enough for his genius and that became, like the sea journey in Melville, the haunted mind in Poe, the puritan conscience in Hawthorne, or the grand metaphor of all-the-world's-a-stage in Shakespeare, both material and point of view, a place where voices spoke to him. He survived many of the typical personal and cultural crises of the early twentieth century, including the crisis of language and the paralyzing tyranny of the imperfect word. He had behind him, as Michael Millgate has shown, good masters, and he also adopted as the models for his stories matchless instances of human endeavor. He learned, early enough, that writing is also the habit of work. And in the face of all the new images and works abroad in the second decade of the twentieth century, when he was going through adolescence and young manhood, it would have been very difficult for him to remain a realist or naturalist and impossible to remain a primitive, though Oxford, Mississippi, to its credit, has had both: Theora Hamblett, whose visionary and memory paintings can still be seen in homes and galleries in Oxford, was truly a primitive, and John Faulkner, William's brother, painted as a primitive and wrote as local colorist, realist, and mild naturalist in books like *Men Working* and *Dollar Cotton.*

One of the comforting things about trying to become an American novelist is to notice how really flawed our classical novels are. Many of our great novelists did not actually know how, in the European sense, to write novels, not having studied them in their youth. Faulkner did have reason to know how,

---

in *The Critical Writings of James Joyce,* ed. Ellsworth Mason and Richard Ellmann (New York: Viking, 1959), 102–5.

because he had studied, and his choices of form and style are deliberate, but his novels may still be slightly flawed, like those of Melville, Hawthorne, Twain, Fitzgerald, and even Hemingway, partly because of the conditions under which he had to write, partly because, as he himself said, of the haste with which he wrote, partly because of the nature of American publishing and of the national literary situation itself, none of which are very conducive to the polished opus. But Faulkner doubtless could appreciate as much as Joyce that art can be both a discipline and a mystery: indeed, that it must be a bit of both and that to be intelligible it must have not only inspiration but also purity of line. Yet he was not tyrranized by the artistic meticulousness that seemed to dog Joyce and, in his review of Hemingway's *The Old Man and the Sea*, he wrote of the danger, "Praise God that whatever made and loves and pities Hemingway and me kept him from touching it any further."[33] This is certainly an instinctive statement, but hardly the irrationality of magic. It expresses a trust in that "logic of the imagination" about which I have already written. Doubtless all of us would like to know what had the most impact, the most effect upon Faulkner when he was trying to become a writer. Was it the symbolists, Eliot, Joyce? Or was it, as is most likely, both bigger and more complex than that? It might have been the realization that writing could be Art, and that he could create it to a high standard, a standard, we will eventually see more plainly, that was deeply informed and shaped by the same nineteenth- and early twentieth-century currents that had affected dozens of other artists in many other countries. What these artists may have given him, above all, is not authority but some comfort and corroboration for his own genius. Authority, I believe, he earned and won. And though it may be true that Faulkner wrote no manifestoes, what he did was to perform them.

    33. Faulkner, rev. of *The Old Man and the Sea*, reprinted in *William Faulkner: Essays, Speeches and Public Letters*, ed. James B. Meriwether (New York: Random House, 1965), 183.

"The Dungeon Was Mother Herself": William Faulkner: 1927–1931

NOEL POLK

My title is taken from the heartbreaking final few pages of Quentin Compson's monologue in *The Sound and the Fury*, before he leaves his Harvard dormitory room for the final time. He has just returned from his outing in the countryside in order to make sure that at least the physical components of his life are in order before he commits himself to the peaceful bottom of the Charles River. After he has washed and changed shirts he turns out the light and goes to the window for a final moment of reflection; it is the same symbolic window through which the shining sun had, that morning, created the shadow on the sash that put him in time again; the curtains brush against his face, reminding him of "someone breathing asleep, breathing slow into the darkness again."[1] What he sees through the window at this significant point in his life, moments before his death, is not, however, the Harvard yard, but home: he sees three members of his family, in characteristic modes, and, in response to the scene, he remembers fragments of a childhood conversation with Caddy:

> *After they had gone up stairs Mother lay back in her chair, the camphor handkerchief to her mouth. Father hadn't moved he still sat beside her holding her hand the bellowing hammering away like no place for it in silence* When I was little there was a picture in one

1. *The Sound and the Fury* (New York: Vintage, 1963), 214. Hereafter *SF*.

I am grateful to Dr. Edmund Berkeley, Jr., Curator of Manuscripts at the Alderman Library of the University of Virginia, and Mrs. Jill Faulkner Summers for permission to quote unpublished passages from Faulkner's manuscripts.

of our books, a dark place into which a single weak ray of light came slanting upon two faces lifted out of the shadow. *You know what I'd do if I were King?* she never was a queen or a fairy she was always a king or a giant or a general *I'd break that place open and drag them out and I'd whip them good* It was torn out, jagged out. I was glad. I'd have to turn back to it until the dungeon was Mother herself she and Father upward into weak light holding hands and us lost somewhere below even them without even a ray of light. Then the honeysuckle got into it. As soon as I turned off the light and tried to go to sleep it would begin to come into the room in waves building and building up until I would have to pant to get any air at all out of it until I would have to get up and feel my way like when I was a little boy. . . ." (*SF,* 214–15)

Several things in this scene deserve our attention: the peculiar significance of the window and the curtain; Quentin's fixation on that particular tableau of complaining mother, helpless father, bellowing brother; the association of that tableau with Caddy and with the honeysuckle, which, as he remembers, filled his bedroom so that just as Benjy's bellowing took up all of the house's space for hearing, the smell of honeysuckle took up the comparable space for breathing. He has to escape, and as the passage continues he remembers escaping not *through* the window and *out* of that house, as Caddy and her daughter do, but merely from his room; he rather moves even deeper into that dark house through the hall and the stairs, to the bathroom, where he apparently has a bowel movement (*SF,* 216). The next thing to note in the passage is the phrase which supplies my title: Quentin's identification of that dark place, the dungeon in his book, with his own mother. This is an image of Caroline Compson subtly reinforced in the final section of the novel by a narrator somewhat more objective than Quentin, who describes her as carrying "a huge bunch of rusted keys on an iron ring like a mediaeval jailer's" (*SF,* 351). It is thus in fact that the whining, self-centered, repressive Caroline Compson presides over the Compson household, making of the house itself a prison, the grounds a fenced compound, which can be escaped only by dying or by climbing through the curtained window. The final thing to notice about the passage is that it is Caddy, rather than Quentin, who wants to "drag" the two faces in that picture book out of the shadows in order to "whip them good." It is not clear whom the faces belong to, but they seem to be the faces of prisoners, like themselves, rather than the faces of their captors, whom she might more logically think of punishing.

Caddy's desire, as a child, to whip those shadow-bound prisoners, to punish someone, may remind us of the adult Addie Bundren's confession of her sadistic pleasure in whipping her pupils: "I would look forward to the times when they faulted," she tells us, "so I could whip them."[2] We can pursue this connection between Addie and Caddy by noting not merely their rhyming names but also the fact that their fathers have a lot in common: Addie's father teaches her that "the reason for living [is] to get ready to stay dead a long time" (*AILD*, 161), a pithy summation of Jason Compson's more discursive nihilism. Further, both women share certain masochistic tendencies. Addie admits that when whipping her students she is really whipping herself: "When the switch fell I could feel it upon my flesh; when it welted and ridged it was my blood that ran" (*AILD*, 162); and it seems from a number of things in *The Sound and the Fury* that Caddy's promiscuity is the product not just of a rampant sexual nature, but of some deep dissatisfaction with herself, of a desire to punish herself for something she herself cannot name: "*There was something terrible in me,*" Quentin remembers her saying; "*sometimes at night I could see it grinning at me I could see it through them grinning at me through their faces*" (*SF*, 138). We don't know whether the "them" through whom she sees that *something* are her parents or the conglomerate faces of her lovers, or something even other than these two possibilities (*SF*, 138).

Let me jump now to a remarkable passage in *Sanctuary*, a novel written between *The Sound and the Fury* and *As I Lay Dying*. In this passage Temple Drake describes to Horace Ben-

2. *As I Lay Dying* (New York: Random House, 1964), 162. Hereafter *AILD*.

bow her incredible night at the Old Frenchman Place. She is at the time of the telling a prisoner in Miss Reba's whorehouse; she is in an upstairs room whose curtained window she spends a lot of time looking out of; she is also lying in a bed to which she ran, immediately after being brought to Miss Reba's, for security; and while she was still bleeding from her injury, she wore in this bed nothing but a towel wrapped around her loins, unmistakably like a diaper; thus it is worth recalling that she was raped in a "crib." Temple describes to Horace a particular fantasy she had as she lay on the cornshuck mattress at the Old Frenchman Place, listening to all the shadowy comings and goings of the mysterious world moiling behind the doors and windows of the old house, just outside her vision: "I hadn't breathed in a long time," she tells him. "So I thought I was dead." Her fantasy gets very specific: "I could see myself in the coffin. I looked sweet— you know: all in white. I had on a veil like a bride." Then she describes her encounter with Popeye, whom she more than once during the novel calls "daddy," and who violates her so grotesquely in that crib:

> I'd lie there with the shucks laughing at me and me jerking away in front of his hand and I'd think what I'd say to him. I'd talk to him like the teacher does in school, and then I was a teacher in school and it was a little black thing like a nigger boy, kind of, and I was the teacher. Because I'd say How old am I? and I'd say I'm forty-five years old. I had iron-gray hair and spectacles and I was all big up here like women get. . . . And I was telling it what I'd do, and it kind of drawing up and drawing up like it could already see the switch.[3]

This is for me an astonishing passage, for in it Temple Drake *becomes* Addie Bundren, right down to the white wedding-dress shroud, the coffin-bed of mattress-shucks, and the veil. (We may here remind ourselves of how often Quentin and Benjy remember Caddy in her veil and in her flowing white wedding gown; neither can we overlook, in this connection, the fact that Nar-

3. *Sanctuary: The Original Text*, ed. Noel Polk (New York: Random House, 1981), 216–17. Hereafter *SO*.

cissa Benbow is almost always seen dressed in white.) Temple
becomes Addie Bundren out of an immediate need to be invulnerable to the slings and arrows of her own outrageous misfortune; significantly, in her fantasy she is not just an older lady, but
a school teacher. Like Addie, Temple wants to strike out, to hit
something, to punish someone; as a teacher she can do this
legally and with impunity. It is, I suggest, the same impulse that
makes Caddy think of being a king or a giant or a general. And
we will not be wrong, I think, if we sense some relationship
between Temple's and Addie's and Caddy's impulse to lash out
at something even more helpless than they and Quentin's own
horrible, sadistic mistreatment of T. P. and Benjy on the day of
Caddy's wedding; he kicks and hits T. P. and thumps him against
the wall, and he forces Benjy to drink so much "sassprilluh" that
it makes him sick (*SF*, 25). In his frustration and helplessness he
picks on an innocent Negro boy and an idiot brother because
they, of all the people he knows, cannot, will not strike back. But
they are substitutes for the one he really wants to punish: himself.[4]

Temple's fantasy of becoming a school teacher is not difficult
to understand: a teacher was a formidable person in Temple's
world, perhaps the only position of authority, outside,
significantly, of motherhood itself, to which a girl of Temple's
time could aspire; the only woman in that society sufficiently
powerful, sufficiently invulnerable, to deal successfully with a
world in which children, particularly female children, were constantly victimized. The other part of the fantasy, the part in
which she projects herself as forty-five years old and having both
"iron gray hair and spectacles" and a huge maternal bosom—"all
big up here, like women get"—is worth a good deal of our time
for she, in one of several avatars—the school teacher among
them—is something of an epicenter in Faulkner's work of this

4. See Freud's "'A Child Is Being Beaten': A Contribution to the Study of the
Origin of Sexual Perversions," *The Standard Edition of the Complete Psychological
Works of Sigmund Freud*, trans. and ed. James Strachey (London: The Hogarth Press
and the Institute of Psycho-Analysis, 1955), 17: 175–204.

period. If she is not in fact at the center of every rumble in the fictional soil of Yoknapatawpha, she is nevertheless at the point just above the disturbance, the point from which the disturbance emanates. She is one, but she is also many: she is grandmother and mother, maiden and widowed aunt; she is often seen framed in windows looking out at the world passing by or at children playing in the yard; she is frequently bedridden, frequently invalid, and she is often seen juxtaposed against the pillow, her hair splayed out, Medusa-like, in grotesque parody of the sexuality she abhors, fears, and represses in herself and in others. She is frequently associated with stairs. She may be an active participant in a particular story or she may be merely part of the story's background. If she is not in fact in *every* story, she is nevertheless *everywhere* in Yoknapatawpha, the county's resident genius of guilt and repression, the root of all problem. She doesn't always have gray hair, she doesn't always wear spectacles, but in one or more combinations and permutations of these elements, she hovers close above huge areas of Yoknapatawpha—iron, imperious, fanatical, frustrated herself, and withal pathetic.

The most potent avatar of this significant character is the mother. In Faulkner's work of this period, mothers are, almost invariably, horrible people: it is difficult to think of a single one who measures up to even minimal standards of human decency, much less to the ideal of mother love as the epitome of selfless, unwavering care and concern. The roll of mothers in this period of Faulkner's career is a long list of women who reject their children outright, or who use and manipulate them to their own purposes: Caroline Compson, Addie Bundren, the redoubtable Mrs. Bland, Narcissa Benbow, Elly's grandmother, Mrs. Boyd, Belle Mitchell, Mrs. Gant and then Zilphia; even Caddy can be counted in this number, finally, because she abandons her own child to the same Compson hell she herself has just escaped; pregnant Dewey Dell Bundren wants nothing more than to scrape her child away. On the opposite side of this coin are the children of these women. If Yoknapatawpha in this period is for the adults a wasteland of frustrated passions and spent, wasted lives, it is for the children a singular and unrelenting torment. There are practically no children in Yoknapatawpha before Chick Mallison, certainly none during this period, who have anything like a normal, even a reasonable, much less a positive and healthy, childhood. Childhood in Faulkner is almost invariably a terrifying experience.

The intensity with which motherhood and childhood are portrayed in Faulkner's work of this period and the almost compulsive frequency with which themes related to the mother/child relationship appear in the work invite, even demand, speculation about their sources, their significance in Faulkner's life and in his work; obviously the possibilities for biographical and psychobiographical study are enormous.[5] I am going to eschew biographical speculation today, however, and pursue these important matters through other channels, channels both within and without the texts themselves. To begin, I want to turn back to *Sanctuary*.[6]

After his trip to Memphis to talk to Temple, Horace Benbow crosses the Jefferson Square, returning home; he is thinking of his experiences in Memphis, particularly of the tale Temple has told him, as "a dream filled with all the nightmare shapes it had taken him forty-three years to invent" (*SO*, 219). This is a highly charged metaphor for Horace to use, since he has, after all, been in a brothel hearing stories of rape and murder and sexual fantasy. All of these "nightmare shapes" become "concentrated" in the "hot, hard lump" of undigested coffee in his stomach, which in turn becomes the immediate physical cause of the nausea that overtakes him only minutes later when he returns to his home

5. See Judith Bryant Wittenberg, *Faulkner: The Transfiguration of Biography* (Lincoln: University of Nebraska Press, 1979). David Minter, *William Faulkner: His Life and Work* (Baltimore: Johns Hopkins University Press, 1980). See also Jay Martin, "'The Whole Burden of Man's History of His Impossible Heart's Desire': The Early Life of William Faulkner," *American Literature*, 53 (January 1982), 607–29.

6. The following discussion of *Sanctuary* is lifted directly from my essay "The Space Between Sanctuary," to be published in the proceedings of the 1982 International Colloquium on Faulkner in Paris, by the University Press of Mississippi. The relationship between this essay and that will be apparent to anyone who cares to read both.

and sees the blurring face of Little Belle in the photograph. In the spectacular conclusion to the scene, Horace vomits. As he does so he *becomes* Temple Drake and Little Belle: *he* "plunged forward and struck the lavatory and leaned upon *his* braced arms while the shucks set up a terrific uproar beneath *her* thighs." Likewise, the coffee he vomits, which is something "*she* watched . . . black and furious go roaring out of *her* pale body" (*SO*, 220; italics supplied), identifies him specifically with Popeye, who to Horace smells black, "like that black stuff that ran out of Bovary's mouth" (*SO*, 25), and with Emma Bovary herself. It also connects him, not incidentally, to other characters in the novel who vomit, Uncle Bud and Temple's Ole Miss co-ed friend. Thus in the nightmarish recapitulation of all that Temple has told him, in a sort of dreamwork condensation of its materials, Horace identifies himself completely with Temple, Little Belle, and Popeye: he is at one and the same time male, female, androgynous; the seducer and the seduced; the violater and the violated; the lover and the protector; father, brother, sister; son, lover, destroyer.

Why does Temple's tale affect him so personally, so physically? There is no answer in the 1931 revised version of *Sanctuary*, in which this scene survives intact. There are passages, however, cancelled in the revision, which give us clues. The first describes Horace passing the jail and looking up at the window in which sit the hands of the condemned Negro murderer. The barred jail window and the Negro murderer are very important points of reference for Horace, as for us, much more important in the first than in the revised version; the first version in fact begins with the description of that window, and of the Negro murderer's hands lying peacefully between the bars. Seeing them, Horace recalls in astonishingly graphic detail the particulars of the Negro's murder of his wife, and of its aftermath: he had "slashed her throat with a razor so that, her whole head tossing further and further backward from the bloody regurgitation of her bubbling throat, she ran out the cabin door and for six or seven steps up the quiet moonlit lane" (*SO*, 3). The curious, indeed almost loving, detail with which Horace remembers the moonlit scene suggests that it is one he has rehearsed many times; it thus stands as a kind of paradigm for something in Horace's own fantasies, some quality of his response to the circumstances of his own life. Part of Horace, I would suggest, admires the Negro's simple solution to his marital troubles; perhaps in his fantasies he wishes he were masculine enough, passionate enough, to solve his own problems so easily; at the very least, perhaps he is troubled by the Negro's capacity for decisive action, an implicit reproach to his own impotence. Likewise, the Negro's present situation, safely incarcerated in the sanctuary of the jail, is one that may attract Horace; unlike Horace, the Negro is free of trouble and worry, free of all striving. He has nothing more troublesome to do than merely wait to die. Further, there may be in Horace's mind some relationship between the Negro murderer and Popeye—that "black man"—who, at the book's end, is also in jail, waiting peacefully, fretlessly, to die. Further still, Horace's identification with the Negro may also be a function of his feeling that he himself deserves, even wants, an appropriate punishment, from an appropriate figure, for his guilt over his murderous and incestuous fantasies, most, as nearly everybody has noted, directed toward his sister, who not for nothing is named Narcissa.

The passage in question is one Faulkner excised when he revised *Sanctuary*:

> Each time he passed the jail he would find himself looking up at the window, to see the hand or the wisp of tobacco smoke blowing along the sunshine. The wall was now in sunlight, the hand lying there in sunlight too, looking dingier, smaller, more tragic than ever, yet he turned his head quickly away. It was as though from that tiny clot of knuckles he was about to reconstruct an edifice upon which he would not dare to look, like an archaeologist who, from a meagre sifting of vertebrae, reconstructs a shape out of the nightmares of his own childhood, and he looked quickly away as the car went smoothly on and the jail, the shabby purlieus of the square gave way

to shady lawns and houses—all the stability which he had known always—a stage upon which tragedy kept to a certain predictableness, decorum. (*SO, 141–42*)

This is a very important passage in the early text, equally for the way it reveals the nightmares which haunt Horace as for the way it reveals his strategies for evading those things he doesn't want to confront directly. What he sees through that jail window, the hands lying between the bars, obviously conjures up some childhood experience so powerful that he looks away immediately, self-protectively, directing his eyes and his body toward the maternal home, back toward what he consciously remembers as "all the stability which he had known always." Yet there is considerable evidence in the original version of *Sanctuary* that Horace's childhood was by no means so serene as he remembers, and that his conscious memories of that childhood as stable and secure are yet another evasion of certain truths, never directly articulated in the novel, that he does not want to face. It is, however, precisely on the way back home that all his nightmares come to life: in the reflecting waters of that mysterious pond, just away from the road, kneeling, a twentieth-century Narcissus, Horace comes face to face with all the conflicting elements that compose his inner life: Popeye, whose face merges with his in the water, and at whom he stares, petrified with fright—or is it fascination?—is much more Horace's double than has generally been allowed: he is at once Horace's twin, his alter-ego, at the same time his id and his superego; he is at once the reductio ad absurdum of Horace's darker sexual impulses and the punishing, vengeful father.

There is yet another scene in the first but not in the second version of *Sanctuary* that may help us understand Horace in this passage. Horace leaves the Sartoris household where his sister and Miss Jenny live, returns to Jefferson determined to open up his childhood home, the house where he and Narcissa grew up, and on which he has secretly paid the taxes for the past ten years. He approaches the old house through a "fence massed with honeysuckle," an association with Quentin Compson we cannot miss; he walks over a lawn whose "uncut grass" has gone "rankly and lustily to seed." As he wanders about the yard he feels it as a "tight and inscrutable desolation" in which he moves "in a prolonged orgasm of sentimental loneliness" (SO, 61). The specific terms describing the foul vegetation around the old house suggest a symbolic relationship, at any rate, between the childhood home and the Old Frenchman Place. The house hardly inspires in him the serenity and stability he thinks he has always known there; quite the contrary. Inside, he examines the windows of the house, which are exactly "as he had nailed them up ten years ago":

> The nails were clumsily driven. . . . Rusted, mute, the warped and battered heads emerged from the wood or lay hammered flat into it by clumsy blows. From each one depended a small rusty stain, like a dried tear or a drop of blood; he touched them, drawing his finger across the abrasions. "I crucified more than me, then," he said aloud. (SO, 61–62)

He pulls the nails with a hammer, opens the shutter, to let in light and, going from room to room, discovers his *conscious* past, a highly evocative tableau, very like Quentin's, his invalid mother in more ways than one at the center of it:

> It seemed to him that he came upon himself and his sister, upon their father and mother, who had been an invalid so long that the one picture of her he retained was two frail arms rising from a soft falling of lace, moving delicately to an interminable manipulation of colored silk, in fading familiar gestures in the instant between darkness and sunlight. (SO, 62–63)

Those windows are Horace's eyes, long since nailed tightly shut upon something, some trauma, some pain, particular or general, associated with his childhood in this house, which he has suppressed from his memory; clearly he has seen something which has traumatized him, something which has filled him not just with fear but also with disgust and self-loathing. Exactly what he has seen we are never told directly; but given Horace's obsessions as they manifest themselves throughout the book, it seems obviously to be something sexual and just as obviously to have happened at home. I would like to propose that Horace has been traumatized by what Freud called the "primal scene," or some variation of it, and that the primal scene is at the root of much of Faulkner's fiction during these early years of his artistic maturity.

There are in fact an arresting number of similarities between *Sanctuary* and Freud's case history popularly known as the "Wolf Man," which was first published in English in 1925, and so could have been available to Faulkner. "An Analysis of Child-hood Neurosis,"[7] as Freud entitled the Wolf Man's case history, is an analysis of a young man who had dreamed of waking in the middle of the night to see the window of his room open suddenly and inexplicably, and reveal to his eyes a tree in which five motionless white wolves were sitting, staring at him. Under analysis, the Wolf Man revealed to Freud that as a child he had awakened from sleep in his crib to see his father and mother engaged in what appeared to be anal intercourse—that is, his mother on her hands and knees and his father behind her. The child's immediate response was to defecate, in his bed. His long-range response was to suppress the incident entirely, both what he saw and what he did. From the patient's childhood dream of the staring wolves, which is much too complicated to go into here, Freud constructs a description of the Wolf Man's inner life which involves the young man's family in ways which ring all sorts of bells for the reader of Faulkner: a mother in ill-health, a depressed and frequently absent father, an older, dominating sister; further, the analysis discovers the Wolf Man's guilt over what he has seen, his shame over his defecation, his incestuous desire to have his father make love to him, and his simultaneous desire to be punished by his father for his sin and his shame. If we can use the Wolf Man as a point of reference, we may be able to understand a number of things only hinted at in *Sanctuary*: when Horace becomes Temple Drake, for example, he is

<hr />

7. Freud, "From the History of an Infantile Neurosis," *The Standard Edition*, 17: 3–122.

fulfilling his own rape fantasy; and it may be that the novel's obsession with defecation and urination and vomiting can be understood best by reference to the Wolf Man.[8] And, as we shall see, the Wolf Man's general sense of self-loathing and self-hatred may help us understand the large number of characters in Faulkner who have tendencies toward self-destruction—they are, of course, legion.

Sanctuary, then, is at least in one sense, Horace's nightmare,[9] the shapes of which it has taken him forty-three years to manufacture; it does not take the form of such a static visual tableau as five motionless white wolves: through his window, the window to his own inner life, he watches as the garden just outside turns into the foul, rank, overgrown jungle which surrounds the Old Frenchman Place where, in the corncrib, Temple, his female self, is violated by Popeye as, in Temple's mind, blind Pap looks on. Horace's dream, then, substituting and transforming and inverting the actual childhood experience, manufactures out of whatever he saw, whatever he felt, whatever he is suppressing, a world of dark fantastic characters and shapes which correspond to something in his hidden life. It is a fantastic world indeed, full of dark places and bizarre, grotesque shapes which make the imagination of Quentin Compson seem, by comparison, a clean, well-lighted place.

There is no primal scene in Sanctuary presented directly, at least partly because that is precisely what Horace would repress, and so the scene appears only indirectly: Horace may at one point get closer to home than he realizes when, responding in

8. See André Bleikasten, "'Cet Affreux Gout d'Encre': Emma Bovary's Ghost in Sanctuary," William Faulkner: Materials, Studies, Criticism (Japan), 5 (May 1983), 1–25, for a discussion of the relationship of Sanctuary and Madame Bovary that has a great deal to say about nausea and vomiting in both novels. Michel Gresset, in his Faulkner ou la fascination (Paris: Klincksieck, 1982) is very good indeed on the 1927–1931 period in Faulkner's career; he too has significant things to say about nausea and vomiting in these works; see especially 237 ff. Gresset's study deals brilliantly with the whole notion of voyeurism in Faulkner, an important element in Faulkner's work.

9. Kubie, "William Faulkner's Sanctuary: An Analysis," Saturday Review of Literature (October 20, 1934), 218, 224–25. Reprinted in J. Douglas Canfield, ed., Twentieth Century Interpretations of "Sanctuary": A Collection of Critical Essays (Englewood Cliffs, N.J.: Prentice-Hall, 1983), 25–31.

the jail cell to Ruby's offer to pay him for his legal services with the only tender she has to offer, he reacts almost violently not just to the idea of sex as payment, but to her embarrassed admission that she would have had to bring the baby with her when she paid. Horace is almost frantic at this: "You mean," he says, "with him at the foot of the bed, maybe? perhaps you holding him by the leg all the time, so he wouldn't fall off?" (SO, 267); and what is it but a reenactment of the primal scene when Popeye stands at the foot of the bed watching, and whinnying, while Temple and Red make love? The primal scene is indeed everywhere implied in the overwhelming emphasis throughout the novel on voyeurism.

There is, however, another scene in the original version of the novel, deleted in revision, which helps define the nature of Horace's relationship with his mother, and so may help the reader understand his neuroses. Sleeping alone in the family house one night, Horace wakes suddenly; if the scene evokes Freud's Wolf Man in any way, I am content:

> On the second night he dreamed that he was a boy again and waked himself crying in a paroxysm of homesickness like that of a child away from home at night, alone in a strange room. It seemed to him that not only the past two days, but the last thirty-five years had been a dream, and he waked himself calling his mother's name in a paroxysm of terror and grief. . . .
>
> After a while he could not tell whether he were awake or not. He could still sense a faint motion of curtains in the dark window and the garden smells, but he was talking to his mother too, who had been dead thirty years. She had been an invalid, but now she was well; she seemed to emanate that abounding serenity as of earth which his sister had done since her marriage and the birth of her child, and she sat on the side of the bed, talking to him. With her hands, her touch, because he realised that she had not opened her mouth. Then he saw that she wore a shapeless garment of faded calico and that Belle's rich, full mouth burned sullenly out of the halflight, and he knew that she was about to open her mouth and he tried to scream at her, to clap his hand to her mouth. But it was too late. He saw her mouth open; a thick, black liquid welled in a bursting bubble that splayed out upon her fading chin and the sun

was shining on his face and he was thinking He smells black. He smells like that black stuff that ran out of Bovary's mouth when they raised her head. (*SO*, 60)

Horace's mother, his sister, his wife, Ruby Lamar, and Emma Bovary, the adulteress, all the objects of his sexual consciousness, become fused with Popeye himself, condensed in his imagination into one horrifying, repulsive image. Thus his repression, all his life, of *something* connected with sex and aggression and death and disgust and his mother is made fairly explicit; we may, then, legitimately wonder whether Horace's mother were not in fact much more akin to Caroline Compson than to the frail, helpless wraith of a woman he insists upon remembering. Given many other relationships between Horace and Quentin Compson, and between the novels in which they appear, we might well look backward to the relationship between Caroline and Jason Compson for some sense of the nature of Horace's parents' relationship, and of their effect on their children; or to Addie Bundren and Anse.

We must look to Freud one more time, briefly, in a related and extremely important matter, to point out the degree to which Oedipal conflicts function as part of the dynamic of *Sanctuary* and other works of this period, and how those conflicts mesh with the problems caused by the primal scene to create the kinds of problems I have described Faulkner's characters as having. I am pleased to quote a letter on this subject from Dr. Ralph Roughton, a practicing psychoanalyst, which may help to make the connection:

> I want to suggest that *Sanctuary* grows out of, and is an expression of, a child's mixed reaction of excitement and horror at having seen, or fantasized seeing, his parents in sexual intercourse. And I'm thinking of this, not so much as one discreet experience, but as the whole murky developmental process of sexual awareness, curiosity, tension, fear, excitement, shattering of idealization and much more. The great mystery that surrounds this in little children, the fantasies that it stimulates (whether they see anything or not). When there is an actual witnessing two adults in sex, it often is interpreted by the child as a fight, or as one doing something bad to the other. Often, of

course, it occurs in the dark, which makes even more mystery, misunderstanding, and distorted fantasying. And often, when a child bursts into their bedroom at such a moment, the child is harshly and hastily dealt with by parents who are angry and/or anxious about the event. Those are some of the realities. Add to this the whole constellation of oedipal desires and fears, jealousy and guilt. Especially in older children, where it is not an accidental event, but an attempt to spy, there is disbelief that his parents would do such a thing. Often a boy will feel his mother has been unfaithful to him; he may experience a shattering disillusionment that his madonna mother would indulge in something so base. Whatever sexual desires he may have himself felt directed at her may produce enough guilt that fear of punishment by father becomes predominant. And I want to emphasize that all this can happen even without an actual "primal scene."[10]

The Oedipus complex is everywhere in *Sanctuary*, everywhere mixed up in the numerous inversions and transpositions of identity which are, according to Freud, the mind's way of dealing with such trauma, which make it possible for Horace in one scene to become Popeye, Temple, and Little Belle, and in yet another to fuse in his suddenly awakened mind his mother, his sister, his wife, Ruby, Popeye, and Emma Bovary; I have suggested in another paper on *Sanctuary*[11] that Miss Reba and Popeye, for example, are inversions of his mother and father, inversions which both hide and symbolically reveal precisely the characteristics of his parents that he is hell-bent on repressing. Horace even jokes, if nervously, about his Oedipus complex, in a scene toward the beginning of *Sanctuary* when Belle accuses him of being "in love with your sister. What do the books call it? What sort of complex?" He evades the issue entirely by punning: "'Not complex,' he said. 'Do you think that any relation with her could be complex?'" (*SO*, 16). Oedipus Tyrannus is himself manifestly present in the entire judicial system enshrined in *Sanctuary* in the numerous corrupt judges, legis-

10. Ralph Roughton to Noel Polk, 21 July 1983. I am grateful to Dr. Roughton for permission to publish portions of his most penetrating letter.
11. See "The Space Between Sanctuary."

lators, lawyers, and police chiefs, who make laws and break them and punish willfully, harshly, wrongfully, implacably: Justice *is* blind. This avatar of Oedipus is as much a hovering presence in *Sanctuary* as the gray-haired bespectacled lady who is the chief subject of this paper; the two, as we shall see, are not unrelated. Further, and finally, Oedipus himself actually makes an appearance in *Sanctuary,* though his two essential characteristics are split between clubfooted Eustace Graham, the district attorney, a father figure who with Narcissa's help does in fact punish Horace, in the courtroom, and Blind Pap, the mysterious figure at the Old Frenchman Place, who with his cane is more than a little like Temple's own judge father and who, in Temple's imagination at any rate, witnesses, without trying to stop, her humiliation and rape by Popeye.

I am not, however, so much interested in the father as I am in the mother, and I'm less interested in both than in the ways in which their children react to them. I want now to go back to that gray-haired bespectacled old lady for a few minutes, to race through a few other works of this period, to suggest the ubiquity of this character, the surprising variety of guises in which she appears; I want to suggest something about the meanings Faulkner attached to her, and to observe the variety of ways young Yoknapatawphans find to deal with the lives their parents have handed them. I apologize for the plot summaries to follow, but that seems to me now the most efficient way to cover a lot of material in a small amount of time.

With one exception, Miss Jenny DuPre is perhaps the best-known of Faulkner's old ladies; she has prominent roles in *Flags in the Dust, Sanctuary,* and "There Was a Queen." She is pretty generally admired by Faulknerians, and it is easy to see her in these three works as merely exercising the privileges of her age in becoming a crotchety and sharp-tongued but finally wise and sympathetic old lady. But she is frequently and unexplainably querulous, rude, impatient, intolerant, and downright mean throughout all these works, and she is in her own way as nihilistic in her pronouncements on the meaning of life as Jason Compson and Addie Bundren's father, though she does have the saving grace of a sense, albeit savage, of humor. Miss Jenny is a war widow; she was married for two years, widowed, and never remarried. So closely is she connected with windows that she even brings one with her, a "narrow" one, "with leaded vari-colored panes,"[12] when she comes from Carolina to stay with her nephew, old Bayard; she brought it to Bayard: along with Miss Jenny herself, the window was, significantly, his mother's death-bed legacy to old Bayard. It is interesting to note that in the manuscript, but not in the book, Miss Jenny is Bayard's sister, not his aunt (*Flags* ms, 27–28): it is not clear why Faulkner changed it in *Flags*, but the significance of the brother-sister relationship there so stuck in his mind that three decades later, writing *The Town*, Faulkner remembered their relationship as that of siblings.[13] Under Miss Jenny's soft graying exterior lurks, we can now imagine, the same sorts of frustrations that we find in other women of her type. She diverts that energy into acceptable channels: she

> enjoyed humanity in its more colorful mutations, preferring lively romance to the most impeccable of dun fact, so she took in the more lurid afternoon paper even though it was yesterday's when it reached her, and read with cold avidity accounts of arson and murder and violent dissolution and adultery; in good time and soon the American scene was to supply her with diversion in the form of bootleggers' wars. (*Flags*, 35)

The manuscript again supplies a telling variant; the final sentence reads: "in good time and soon the American scene was to furnish her with soul's ease in the form of bootleggers' wars" (*Flags* ms, 29). Clearly her sharp tongue, her avidity for the sensational, are vicarious thrills, substitutions for a kind of expe-

---

12. *Flags in the Dust*, ed. Douglas Day (New York: Random House, 1974), 34. Hereafter *Flags*.
13. *The Town* (New York: Random House, 1957), 139.

rience which she has been denied, but for which, at some psychological level, she longs. It is not absolutely clear why she dies at the end of "There Was a Queen," except that it is clearly related to her adamant and self-righteous disapproval of Narcissa's liaison with a Jew; how much of envy is involved is impossible to say, but one early version of "There Was a Queen" is entitled "Through the Window."

In *Flags in the Dust* Narcissa Benbow is associated many times with windows, both those she looks out of and those through which she is spied upon. It is manifestly clear throughout *Flags* that her feelings for Horace are more maternal than sexual; in one scene which suggests her true place in Horace's psyche and her part in the pattern I'm trying to describe, Horace comes to her to talk while she is lying in bed, "beneath the shaded light, with the dark splash of her hair upon the pillow, and only her eyes moved as he crossed the room . . . watching him with sober interrogation" (*Flags*, 241).

In *The Sound and the Fury* Quentin takes Little Sister Death into a bakery where they are greeted by a lady who thoroughly disapproves of the Italian girl's presence in her store, though perhaps Quentin interprets her disapproval somewhat otherwise; she appears in "her neat grey face her hair tight and sparse from her neat grey skull, spectacles in neat grey rims riding approaching like something on a wire. . . . She looked like a librarian" (*SF*, 155); a deleted line in the manuscript adds, "or at least, a school teacher" (*SF* ms, 58). She glares at Quentin: "She just needed a bunch of switches, a blackboard behind her 2 × 2 e 5," he says (*SF*, 156). She does give the little urchin a loaf of bread; but she does so so ungenerously as to render the gift devoid of any charity.

In *Sanctuary* one of the prim Madames who sits around with Miss Reba after Red's funeral swilling gin and beer and talking about their trade is a woman "primly erect, in gold nose-glasses on a gold chain and neat iron-gray hair. She looked like a schoolteacher" (SO, 246). Temple herself is described in Miss Reba's bed, "the covers to her chin and her face small and wan, framed in the rich sprawl of her hair" (SO, 170; see also 175).

In "The Brooch," Howard Boyd's invalid mother controls his life and his wife's from her bedroom, at the top of the stairs behind a closed door. When they see her, or even when they imagine her, she is "high-propped on the pillows, with her tallow face and dark inscrutable eyes and the hair which Amy said resembled weathered cotton."[14] Howard's way out, like Quentin Compson's, is to commit suicide. Her constant observing presence is symbolized by the light from her room at the top of the stairs shining through the transom over her door.

"Miss Zilphia Gant," whose existence can be traced to December of 1928, less than a month before he was to start the final push to finish Sanctuary, is perhaps Faulkner's least subtle and so most revealing treatment of these themes. Zilphia's father is a travelling man who leaves home for another woman; Zilphia's mother hunts him down with a shotgun, and kills him; she seeks him "with the capability of a man, the pertinacity of a Fate, the serene imperviousness of a vestal out of a violated temple, and then returned to her child, her face cold, satiate and chaste."[15] She rears Zilphia in a house which is literally a prison, even to the barred windows. The townspeople see Zilphia's "wan small face watching them, or, holding to the bars, coughing" (US, 371). Mrs. Gant cruelly examines Zilphia for signs of puberty by making her "strip naked [each month] and stand cringing before her while the savage light fell through the bars" (US, 373). As she gets older, Zilphia becomes a "neat woman, with neat hair. Her skin was the color of celery and she was a little plump in a flabby sort of way. Her glasses lent a baffled, ascetic look to her face" (US, 375). She becomes enamoured of a housepainter who first

14. "The Brooch," in Collected Stories (New York: Random House, 1950), 655. Hereafter CS.
15. "Miss Zilphia Gant," in Uncollected Stories of William Faulkner, ed. Joseph Blotner (New York: Random House, 1979), 370. Hereafter US.

sees her and then continues to stare at her through the window as she sits sewing, and at whom she obviously stares through the same barred window; she dreams at night of things which "the painter performed monstrously with his pot and brush." To make sure that we don't miss the implications of this dream, Faulkner tells us that now and then "she dreamed of the pot and brush alone. They would be alive, performing of themselves actions of monstrous and ritualled significance" (*US*, 375). She marries the painter, but her mother, again with shotgun, denies him entrance to the house, and intimidates Zilphia into staying with her; though the painter begs, Mrs. Gant maintains a vigil, "in a chair at the front window, the shotgun leaning at her hand. For three days she sat there, rigid, erect, her eyes closed, sweating slowly . . . . That night Mrs. Gant died, erect and fully dressed in the chair" (*US*, 378).

Alone, Zilphia hires a detective to follow her husband's life, and lives vicariously through the reports. "Sometimes at night she would become one of the two of them, entering their bodies in turn and crucified anew by her ubiquity, participating in ecstasies the more racking for being vicarious and transcendant of the actual flesh" (*US*, 380); a passage deleted from the manuscript tells us that when she received word that the wife was pregnant, she "dreamed that night that she was shackled to the wall of their bedroom, her eyelids wedged [open]" ("Miss Zilphia Gant" ms, 9). She tries to commit suicide, but fails. She spends ten years dreaming and weeping. Then she begins to realize that "for some time now she had been dreaming of negro men. 'Something is about to happen to me,'" she thinks, like Temple Drake and Joe Christmas. Like Minnie Cooper, she fantasizes a sexual experience with a black man. When she learns that both her husband and his wife are dead, she goes to get the child, brings her to Jefferson; repeating her own life, she becomes her own mother and begins to rear the little girl as she had been reared, in a house with barred windows.

Miss Minnie Cooper, in "Dry September," also fantasizes about Negro men; the fantasy becomes so real that she accuses one of raping her and so causes the death of Will Mayes. Minnie is "thirty-eight or thirty-nine." She lives in a "small frame house with her invalid mother and a thin, sallow, unflagging aunt,"[16] a very uneventful existence, life and lovers having passed her by. More significant is the interest her friends have in her experience: "Do you feel strong enough to go out?" they ask her when they come to take her to a movie, "their eyes bright too, with a dark glitter. 'When you have had time to get over the shock, you must tell us what happened. What he said and did; everything'" (CS, 180). Clearly their fantasies have taken routes similar to hers.

"Elly" is particularly revealing, in that Elly is compounded of parts of Temple Drake, Caddy, Miss Quentin, Addie Bundren, Zilphia Gant, and Minnie Cooper. She is an eighteen-year-old girl who lives in Jefferson, in a "dark house"—a designation emphasized several times throughout the story—with her parents and her deaf grandmother who, she feels, watches her all the time. She is, like Caddy and Quentin, a very promiscuous young lady, lying "almost nightly" in the shadows created by the house's "deep veranda with screening vines and no lights,"[17] with just about any male, although she will go no farther with them than heavy necking, out of fear of becoming pregnant. After such sessions, she has to walk up the stairs to her room; at the top of the stairs is her grandmother's room, from the door of which "a single square of light" falls "upon the upper hallway." She passes the room and sometimes looks in, sometimes not, to where the grandmother sits in the bed, "erect, an open book in her hands, facing the hall" (CS, 208). What part her parents play in her life we do not know, except that her grandmother's most potent threat, what Elly fears most, is that she will tell Elly's father. Elly, however, apparently is promiscuous through no pleasure that it gives her; she is simply striking back at her

16. "Dry September," CS, 173.
17. "Elly," CS, 208.

grandmother. She stares at herself in the mirror, sees her face
"flattened . . . and weary and dulled with kissing," and she
thinks with disgust:

'My God. Why do I do it? What is the matter with me?' thinking of
how tomorrow she must face the old woman again with the mark of
last night upon her mouth like bruises, with a feeling of the pointlessness and emptiness of life more profound than the rage or the
sense of persecution. (*CS*, 209)

The fact that she feels the pointlessness and emptiness of her life
to be more profound than her rage or her sense of being persecuted is an important index to her character, and has implications for our discussion, in a moment, of *Light in August*. She
says "My God. How could I. How could I. I don't want any man,
anything" (*CS*, 211). At a crucial moment in the story she repeats
the action of so many of Faulkner's characters, of looking out a
window at a burgeoning world which both attracts and repels
her: from her mother's bedroom window, she watches the
"infinitesimal clematis tendrils as they crept and overflowed up
the screen and onto the veranda roof with the augmenting summer" (*CS*, 214). Part of her rage, part of her frustration, is that
she is about to be married to a very dull childhood friend, a
cashier in the bank. She thinks of that marriage in language like
Addie Bundren's, "with quiet despair and resignation. 'Anyway I
can live quietly now,' she thought. 'At least I can live out the rest
of my dead life as quietly as if I were already dead'" (*CS*, 213). It
is not just her present life in that dark house which causes her
grief, then; more than anything, she despairs over the long life
to come, married to her banker, in which she will continue to
live in such a prison. When her grandmother interrupts her first
attempt to have sexual intercourse, she is driven to rage against
the old lady. But she is frustrated more than anything else because the grandmother caught them *before* they had a chance to
do anything: "At least, I would have had something, something
. . ." (*CS*, 212). Her decision, then, to give her virginity not just
to someone besides her husband but to a Negro, Paul de Mon-
tigny, is the fulfillment of Minnie Cooper's and Zilphia Gant's

fantasies, a doubly intense sin, a doubly intense entry into the
forbidden, a sin no less potent than incest. It is not just an act of
rebellion against her grandmother and the mores of Jefferson,
nor is it for her an attempt to escape from that life; sex with the
Negro, with the forbidden, is more in the nature of a momentary
reprieve, a chance to store up some excitement, some quality of
living, that she will have as a memory in the long, dull life to
come. It is not, however, a decision which makes her very happy
with herself; she cannot escape feelings of guilt, however strong
her feelings of resentment are.

   She has a very special relationship with her grandmother
which may tell us something about her. She is named for her—
Ailanthia—and they are frequently depicted as staring into each
other's eyes in ways which may remind us of Popeye's and
Horace's two-hour séance across the pond. Since she is deaf,
Elly must communicate with her by writing on small cards;
during one of their fights they have a tug of war over one of the
cards: it connects them, the narrator tells us, "like a queer umbilical cord" (CS, 218). We can best understand Elly, then, if we
see her grandmother operating in her life in two ways: she is first
the very model of what Elly is afraid she herself will, in time,
become: this terrifies her. Second, and more obviously, the
grandmother represents the part of Elly's own consciousness
which gives her more trouble than anything, her conscience, the
part that disapproves of her, that forces her to hate herself: when
she and Paul and her grandmother ride back home, the grandmother sits significantly between them, between Elly and the
object of her shame and degradation. In trying to horrify her
grandmother, by flaunting her liaison with a Negro, she is, like
Quentin Compson, begging for punishment. Thus when she
schemes to kill her grandmother, it is herself whom she wants to
punish.

   "A Rose for Emily" is perhaps the classic study of this character type. We know nothing of Emily's mother, but her father is
cast from the same mold as Temple Drake's father, Zilphia

Gant's mother, and Elly's grandmother. He drives her potential suitors away. The town thinks of Emily and her father "as a tableau": "Miss Emily a slender figure in white in the background, her father a spraddled silhouette in the foreground, his back to her and clutching a horsewhip, the two of them framed by the back-flung front door."[18] Long after her father dies, she keeps his portrait on a gilt easel before the fireplace, doubtless a portrait she herself has painted, though we are not told certainly. The town sees her over the years sitting in one of the many windows of that huge dark house, "the light behind her, and her upright torso motionless as that of an idol" (CS, 123). The city fathers who come to call on her about her taxes, find her

> a small, fat woman in black, with a thin gold chain descending to her waist and vanishing into her belt, leaning on an ebony cane with a tarnished gold head. . . . She just stood in the door and listened quietly. . . . Then they could hear the invisible watch ticking at the end of the gold chain. (CS, 121)

The ebony cane with the gold knob is like the one flourished by Temple Drake's father; and I wonder whether in dressing Miss Emily in black, and in giving her that thin watch chain and watch, Faulkner somehow connected Miss Emily and Popeye: a number of other characters, including Simon McEachern, are characteristically dressed in black. It is a possibility worth some thought.

Emily dies "in a heavy walnut bed with a curtain, her gray head propped on a pillow yellow and moldy with age and lack of sunlight" (CS, 129). The townspeople who come to the house out of curiosity to look at her body find her laid out in the parlor, "with the crayon face of her father musing profoundly above the bier" (CS, 129); and, of course, they find upstairs, on the pillow beside Homer Barron's skeleton, the gray-haired evidence of Miss Emily's necrophilia.

It is more than mere necrophilia, however; Homer Barron—

18. "A Rose for Emily," CS, 123.

whose name signifies not just "barren home" but perhaps also blindness, perhaps Oedipus—can also be seen as a substitute for her father. Like her father, he carries a "whip in a yellow glove" when they ride through the streets during their "courtship"; more significantly, she completes with Homer's body the gesture she began when her father had died, of simply refusing to give up the body to the necessary authorities. Whether she actually makes physical love to this "father" before he is murdered is not clear; but there can be no doubt that after his death she symbolically and repeatedly consummates the Oedipal dream. The townspeople are more correct than they know when they surmise that "with nothing left, she would have to cling to that which had robbed her, as people will" (CS, 124). This is a summation that seems to me to be central to an understanding of many of the tormented characters in Faulkner's fiction of this period.

I want to conclude with a discussion of *Light in August*, which is not so far out of the range of our 1927–1931 time period as its 1932 publication date would indicate. It was in fact written, according to dates on the manuscript, between mid-August of 1931 and mid-February of 1932. It stands as the premier exemplar of nearly all of the themes I have been discussing. They and the images that underlie them are laid out just as plainly, if by no means so crudely, as in "Miss Zilphia Gant." I will only remind you, if I need to, that the manuscript of *Light in August* bears the deleted title *Dark House*.[19]

Joe Christmas's childhood is so dreary and bleak as to make of it a kind of reductio ad absurdum, almost in some ways a parody, of all childhoods in Faulkner. It is so bleak that Joe represses most of it from his conscious mind; the long flashback in chapter

19. In this discussion of *Light in August*, as well as in that of *Sanctuary*, I am moving in directions already provocatively mapped out by André Bleikasten in his important new book, *Parcours de Faulkner* (Paris: Editions Ophrys; Association des Publications près les Universités de Strasbourg, 1982). I am particularly grateful to him for suggesting that I look into Freud's Wolf Man.

6 which recounts his earliest years is in fact specifically presented as the work of his *unconscious:* "Memory believes before
knowing remembers."[20] Embedded in his unconscious is the
prison world wasteland of the orphanage: "a corridor in a big
long garbled cold echoing building of dark red brick soot-
bleakened by more chimneys than its own, set in a grassless
cinderstrewnpacked compound surrounded by smoking factory
purlieus and enclosed by a ten foot steel-and-wire fence like a
penitentiary or a zoo" (*LA*, 111). The building has "bleak windows where in rain soot from the yearly adjacenting chimneys
streaked like black tears" (*LA*, 111).

If the narrative indirection of *Sanctuary* makes it impossible
to do more than speculate about the primal scene, there can be
no doubt that it is the central episode in Joe Christmas's childhood, the event of which all the misery of his later life is a
repercussion. Joe actually witnesses, or rather hears, the primal
scene, the intercourse between the dietitian and the young intern, who have been rather carefully set up as substitute parents
of the orphaned child—the dietitian through her constant association with Joe's food, a common factor among all of the women
Joe deals with; and it is of course the intern who finds him on the
orphanage's steps on Christmas Eve. At any rate, the primal
scene itself is clear enough, and Joe's experience follows the
pattern established by the Wolf Man: the Wolf Man defecates,
Joe vomits, symbolically the same thing. Like the Wolf Man, Joe
after this associates all things sexual with filth and shame: recall
the image of the cracked urn. He kicks and beats the young
Negro girl he and the other boys are about to have sex with, and,
later, he thinks of his relationship with Joanna Burden "as
though he had fallen into a sewer" (*LA*, 242); such associations
may be what causes Quentin Compson to want to smear mud on
himself and on Caddy when Caddy, for example, catches him
with Natalie. Joe torments the dietitian by constantly putting
himself in her way, to get his punishment over with; he in fact

20. *Light in August* (New York: Harrison Smith & Robert Haas), 111. Hereafter *LA*.

spends the rest of his life unconsciously looking for it. As an adult he constantly seeks ways to get himself beaten up. As a child and adolescent, he invites regular beatings from his foster father, and accepts them not just as his due, but as something he positively must have; Simon McEachern is, of course, more than happy to oblige him. In the well-known scene during which he is being punished for refusing to learn his catechism Joe stands erect, holding the pamphlet containing the catechism, "his face and the pamphlet lifted, his attitude one of exaltation" (*LA*, 140).

Mrs. McEachern, who tries to be kind to him, is physically at least a prototype of the woman we have been describing. Joe first sees her, when he arrives, waiting for him:

> waiting on the porch—a patient, beaten creature without sex de-marcation at all save the neat screw of graying hair and the skirt. . . . It was as though instead of having been subtly slain and corrupted by the ruthless and bigoted man into something beyond his intend-ing and her knowing, she had been hammered stubbornly thinner and thinner like some passive and dully malleable metal, into an attenuation of dumb hopes and frustrated desires now faint and pale as dead ashes. (*LA*, 155)

She, however, oppresses Joe more with her long-delayed mothering than does McEachern with his harsh uprightness; he perceives her as one of his "enemies" (*LA*, 194). Like Caddy and Quentin and Lena Grove, he escapes periodically from that house through the window, by means of a rope he maliciously allows Mrs. McEachern to help him hide. After he has killed McEachern, and prepares to make his final escape from this world, he returns to steal the money she has hidden, and to repudiate her along with the father. She is standing in the door-way when he arrives: he "swept her aside as he might have a curtain across the door" (*LA*, 194), symbolically destroying the curtain, the veil, that so imprisons Horace and Quentin and Elly, and so many others.

Joe escapes the McEachern house; but he never escapes those patterns of reaction that were established in him during his childhood. Faulkner is at pains, then, to suggest that his appearance at the house of Joanna Burden—a name that we can now see has as much to do with Joe's problem as with Joanna's, or the South's—is symbolically, a return to the McEachern home; in Joanna are combined all the most potent characteristics of his foster parents, Simon's rigid puritanism, Mrs. McEachern's frustrated and hopeless female life. Joe thinks of the McEacherns at crucial times in his relationship with Joanna: stealing the cold peas from the stove, and climbing in and out of her windows; the scene in which he throws Joanna's proffered food on the floor is significantly a repetition of his earlier rejection of Mrs. McEachern's plate. There may even be some reason to see in the similarity of their names—Joe and Joanna—an attempt to suggest a sort of mirror relationship, perhaps that of brother and sister, in the two lovers-to-be, so that in some ways Joe is also fulfilling the incestuous fantasies of Quentin, Horace, and Darl.

Joe first sees Joanna Burden through the window of her dark house as a shadow moving across the wall of the only lighted room (*LA*, 215). He climbs through the window to steal food from the kitchen. Curiously, the window is open, and we surmise later that Joanna has, all of her life, fantasized about just such an occurrence: like Elly, like Miss Zilphia Gant, like Minnie Cooper, she fantasizes about Negro men. Nor, in her sexual frustration and loneliness, is she by any means alone in *Light in August:* she has many sisters. There are two scenes worth mentioning. The first occurs in the opening chapter, in the Armstid home after Henry has taken Lena Grove there. Mrs. Armstid has a "savage screw of gray hair at the base of her skull and a face that might have been carved in sandstone" (*LA*, 15); she is a "gray woman not plump and not thin, manhard, workhard, in a serviceable gray garment worn savage and brusque, her hands on her hips, her face like those of generals who have been defeated in battle" (*LA*, 14). She is hospitable to Lena, even gives her money; but she is not *kind.* While Lena is her "guest" she is "savage": she cooks with "an amount of attention out of all

proportion to the savage finality with which she built the fire"
(*LA*, 14–15). The intensity of her hospitality suggests a tumultuous ambivalence as she contemplates Lena's presence in her
respectable house: at the top of her reaction is her moral outrage; just under the surface of the outrage, however, and bubbling furiously, is a lot of envy—perhaps unconscious, certainly
never verbalized—of Lena's youth, of her freedom, and perhaps, even though Mrs. Armstid has herself borne several children, of Lena's untroubled sexuality. Lena's presence, then, fills
her with a hatred of her own life. The second scene occurs as the
townsfolk gather around Joanna's burning house, the scene of
the crime. They come out, grateful to Joanna for supplying them
with an "emotional barbecue," a "Roman holiday almost." They
hope that Joanna has been raped as well as murdered, though
this hope is not so coldblooded and heartless, nor the townfolk
so pitiless, as the mere words suggest; for there is not so much
hatred as envy in their hearts. The women come,

> the idle ones in bright and sometimes hurried garments, with secret
> and passionate and glittering looks and with secret frustrated breasts
> (who have ever loved death better than peace) to print with a myriad
> small hard heels to the constant murmur *Who did it? Who did it?*
> periods such as perhaps *Is he still free? Ah. Is he? Is he?* (*LA*, 273)

Such are their own lives that death, particularly a violent, sexual
death, is better then peace.

Unlike Minnie Cooper and Zilphia Gant, Joanna is with Joe
able actually to live out her fantasies, all of them; Joe plays her
games, eats her food, listens to her use the foul forbidden
epithets that so excite her as they make love. But both live in a
state of constantly growing shame. Her guilt at last overpowers
the relationship. Joe goes to her bedroom and finds her, not in
bed, but at her desk: her hair, he notices, is "just beginning to
gray" and it is "drawn gauntly back to a knot as savage and ugly
as a wart on a diseased bough. . . . she looked up at him and he
saw that she wore steelrimmed spectacles which he had never
seen before" (*LA*, 260). Having assumed the mantel of guilt and
repression, she proceeds to try to make Joe do the same, just as

McEachern had done, by making him pray. Thus Joanna is for Joe Mother, who feeds him and cares for him for a long time without asking or expecting any return; but she is also Father, in whom are imbedded those hard manlike puritanical qualities that Joe is so conscious of when they make love: "My God . . . it was like I was the woman and she was the man" (LA, 222), he thinks. When they make love, Joe fulfills not only his own Oedipal fantasies, but also, and quite specifically, it seems to me, the Wolf Man's desire to be made love to by his father.

The final confrontation takes place with Joanna "sitting up in the bed, her back against the headboard" (LA, 266). In killing her, Joe not only rekills his father, who will not stay dead, but also kills that mother, the source of much of Yoknapatawpha's grief; it is a slaying many characters in Faulkner might applaud.

But of course Joe still cannot escape himself. All of his running after the murder is, like his efforts to get the dietitian to beat him, simply an effort to get caught, to get his punishment over with; he walks up and down the streets of Mottstown, waiting for somebody to recognize him (LA, 329). Nor can he escape the unceasing maternal Erynnis. Safe, he thinks, in jail, awaiting his trial and execution—like another black man, in Sanctuary, in the same jail, awaiting execution for the same crime of cutting his wife's throat—safe, he thinks, his sanctuary is violated by Mrs. Hines, a woman claiming to be his actual grandmother, who has the audacity to tell him that she is going to interfere, to help him by getting Rev. Hightower to lie for him—the same sort of slimy collusion that he so detested in Mrs. McEachern. Thus, I suggest, the reason he runs from the police guard on his final day is not, as Gavin Stevens pontificates, because of the conflict between his black and his white blood: his running is a desperate ultimate repudiation of the mother, one last attempt to get the punishment he deserves. What more appropriate punishment than castration and death for one who has sinned as he has?

There is much more, too much to deal with it all; but I cannot close without one brief word about Gail Hightower, who also spends an abnormal amount of time looking out his study window. You may not be surprised, by this time, to learn that Hightower too had a mother who was an invalid for twenty years before she died; presumably she was an invalid when she gave birth to Hightower, so there may be some reason to wonder about the cause of her invalidism. He remembers her and his father in a passage which in effect sums up the meaning of mother—indeed, of family, of the Oedipal triangle itself—in the Faulkner of this period. He remembers her

> first and last as a thin face and tremendous eyes and a spread of dark hair on a pillow, with blue, still, almost skeleton hands. . . . at eight and nine and ten he thought of her as without legs, feet; as being only that thin face and the two eyes which seemed daily to grow bigger and bigger, as though about to embrace all seeing, all life, with one last terrible glare of frustration and suffering and foreknowledge. . . . Already, before she died, he could feel them through all walls. They were the house: he dwelled within them, within their dark and all-embracing and patient aftermath of physical betrayal. He and she both lived in them like two small, weak beasts in a den, a cavern, into which now and then the father entered—that man who was a stranger to them both, a foreigner, almost a threat: so quickly does the body's wellbeing alter and change the spirit. He was more than a stranger: he was an enemy. He smelled differently from them. He spoke with a different voice, almost in different words, as though he dwelled by ordinary among different surroundings and in a different world; crouching beside the bed the child could feel the man fill the room with rude health and unconscious contempt, he too as helpless and frustrated as they. [*LA*, 449–50]

I have sped rather quickly through a lot of material, necessarily hitting only the high spots and drastically oversimplifying. I have by no means exhausted the high spots or even mentioned numerous of the other images which also crop up with compulsive regularity in the fiction of this period, and which bear directly on the subject of this paper. There are many more, which with the gray-haired bespectacled matron of our deliberations form a substructure to the works of this period, and perhaps

beyond, a base which all the works, or nearly all, touch at sometimes one point, sometimes many. Taken together, all the elements of this substructure, in their various configurations, open
a window, if you'll pardon me, into a world of sexual frustration,
of violence, that we have to be sure written a great deal about.
But we have tended to define the frustration and impotence, the
emptiness, the loneliness, the meaninglessness, the masochism,
in terms of twentieth-century cultural disorders—the postwar
malaise, the Waste Land, the modern world, the decline of the
Old South, apply whatever rubric you will. The window now
opened makes it clear, I believe, that for Faulkner at least these
disorders are considerably older than the modern world, older
than culture, older even than myth: they take us right back into
and even beyond the womb itself, into the "den . . . cavern" we
all, with Gail Hightower, shared with our mothers (*LA*, 450),
right back into the "old fetid caves where knowing began" (*LA*,
272).

An Anthropological Approach
to Yoknapatawpha

BERNDT OSTENDORF

The idea of this paper, which the title broadly, but clumsily embraces, is simple: that there is a similarity between the writing of anthropology and the writing of fiction, a similarity in the structure of desire, the logic of discovery, and the logic of demonstration. The established division of labor between anthropology and fiction, that is, between scientific and artistic knowledge about man, is due to an arbitrary separation and hence to a superficially separate socialization pattern of these identical twins of Western curiosity, a common parentage which led to a parallel development of the novel and of anthropology. The passion that inspires anthropologists to do what they do is fueled by motives that also make novelists write, and the way both go about finding their objective world—that choreography of perception, selection, and combination—confirms their kinship. Anthropology and fiction share a basic stock of what Northrop Frye calls pregeneric myths, and a common philosophical purpose emerges in the very forms they use to put their respective knowledge on paper, in narratives, scenarios, stories, plots, genealogies, or other socially structured wholes. A second idea, more specifically related to the concerns of this conference, is that among the modern American writers of fiction Faulkner has the most significant things to say to anthropologists of Southern culture. Conversely, an anthropological frame might afford a different perspective on the accustomed picture of Yoknapatawpha. Faulkner's preoccupation with a whole way of life and a complex culture of a particular region and his imaginative

94

reconstruction of how that culture came about through man's interaction with nature and through the historical consequences of this interaction are of interest to the cultural anthropologist. Yet, more than these common interests and approaches, it is Faulkner's awareness of the centrality of storytelling as man's most essential structuring activity, his idea that man creates himself and decodes himself through imaginative webs of significance, which makes his work appealing to the contemporary anthropologist.

The kinship of literature and anthropology is manifested in the many writers who have written quasi-anthropological novels—say Cary, Conrad, Kipling, Melville—and the many anthropologists who have written poetry and novels, often furtively in order not to jeopardize their scientific credibility. Ruth Benedict, Zora Neale Hurston, and Edward Sapir come to mind, or Stanley Diamond and Laura Bohannan in our time.[1] I would like to begin my paper with an ethnographic fiction written by Laura Bohannan, an anthropologist known for her work on Africa. She also wrote a remarkable novel, *Return to Laughter* (New York, 1954), but under her *nom de plume* Elenore Smith Bowen—an interesting anthropological phenomenon, this division of the writing personality into a body natural and a body fictional. The ethnographic fiction I am going to examine was published under her real name. Under the established rules of the game which Bohannan previously endorsed this could be taken as a marker for nonfictionality; but the story is, to paraphrase Aristotle, too plausible to be true, a well-known contradiction in Faulkner's storyland.

The story is a sort of epistemological tale which makes a number of points about anthropology and fiction, about "reading" a culture from a foreign perspective, about the operation called "verstehen," and about cultural bias, point of view, and author-

---

1. When asked why he chose anthropology as a profession, Stanley Diamond answered "I had selected it because it was the next best thing to poetry." Quoted in Dan Rose, "In Search of Experience: The Anthropological Poetics of Stanley Diamond," *American Anthropologist*, 85 (1983), 348.

ity. Chief protagonist on this level of the story is Hermeneutics itself. What should interest Faulkner scholars is that the story reconstructs and dramatizes a *storytelling event* set in West Africa among the Tiv, an isolated African tribe far away from the corrosive effects of Western civilization, where Bohannan did field work as a budding anthropologist. One rainy day she and the Tiv elders sit around and drink beer, telling stories, which they explain, analyze, and comment on, an event quite similar to a Faulkner conference. These are noisy occasions requiring large quantities of beer, and the ensuing battles of interpretation, Bohannan gradually learns, are just as important as the stories themselves. We begin to realize, as we enter the story, how Bohannan and the Tiv, how text and context, the native and alien point of view depend on each other and are dialectically intertwined, albeit under conditions of hegemony, which means that the final interpretation depends just as much on power as on plausibility. Gradually the tacit presumption of Western power (i.e., of that scientific superiority which brought Bohannan to the Tiv as an anthropologist and not as a true partner in dialogue) evaporates; the security of her rational point of view, buttressed by centuries of literate imperialism and dominance over "lesser people without the law," vanishes before Tiv logic, friendship, and local authority. She becomes confused, like Quentin in *Absalom, Absalom!*, and does not know what to make of it. The very fact that the Tiv not only interpret Western culture within Tiv logic, but by virtue of their local authority also foist it upon her, throws a new light on the dubious presumption of Western, or any, logic that it can understand a foreign culture better than the natives—a presumption under which we are happily assembled here in Yoknapatawpha.

The story, which is entitled "Shakespeare in the Bush," begins in Oxford, England.[2] At a party in her honor Bohannan, an American, reacts rather testily to the claim of her British hosts

2. *Natural History*, 75 (August–September 1966), 28–33. "Shakespeare in the Bush" is reprinted in *Everyman His Own Way*, ed. Alan Dundes (Englewood Cliffs, N.J.: Prentice Hall, 1978).

that one has to be born British to really understand Shakespeare. Angry at such cheek and arrogance, Bohannan argues the universality of certain stories, myths, and human interactions. Her hosts are not convinced and present her with a copy of *Hamlet*, which they urge her to read while she is doing field work among the Tiv. With this controversial point fresh in her mind (i.e., the universality or diversity of culture), she starts out for West Africa and begins her field work. One evening the elders watch her reading a book and ask her why on earth she is looking at this piece of paper, for they know paper primarily in the form of tax receipts. She answers that she is reading one of the important stories of her people. "Tell it to us," they urge. She is not in the mood to drink beer and refuses. Now they give her an ultimatum. They will no longer tell her any of their stories if she will not reciprocate and tell them one of her tales. It is interesting to note here that the Tiv implicitly protest against the one-directional flow of communication (i.e., the anthropologist's drawing stories out of the Tiv, but giving nothing in return), which characterizes all anthropological inquiry. The Tiv at any rate will not tolerate this subtle brain-drain, or rather story-drain, and insist on dialogue. Bohannan protests again, and ironically, pleads inferiority and inexperience when in fact she has been dominating the Tiv in her role as anthropologist. The Tiv insist on being met on their own ground and on their established conditions. These, however, are hard to meet—as Bohannan knows—for the art of storytelling is highly regarded among the Tiv. Standards are high, competition is fierce, and critical habits rough. The Tiv elders, aware of her fears, give her a symbolic thirty yards' headstart by telling her that they, being the elders, will not only help her if she should get stuck, but also will correct her mistakes which she, being young and a woman, is obviously entitled to make.

> I began in the proper style, "Not yesterday, not yesterday, but long ago, a thing occurred. One night three men were keeping watch outside the homestead of the great chief, when suddenly they saw the former chief approach them."

"Why was he no longer their chief?"

"He was dead," I explained. "That is why they were troubled and afraid when they saw him."

"Impossible," began one of the elders . . . "Of course it wasn't the chief. It was an omen sent by a witch. Go on."

Slightly shaken I continued. "One of these three was a man who knew things"—the closest translation for scholar, but unfortunately it also meant witch. The second elder looked triumphantly at the first.[3]

Bohannan continues the story by saying that Horatio, not knowing what to do, takes Hamlet into his confidence since the matter is of vital importance to him. The elders look at each other in disgust. Such omens, they say, should be dealt with by the elders in consultation with the king's brother. Did not the king have a brother, they ask. Bohannan, feeling the story slip away, is getting slightly desperate.

"In our country the son is next to the father. The dead chief's younger brother had become the great chief. He had also married his elder brother's widow only about a month after the funeral."

"He did well," the old man beamed and announced to the others: "I told you that if we knew more about Europeans, we would find they really were very like us. In our country also," he added to me, "the younger brother marries the elder brother's widow and becomes the father of his children."

With one of the central structural pillars of *Hamlet* knocked clear out of the picture, Bohannan picks up the pieces.

I decided to skip the soliloquy. Even if Claudius was here thought quite right to marry his brother's widow, there remained the poison motif, and I knew that they would disapprove of fratricide. More hopefully I resumed, "That night Hamlet kept watch with the three who had seen his dead father. The dead chief again appeared, and although the others were afraid, Hamlet followed his dead father to one side. When they were alone, Hamlet's dead father spoke."

3. The semantic identification of knowledge with witchcraft is not altogether new or unknown to Western thought. After all, Socrates' self-knowledge is personified in "demons," and "daimones" in ancient Greek means "the knowing ones." Cowley mentions that Faulkner spoke of his "demons" or "voices" as an incorruptible part of his personality, the cursed alter ego, as it were.

"Omens can't talk!" The old man was emphatic.
"Hamlet's dead father wasn't an omen. Seeing him might have been an omen, but he was not." My audience looked as confused as I sounded. "It *was* Hamlet's dead father. It was a thing we call a 'ghost.'" I had to use the English word, for unlike many of the neighboring tribes, these people didn't believe in the survival after death of any individuating part of the personality.
"What is a 'ghost'? An omen?"
"No, a 'ghost' is someone who is dead but who walks around and can talk and people can hear and see him but not touch him."
They objected. "One can touch zombis."
"No, no! It was not a dead body the witches had animated to sacrifice and eat. No one else made Hamlet's dead father walk. He did it himself."
"Dead men can't walk," protested my audience as one man.
I was quite willing to compromise. "A 'ghost' is the dead man's shadow."
But again they objected. "Dead men cast no shadow."
"They do in my country," I snapped.

There is an interesting reversal in the relationship between Bohannan and the Tiv, a reversal of roles, of the flow of communication, of text and context, and of power. Under conditions defined by anthropology the Tiv are the informants, Tiv stories acquire meaning within Western rational discourse, and the anthropologist-as-scientist calls the shots, or defines standards of meaning. In that set-up the Tiv, like all natives, are at a clear disadvantage. However, now Bohannan is the informant, *Hamlet* is at the mercy of Tiv contextuality, and the elders lord it over the young female apprentice. The moral is simple: it all depends on who has the power to call the shots and who controls the encompassing cultural situation, within which the story is interpreted.
Like all cultures, Tiv culture is primarily self-centered and self-validating. We realize, reluctantly perhaps, that Western thought, too, may be such a prison house or labyrinth with intrareferential signposts controlled by *our* common sense. Bohannan finds herself involuntarily cast in that role which she had naively assigned to the Tiv, and she realizes that though she

controls the telling of *Hamlet,* she is still at the mercy of the encompassing Tiv discourse. In her growing panic she begins to understand that Hamlet through her use of Tiv language looks more and more like a Tiv chief's son and that the story acquires a resonance of contextual meaning which it did not have in Stratford and—more important—over which the elders, not she, have control. Clearly the words of her British hosts who claimed the particularity of cultural knowledge ring in her ears.

Hamlet's alleged madness is eagerly discussed by the Tiv elders, but who, they ask, would have an interest in bewitching him—for in the Tiv world madness is caused by witches. The solution is found, after much deliberation and "crossing of wires," in the scene with Hamlet in Gertrude's parlor with Polonius hiding behind the curtain. Hamlet, believing it is Claudius, yells "a rat" and runs his dagger through the cloth, stabbing Polonius. The elders call Polonius a fool. Why did he not yell, "It's me, Polonius"; for the Tiv being avid hunters have a habit of identifying themselves when hunting. When they see game stirring in the high grass they will yell "game" to make sure it is not one of the hunters, then take aim and shoot. Hamlet, being a good hunter, had yelled "a rat." But that Hamlet had intended to kill Claudius gives them some alarm. "'For a man to raise his hand against his father's brother and the one who has become his father—that is a terrible thing. The elders ought to let such a man be bewitched,'" the Tiv conclude. Now Hamlet's derangement makes some sense to them.

> "But if his father's brother had indeed been wicked enough to bewitch Hamlet and make him mad that would be a very good story indeed, for it would be his fault that Hamlet, being mad, no longer had any sense and thus was ready to kill his father's brother."
> There was a murmur of applause. *Hamlet* again was a good story to them, but it no longer seemed quite the same story to me.

The Laertes-Ophelia relationship is reconstructed in terms of Tiv kinship, it makes Tiv-sense (in German Tiv-Sinn). According to Tiv belief people do not drown—water being harmless—but are made to drown by witches. Again the problem needs to be addressed as to who would have an interest in drowning Ophelia.

> "Listen," said the elder, "and I will tell you how it was and how your story will go, then you may tell me if I am right. Polonius knew his son would get into trouble, and so he did. He had many fines to pay for fighting, and debts from gambling. But he had only two ways of getting money quickly. One was to marry off his sister at once, but it is difficult to find a man who will marry a woman desired by the son of a chief. For if the chief's heir commits adultery with your wife, what can you do? Only a fool calls a case against a man who will someday be his judge. Therefore Laertes had to take the second way: he killed his sister by witchcraft, drowning her so he could secretly sell her body to the witches."

Bohannan is increasingly powerless to argue against Tiv sense, for in the Tiv universe *Hamlet* does find a place and ends up making perfect sense. Here as in Britain she is at a territorial disadvantage. On British soil her British hosts claimed the right of interpretation, held the monopoly, as it were, and argued the particularity of all cultural knowledge on the basis of alleged American misreadings of Shakespeare. Now her own argument of the universality of certain myths goes out the Tiv chimney. In fact, the Tiv elders remind me of an assembly of Faulkner specialists, say in a Ph.D. qualifying examination. For they, quite like their Tiv opposite numbers, hold the monopoly of interpretation. After the story is told and analyzed the Tiv dismiss Bohannan, just as a female Ph.D. candidate might be dismissed with a passing grade "nice try," but they fault her on her grasp of anthropological theory:

> "You tell the story well, and we are listening. But it is clear that the elders of your country have never told you what the story really means. No, don't interrupt! We believe you when you say that your marriage customs are different, or your clothes and weapons. But people are the same everywhere. . . ."

The various layers of meaning in this story are at cross purposes and generate Socratic irony—that is, the type which creates self-knowledge and teaches, as Nietzsche says, a wholesome humility before the other. The storytelling event and the content of the story are dialogically at odds or enmeshed in a dialectic of ironies. They dramatize antiphonally the deep philosophical polarity or ambiguity of all cultural knowledge, anthropological or fictional. Clifford Geertz captured the tension of hermeneutic passion:

> Both literary critics and anthropologists . . . pursue their vocations haunted by a riddle quite as irresolvable as it is fundamental; namely, that the significant works of the human imagination . . . speak with equal power to the consoling piety that we are all like to one another and to the worrying suspicion that we are not.[4]

I would like to pursue this dialectic, or better dialogic frame, and branch out into a variety of areas where Faulkner's work touches the concerns of anthropologists or where anthropological questions might enlighten Faulkner scholarship.

UNIVERSALITY

The interpretation of *Hamlet* by the Tiv is a dramatistic event structured as a competing dialogue which on a metalevel is an indication that the Tiv are not only willing to talk, but willing to learn and to be informed while defending their point of view. Bohannan and the Tiv negotiate every point, as if they were at the SALT talks, and this negotiation or battle of modelling systems very quickly calls into doubt that there are universals or truths *outside* such modelling systems, that there is, for example, one common universal rationality which stands beyond specific cultures, that there is one structure of clean objectivity outside the messy Babel of conflicting discourses. Yet, it also demonstrates that there is common ground: what unites these two modelling systems, Bohannan's and theirs—and what unites all cultures—is not some sort of essential, or ontological, universal content such as humanism, but the ability and competence of all cultures to connect, to make sense, to interpret, to engage in

4. Clifford Geertz, "Found in Translation: On the Social History of the Moral Imagination," *The Georgia Review*, 31 (Winter 1977), 796. See also his *The Interpretation of Cultures* (New York: Basic Books, Inc., 1973).

dialogue, however incongruous the conflicting universes of discourse. This metacultural competence is the key that will let us out of the prison house of our particular language; it is the capacity which will enable us not to fully understand, but to make contact with the alien context, and embark on the road to understanding which never ends. This activity of connecting, interpreting, and making sense proceeds clearly from within one's own cultural presumptions and prejudices; and the root prejudice is that one's own convictions either are, or at least ought to be, universal—but that is normal. According to Lévi-Strauss, the only true universal is ethnocentrism of that sort. But once the journey into the unknown begins and the conversation between conflicting cultures is opened, the continuing battle itself will take care that those prejudices begin to erode and break down. However, for this to happen, the drama must continue unchecked by roadblocks parading as universals, and that the conversation must not end by some proverbial fiat or sentiments attributed to some elderly white male philosopher or Christian god. One look at Faulkner's characters tells us that he hated principled people or fundamentalists who stopped asking questions and had their minds made up once and for all, particularly when they stubbornly held on to empty abstractions or acted in a predetermined, mechanical fashion like robots or machines. Faulkner's original sin is stasis, rigidity, fundamentalism, and egocentrism, which in culture contact translates into ethnocentrism. As Ellison said of Faulkner's portrayal of blacks, he may have begun with the rigid stereotype but then he struggled on, at great pains, to discover the human being behind it.

Ultimately all interpretation relates to power; it depends on who has the right to foist his "universals" on others, a problem Faulkner was keenly aware of. When the Tiv and Bohannan are through interpreting *Hamlet,* the elders have won simply because they have the power. Like the Catholic church in doctrinal matters, they hold the *imprimatur: Roma locuta, causa finita.* Thus the tale is also a parable about the role of power and authority in interpretation. The evolving moral of the story is that anthropological interpretations are ultimately validated not by rationality, greater plausibility, or closer adherence to principles, but by power. As Humpty Dumpty put it so well, the question is not what words mean, but who has the power to say what they mean. That is why the "elders of interpretation" continue to be assailed and attacked at regular generational intervals, in Faulkner criticism as among the Tiv.

One could continue to draw interesting if not dangerous parallels between what happens in the story and what happens at literary conferences: Clearly it is remarkable that the efforts on the part of natives and nonnatives to make sense of the strange world of Yoknapatawpha on the basis of elusive tales and narratives of great semantic ambivalence continue, and that five decades of concerted effort on the part of the Faulkner priesthood have not exhausted Yoknapatawpha's interpretability. It is as if Faulkner intended to make just that point, that knowledge is an unending process which begins in misunderstanding. Clearly the point Bohannan tries to get across about the nature of anthropological knowledge is identical to Faulkner's larger epistemological purpose.

FROM THE NATIVE POINT OF VIEW

The reverse anthropological inquiry—the world of the anthropologist seen from the native point of view—creates what one might call the *lettres persanes* effect: it holds up a mirror to our tacit ethnocentrism camouflaged as universalism which, as Faulkner reminds us, gave much greater comfort to the early American settlers than to the Indians; it prohibits the naive comfort of what Nietzsche called the dogma of immaculate perception, and it throws into doubt our tendency to universalize our current ideological preference, our way of life.

Now it is common knowledge that anthropological monographs about the Kwakiutl, the Eskimos, the Mexicans, or the Samoans written in this century by Americans have that same *lettres persanes* effect. Getting to know a foreign culture (however subtly prejudiced the operation itself may be) makes one

look at one's own culture in a different, usually, but not necessarily, in a more critical light. My thesis is that Margaret Mead
was not unscientific or insufficiently rigorous in her methods,
but merely honest enough to articulate this phenomenon, even
to acknowledge it in a subtitle, thus naming an epistemological
hazard which others studiously ignore or sweep under the car-
pet of alleged objectivity. Objective understanding of a foreign
culture is itself a fiction. One can never read a culture clinically
without bringing in oneself and one's point of view. "Ethnog-
raphies are complex realistic fictions derived from research in
historical circumstances that can never be fully controlled,"[5]
writes the anthropologist James Clifford in defense of Margaret
Mead; and Giles Gunn says about poetry: "reading a poem, like
interpreting another culture, thus depends upon a fundamental
distinction between all that we are and all that we are not,
between all that we could be and that we cannot be or will not
be."[6] Faulkner could have said that.

Yes, it all sounds so familiar to the reader of *Absalom, Absalom!, The Sound and the Fury,* or *Go Down, Moses.* And it
speaks to the non-American reader of Faulkner's work who
draws comfort from the fact that this preoccupation with the
problem of knowing—the central concern of anthropology—is
precisely the pervasive theme of the classic Faulkner work: how
can we know the past, blacks, Indians, nature, culture and—by
a sort of *lettres persanes* effect—ourselves? And once we have
that knowledge, how can we turn it into language, text? Faulkner buries the *lettres persanes* effect in the structure of his
narrative, thus imposing the task of defining fictional knowledge—what Faulkner means—to the reader. The reader becomes Faulkner's anthropologist by being forcibly assigned the
role of interpreter, having to make sense of a strange and foreign
world without the benefit or security of point of view or fatherly

5. James Clifford, "The Other Side of Paradise," *Times Literary Supplement* (May
13, 1983), 475.
6. Giles Gunn, "The Semiotics of Geertz and the Moral Imagination," *Studies in the
Literary Imagination,* 12 (Spring 1979), 128. This essay I found particularly inspiring.

assistance from the author. Often the highest plausibility of a story (say Shreve's clear-headed plot-reduction of the Sutpen maze) has the least or lowest validation in fact. This is in itself a Faulknerian comment on the problem of understanding a foreign culture, or any culture.

It is interesting to note that Faulkner's caveats about ego- or ethnocentrism are today widely discussed in anthropological circles, but he voiced them—surely without having read Dilthey or Cassirer—in the thirties, far ahead of the pack of the paradigm changes, once again proving what Simmel, Boas, or Weber knew: that art is always in the vanguard of social thought, an old truth heavily underscored quite recently by Robert Nisbet in his book *Sociology as an Art Form.*

THE PROBLEM OF AESTHETIC AND CULTURAL DISTANCE

The proverbial wisdom that one cannot see the wood for all the trees states the need for distance in order to perceive or to make sense. Distance is indeed an analytic and poetic necessity to perceive significance in what would otherwise remain unconnected. Lack of distance, overwhelming immediacy, is Rosa's curse; her refusal to translate or work off Sutpen's violation of her integrity into some sort of retrospective abstraction is comparable to the refusal of undergraduates to read a text a second time; both refuse distance—or knowledge, and prefer the obstinate comfort of the "sentient meat."

It is, of course, one thing to read and understand the literature of one's own country of origin and quite another to read the literature of foreign places, whether in a foreign tongue or in translation. Surely, understanding the literature of one's own country is not genetically guaranteed or programmed; it too requires a distancing, an effort of estrangement as one important thrust of all hermeneutic practice. On a more mundane level, on that of reader response, one could argue that one reason why some authors are more readily accepted abroad than at home may have to do with cultural distance. Prophets are not appreciated at home, for their revelations are too near the native bone. The outsider will more easily accept the prophet since he is not weighted down by the burden of foreknowledge like Quentin, or rendered myopic by taboo, blinded by the quotidian and habituated to repress undesirable truths. At the same time Faulkner's work is not totally distant to the foreigner. His drive for the larger philosophical and anthropological contradictions, his handling of narrative strategies, his attention to the dynamics of emplotment rather than to stable plots, and the aura of the melodramatic which hovers over his work—all these translate easily into a variety of cultural frames.

The strategy of translation of course involves more than finding the *mot juste* or achieving an exact fit; it brings into focus the problem the Tiv had with *Hamlet*. Language is always bound into cultural structures of meaning; these are highly specific and fiercely local webs of significance which validate local human praxis. Meaning depends on doing, and the Tiv do things differently. Thus translation needs to reconstruct the doing of one culture within the frames of another culture. Translation—both metaphorical and real—has to negotiate, bargain, and settle disputes between two competing languages, just as Nabokov and Wilson fought over the issue of which language, Russian or English, should have poetic priority. By necessity it places the particulars of experience of one culture—how one eats, works, mates, and dies—in the context of how things are done in the other culture. Very often the translator has to translate the particulars of one culture into a more general framework or into an even more attenuated and particular frame of reference: too often translation means semantic attenuation, to speak Faulknerian. Being incapable of rendering the exact correlative of smell, sound, texture, and taste of specific Mississippi resonances, the translation, say into German or Japanese, has to fall back on the next best universalization that the experiential range of the receiving language permits, unless of course the translator becomes himself a writer by entirely recreating the text from within the native structure of feeling or by creating smells, sounds, textures, and tastes which have never before been expe-

rienced in his language. The latter choice invites an exotic response on the part of readers, the former leaves the original too
far behind. The conflict remains and must be negotiated.

All this while I am pretending that we know clearly what
Faulkner means in his very own language. Faulkner—I need not
belabor the obvious—uses a strategy of deliberately delayed
meaning, of partial disclosure, and of semantic obfuscation.
Even those who think they are natives must therefore translate,
must overcome a distance between Faulkner's semiotic island
and their own. James Merrill, the poet, says "all is translation/
And every bit of us is lost in it."[7] By another, more radical turn of
the screw, translation and distance bring us to a central concern
of modernist authors who tried to break the bounds of the
merely expressible and who doubted the referential power of
language. They need not have read Wittgenstein or Saussure,
for poets were first in their critique of a naive view of language
or form. Faulkner's language alone would mock his classification
as a realist. His radical doubt of fixities and rigidities is the
principle which may be found on all levels: the multiple, ambiguous points of view, compounded by hearsay and projection,
are mirrored in the polysemous softness of language, the soft
focus of his words which he uses in chorus rather than alone. A
chorus of words and a chorus of voices. Kafka writes: "You cannot
express what you are, for that you are; you can communicate
only that which you aren't, namely the lie. Only in the chorus
there may be some truth."[8] The reader therefore accepts a severe liability when he enters Faulkner territory of having to find
his own web of significance within that chorus of lies. "I would
think how words go straight up in a thin line, quick and harmless, and how terrible doing goes along the earth, clinging to it,
so that after a while the two lines are too far apart for the same
person to straddle from one to the other." Addie Bundren may
just as well have been speaking for the reader of Faulkner. Here

7. Quoted in Geertz, "Found in Translation," 805.
8. This theme is further developed in my article "Faulkner, *Absalom, Absalom!*" in
Der amerikanische Roman, ed. Hans Joachim Lang (Düsseldorf: A. Bagel, 1972).

we are dealing with the most central concern of anthropologists in presenting a foreign culture, foreign doing, through the grid of not only Western discourse, but also scientific rationality. All such scientific anthropology must result in a misreading; and the misreading will increase in proportion to the degree of scientific objectivity. For the scientific grid of a highly stratified *univers du discours,* characterized by a high degree of semantic division of labor, cannot do justice to holophrastic, preindustrial, other-cultural experience, and perhaps it should not even try. What it can do is to make its own scientific connections, its own type of sense. *Absalom, Absalom!* in particular speaks to the anthro-pologist, for it articulates the problem of knowing and names the price we pay for knowing.

FICTION AS AUTOETHNOGRAPHY

In recent years there has been a revolution in anthropological praxis both for external and internal reasons, which brings its concerns much closer again to what Faulkner has been doing all along. Faulkner is again ahead of paradigm changes. The newest preoccupation is autoethnography, also called indigenous an-thropology or anthropology at home. This is in fact what the Center for the Study of Southern Culture here at Oxford is all about. An older type of anthropology or ethnology was by definition the meeting of a Western, enlightened scientific dis-course and disposition with a foreign, mostly "primitive" cul-ture. The farther away and the more primitive the better, a principle which made the Australian aborigines alltime favorites in the field. Anthropology arose from the meeting of Western reason with foreign cultures, says Foucault. The question re-mains: why would Western civilization develop an interest in foreign cultures when the Chinese and Islamic worlds, which had the scientific and practical wherewithal for exploration and conquest, were notoriously disinterested in other people? Christian "reconquista," the search for the primitive, the flight from civilization, pastoral yearning, seafaring, imperialist greed, pursuing some abstract design such as a city on the hill or a common wealth—all these motives surely played a role. And the so-called "discovery" of America—the terminology itself is eth-nocentric—has a lot to do with the rise of anthropology. There are more anthropologists in America than in the rest of the world; it seems therefore safe to say that it is a very American concern.

The new type of anthropology, anthropology at home, arose for two reasons. First, Americans began not only to discover their own natives as discrete ethnic groups, but also themselves as being inextricably intertwined ethnically and culturally with the victims of their own abstract designs. Ellison says that Southerners cannot walk, talk, sing, breathe, eat, or die without making some reference to blacks (or New Yorkers to Jews, and Midwesterners to Germans, one might add). At the same time the once friendly natives of the Third World have become posi-tively hostile when they see anthropologists coming and refuse to be studied under whatever pretext of scientific objectivity. They fear quite rightly that the anthropologist has too often been the vanguard of any number of capitalist Snopeses. Therefore many anthropologists brought their "vision" and craft, their par-ticular sense of the object, their ability to wonder and their logic of discovery home to roost and began looking at their own cul-ture the way they had learned to look at foreign cultures, as something to be discovered, as something essentially new and strange which ought to be made visible and which ought to be lifted from the unconscious and quotidian into visibility and discourse. And many of them, Faulkner among them, made the observation that the natives at home become mighty hostile, too, if you begin to tell the whole truth about the way they carry on. There is in fact something essentially alien in the craft of the fiction writer and the anthropologist, both children of the larger period of modern history which begins in the age of discoveries. In a much larger sense then anthropologists and Faulkner are united in their resolve to discover, to make visible, to uncover, to restore to the people what Robert Penn Warren describes as "some truth about the South and their own Southernness that had been lying speechless in their experience." We are after all children of Marx, Freud, and Nietzsche, the troika in search of hidden motives. "Wo Lafayette war soll Yoknapatawpha sein" ("Where Lafayette was there shall be Yoknapatawpha").

If modernist authors were involved in a version of autoethnography, thus anticipating the *nouvelle vague* in anthropology, why did so many flee from home in order to be able to write about it? This again is a variation on the theme of aesthetic and cultural distance. They sought out the alien context for the absence of sociocultural restraints on their muse. Joyce chose Switzerland and Italy, Americans preferred Paris, both less forbidding than Dublin or Wyoming. Some of these authors commented on the need for exile in order to sever the libidinal ties that bound them and their language to the place, to shake off the inhibiting burden of personal, often traumatic connotations. They freed their language from the social context and the context of their socialization in order to give it free poetic rein; they took their muse "away from it all," sneaking away with their love, as it were, flying by the nets of family, church, and nation, as Stephen Dedalus puts it. While many anthropologists go abroad primarily in order to understand a foreign culture (though the nature of their quest may imply a criticism of their own civilization), modernist authors fled from their culture in order to come closer to it by way of language. They escape to make it *new* by making it *strange*, we might say echoing Pound and Sklovsky. Those who have spent a year away from their own language will readily grant that this has a liberating effect. What motivates authors and anthropologists to go to Paris, to Melanesia, or to some *Afrique de l'esprit* is the desire to cut that umbilical cord, to get rid of "castrating mothers or fathers" and the demands of the cultural superego which are, invisibly, crowding the memory and occupying their linguistic space. Culturally and linguistically speaking, exile is an escape into poetry, a search for qualities lost at home. Here is the anthropologist Horton trying to explain the powerful hold which Africa has on him:

> As a scientist, it is perhaps inevitable that I should at a certain point give the impression that traditional African thought is a poor, shackled thing when compared with the thought of the sciences. Yet as a

man, here I am living by choice in a still-heavily-traditional Africa
rather than in the scientifically oriented Western subculture I was
brought up in. Why? Well, there may be lots of queer, sinister, un-
acknowledged reasons. But one certain reason is the discovery of
things lost at home. An intensely poetic quality in everyday life and
thought, and a vivid enjoyment of the passing moment—both driven
out of sophisticated Western life by the quest for purity of motive
and the faith in progress.[9]

Pynchon captures in a nutshell the structure of anthropological
desire.

—wait, wait a minute, yes it's Karl Marx, that sly old racist skipping
away with his teeth together and his eyebrows up trying to make
believe it's nothing but Cheap Labor and Overseas Markets. . . .
Oh, no. Colonies are much, much more. Colonies are the outhouses
of the European soul, where a fellow can let his pants down and
relax, enjoy the smell of his own shit. . . . Christian Europe was
always death, Karl, death and repression. Out and down in the
colonies, life can be indulged, life and sensuality in all its forms,
with no harm done to the Metropolis, nothing to soil those cathe-
drals, white marble statues, noble thoughts.[10]

Escape from the context which corsets the self in order to find
the self, this has been the flight and quest myth of the West, that
circular journey of Ulysses. This yearning is transformed into
ideology and becomes a powerful projection which then drives
the quest. Perhaps the pastoral urge, first spelled out in Vergil's
fourth eclogue, from which the motto on the dollar bill ("Annuit
Coeptis—Novus Ordo Seclorum") is taken, provides a good example. The city flees to the country in order to find *not* what the
country *is,* but what the city *lacks* and *is not.* It is an appropriation of the other in terms of personal want. Since Michael Millgate single-handedly lifted the taboo on autocitation, I will
quote myself without *ayenbite of inwit:* "Pastoralism arises from
a genuine want and desire. Suffering from overcivilization the
dominant, urban group turns to its agrarian, rural subculture.
By saying to the rural poor and oppressed 'Stay where you are,

9. Quoted in Jurgen Habermas, *Theorie des kommunikativen Handelns* (Frankfurt: Suhrkamp, 1981), 101–2.
10. Thomas Pynchon, *Gravity's Rainbow* (New York: Viking, 1973), 371.

you've got it so much better' pastoralism soothes the bad conscience of the oppressor and makes the oppressed feel better.
The exhortation 'Don't become like us, we're so alienated up
here' makes sure that things stay that way."[11] What I said here
about the tension between urban and rural applies equally to the
structures of desire which drives civilized anthropology to
primitive societies.

Here my analogy runs into a snag. For Faulkner never fled
from home. However, with a little dialectic magic I can make
him fit my theory. For wasn't he always a sort of stranger in
town, "Count No 'Count," a marginal man? It is true that any
writer—particularly in a rural environment—tends to be marginal, unless he writes poetry for weddings and the unveiling of
plaques. But Faulkner deliberately cultivated his role as outsider and kept his distance even at some cost to his friends and
his family. He had to invent invisible distancing strategies, draw
boundaries, flee into an alienating privacy in order to make up
for not having been abroad.

ANTHROPOLOGY, KNOWLEDGE, AND HUMAN INTEREST: A TENTATIVE CONCLUSION

Both fiction and anthropology are motivated by the "consoling
piety that we are all like to one another" and "the worrying
suspicion that we are not." This is the largest common de-
nominator of Western curiosity, the modern urge to know.
Which direction does that interest, that desire to know, take?
The attraction of the novel and the attraction of anthropological
writing lies in the hermeneutic tension which characterizes both
enterprises: both try to achieve integration *and* differentiation,
work macrologically *and* micrologically, focus on the universal
and the particular, pursue the manifest *and* the latent, and
finally try to bring into one horizon the alien *and* the self.

---

11. The whole question of symbolic exploitation and of literate imperialism needs
more attention. This quotation is from my book *Black Literature in White America*
(Brighton, Sussex: Harvester Press, 1982), where the relationship between black and
white, rural and urban groups is discussed in the context of minstrelsy.

THE UNIVERSAL AND THE PARTICULAR

Anthropology—as philosophy—is concerned with the entire spectrum of social action, with all that man does or ever has done. It therefore holds on to an idea of totality, or to some sort of coherent whole. As *one* generic *history* of mankind anthropology tries to understand how Man organizes his relationship to nature, to his self-created environment, to his fellow human beings, and how he understands himself both as *product* and *producer* of this history. Therefore this large-scale anthropology is the basis of all social theory; it moves all human curiosity, including that of Faulkner. This larger notion of anthropology incidentally was mostly inspired by the consoling piety that we are all the same.

But then the anthropological frame of reference is not only circumscribed by one generic history (time), but, speaking synchronically and geographically, by *one globe* (place), which houses not one culture (singular) but a diversity of cultures. Culture is not seen not as sameness, but as precisely the marker of diversity. (As an aside, it is interesting that this contradiction emerges in the "new American ethnicity" and the new sense of cultural difference which gives the lie to that old flagship of the American egalitarian creed "regardless of race, creed, or national origin.") Micrological descriptions of human praxis, kinship systems, eating habits, medicinal lore, cockfights in Bali, how to order a beer in Subanum—nothing is too small to escape the scrutiny of the differential anthropologist. When such anthropologists meet over beer and discuss their field work you will often hear "but my people do it differently."

Faulkner plays with both anthropological frames. Clearly there is in his work a conscious or unconscious drive for totality, an attempt to create a sort of centripetal superplot which encompasses all situations and characters, as Michael Millgate has shown. Though these situations and characters have a strong particularity, they are more than mimetic transcripts of the actual world. Sutpen surely fits the prototype of "homo novus Americanus" as drawn by Schlesinger and Brooks, but, to quote

Northrop Frye again, we don't study *Macbeth* for Scottish history, but "to learn what a man feels like after he's gained a
kingdom and lost his soul." At the same time, however, one
ought not to denigrate his passion for details. The German saying "Der liebe Gott sitzt im Detail" translates loosely as "the
most universal principle resides in the smallest detail." Protected by his poetic license and armed with the visa of
fictionality, Faulkner has entered uncharted and forbidden regions of the American experience and has mapped these in micrological detail. One such abiding theme in Faulkner's work has
been the cluster of race relations, kinship, and legitimation.
There is no decent new scholarship on miscegenation excepting
a new book by Joel Williamson on mulattoes. But given the
enormity and centrality of the problem, the scholarly reluctance
of historians and anthropologists to deal with it is striking.
Hardly anyone has elaborated in such detail as Faulkner the
actual *process* of miscegenation. In *Absalom, Absalom!* alone we
find Charles Bon, Eulalia Bon (his mother), his octoroon mistress, his son (Charles Etienne Saint Valery Bon), Clytie, and
Jim Bond. In *Go Down, Moses* we follow the thinning out of the
family tree, a tragic kinship system between black and white
wherein Ike tries to locate his right to exist. These are clearly
themes that need to be addressed with some anthropological
sophistication; without such know-how critics will too often
come up with ideological position papers. That entire area of the
human imagination between *Purity and Danger*, which Mary
Douglas has charted, would enrich the discussion of mongreliza-
tion (Lion, Sam Fathers) or the relationship between money and
miscegenation. Dealing with the particulars of Faulkner's texts
the literary critic might find inspiration from the questions of
anthropologists.

THE MANIFEST AND THE LATENT

Social anthropology, particularly its British variant as represented by Evans-Pritchard, was interested in the manifest functioning of social relations. These scholars asked how does the
ensemble of social relations, say among the Dinka or Nuer,

work? How do kinship relations, religious beliefs, and power structures stabilize each other into homeostatic systems, and what causes their breakdown? The colonial administration, in whose mighty shadow most of these anthropologists worked, had a political stake in stability and order, both at home and abroad. Their mood was one of cultural orthodoxy, which the anthropologists also adopted. Meanwhile across the Atlantic, American cultural anthropologists, who owed much more to romantic (i.e., dynamic rather than static) modes of thought, went underground. American cultural anthropology began as an attempt to rescue vanishing Indian cultures, many of which had been literally plowed under, and to reconstruct not the social structure (which was irretrievably gone), but the structures of experience of defunct groups. American anthropologists could rarely observe actual, untouched Indian cultures, but had to refashion "from a few mouth-to-mouth tales" what might have been: *potential* cultures. This requires a great deal of imaginative writerly skill, and an understanding of the covert forces which make cultures function, of latent norms and patterns which guide and structure life. Ruth Benedict's *Patterns of Culture*, which became a bestseller, focused not on the behavior itself, but on *patterns* of behavior, the strategies and programs, the resources and deeper charters of behavior. The Sapir-Whorf discussion is merely a symptom of this pervasive interest to understand "was die Welt im Innersten zusammenhält." Concepts such as the "oversoul" or the "superorganic" or the "hidden dimension" attest to this passion for the latent in America's history of thought.

   It is curious how the difference between British and American anthropology is mirrored in the novelistic traditions. Clearly the British novel has been and is more concerned with manifest social relations, whereas the American novel, like American art forms in general, deals with dimensions of experience which are normally hidden from view. There may have been very pragmatic reasons for "going romantic," those advanced by Cooper and Hawthorne, which James summarized as "the paucity of social ingredients" in American life, but I think the main reason

lies in America's philosophical passion for the latent. This preoccupation might also explain the French interest in Faulkner. For
French social thought never had much patience with surfaces,
the manifest and obvious. The French go even deeper than the
Americans: Durkheim's notions of "collective representations,"
Mauss's system of reciprocity, Lévi-Strauss's interest in deep
thought structures, myths, and exchanges, and Foucault's yeasty
archeology come to mind. It is no accident therefore that an
almost stereotypical complaint of British social scientists about
their French colleagues has to do with their magisterial disdain
for the actual fact.

Faulkner's Yoknapatawpha may be mined for both kinds of
truth. There is enough manifest material which may be system-
atically collected in real-life taxonomies, such as Faulkner's detailed kinship systems. Yet, it is telling that often one has to
consult his appendices or maps for clarification which his texts
deny. On the level of the manifest, Faulkner is primarily interested not in the functioning, but in the disfunctioning of family
or state systems. I do not have to list the many examples of
decline, devolution, disaster, or attenuation. The Faulkner criticism devoted to the charting or retelling of the manifest is in my
opinion not terribly well-informed, for it tends to forget that
Faulkner through his use of narrative and language constantly
perforates the manifest. The positivistic attention of such critics
to "what can be proven to be there" implicitly postulates an
ontological priority of context over text, of Lafayette over Yoknapatawpha, thus working against Faulkner who wrote all his life
to put Yoknapatawpha where Lafayette was. In the realm of
thought the most manifest positions are often voiced by his least
lovable or reliable characters. Clearly the "face value" of the
manifest has a low priority in Faulkner's universe. Faulkner
deplored stasis, including that of mimesis.

THE ALIEN AND THE SELF, PRIMITIVISM AND CIVILIZATION

Last but not least, anthropologists in search for the primitive
often come home with a vigorous criticism of civilization. Faulk-

ner sought out the hidden dimension in America's repressed geography, the primitive subsoil of American culture. And this so-called primitivism is implicitly a criticism of civilization. *Go Down, Moses* has been quoted to death on this score. The dualistic drive which has inspired anthropology from its inception—half utopia and half quest for power, half pastoral yearning and half violence, half search for the primitive and half criticism of civilization—is felt in much of his writing. Again we should not forget that Faulkner wrote complicated narrative stories in which nothing is unequivocally clear. His criticism of civilization is also an implied criticism of the critic. Surely Ike, who is the mouthpiece of such criticism, is afflicted by a certain lack of resolve; there is something self-congratulatory about him, which today might be called narcissistic. Or take Rosa's father, who may have lofty convictions but the wrong personality.

My point is that Faulkner pursued those questions which characterize the contemporary discussion in anthropology, and he choreographed and dramatized those questions in interlocking dialogic structures, using a chorus of antiphonal voices, which deepen, but do not conclusively answer anyone of them. He dealt quite consciously with the chief epistemological problems of his day: how can we know and how can we put it into believable discourse? He attacked and made visible the tacit background assumptions of naive anthropologists or critics who continue to adhere to the dogma of immaculate perception, to the universality of their cultural preferences, and to forms of knowledge outside the unending process of storytelling. He would probably agree with the German philosopher who defined modern man as being "in Geschichten verstrickt." Certainly, this is a fitting epitaph for Faulkner's Laocoon, Quentin Compson.

Faulkner's Relationship to Jews: A Beginning

ILSE DUSOIR LIND

Although Jewish characters play only minor roles in Faulkner's great Yoknapatawpha fictions, appearing there fitfully, if at all, Jews are assigned major parts in *Mosquitoes* (1927) and *A Fable* (1954), suggesting that Faulkner's interest in Jews as a fictional subject engaged his imagination throughout the entire span of his literary career. His artistic handling of Jewish characters in his work is, like everything else in his fiction, marked by subtlety of aesthetic motive and artistically strategic indirection. Thus it has been impossible to come to any generalized conclusion as to what his attitude towards Jews may be, insofar as his work may be said to convey one. Biography has cast more light than criticism on this question, especially Joseph Blotner's two-volume *Faulkner, A Biography*, because of the account it gives of the many close relationships Faulkner had with individuals of Jewish background.[1] But even in his immediate experience with Jewish individuals, Faulkner confronts us with troubling responses on his part. In *Selected Letters*, for example, he expresses both pro-Semitic and anti-Semitic sentiments in relation to specific individuals.[2]

Clearly a need exists to study Faulkner's attitude toward Jews, in both his work and his life.

Such a need has been urgent, in fact, ever since Michael N.

1. New York: Random House, 1974.
2. *Selected Letters of William Faulkner*, ed. Joseph Blotner (New York: Random House, 1977), 66 and 175.

119

Dobkowski's *The Tarnished Dream*, a sociohistorical study of the way anti-Semitism is kept alive in American culture through the perpetuation of anti-Semitic stereotypes by American writers.[3] Dobkowski's book as a whole presents the disturbing finding that the American literary heritage is contaminated throughout by repugnant Judeophobic images, which appear even in the work of Hawthorne, Twain, Henry James, and Dreiser—to name only a few. Faulkner does not escape condemnation on this score by any means; he is found to be as guilty of anti-Semitism as T. S. Eliot, Fitzgerald, or Hemingway. Such a judgment, however, does not seem warranted in Faulkner's case, for a thoughtful reading of his work leaves the general impression that he stands far clearer of anti-Semitic prejudice than most of his great American contemporaries—obviously clearer than Pound and Eliot, because he never promulgates anti-Semitic ideology, and distinctly clearer than Hemingway and Fitzgerald, both of whom have created memorable fictional characters who arouse anti-Semitic emotions in the reader, characters like Robert Cohn of *The Sun Also Rises* and Meyer Wolfsheim of *The Great Gatsby*.[4]

In Faulkner's work, memorable characters arousing negative emotions of an intense kind, like Jason Compson or Flem Snopes, are almost invariably Protestant. Unequivocally negative Jewish characters—like H. I. Feinman of *Pylon*, for example, are not markedly embellished and tend not to carry a strong emotional charge.

The evidence Dobkowski cites cannot be lightly dismissed, however. Drawing upon a previous study, "Faulkner and the Jews," by Alfred J. Kutzik,[5] he points to Judeophobic characterizations or anti-Semitic references in *Soldiers' Pay, Mosquitoes, The Sound and the Fury*, and the short story "Death Drag."[6] The stereotype that he finds to predominate in these works is the one

3. Westport, Connecticut: Greenwood Press, 1979.
4. Josephine Z. Kopf, "Meyer Wolfsheim and Robert Cohn: A Study of a Jewish Type and Stereotype," *Tradition*, 10 (Spring 1969), 93–104.
5. *Yivo Annual of Jewish Social Science*, 13 (1965), 213–26.
6. Dobkowski, 103.

which appeared with greatest frequency in the Gilded Age, that of the money-obsessed Jew, or Shylock. Kutzik, in his lengthier treatment of this subject, cites additional works which he finds to contain offending references: *Sanctuary, Pylon, The Hamlet, The Wild Palms, Intruder in the Dust, Requiem for a Nun, A Fable,* and—among the short stories—"There Was a Queen," "Honor," and "The Bear." The stereotypes which Kutzik finds are more varied, and include—besides the unscrupulous businessman or the shyster, images of the criminal Jew, the sexually sinister Jew, the unpatriotic Jew, the Jew as flashy and vulgar dresser, and the unwashed immigrant Jew of the lower classes— "the coastal spew of Europe."[7] In addition, he finds the common physical stereotype, featuring the exaggerated long hooked nose, to appear frequently in Faulkner's work. Like Dobkowski, Kutzik views Faulkner's anti-Semitism as being intense, especially during the first phase of his career. He differentiates two distinct phases, as far as Faulkner's attitude towards Jews is concerned, a first phase extending to approximately 1950, in which negative attitude towards Jews is in excess of that which prevailed in the environment, and a second phase, in which Faulkner attempted to compensate for his negative characterizations of Jews by replacing them with positive ones, as in the creation of the heroic airman Levine of *A Fable* to replace that of the mercenary airman Ginsfarb of "Death Drag." Faulkner's complete reversal of attitude is for Kutzik so extreme as to be explainable only in terms of outside factors, like his possible admiration of the military prowess of Israel in the 1956 war, or the (possible) influence of his reading of John Hersey's *The Wall.*

Closer inspection of Faulkner's work for the purpose of detecting references to Jews shows that the lists compiled by Dobkowski and Kutzik are still not complete, for it is necessary also to name *The Mansion* and *Knight's Gambit* as containing significant reference to Jews, and it is to be expected that further

---

7. Cited by Kutzik from *Intruder in the Dust.*

Faulkner titles will need to be added because very small verbal units are sometimes involved, occasionally only single words or phrases, which come to notice only gradually. The total number of works involved, therefore, is by no means negligible. The task of evaluating this material in order to arrive at an understanding of Faulkner's attitude towards Jews, on the basis of which a response to the charge of anti-Semitism can be made, is not to be avoided.

How is this problem to be approached? The first temptation is to view whatever anti-Semitic references there may be in Faulkner's work as simply reflexive of Southern culture, of which anti-Semitism is a component, as in most other regions of the United States.[8] Reflexive anti-Semitism constitutes passive transmission of such prejudice as is imbedded in language itself. Because anti-Semitism dates from the time of Christianity, its assimilation into the English language and English culture occurred very early. The first American settlers brought it to this country as part of their cultural baggage, and the Protestant bias of Puritan thought reinforced it. Many of the American writers whom Dobkowski finds to be carriers of this social virus appear to have derived their anti-Semitism unconsciously, without themselves subscribing to anti-Semitic ideology. Faulkner may be another instance. If so, a certain allowance should perhaps be made for this.

But in Faulkner's case there are at least two reasons why such elements in his work as may appear to be anti-Semitic cannot simply be accepted as being the unwitting reflection of background. The first is the particular interest Faulkner evinced in the complex relation existing between an individual and his milieu. Given his awareness of the influence of place and com-

---

8. Leonard Dinnerstein, "A Note on Southern Attitudes towards Jews," *Jewish Social Studies*, 32 (January 1970), 93–99, and *Jews in the South*, Leonard Dinnerstein and Mary Dale Palsson, eds. (Baton Rouge: Louisiana State University Press, 1973). Comparative judgments as to which regions of the United States are more anti-Semitic than others are impossible to make with any accuracy on the basis of reliable historical research at the present time. Organized anti-Semitism dates from the early 1920s. Earlier manifestations show great variation with social class and region.

munity upon character in his fiction, is it likely that he was oblivious to the impact of his cultural environment upon himself? This seems hardly likely.

The second reason is the essential integrity of his artistic vision, so often noted by his critics. By this I do not mean that his work finds its justification in the centrality of its moral concern, or in its fidelity to external reality in the manner of social realism, but rather that it takes human beings and their doings seriously, differentiating one person from another with minute accuracy. No matter how individuals cope with life, their manner of doing so is viewed by Faulkner as having significance in terms of their life's circumstance and their specific motive at a given moment, within a precise social context. Such specificity is inconsistent with the tendency to think in terms of racial stereotypes, which blurs the truth of individual difference rather than elucidating it. Thus, all the evidence bearing on this question needs to be evaluated very thoughtfully and with extreme care.

But it is erroneous to think that Faulkner's social attitudes can be defined without first acknowledging the complex relation which exists in his work between social reality and imaginative reality.[9] The autonomy of Faulkner's fictions as modern artistic creations renders them inaccessible to direct probing and makes generalization about his social ideas extremely hazardous. In order to do justice to this subject one cannot institute an inquiry on the model of a legal investigation. The only way to proceed is by pursuing an oblique course—as oblique as that of Faulkner's art itself, moving in a kind of zigzag fashion—from appreciation of any given work in its aesthetic unity, to consideration of the questions about the circumambient social reality that it raises; from consideration of the personal relation of the creative artist himself to whatever he may be presenting in a given work back

9. For this important distinction, I am indebted to Robert Alter, *Defenses of the Imagination* (Philadelphia: Jewish Publication Society, 1977). Alter makes it clear that deductions about racial attitudes cannot be made without full consideration of the style of modernist authors. He also suggests that this subject, if carefully pursued, may offer a key to aspects of an author's work as a whole.

to the work again as an aesthetic entity in hopes of gaining an enriched reading.

Because Faulkner's works are modernist, they demand an unusually active collaboration on the part of the reader in every way, not only where psychological and sexual meanings are concerned, but also in relation to their social and historical import. Where the circumambient milieu and Faulkner's personal relation to it are being examined, such investigation cannot be conducted wholly within the linguistic prison house of the verbal text of any work; it must also go beyond this, into exploration of the external realm to which the text makes allusive reference. For although Faulkner's work lends itself rewardingly to the type of critical analysis that proceeds primarily in an inward direction, it also exists in dynamic relation to the particular outer world which it continuously reflects. Faulkner's habit of sublimating the actual into the apocryphal suggests that we, too, can gain by examining the social and historical actuality that he transmutes into imaginative form.

The impetus to such study is, in fact, provided by Faulkner's style itself, in its discrepancies, blatancies, and inconsistencies, which demand that we go beyond the text in order to resolve many questions to which the text itself does not give answers. These irregularities serve as stimulants to exploration of the social and historical background, as a source of further illumination of the literal import of certain passages. When we embark on such researches, we inevitably discover that the historical and social reality of the past is in the process of corroding and crumbling; already, it is no longer recoverable, in many instances. Nevertheless, if we wish to resolve the question of Faulkner's attitude towards Jews, insofar as his work reflects one, there is no avoiding a serious study of this background and of undertaking a critical reading that is oriented to the social and historical realities as much as possible.

In pursuing such an inquiry, in other words, it is necessary to encompass not only the usual critical approaches, but also sociohistorical and biographical perspectives. Certain fundamental questions must be asked which cannot be answered by analyzing the texts of the fictions alone. What, for example, was Faulkner's relation to Jews during his formative years? What view did he hold of the anti-Semitism of his own culture? How did his attitude change during a career that spanned many decades, taking him into an everwidening world, which included the Holocaust? In order to answer such questions, it is necessary to cast a wide net, to run the risk of appearing to be undisciplined while in the very act of attempting to apply more than one discipline.

The present occasion serves as an opportunity to set forth the beginning of what has proved to be a fascinating and rich inquiry into this subject. In what follows, I shall be dealing only with the Oxford milieu insofar as this bears on Faulkner's early contact with certain Jewish individuals. By way of suggesting the usefulness of such knowledge to critical reading, I shall conclude with some brief comment upon one or two short passages in *The Town* and *The Mansion* which an understanding of this background helps to place in clearer perspective.

I. THE OXFORD MILIEU

Concerning the experience of Jews as a social minority in the predominantly Protestant culture of the South, it has been said that the single Jewish families who settled in small Southern towns enjoyed a warmer and more socially interactive relationship with their communities than did those who settled in New York City, especially where such families were the only members of their ethnic group.[10] One is inclined to doubt generalizations of this kind, however, not only because a latter-day sectionalism often seems to tinge them, as here, but also because dependable research on this subject is sparse and unreliable. Only now is formal study of the history of Jews in the South

---

10. See *Jews in the South*, Dinnerstein and Palsson, eds., 13; Leo E. and Evelyn Turitz, *Jews in Early Mississippi* (Jackson: University Press of Mississippi, 1983), xiv; and Peter I. Rose, "Small-Town Jews and Their Neighbors in the United States," *Jewish Journal of Sociology*, 2 (1961), 174–91.

beginning to be undertaken and recognition being given to the complexities of Southern history, as compared to Northern, in their effect upon the interrelation of Jews and Gentiles within differing social contexts in the South.

In the absence of systematic and dependable sociohistorical studies, therefore, it is essential to work from firsthand evidence as much as possible in relation to the Jewish family that lived in Oxford from the time of Faulkner's boyhood. Luckily, such firsthand evidence exists, obtainable from descendants of the original family, their friends, and members of the Oxford community who remember them.[11] In addition, the fine detail of Blotner's biography serves to enrich the picture, making this a rare instance where the literary scholar is in a position to serve the cultural historian by providing more information than usual about a group of Jewish individuals in a Southern community who are not often chronicled with close attention.

The Friedmans of Oxford (they were actually two families, a pair of brothers and their wives and children) who settled in Oxford at the turn of the century, were, in fact, the sole members of their ethnic group in the town for many decades, and their relationship with the community was, according to all evidence, extremely harmonious. Leo and Evelyn Turitz, in their recent collection of photographs of Jews in early Mississippi, include a studio portrait of Joseph Friedman and his wife which conveys, through the presence of the couple before the camera and the quality of their attire, the sense that their status in the Old World was at least middle class.[12] The majority of Jewish

---

11. I am especially indebted to Dr. Ralph Friedman (son of Joseph) for the outlines of the Friedman family history and for the remembered incidents cited. I am also indebted to Rosemary Schiff, granddaughter of Hyman Friedman, for recollections of his settlement in Oxford in early years and for other remembered incidents, and to Mrs. Louis Doerflinger, daughter of Hyman Friedman. In addition, I wish to express my thanks to Mrs. Edith Brown Douds for the information generously supplied by letter and to Dr. Calvin Brown for his helpful exchanges on this topic. Also providing information relating to the Friedmans in interviews are W. McNeill Reed (August 4, 1982) and Mrs. Marvel Sisk (August 5, 1983). The views that Hyman was exceptionally learned and that the Friedman brothers were an asset to the community were held unequivocally by all who remember them.

12. Turitz, 79.

settlers in Mississippi were of German origin, but the Friedmans
were Eastern Europeans. As such, they differed from the large
numbers of Eastern European Jews who immigrated to America
in massive waves around the turn of the century, most of whom
settled in New York, many of whom were impoverished and
illiterate. Only the more strongly inner-directed of these immi-
grants went South to settle; for as Harry Golden has said, only
the extremely hardy could travel one-fourth of the way around
the globe to get to New York and then still venture thousands of
miles farther into an unknown region of the United States,
where they would expect to live as isolated members of their
religious faith.[13]

The pioneering adventurer of this family was Hyman Friedman, the elder of two brothers, who immigrated to the United
States from Russia (now Latvia) in the mid-1890s. In Russia he
was beginning training for the rabbinate at a time when pograms
were at their height. While he was still growing up, he had seen
thirteen children burned to death in fires set by the Czar's
soldiers during pograms.[14] Deciding that the time had come
when he must flee, he landed first in New York. There he
worked in a clothing factory for several years, marrying his em-
ployer's daughter. When he had accumulated enough money, he
set forth for Memphis, where relatives of his wife were established in the clothing business. Here he again worked until he
had accumulated enough money to make a move, this time planning to set up a business of his own. Discovering that there was a
town less than a hundred miles away adjoining a state university,
where he would be able to get good education for his children,
he decided to put down roots there. The high level of his intellectual interests led him to dream of applying for a post at the
university, but being doubtful of the appropriateness of indicating a desire to pursue such a career, he resisted the impulse to
present himself. All his life, however, he retained a respect

13. Harry Golden, *Our Southern Landsman* (New York: G. P. Putnam's Sons, 1974),
33.
   14. As recalled by Rosemary Schiff.

verging on awe for the pursuit of learning at the advanced university level.[15]

The town already had a department store, Neilson's, founded in 1839, which catered to the quality trade, and he did not offer serious business competition to it by setting up a small retail store offering cheaper ready-to-wear garments of the kind needed by the poorer working people of the town, and the Negroes and country folk who came into Oxford in large numbers on Saturdays. By the year 1902, when William Faulkner with his parents were making their way from Ripley, Mississippi, into Oxford, Hyman's store on the Courthouse Square was already a fixture there, and Hyman himself a colorful, well-known local personality. Within a few years, he was doing well enough in business to be able to send for his brother Joseph, finding him work as a tailor in a small shop situated on an upper floor on the Square. After Joseph had saved enough money to enter into a business partnership with him, he and Joseph opened a second store on the Square, offering a wider selection of merchandise and catering to the same type of clientele.

Hyman was satisfied with his choice of a new home and immersed himself in the town's life. He enjoyed assuming responsibility in civic projects and taking initiative in worthy causes. One incident illustrating his spontaneous benevolence concerns a poor farmer and his horse. The farmer had driven into the Square and was about to hitch his wagon to a post when the animal collapsed within its traces. A crowd assembled, Hyman running out from his store to see what was the matter. The horse, it appeared, had simply dropped dead. Everyone exclaimed how sorry they felt for the distressed farmer, who clearly could not afford to buy another horse. Quickly appraising the situation, Hyman reached into his pocket, took out a five-dollar bill, and holding it high in the air said: "I am five-dollars-worth-sorry. How many dollars-worth sorry are you?" The moral

15. Hyman's reverence for learning and for its pursuit at the university level is recalled by Dr. Ralph Friedman.

arithmetic of this resembles the Snopesian calculations as to who should be what-percent ashamed in the matter of Ike and his cow in *The Hamlet*. Whether Faulkner himself was present when the incident occurred we cannot verify, but we can ascertain that Hyman's amusing quantification of emotion is still locally remembered.[16]

Hyman enjoyed sharing his knowledge and experience in all areas, including business, and when he hired young men to assist him behind the counter he also taught them how to keep books, attend to customers, and avoid waste. To illustrate the latter, he sometimes told them the story of the one-legged Negro who came into the store to buy a shoe. It was his left leg that he had lost, so Hyman sold him a right shoe, breaking a pair to accommodate him. Within the month, another Negro who had suffered an amputation of the leg came in, but this one had the right leg missing. Hyman took out the left shoe that he had kept in stock, and—as by a miracle—it proved to be exactly the needed size.[17]

It was soon recognized by members of the business community that Hyman's practices as a merchant were ethical and that his management of his affairs showed good business judgment. Also, he was extremely well liked. He was therefore invited to become a member of the board of directors of the First National Bank of Oxford—the same bank of which William Faulkner's paternal grandfather was president. Eventually, he also became president of the school board. Joseph, too, was respected as a businessman, recognized as being scrupulously ethical, and invited to join the Rotary. In time he also became a member of the board of directors of the First National Bank of Oxford.

All the Friedman children attended the local schools and the university. Close ties naturally developed between them and certain of their teachers and classmates. Dr. Calvin Brown,

16. As recalled by Dr. Ralph Friedman. Mrs. Marvel Sisk still remembers this incident and Hyman's remark.
17. As recalled by Rosemary Schiff. Dr. Ralph Friedman suggests that this anecdote probably relates to Joseph, rather than to Hyman, but in their approach to business management and customer relations the two brothers were similar.

Chairman of the Department of Modern Languages and adjacent neighbors of the Faulkners in their home on campus, taught most of them their required languages. The Brown children and the Friedman children—both of whom had learned fathers—were congenial, Edith Brown (now Mrs. John B. Douds) and Rosalie (Joseph's younger daughter) becoming best girlfriends. Mrs. Doud must be approaching eighty now, but she can still recall the many visits to each others' homes, the fun of "stay-the-nights" at Rosalie's, and the delicious meals served by Rosalie's mother who—unlike most Oxford mothers—worked outside the home in the family store. When I asked Mrs. Douds whether anti-Jewish attitudes of any sort complicated her relationship with the Friedmans, she replied: "Certainly not. In my memory, the Oxford of the teens and early twenties knew about anti-Semitism only from books. To us—and I would think to Bill Faulkner as well—it was as remote as the hatred of the Turks for the Greeks."[18]

The "us" to which Mrs. Douds refers consists of those who lived within the humanistic aura of the university. Residing on campus and pursuing his mental interests, Faulkner was thus sheltered from anti-Semitism, a fact that is extremely important to be able to establish with reasonable definitiveness. At the same time, it is doubtful that anti-Semitism was remote from him entirely, for his work suggests otherwise. In the short story "There Was a Queen,"[19] he shows that the anti-Semitism of older important Southern families was definitely not remote from him. To judge by his story, the hatred of Jews among certain members of this class was virulent. Although there has been almost no study of the anti-Semitism of Southern patricians as a group, it seems to have been even more intense than its Northern counterpart in families like the Lowells, Adamses, and Eliots, who reacted against Jews with marked intensity when

18. Quoted in a letter from Mrs. Edith Brown Douds to me on this subject, February 12, 1982.
19. *Collected Stories of William Faulkner* (New York: Random House, 1950), 727–44.

their economic and social status was threatened as a consequence of the rapid changes in the American economy which
took place during the nineteenth century.[20]

In "There Was a Queen," Faulkner presents the ninety-year
Miss Jenny, who refuses to sit at table with a Jewish lawyer who
has come to call. The young man is college-educated and obviously intellectually superior; like Gavin Stevens, he wears a Phi
Beta Kappa key. Miss Jenny orders herself to be removed from
the table and wheeled to her bedroom in her wheel chair rather
than remain at table to suffer the effrontery of a Jew who has
dared to present himself as a guest at the Sartorises' table (Jenny
is John Sartoris's sister.) After she learns that Narcissa has given
herself to the lawyer sexually, during an assignation which her
grandniece made with him in Memphis, she is so upset that she
dies from the stress engendered by this event. Her antipathy to
Jews is presented by Faulkner as an unchangeable, irrational
condition of mind, inseparable from her strong will and her
"queenliness" as a Sartoris. Inasmuch as Faulkner identified
himself with the old Sartoris line in his fiction, such anti-
Semitism was clearly not remote from him, even though the
blind intensity of Miss Jenny's prejudice typified that of a by-
gone generation of Southern aristocrats.

While Faulkner obviously admires Miss Jenny despite her
anti-Semitism, it does not follow that he approves her bigotry.
His reservations are expressed in the secondary action of the
story, involving Jenny's grandniece. Narcissa assumes that the
lawyer's sole purpose in bringing the letters in person is to
blackmail her into having a sexual affair with him. Kutzik, in
judging this story as an example of Faulkner's anti-Semitism,
also accepts this assumption.[21] However, the more likely possibility exists that Narcissa is projecting the assumption of sexual
blackmail on the lawyer. The story supplies many hints relating

20. Dobkowski discusses patrician anti-Semitism in its Northern manifestations at
considerable length (112–42), but does not deal with its approximately equivalent manifestation in the South.
21. Kutzik, 215–16.

to Narcissa's morbid sexuality, while it gives almost no information about the lawyer's motives beyond his initial statement that
he thinks the addressee of the letters may provide a clue to the
unsolved bank robbery which took place twelve years ago. In
the story, it is not the lawyer who proposes a Memphis assignation, but Narcissa who first mentions such a meeting on the
assumption that he demands it.[22] Originally, she had kept the
pornographic letters because she derived excitement from reading them: this is the reason they still exist, as an object to be
stolen and as a source of potential embarrassment to her. Her
idea that the lawyer has sought her out because he has been
aroused by them reflects her own psychological frame of mind; it
does not necessarily reflect his. The sexual neuroticism of Southern white women of good social standing who desire relationships with sexual partners—either real or fantasied—belonging
to a social group that is held in contempt by their own class is a
theme Faulkner treated on more than one occasion, and, in this
story, Narcissa appears to be manifesting such neuroticism, as
well as imposing on the lawyer a prevailing stereotype about
Jewish males—that they are licentious and sexually sinister. The
fact that the lawyer may be governed by conscientious motives
cannot be ruled out, and if he has come strictly on business, as
he says, it is necessary to consider that Narcissa's view of his evil
intentions puts him in an extremely awkward position.

The more common type of anti-Semitism which derives in the
South from broad cultural tradition, agrarian xenophobia and
the need to find a scapegoat upon whom to vent personal frustration, was not remote from Faulkner either, to judge by a passage
in *The Sound and the Fury.*[23] When Jason asks a passing drum-
mer who happens to have a hooked nose whether he does not
agree that "Jews produce nothing," he is voicing a cliché of
agrarian anti-Semitism, rooted in Populist anti-Semitic ideology.

22. Miss Jenny's recognition that Narcissa, as a young widow in the prime of life,
needs a man and should marry again lends support to the interpretation that Narcissa's
sexual initiative is being emphasized, rather than the lawyer's.
23. New York: Jonathan Cape and Harrison Smith, 1929, 237–38.

The ugliness of it is not lost on the reader who recognizes Jason's general mean-spiritedness. The fact that Faulkner's father also ran a hardware store suggests that this conventional type of anti-Semitism was known to him because Faulkner drew upon the hardware store as a setting in the Jason section of *The Sound and the Fury*. Doubtless he heard anti-Semitic remarks of this type made there.[24] The example provided in *The Sound and the Fury* is, of course, meant to be construed ironically. Dobkowski is thus inaccurate in classifying this as an instance of Faulkner's own anti-Semitic bias,[25] as is Kutzik when he also classifies it as an another illustration of Faulkner's anti-Semitic prejudice, even though he recognizes the irony.[26]

To return to the story of the Friedmans of Oxford—like most Southern Jewish settlers of this period and earlier, they maintained their religious identity, observing the customary practices as far as possible. When the Jewish New Year came round, they placed a notice in *The Oxford Eagle* stating that their stores were closed. On this and other major Jewish holidays, they packed their families, including all the children, into carriages—later automobiles—and made the long trip to Memphis to worship in the synagogue. As the children became older and as Jewish students began attending the university in small numbers, they more often observed the holidays at home, inviting these students to join them. Joseph's home, in time, became known as the place where Jewish travelers from all over the state were welcome to spend the night and join the family for meals.

The Friedman stores did well, but the Friedman business operation was not enlarged to any extent over the years. By 1914, Hyman and Joseph were able to bring over to this country the two sons of their remaining brother, Louis and Sam, who were reaching an age when they would be conscripted into the

24. Since delivering this paper I have learned that Faulkner's mother identified her own husband as having made this remark. If so, this type of anti-Semitism was even closer to Faulkner personally than suggested and shows him rejecting such bigotry on the part of his own father.
25. Dobkowski, 103.
26. Kutzik, 214–15.

Russian Army. Deciding to share the responsibility equally, the brothers each took one of them, Hyman housing Louis and Joseph, Sam. These Russian-speaking younger Friedmans grew to manhood in Oxford and established two small businesses there as well, first a furniture, and later a dry goods store.

It has been necessary to relate the story of the Friedmans in such detail in order to pose the necessary question: to what extent was Faulkner aware of them, as a family and as individuals?

Definitely aware of them, one surmises. Besides holding a position as officer in the bank, Hyman owned one of the first automobiles in town, as did Faulkner's grandfather, and one of the first radios. He spoke English inventively, adapting Russian syntax in a way Faulkner found amusing: Blotner tells us that he adopted for his own use Hyman's manner of calling the golf course, "the golfing pasture."[27] Hyman's daughter Florrie was an exceptionally bright student, at ease with the brilliant Phil Stone who served Faulkner as a local mentor for a number of years. Because she was a close friend of Katrina Carter, whom Phil was dating at the time, she and Faulkner, along with Phil and Katrina, made a foursome on more than one occasion. Faulkner also took Florrie and Katrina on a possum hunt which he directed in full style, seeing to it that it included a picnic at midnight in front of an open campfire. During evenings at the home of the local music teacher, he sought Florrie out as a partner with whom to play Five Hundred. Florrie and Estelle Oldham were friends during the years that Florrie was an undergraduate, their relationship continuing long after Estelle and Bill married and settled at Rowan Oak, where she was always a welcome visitor.

Rosalie (Joseph's daughter and a college generation younger) was Faulkner's favorite as a member of the group of collegians called "The Bunch," in whom Faulkner and Phil Stone took an

27. Blotner, *Faulkner: A Biography*, I, 243.

avuncular interest.[28] And Faulkner once took special note of Louis Friedman, the nephew of Hyman and Joseph, shortly after Louis arrived in Oxford, while he still understood very little English. Approaching Louis on the street one day, Faulkner said to him with strong emphasis, "You have ancestors!" Louis, whose English vocabulary still did not include the word "ancestors," thought Faulkner was accusing him of having some dreadful disease and ran home to get reassurance.[29]

What impression did the Friedmans make on Faulkner as Jews? We cannot know; we can only say that they were part of the web of his existence during formative years, that they were not abstractions to him but real people, people he had feelings about, people with whom he interacted and whom he had ample opportunity to observe. It could not have failed to be obvious to him that they were a close, mutually supporting family (more so than his own in some ways), that they were devoted to learning and the arts (they never missed a classical concert in Memphis), that they were ethically conscientious in the extreme, and faithful in their observance of their religion. In sum, it seems safe to say that they provided him with a base upon which further feelings towards Jews as individuals, rather than as stereotypes could be established.

II. JEWS IN YOKNAPATAWPHA

The Friedmans appear in Faulkner's fiction a half-century after he first saw Hyman Friedman's store on the Square, receiving mention in *The Town* when Chick Mallison reminisces about his own boyhood, saying:

> We had a Chinese laundryman and two Jews, brothers, with their families, who ran two clothing stores . . . one of them had been trained in Russia to be a rabbi and spoke seven languages including

---

28. Edith Brown Douds, "Recollection of William Faulkner and the Bunch," in *William Faulkner of Oxford*, ed. James W. Webb and A. Wigfall Green (Baton Rouge: Louisiana State University Press, 1965), 48–53.
29. Anecdote related by Dr. Ralph Friedman.

ancient Greek and Latin and worked geometry problems for relaxation.[30]

Kutzik sees Faulkner's exaggeration of rabbinical erudition here as another instance of his ridiculing of Jews,[31] but knowledge of Hyman Friedman's outstanding intellectuality enables us to understand that Faulkner is not making reference to rabbis in general; he is thinking of a learned Jewish man in that environment who had an actual existence. Chick's manner of speaking about his mental prowess suggests that this man's deep and intensive learning had become a local myth. But a few lines further on we discover, to our complete bafflement, that what Faulkner knew about the Friedmans and what Chick knows about the Jewish family modeled on them is radically divergent, as indicated by Chick's further comment that "the older brother and his family all attended, were members of the Methodist church and so they didn't count."[32] When Alice Friedman, Joseph's oldest daughter, first came upon this statement in her reading of *The Town*, she was outraged. She could not believe that Bill Faulkner could ever think such a thing about her family, much less say it.

And of course Faulkner did not think this. In *The Town* Faulkner is employing Chick as a persona; he is not speaking in his own voice. Chick is twelve years old at this time, and he is caught up in the climactic developments relating to Eula and Manfred de Spain, whose adulterous love he has come to view sympathetically through Stevens's compassion for Eula in her marital dilemma. At this point in the novel, the lovers have been discovered, and Chick knows that it will not be long before the self-righteous members of the community will enjoy the pros-

---

30. *The Town* (New York: Random House, 1957), 306.
31. Kutzik, 219.
32. *The Town*, 306. As a historical tendency, the assimilation of Southern Jews into the predominantly Protestant culture occurred steadily over the years, but Faulkner does not seem to be using Chick here to point to this historical trend, since such assimilation took place more frequently through intermarriage than through direct religious conversion, as in the reference to the "other Jewish brother" not merely attending but becoming "a member of" the local Methodist church.

pect of the retribution to be visited on the couple. Chick hates the moral judging which they will indulge in now, in which he foresees all the white members of the community participating except the former rabbi, whose intellectuality sets him in a class apart, and his brother, who, though he has converted to Methodism, is still a Jew in the town's eyes and hence does not "count" in the tallying of such judgments. While Chick condemns the townsfolk for their lack of feeling for the lovers, he still reveals himself to share negative prejudices with them in relation to Jews, for in speaking about the second Jewish family he mentions the way they looked "in *our* eyes" [emphasis mine], thereby identifying himself with them in their ethnocentrism. At age twelve, he is still too young to be aware of this social bigotry, which he shares with them.

It is important to bear in mind, in attempting to evaluate Chick's attitude towards the Jewish families to whom he makes reference, that Chick differs from Faulkner himself in the influences that shaped his attitudes about Jews. Born about ten years later than his own creator, Chick grew up in the county seat of Yoknapatawpha, Jefferson, a town which does *not* adjoin a university but is more typical of the small American Southern town.[33] Like all small towns, this town has its social hierarchy and certain prescribed events that give it ritual expression, like the annual Cotillion Ball. The extent to which Jews were excluded from participation in this social hierarchy on the basis of purely ethnic—not religious—grounds is revealed in these few remarks by Chick about the only Jews he knows, whom he obviously does not know personally. The Chick of *Intruder in the Dust*, whose lively moral sense in relation to the black race problem makes him a symbol of the best of the younger generation in the South, is no less morally eager in *The Town*, but Faulkner here takes pains to indicate the negative influence of

33. Faulkner's use of local fact combined with departure from it for obvious artistic reasons finds parallel in similar examples in *Light in August* and *The Reivers*, as pointed out by Calvin S. Brown in *A Glossary of Faulkner's South* (New Haven: Yale University Press, 1976), 223–41. For differences between Jefferson and Oxford, see also Calvin S. Brown, "Faulkner's Geography and Topography," *PMLA*, 77 (December 1962), 652–59.

his homogeneous social and cultural background, insofar as it affects his responses to Jews.

Kutzik, in attempting to fathom the reason that Faulkner's later works are strongly philo-Semitic, does not hypothesize the probable influence of the Holocaust. For a man of Faulkner's sensibility, who had known Jews from the beginning as individuals, the Holocaust inevitably registered with shattering impact. Besides his initial personal orientation to Jews, he had formed numerous important relationships with individuals of Jewish background over the years. The need to express himself in relation to the monstrous extermination of Jews by Hitler therefore became increasingly urgent after World War II, when the full scope of the Nazi atrocities became known. The Snopes story, from its first inception in *The Hamlet*, had illustrated the existence of ugly emotions in certain members of the human race. In resuming work on it in the 1950s, it therefore seemed to him an apt vehicle to depict contemporary social ugliness. Thus, while keeping the immediate story of Flem Snopes and his family in central focus, he depicted, through a continuous subtheme in the two final volumes, the dangers of Southern ethnocentrism, giving attention to the ominous political tendencies of his region which were latently protofascist—the emphasis upon the Nordic racial origins of Southerners, the pervasive paranoid suspicion of liberals and Jews, the continuing racist demagoguery, and the rise of the Silver Shirts.

While *The Mansion* serves more as a vehicle for Faulkner's strong emotions relating to these social and political issues than does *The Town*, the theme of Southern ethnocentricity is integrated into this earlier novel as well, through Faulkner's ingeniously modernist device of drawing upon familiar characters from previous works to stimulate questioning about Southern ethnocentrism and its implications. Chick is utilized in this way in *The Town* when he describes the Jewish family in his town in the manner he does. Gavin Stevens is exploited by Faulkner in a similar way when he talks in his own character, at the same time that he expresses opinions that represent Faulkner's own strongly felt attitudes during the 1950s. For example, in *The Town*—almost a half century after the event, and decades after Stevens's education was first mentioned in Faulkner's fiction— Stevens explains why he did not fight on the side of the Germans in World War I, even though he had been pursuing a Ph.D. at Heidelberg when the war broke out. Originally, he had planned to be a stretcher-bearer serving with the German army, but the irrational racial mysticism of the Germans seemed to him to impair the integrity of German culture as a whole, and he changed his mind.[34] Thus Faulkner, after the Holocaust and through Stevens, expresses his animus against the country that instigated the Holocaust.

Faulkner also makes use of his familiar and beloved character, Ratliff, to the same end in *The Town* when he suddenly reveals the names that Ratliff's initials stand for. Ratliff, who in his appearances in previous fictions had established a reputation as the character in the Faulkner canon who most represents the ideal plain American, had seemed physically to resemble a character Chaucer might have drawn. Without his racial origins being specified, he had seemed to be a character of Nordic racial ancestry. Now, quite unexpectedly, Faulkner endows him with Russian ancestors! His initials, it appears, stand for the names Vladimir and Kyrilytch. He has had to suppress this Eastern European heritage in order to survive in Yoknapatawpha, because, as the text informs us, no man named Vladimir could hope "to make a living selling sewing machines or anything else in rural Mississippi."[35] Thus Faulkner comments once more on the ethnocentrism of the middle-American South, utilizing one of his most ideal characters to make the specific point that the best Americans do not necessarily come from Nordic stock.

The Mansion is often thought to betray Faulkner's waning creative energies, but in evaluating this novel it is essential to remember that the passions which brought it into being, were—

34. *The Town*, 103.
35. Ibid., 322–23.

to a significant degree—negative ones, involving a response to such horrendous contemporary events as the Holocaust. Like Picasso's *Guernica,* which is also a response to unthinkable disasters which have occurred in modern history, there is a similar draining of color, an unpleasant jaggedness and flatness in the execution of the whole, at the same time that Faulkner's vision is not utterly dark—as Picasso's is in *Guernica*—but mixes dark and bright in different proportions than earlier.

In *The Mansion,* Faulkner's objection to Southern ethnocentrism is markedly intensified. At the beginning of the novel Gavin Stevens does not yet realize what he knew in a previous work, *Knight's Gambit*—that the Germans had "ruined a continent and were rendering a whole race into fertilizer and lubricating oil."[36] All he knows of Hitler early in the 1930s is that there is a dictator on the rise in Germany who is far more dangerous than Mussolini or Franco because he has the German people to help him.[37] His fear now is that the Southern people will not be steadfast in their belief in democratic American pluralism, that native fascist leaders may be able to exploit the mystic bond which Southerners are forging between American "Nordics" and German "Aryans." For at this time, the doctrine of one-hundred-percent-Americanism was gaining adherents at an alarming rate, in the South as elsewhere in the United States.

Faulkner's personal reaction to this drift was violent, and it led him to call upon Stevens in *The Mansion* to expatiate still further on the dangers of German racism and to explain once more why he came to reject all of German culture, including German philosophy and music.[38] Such a position, on Stevens's part, had been a radical one in 1914, and its radicalism at this early date conveys Faulkner's own animus against Germany following the Holocaust.

Contributing further to the theme of Faulker's objection to fascism, anti-Semitism, and Southern ethnocentrism is Faulk-

36. *Knight's Gambit* (New York: Random House), 243.
37. The Mansion, 160.
38. Ibid., 131–32.

ner's decision to endow Linda Snopes Kohl in *The Mansion* with
a Jewish husband, a New York sculptor who joined the Communist party to fight in Spain on behalf of the Loyalists during the
Spanish Civil War. Barton Kohl is a Jewish character who is
rendered with unabashed philo-Semitism of the kind that Kutzik
has noted, but not for the purpose he proposes. For in actuality,
the dichotomy which Kutzick conjectures does not exist, as we
have seen. In *The Mansion*, the pro-Jewish characterization of
Kohl is not a replacement for anti-Semitic characterizations in
earlier works, but integral to *The Mansion* itself, and in more
than one way.

To begin with, Linda's marriage to Kohl provides a means by
which Faulkner registers the reaction of the residents of Yoknapatawpha to a Jew who decided that it was important to fight
fascism abroad by volunteering in the Spanish Civil War. For
when Linda returns to Jefferson as a widow, they do not respect
his idealism but harass her because she was married to a Communist and a Jew, even though they have never seen him. Because they have heard that Barton Kohl is a New York Jew, they,
stereotypically, think that Linda is rich, Faulkner exposing the
fact that the Shylock image still gives no sign of fading from the
inland Southern consciousness. Faulkner illustrates the presence of anti-Semitism in the region during these decades by the
fact that Kohl elicits it, even though he is dead.

More central to the main theme of the trilogy is the contrast
Kohl affords to Flem Snopes in every way. For although Kohl's
marriage to Linda Snopes was very brief, as contrasted to Flem's
marriage to Eula, he brought such happiness to his wife that he
made her realize the worth of marriage as a social institution.
Eula's life with Flem, as we know, brought her to the opposite
conclusion. Also, unlike the money-obsessed Flem, Kohl at-
taches no particular importance to material wealth. He is not
obsessed with acquisitiveness, nor is he physically or emotionally sterile. He is, in every sense, a complete man—creative,
principled, courageous, and humanly warm. "He was a big
man," Faulkner says, "I dont [sic] mean just a hunk of beef, but

virile, alive . . . a man who loved what the old Greeks meant by laughter, who would have been a match for, competent to fulfill any woman's emotional and physical life too."[39] He is more of a man, in other words, than almost any Protestant male in Yoknapatawpha county. Though presented only briefly and drawn one-dimensionally, he is deliberately idealized in an exaggerated way, Faulkner utilizing this characterization of an artist-Jew, with whom he is obviously also self-identified, to counter more than one anti-Semitic stereotype relating to Jewish males.

The Mansion, then, may be said to embody—and not for the first time in Faulkner's fiction by any means—a criticism of Southern whites for their sense of Nordic racial superiority and an unqualified proclamation of the worth of Jewish individuals. During the time that *The Mansion* was written, a topic of great concern in America was whether what had happened in Germany could happen here. This is a question that worries Gavin Stevens when he wonders what mankind needs in order to avoid the kind of racial prejudice that led to German Nazism. In one of his conversations with himself on this subject he gropes for an answer. "Man must have light," he says, "he must live in the fierce full constant glare of light, where all shadow will be defined and sharp and unique and personal."[40]

In articulating this idea, Stevens is searching for a principle that will help mankind in the future. But he is describing as well the luminosity of that Mississippi in the teens and early twenties of this century. Here, if shadows of anti-Semitism lurked, they were sharply defined as to their location and source. Here Faulkner formed his own unique relation to a Jewish family that lived in Oxford. And here, despising anti-Semitic bigotry, he established his relationship to Jews on a firm foundation, in terms that were both principled and personal.

39. Ibid., 218.
40. Ibid., 132.

"Topmost in the Pattern": Family Structure in Faulkner

ARTHUR F. KINNEY

"This novel is the portrayal of a family," an anonymous copywriter sums in a singular attempt to condense an early, sprawling Faulkner novel into the size of his own postage stamp in order to promote it on the back dustjacket flap of *The Devil Beats His Wife*, the novel of Faulkner's friend and agent Ben Wasson.

> This novel is the portrayal of a family. Impatient and violent, the men have gone out to battle and returned to their homes. There are scarcely any words of fighting spoken by them, yet they have brought back to the Sartoris-by-marriage women the smell of cannon fire and the wounds of their hearts. These women must bear with them, heal them, and smile to themselves a little at the childishness of all men folk. Through the close-knit story runs a sinister thread; there is meanness and fatality, but also life, color, and a quiet and sometimes almost hilarious humor, with a Sartoris always topmost in the pattern.
>
> These people will, as time moves by, be succeeded by the more worldly and pushing Snopes family. A hint is already given here of that victory without battle when peanut farmers supersede a fine Southern tradition. But now we have them before us—both white and black, for even negroes associated with the family take on their characteristics. Mr. Faulkner has painted a big canvas with many fine portraits.[1]

This bold précis has not been bettered—not by George Marion O'Donnell in his classic essay on "Faulkner's Mythology" in the first volume of *The Kenyon Review* in 1939 which divided all of

---

1. Quoted in Ben Wasson, *"Count No 'Count": Flashbacks to Faulkner* (Jackson: University Press of Mississippi, 1983), 95.

143

Yoknapatawpha into a "universal conflict" between the twin
forces of the Sartorises and the Snopeses—

> The Sartorises act traditionally; that is to say, they act always with an
> ethically responsible will. They represent vital morality, humanism.
> Being anti-traditional, the Snopeses are immoral from the Sartoris
> point-of-view. But the Snopeses do not recognize this point-of-view;
> acting only for self-interest, they acknowledge no ethical duty.
> Really, then, they are a-moral; they represent naturalism or animal-
> ism. And the Sartoris-Snopes conflict is fundamentally a struggle
> between humanism and naturalism[2]—

nor, more than a half-century after *The Devil Beats His Wife*
publicly announced *Sartoris*, the most recent critical work to
appear on Faulkner, that by Hugh M. Ruppersburg, who writes
that

> Faulkner's earlier novels evinced a particular concern with the fam-
> ily: the Sartorises, Benbows, Goodwins, Compsons, Bundrens, and
> others. They often focused on relationships among family members
> and their varying individual perspectives on the world.[3]

Thinking of the Snopes trilogy *(The Hamlet, The Town, The
Mansion)* or the Stevens, Mallison, or Priest families, we might
amend this to say all his novels evince this particular concern
with the family, both as fact and as metaphor. "The complex and
contorted genealogies of William Faulkner's inhabitants of Yoknapatawpha County," Susan Gallagher writes,

> often summarize each family's story. The Compson line shows a
> thin, downward progression, the Snopeses proliferate on a horizon-
> tal line, and the McCaslin tree is noteworthy for its interconnecting
> branches. The idea of family is crucial to the Yoknapatawpha saga.
> Faulkner always centers these stories on a specific family and its
> relationships. Frequently a brother/sister pairing occurs, which is
> identifiable either because of a special relationship existing between
> the two or because they are the only two siblings present in the
> book. The former situation occurs with Quentin and Caddy Comp-

son and Darl and Dewey Dell Bundren; the latter occurs with pairs
as varied as Henry and Judith Sutpen, Jody and Eula Varner, and
Horace and Narcissa Benbow.[4]

Such a persistent observation, at once basic to understanding
Faulkner's narrative poetics and all-embracing in its applicabil-
ity to the Faulknerian canon, draws together both the Yoknapatawpha fictions and, with *Pylon, The Wild Palms,* and *A
Fable,* those works that stretch beyond his mythic kingdom of
which he remains the proud, self-proclaimed proprietor.

In the first of a series of new books on Faulkner's families,
Donald M. Kartiganer remarks that

> more perhaps than the chronicler of a mythic corner of Mississippi,
> Faulkner is the premier American novelist of family. His people,
> however uniquely and memorably portrayed, invariably trail behind
> them clouds of familial qualifiers: the grandparents, parents, and
> siblings whose cumulative identity is the indispensable context of
> individual character. The bulk of Faulkner's people are not so much
> single, separate persons as collective enterprises, the products and
> processes of family dramas apart from which the individual actor is
> scarcely intelligible. Confronting the single member of the Sartoris,
> Compson, McCaslin, or Snopes lines, or even of the less amply
> elaborated lines such as Bundren, Hightower, Sutpen, or Varner, we
> soon find ourselves addressing family complexes, synchronic and
> diachronic systems whose individual units take their meanings from
> their transactions with each other.[5]

Indeed, when Faulkner told Jean Stein vanden Heuvel in 1956
that "beginning with *Sartoris* I discovered that my own little
postage stamp of native soil was worth writing about and that I
would never live long enough to exhaust it"—perhaps over the
years Faulkner's best-known comment on his own work—it is
difficult to know, save for the tell-tale italics, whether he means
the novel or the family when he talks of *Sartoris.* Faulkner himself makes the transference apparently without knowing it. Yet it

4. "To Love and to Honor: Brothers and Sisters in Faulkner's Yoknapatawpha
County," *Essays in Literature,* 7:2 (Fall 1980), 213.
5. "Quentin Compson and Faulkner's Drama of the Generations," in *Critical Essays on William Faulkner: The Compson Family,* ed. Arthur F. Kinney (Boston: G. K.
Hall & Co., 1982), 381.

is crucial to understanding his work. Here, then, is the full passage, which is very seldom quoted, from which this single sentence is frequently but unrepresentatively drawn; note how his subject once he mentions *Sartoris* changes from *books* to *people* and through *characters* to *purpose:*

> Beginning with *Sartoris* I discovered that my own little postage stamp of native soil was worth writing about and that I would never live long enough to exhaust it, and by sublimating the actual into apocryphal I would have complete liberty to use whatever talent I might have to its absolute top. It opened up a gold mine of other peoples, so I created a cosmos of my own. I can move these people around like God, not only in space but in time too. The fact that I have moved my characters around in time successfully, at least in my own estimation, proves to me my own theory that time is a fluid condition which has no existence except in the momentary avatars of individual people. There is no such thing as *was*—only *is*. If *was* existed there would be no grief or sorrow. I like to think of the world I created as being a kind of keystone in the Universe; that, as small as that keystone is, if it were ever taken away, the universe itself would collapse. My last book will be the Doomsday Book, the Golden Book, of Yoknapatawpha County. Then I shall break the pencil and I'll have to stop.[6]

For the Doomsday Book, as Faulkner knows, is a genealogical listing, the skeins of people composing the pattern, the design, and the significance of the whole.

Let us take counsel, then, from the anonymous publicist who wrote copy for the jacket of the Wasson novel and take a look at *Sartoris*. When we do, we discover it focuses not on one family but, actually, on six—the Sartorises, the Benbows, the Mitchells, the MacCallums, the Peabodys, and the Snopeses—and that it always looks at individual members of the families as, *concurrently, representatives* of those families. In all six families, Faulkner shows more than one generation; with the Sartorises, he portrays five generations. So while the action of the novel occurs in slightly more than a year, the memories of

---

6. Rep. in *Lion in the Garden: Interviews with William Faulkner, 1926–1962*, ed. James B. Meriwether and Michael Millgate (New York: Random House, 1968), 255.

living characters broaden the scope backwards in time, enlarging the concerns of the novel while suggesting that, in the narrowing reductions of present time, there is significant diminution. By entering the novel through the family lines—through any of the six family lines, in fact—we shall come rather swiftly to its emphatic and repetitive theme: what we are to make of a diminished thing.[7] And what was true of the truncated *Sartoris* is equally true of the novel in its parent form as *Flags in the Dust*, at present rescued for us in one rather peculiar conflation by Douglas Day (1973). Earlier this year, too, Walter Taylor has made a similar judgment in his rather compact introduction to this longer, original, and more important text:

> By the time Faulkner submitted *Flags in the Dust*, the geopolitics of Yoknapatawpha County was clearly delineated. The white population was neatly divided among patricians and their dependents, who lived in the foothills and valleys; upwardly mobile poor-white tradesmen, who lived in Jefferson and had close ties to hill folk; and poor whites, who lived in the hills. These latter two groups were infiltrated by Snopeses. Byron Snopes, bookkeeper at old Bayard Sartoris's bank, was a "hillman" (*FID*, 7). He was a cousin of Flem Snopes, who recently "to old Bayard's profane astonishment . . . became vice president of the Sartoris bank." These hillmen were "from a small settlement known as Frenchman's Bend"; they were "a seemingly inexhaustible family which for the last ten or twelve years had been moving to town in driblets." Their presence was deplored by the old guard—according to one patrician lady, "General Johnston or General Forrest wouldn't have took a Snopes in his army" (*Sar*, 172, 174). These Snopeses were background figures, but Faulkner's implication was clear: if the Sartorises were dying out, the Snopeses were waiting to take over, and it was going to be a smaller world when they did.

Taylor, we see, cannot tell us about *Flags in the Dust* without concentrating on family. He goes on:

7. Several of the foregoing statistics and observations are paraphrased from the unpublished dissertation of James B. Meriwether, "The Place of *The Unvanquished* in Faulkner's Yoknapatawpha Series" (Princeton, 1958), 17. I am grateful to Professor Meriwether for lending me a copy of this study.

The Sartoris place, screened off from Jefferson by "upland country," occupied the Yoknapatawpha equivalent of Delta land, "a valley
of good broad fields." Tradition sat heavy on this house that Colonel
John Sartoris had built. "In the nineteenth century," Colonel John
had told old Bayard, "genealogy . . . is poppycock"; that was true
"particularly in America," he said, where nobody could be sure of
his ancestry. But John Sartoris was proud of his own. People who
were not were "only a little less vain" than those who were, and,
besides, "a Sartoris can have a little vanity and poppycock if he
wants it." Poppycock or not, they seemed locked into their traditions—a "funny family," one friend commented, who were "always
going to wars, and always getting killed." They inherited their
bizarre behavior from Colonel John, onto whom they projected what
his sister, Miss Jenny Du Pre, thought of as "a glamorous fatality."
Colonel John's mystique prevented them from dealing with their
own lives objectively; the Colonel was an "arrogant shade" who still
"dominated the house and the life that went on there" (*Sar,* 6, 92,
167, 380, 113).[8]

I think we can readily agree with my enumerative summary of
six families in *Sartoris,* a point which I have actually paraphrased
from a very useful if unpublished dissertation by James B.
Meriwether, and with Walter Taylor's compressed version of
Flags in the Dust. But when we turn to either textual version
directly, we shall find nothing like either of these—not in Old
Man Falls's recollections, Simon's borrowed behavior, Aunt
Jenny's recollections, or Young Bayard's broodings. While
genealogical truths are imperative for us, they are deliberately
avoided (or exaggerated) by the family members themselves.
And Horace Benbow and Belle Mitchell are no nearer the mark
on themselves or their relations than Aunt Jenny or Old Bayard.

Still, this way of looking at Yoknapatawpha is significantly
similar to the way Southerners have from their social origins to
the present looked at themselves and, on occasion, judged
themselves. Clan is more important, in fact, than either caste or
race because clan *includes* both caste and race. At the main

8. Walter Taylor, *Faulkner's Search for a South* (Urbana: University of Illinois
Press, 1983), 27, 27–28.

crossroads in Oxford, Mississippi, a sign points to Oxford Ceme-
tery by way of the famous persons who are buried there; two
short blocks south and east, near the intersection of Buchanan
and South 13th Streets, the original of the Compson house is
referred to locally not by the street address but as "the Thomp-
son-Chandler house." Rowan Oak, despite that European over-
lay, is known here as the Faulkner home. Patronymic names
become everyday labels. For as the distinguished sociologist
John Dollard has noted, "the monogamous patriarchal family"
remains "the prime character-forming agent" in Southern society.[9]

Dollard's classic study of the South, *Caste and Class in a
Southern Town*, was published by Yale University Press in 1937
but, essentially unchanged, it was reprinted by Harper and
Brothers in 1949 and was made a Doubleday Anchor Book, in a
current third edition, in 1957. Dollard was a Northerner, a professor of psychology at Yale, who used as a research site for
examining Southern mores and perspectives—though his real
focus became race—an unidentified town he called Southerntown in analogy to the then-current study of Middletown USA
by Robert S. and Helen M. Lynd. In one of very few examples
of raw data which he compiled, he transcribes this note made on
a spontaneous conversation during a train ride.

Met a young man on the train last night and fell into conversation.
Apparently he comes of a well-known family here. Says grandfather
told him about having been a courier for General Hood in the Civil
War. Says when they say "war" down here, they mean the Civil War,
not the World War. Says northern people feel that southerners are
mean toward Negroes; says this is not so, his family have always had
Negro slaves and servants and have loved them. Gives example of
personal services to Negroes. Feels people have not gotten over the
Civil War. He wanted me to learn about the "real South," says
southern hospitality is not a myth but exists in the small upper
group. Wishes I could see it as he knows it from his own home. Said

9. John Dollard, *Caste and Class in a Southern Town* (Garden City, N.Y.: Doubleday Anchor Books, 1957), 434–45.

that he wished that his family were still prosperous so that he could take me to his home and show me the real thing. Despaired of communicating the real South to me by word.[10]

It was, in fact, this matter of clan that especially concerned this Northern scholar, that became his means of conducting investigation. In connection with this note taken in the field, he writes,

> To be an upper-class person is to have a certain kind of memory of the past and to hold a certain rôle in the eyes of others with similar memories. If, on meeting a southern person, the stranger could by chance open a history book and ask him to thumb through it, and if the southerner stopped now and then to say, "Oh, yes, that is Governor So-and-so; he was my grandmother's brother," or "General Blank married a second cousin of my mother, she was of the South Carolina Blanks, you know," he would be dealing with an upper-class person. Originally, no doubt, membership in this class was based on a strong position in the economic system and entry to it was often secured by possession of special social skills and money. Like all aristocratic traits, however, class membership tends to be socially inherited and does not continually need the underpinning of actual economic pre-eminence. In its day this was a functioning class leading in statecraft and agriculture, and disciplining its individuals for leadership. Nowadays it seems to be based largely on memories of interrelationship with other leading families of the past, rather than on current achievement. It still differentiates sufficiently the behavior of those who are born into it so that it is a formative force in the culture.[11]

A number of scholars and writers since Dollard—and Faulkner can be counted among them—have noted that aristocratic behavior was not characteristic of those who founded Mississippi; they were rough frontiersmen such as those described in the opening pages of *Requiem for a Nun* or in the Appendix to *The Sound and the Fury* written in 1946, but it is nevertheless important to note that Southerners, including Mississippians, have no doubt nurtured the myth of aristocracy because it reflects the centrality of families in their history and culture. Settled in the

10. Ibid., 81.
11. Ibid., 79–80.

true sense of that word, Southerners intermarried, became in-
terrelated, and found that genealogical ties united with genetic
strains produced identifiable units called families. As William
Stadiem writes at the close of a recent book-length survey,
"Families created the South. They molded its character and
captured its imagination. Southerners are a close-knit lot. *The
family is the South's most important institution, and the great
families are its most cherished icons. Despite the beckoning
future, Southerners enjoy living in the past. Despite every concept of democracy, Southerners enjoy doting on their aristocracy. Old times, it seems, are simply not forgotten.*"[12] Myths
aside, however, this basic interrelationship of people as the fundamental means of organization, association, growth, and development has, through the nearly two centuries of Southern
history, pervaded all classes: it is as true of the land-locked
Bundrens and the carpetbagger Burdens as it is of the aristocratic Sartorises, the middle-class Benbows, and the poor white
Snopeses.

The Falkners well illustrate the importance of families in
Southern life. "In 1859," John Pilkington has recently summed,

> when Faulkner's great-great-great-uncle, John Wesley Thompson,
> joined the Book and Tract Society of the Memphis Conference of the
> Methodist Episcopal Church South, he received a "genealogical
> family Bible and case." In his will, he provided that the Bible should
> descend in the family through the eldest son. William Faulkner
> inherited this Bible at the death of his father on August 7, 1932, and
> in it made new entries in some of the genealogical tables, charac-
> terized by Faulkner's biographer as "literally hundreds of pages
> bound into the Bible between the Old and New Testaments." In the
> South, a man's knowledge of his ancestors helped him to answer the
> question Who am I? It gave him a sense of continuity. The family
> reputation defined his position in the community. The comment in
> *Sartoris*—"the man who professes to care nothing about his
> forebears is only a little less vain than the man who bases all his
> actions on blood precedent"—falls considerably short of rendering

12. *A Class by Themselves: The Untold Story of the Great Southern Families* (New
York: Crown Publishers, Inc., 1980), 263.

Faulkner's absorption in family tradition, family legends, family stories, and, particularly, the career of Colonel William Clark Falkner, the novelist's great-grandfather.[13]

John Faulkner, in his "affectionate reminiscence" called *My Brother Bill* begins with a chapter describing Faulkner's death that is heavily dependent on family references and involvement:

> I went over to Bill's house. It was about two-thirty. Jimmy, my oldest son, was already there. He met me at the door. Estelle, Bill's wife, had called him as soon as the hospital had called her. They had not had time to summon her to the hospital. They were all too busy working with Bill. Jimmy, as soon as she called, had called me and Chooky, my younger son, and my older brother, Jack, in Mobile. Chooky was not there yet. Jimmy had called me first and he had not quite had time to arrive.[14]

When, in chapter 2, he turns to Faulkner's life, that too is thick with family references to secure its meaning.

> The first memory I have about my brother Bill is what Mother told me about his colic. For his first year he had it almost every night. We lived at the time in New Albany, a town about thirty miles northeast of Oxford. At least Mother and Dad and Bill lived there. Jack and I and Dean hadn't come along yet. We were born later in Ripley and in Oxford.
>
> Dad was working for the railroad then. He was general passenger agent at New Albany. It was Grandfather's road. The Old Colonel, my great-grandfather, the first W. C. Falkner, had built it and Grandfather and his half sisters had inherited it when my great-grandfather died. After that Grandfather became president and managed it until 1902, when he sold it because he did not have the time to attend to it. It was called the Gulf and Chicago then; the Gulf, Mobile and Northern now.
>
> Grandfather had not wanted the railroad to begin with. He had an extensive criminal practice at the law that left him no spare time to manage anything else, let alone a railroad. Dad was the only one who wanted it and except for a misunderstanding would have bought it when Grandfather sold it in 1902.[15]

13. *The Heart of Yoknapatawpha* (Jackson: University Press of Mississippi, 1981), 12–13.
14. (New York: Trident, 1963), 2.
15. Ibid., 9.

As for Jack himself—Murry C. Falkner—when "the LSU Press had asked me to write a book of my own," he says, "I decided to try my hand at it—to write not only about Bill but about my other two brothers and myself as well: the story of a Mississippi family."[16] Consequently, *The Falkners of Mississippi* opens with a genealogy[17] and stresses from the outset the family setting and family relationships: "How kind they were, those years of long ago; how gentle the life and how pleasant the memories of it. I can almost see us now: the day is done and we are all about the fireplace in the living room—Mammy in her rocking chair, Father with the paper, Mother sewing, and Bill, John, and I listening to Mammy telling us again and again about the War— still, as always, the only one., We were all there, each belonged, was loved, and loved in return."[18]

It is not surprising, then, that an interest in the structure and dynamics of the family was central to Faulkner's fiction from the first. *Soldiers' Pay* sharply contrasts Donald Mahon both as a wounded veteran who once had the potential to extend his family line and also as a dying man. This central conflict is realized in many ways: in his father's conflict as his parent and as his rector; in the recollections of Cecily and Emily which juxtapose the old Donald and the new, the normal and the maimed; and in Mrs. Powers's marriage to Donald to assuage her own guilt. By appealing to a more limited sense of family, both Cecily and Margaret Powers demean Donald himself, while his weakened condition enables the Reverend Mahon, as well as Joe Gilligan, to grow in spiritual understanding. In *Mosquitoes* both the biological and spiritual senses of family are mercilessly mocked in Mrs. Maurier's inept and pathetic attempt to gather about her a nuclear family in her yacht on Lake Ponchartrain: personal relationships are mocked in the adolescent fumblings of Pat and Josh and of Miss Jameson and Mr. Talliaferro while spiritual growth is parodied through the effete behavior and discussions

16. *The Falkners of Mississippi: A Memoir* (Baton Rouge: Louisiana State University Press, 1967), xviii.
17. Ibid., xxv.
18. Ibid., 16.

of the artists who would replace transcendent awareness with grandiose verbiage.

Both of these apprentice novels lack the sudden power of *Sartoris/Flags in the Dust* despite their shared interest in the family and in family relationships because they remain rooted in the fable-making imagination. The Sartoris saga gains force, however, since it has the authenticity of fact—of very recent fact—and of Faulkner's own obsessive concern with his own family roots. Walter Taylor sums the work of Meriwether, Joseph Blotner, David Minter, Judith Bryant Wittenberg, and other helpful critics this way:

> John Sartoris was modeled on Colonel William Clark Falkner. Ignoring the Old Colonel's origin as a penniless runaway, Faulkner focused on his image as wartime guerilla, scourge of carpetbaggers, railroad builder, and duelist. And he made a significant decision. His readers would experience Colonel John as Faulkner had experienced the Old Colonel, who had died eight years before his own birth—through the patchwork of memory and legend passed on by his survivors. . . .
>
> Colonel John's sister, Virginia Du Pre, preserved and embellished the family legends. This formidable lady, modeled on "Auntee" Holland Falkner Wilkins who kept the Young Colonel's house after his wife's death, had come to live with her brother "two years a wife and seven years a widow at thirty." It was Miss Jenny who spun tales of the glamorous, foolhardy Carolina Bayard Sartoris. . . .
>
> [But] The Sartoris man she had had to contend with longest was Colonel John's son, Bayard. Faulkner, ignoring his grandfather's reputation as senator and county boss, had constructed old Bayard's portrait around J. W. T. Falkner's image as banker and man of conservative tastes.[19]

By extension, then, the Sartorises are distantly autobiographical explorations by Faulkner, but in decidedly familial terms. What is even more telling than what Faulkner determined to preserve in the amber of his fiction is what he left out. As Taylor puts it,

> In Miss Jenny and old Bayard, Faulkner had done a remarkable job of "sublimating the actual" of his family's experience "into apoc-

19. Taylor, 28–30.

ryphal," and he had accomplished this with convincing objectivity. Now he made a surprising choice: the twins' parents, he reported, were long dead. This decision allowed Faulkner to suggest something that all the Falkner boys must have felt. Murry Falkner [their father] had not followed in the very large footsteps of J. W. T. Falkner and the Old Colonel, and Miss Maud [their mother] came from a different kind of family; "the Big Place," where Auntee Wilkins presided over the Young Colonel's household, had been like a second home to the boys, and that house and its aging inhabitants symbolized the family traditions. Telescoping the Sartoris generations thus allowed Faulkner to write as though he were J. W. T. Falkner's *son* rather than his grandson.[20]

And, as if to underscore the point, it is the generation based on Faulkner's own parents that is the single generation that is all but omitted from any of the accounts supplied in *Sartoris/Flags in the Dust* of Sartorises past and present—except for the livery stable, a distant allusion to one of Murry Falkner's best-known associations. What is important to Faulkner, then, what seems to energize his creativity, is the bold and matchless vision of his great-grandfather, who, beginning penniless and alone rose to great fortune, transformed himself from an alien boy in Ripley to that town's most powerful politician and its most colorful citizen, who turned defeat in Army leadership into triumph as a blockade runner during the War Between the States, and who had the ability to say let there be a railroad in a land of unpaved roadways and saw to it that there soon was one. It is, I think, this imagination to shape a life to the contours of fiction that great-grandfather and great-grandson share in real life; the genealogical force of it is tested through the failure of final heroism—"*For man's enlightenment he lived / By man's ingratitude he died*" is the epitaph of Colonel John Sartoris, C.S.A.[21] while Young Bayard dies an inglorious and obscure death in the test flight of a poorly designed plane—that makes both generations of Sartoris similar and perhaps inferior to the two generations of Falkner. This explicit examination of Sartoris/Falkner shows how urgent and how vital a sense of family was to Faulkner's perspective and

20. Ibid., 30–31.
21. *Flags in the Dust* (New York: Random House, 1973), 428.

to his fiction. Indeed, the concern with Sartorises surges
through the later fiction like some vital undercurrent, surfacing
in *Sanctuary, Absalom, Absalom!, The Unvanquished, The
Hamlet, The Town, The Mansion, Knight's Gambit,* and *Requiem
for a Nun;* in "Ad Astra," "A Rose for Emily," "All the Dead
Pilots," "There Was a Queen," "The Bear," and "With Caution
and Dispatch," and even in the film script for *War Birds.*

Faulkner also employed the Compsons—as he did the Sartorises—in many of his works: in *The Sound and the Fury, Absalom, Absalom! The Unvanquished, Go Down, Moses, Requiem
for a Nun, The Town,* and *The Mansion;* in "That Evening Sun,"
"A Justice," "Lion," "Skirmish at Sartoris," "My Grandmother
Millard," "Vendée," "Retreat," "Raid," "A Bear Hunt," "The Old
People," "The Bear," and "Delta Autumn," and, perhaps most
significantly, in "Compson," the 1946 Appendix to *The Sound
and the Fury* which was to appear before the novel itself actually
began.[22] The Compson line stretches backwards and forwards in
time well beyond the Sartoris line. And the Appendix "Compson" begins not with the white Scottish line of that name, but
with the Indian chief Ikkemotubbe. Although he calls himself
"L'Homme," later "Doom," he corrupts more than his name
since he uses intimidation and exploitation to rule his Chickasaw
people. As a result, he becomes in time "a dispossessed American King."[23] His brief biographical sketch is that of a gambler
whose greed finally causes his defeat (in exile); in this way he
anticipates several Compsons. His life story is followed by a
sketch of Andrew Jackson, pictured as sentimental, idealistic,
naive. His innocence is the other side of Ikkemotubbe's crafti-
ness, as it foreshadows the other sort of Compson. Then come
the Compsons themselves—a gallery of the dispossessed—who
alternate between the naive idealist (Quentin Maclachan, or
Quentin I, who rebels against the King of England; Charles
Stuart, who rebels against the United States; Jason II, or Gen-

22. *Selected Letters of William Faulkner,* ed. Joseph Blotner (New York: Random
House, 1977), 220–21.
23. *The Sound and the Fury* (New York: Modern Library, 1956), 403.

eral Compson, who suffers the Confederates' defeat at Shiloh and Resaca; Jason III, Mr. Compson, who fails as a lawyer and father; and his son Quentin III) and the corrupt gambler (Jason Lycurgus, or Jason I, the Old Governor, who trades a racehorse for the Compson Domain, a square mile of the best land in Jefferson; Jason IV, who extorts his niece and sister and steals from his mother). The long lists of public accomplishments and gestures of heroism in "Compson" limn a long line of men internally weak or corrupt. Together, they people a decadent aristocracy through generations of family breeding, one weakened by nature as well as by activity (or inactivity). The family history thus writ large remains a history of sound and fury signifying little. Indeed, it may signify little because the Compsons have no Aunt Jennys (nor any old man Falls) to make at least a part of the lineage mythically admirable.[24]

The House of Sartoris concentrates largely on the War Between the States and Reconstruction, but the House of Compson traces with pride its European beginnings; and we cannot understand the House of Sutpen without seeing that all of its peculiarities—Thomas Sutpen's lessons of aristocracy in the Tidewater, his meager beginnings in Yoknapatawpha, and the incest which Henry if not Thomas might perhaps allow—all fulfill family traditions that in and of themselves established Sutpen primacy and authority. If Thomas Sutpen's hasty drive towards respectability annoys and exposes Mr. Compson, it is not because it is essentially different but because it can be (apparently) so easily arrived at, in a single generation, by one domineering visionary.

If Faulkner is the premier novelist of family, then *Absalom, Absalom!* is his premier work. Faulkner knew the book was a study of Thomas Sutpen and Thomas Sutpen as a family man. He remarked in a graduate course at Virginia that "the central character is Sutpen, yes. The story of a man who wanted a son

24. This paragraph paraphrases an earlier account in my *Critical Essays on William Faulkner: The Compson Family*, 9–10.

and got too many, got so many that they destroyed him. It's incidentally the story of Quentin Compson's hatred of the bad qualities in the country he loves. But the central character is Sutpen, the story of a man who wanted sons."[25] The long mid-section of the novel which details the Sutpen biography primarily in terms of founding a dynasty—the definition of the House of Sutpen as the formation of family—is bounded at the start by the effects of founding families, at the close by the causes for needing them and the cultural causes that seem to prevent Sutpen from obtaining what so many Mississippians from the Eastern seaboard had managed to do with no greater resources and with far less imagination, if not less drive. Indeed, if Sutpen's ambitions were not so rooted in cultural perspective, he would not have been so attractive to the earlier Compsons and Coldfields nor so seductive to Rosa. He embodies the sense of family they cherish. His grand sense of the South—which incorporates joining the Confederate Army and reestablishing his plantation after Appomatox—are what they peculiarly treasure. So all would be a part of that family by intermarriage into it or by witnesses of it: even General Compson is Sutpen's friend. What goes wrong, of course, is that the pure drive for family as a cultural construct leaves out the human integers from which it must be built. There is a marvelous way in which the novel, like Sutpen, disembodies Rosa, Charles, and even the Haitian wife, in its compulsive drive towards self-destruction, while the vision of what denies their humanity seems to shine all the more relentlessly, to Rosa in her darkened parlor, to Mr. Compson on his humid front porch, and to Quentin and Shreve in their chilled dormitory room.

But *Absalom, Absalom!* admits other families even as it concentrates on the rise and fall of the House of Sutpen. There is, first of all, Bon's family. We never know how much Charles knows of the marriage of his parents, but we do feel the pull he

25. *Faulkner in the University: Class Conferences at the University of Virginia, 1957–1958*, ed. Frederick L. Gwynn and Joseph L. Blotner (Charlottesville: University of Virginia Press, 1959), 71.

must feel towards his father and his half-brother and half-sister. His marriage would partly repair what Sutpen has tried to put asunder. There is also the Coldfield family. Rosa is drawn to Sutpen not because she would succeed (or displace, therefore) her sister Ellen but because Sutpen's sense of aristocracy amends Coldfield's compromise with the ordinary. All that Rosa does during the war, in fact, at the side of Judith and Clytie in the hard hot fields and in the sprawling house, is to maintain family—if she is not childbearing, as her older sister Ellen is, she is at least supportive to her sister's children. It is a good part of her motive to enter a family where she can find satisfying purpose and function. As for the objects of her adoration, Henry and Judith (and later Bon), we do not know whether they return her concern. We do not know, either, whether they know that in their love of Charles they are being drawn to their own kin. What we do know is that they would embrace Charles into their family, an act of marriage which is seen by both Sutpen children as an addition to the family which augments and enhances, but does not necessarily change, as it does not diminish, the family. At least, not until Henry presumably thinks of Charles as black, and therefore ineligible, by force or otherwise, to join the family line. Nor should we forget the Jones family in thinking of *Absalom, Absalom!* Wash's desire to breed Milly by Thomas is not simply an ignorant poor white's dream but the need to continue a family line which seems at an end. When we see Wash, moreover, we see a man who respects Sutpen's values more than his money—and one whom Wash finds a father surrogate every bit as much as Henry, Judith, Charles, *and Rosa* do. In fact, it is Sutpen as the mythic Southern father, head of household, that seems also to attract Quentin; if his final association comes more easily and naturally with Henry—the one Sutpen he has met and conversed with—he nevertheless through the four long chapters that close *Absalom, Absalom!* clearly finds in Sutpen a man who makes something of himself as Quentin's own father did not. Against the action which Sutpen embodies in chapters 2 through 4 Faulkner (and Quentin) places the mocking perspective of Mr. Compson who, unlike his own father, General (Grandfather) Compson, refuses to give Sutpen any praise, although clearly the two men should have common values and, after the war, even common cause. *Absalom, Absalom!*, then, is the story about the failure of the South seen as the failure to produce a viable family—whether because of incest, racism, jealousy, or inhumanity—a failure that is shared by the Sutpens, the Bons, the Coldfields, the Joneses, and the Compsons. This need to *have* a family, and the need to understand why the best intentions failed, may also explain why the one character without a family portrayed in the novel—Shreve—finds such compelling fascination in the story of Sutpen and his family and why, in the end, he too wants to be involved. "'Wait,'" he exclaims, "'For God's sake wait'"; "'Let me play a while now,'" he pleads.[26]

And what Shreve forces upon Quentin—and what is urgently insinuated throughout the book upon us—are questions regarding race. In tracing the history of the South as, fundamentally, the development of its families, Faulkner is no longer able to avoid such questions as those surrounding miscegenation. In his fictional study of the last major Yoknapatawpha family with historical claim to some kind of privilege, the McCaslin-Beauchamp-Edmonds family, such matters are a central focus. The long-time custom of whites and blacks constituting a larger single family is something Faulkner took for granted in his early years because of his own relationships with family servants, and especially with Callie Barr. It was, after all, Southern family tradition. Hodding Carter reminds us of this when he describes Son McKnight, the black boy who joined his family when both children were nine: like Ringo and Bayard or, later, Lucas and Zack, they grew up together, not worrying about the fact that there would be only limited ways that, as adults, they might associate with one another.[27] After describing their child-

26. *Absalom, Absalom!* (New York: Modern Library, 1951), 216, 280.
27. Hodding Carter, *Southern Legacy* (Baton Rouge: Louisiana State University Press, 1950), 39–42.

hood experiences, Carter tells of Son's requiring an invitation to his all-white wedding, and of how he managed to slip past the guests, stand on a chair, and wave a greeting that is Hodding Carter's sole memory of the occasion. And how, later, when he and his bride had settled down, and the night turned cold, Son took a skeleton key, let himself in, and began kindling a fire to keep the newlyweds warm. Such anecdotes, told with affection, bear out in exacting detail Dollard's accumulated data which talk of blacks and whites co-existing in Southerntown by both races accepting paradigmatic *family* relationships: the whites, he says, speak of Negroes as children, talk of taking care of them, and provide furnishings that become their home.[28]

Go Down, Moses seems by hindsight to be the necessary and logical sequel to *Absalom, Absalom!* because in its examination of the House of McCaslin it takes up both the white and the mulatto lines. As critics frequently note, the central scene of that novel is the long debate in the commissary between Ike McCaslin (of the male McCaslin line) and Cass Edmonds (named for McCaslin, but from the female side) who view quite differently the ledgers of their common ancestry: to Ike, they are intimate moments in the family diary; to Cass they are business transactions that form the basis for the farm and the family he manages. It is a difference of interpretation, Faulkner implies, that cannot be reconciled. Both come by their viewpoints honestly. We understand Cass's when we recall that the first mention of him—as the narrator of "Was"—is as a child who learned from Buck and Buddy that lives consist of managing blacks like Tomey's Turl for work and amusement, much as one would command a labor force, even if he is one's half-brother. Ike, on the other hand, taking his lessons from Sam Fathers, himself a man of mixed blood, learns what Sam calls humility and sacrifice. Ike's personal relationships, twisted by memories of the racial behavior of his ancestors if not his own treatment of Lucas and Fonsiba, abort his desire to have children of his own, because they abort a pattern for marriage and childrearing

28. Dollard, 435–38.

which make him only the true descendant of other bachelors, like Uncle Buddy, like Uncle Buck (for much of his life), like Sam Fathers and Boon. Against such sterile and unproductive white men, whose burden of guilt seems to prevent their freedom to give, are the blacks. They have a natural and fertile family life, like Lucas and Molly, or are fertile until corrupted, like the doomed Eunice who *"Drownd herself"* *"in Crick Cristmas Day 1832,"*[29] or, most tragically of all, have their natural family life cut short, like Rider and Mannie, as if there is no place for normal relations when whites cheat blacks at their hidden stills or in their crooked crap games or among posses and crooked sheriffs. Racism so corrupts the family of man that reproduction itself is at times denied. *Go Down, Moses,* like *Sartoris/Flags in the Dust, The Sound and the Fury,* and *Absalom, Absalom!,* is fundamentally, incisively, and finally a novel of family; and it is no accident that in concluding with still another bachelor, Gavin Stevens, who feels he can buy off the guilt of the Butch Beauchamps with a decent ride in a hearse as Ike could buy off his black kin with bank accounts, shows how nothing less than the family of man as the aim for families of the South lies at the heart of Faulkner's fiction. Nevertheless, what the *family* first began—unequal treatment and the refusal to recognize one's kin, as Thomas Sutpen refuses to recognize Charles Bon— both Cass and Ike feel the *family* must resolve. But without family precedent, Ike can find no way to do it within the family structure; *Go Down, Moses* keeps insisting that the failure of the South comes in the failures of its families.

Faulkner's extended interest in the families of Yoknapatawpha causes him to examine also those that are not members of the aristocracy. A good deal of attention is paid to the professional and middle-class families in Jefferson, for instance. Horace Benbow's urgent need to locate an absolute justice—one that can hold for poor whites and common-law marriages despite Aunt Jenny's scornful warning and Narcissa's cynical behavior—is in-

29. *Go Down, Moses* (New York: Random House, 1973), 267.

explicable unless we see it in the context of those middle-class values which have been slipping away from Horace's life ever since he left a sister of whom he was inordinately fond for a wife who mocks him as husband and father. The respectability he would recover for Belle and himself, as a lawyer, is the respectability he yearns to find in Temple Drake, whose father is a judge, and his sister, whose friend is the district attorney Eustace Graham; when he finds Temple, in her Memphis whorehouse, apparently a prostitute by inclination, it is striking that he mingles his memory of her face with the portrait of his stepdaughter and, eventually, memories of his sister and wife. Tainted family connections both by birth and by marriage pen Horace in. The same sort of biological determinism seems to be at work in Joanna Burden; it is not possible to appreciate the fanatacism she maintains for the Negro and for her affair with Joe apart from the abolitionist heritage that defines her past and shapes her present-day attitudes. Nor can Doc Hines's mad behavior concerning Joe nor Hightower's religion of Confederate bravery be understood apart from the family values which circumscribe their understanding.

Perhaps the greatest anxieties of all in Faulkner come from those who cannot find family ties or, yearning for them, develop ties that have no basis in blood or lineage. Joe Christmas is an example of how family is for Faulkner an overriding concern in all his fiction. Without family, as an orphan, Joe is without identity. And, Faulkner told the students at Virginia:

That was his tragedy, that to me was the tragic, central idea of the story—that he didn't know what he was, and there was no way possible in life for him to find out. Which to me is the most tragic condition a man could find himself in—not to know what he is and to know that he will never know.[30]

Joe's inability as a child to establish a sense of kinship forces him to begin his own sense of family, with Bobbie Allen. That he is unsuccessful causes him, it seems, to assault women physically

30. *Faulkner in the University*, 72.

and sexually, as if to deny their function as childbearing, and so family-forming, creatures. This impossible polarity, to love and to hate women, is executed by his ability to move by pronouncement from one racial heritage to another. Only in Joanna Burden does he meet another human being who, like him, is at the end of a family line and in a state of frantic isolation. The loneliness felt by Joe and Joanna is shared by others whose lives make up this novel—by Hightower, who cannot reconstitute the glorious family line of his grandfather and so neglects his wife that she commits suicide; Byron, who substitutes labor for the family he can neither locate nor create for himself; Lena, whose concern is to establish a traditional family, to find a father for her chap. The novel *Light in August* suggests that, despite its title, there is only darkness in August because there is no possibility of family—unless Byron's pursuit of Lena provides some final suggestion of light.

The canon of Faulkner, like that of any great writer, cannot be neatly divided into portions, but there are emphases. After the early explorations of the significance of blood ties in *Soldiers' Pay* and the artificial family in *Mosquitoes*, Faulkner turned his attention in the early Yoknapatawpha works to tracing those blood lines that provided the foundations of his society. Soon thereafter Faulkner also began to explore the yearning of those without families to create one. The common-law marriage of Lee and Ruby Goodwin is one such instance. It is a relationship which in its unconventionality threatens Temple and later Horace, yet Ruby is at pains to demonstrate that her love for Lee runs so deep that the certificate of marriage is superfluous. Indeed, the naturalness of their devotion to others less fortunate even than themselves at first disturbs Horace, who has just felt the rebuff of his own broken family, and later captures his entire attention in a mixture of respect and envy. Ruby is setting the dinner table with an extra plate for Horace when

> Goodwin entered. He wore muddy overalls. He had a lean, weathered face, the jaws covered by a black stubble; his hair was gray at the temples. He was leading by the arm an old man with a

long white beard stained about the mouth. Benbow watched Goodwin seat the old man in a chair, where he sat obediently with that
tentative and abject eagerness of a man who has but one pleasure
left and whom the world can reach only through one sense, for he
was both blind and deaf: a short man with a bald skull and a round,
full-fleshed, rosey face in which his cataracted eyes looked like two
clots of phlegm. Benbow watched him take a filthy rag from his
pocket and regurgitate into the rag an almost colorless wad of what
had once been chewing tobacco, and fold the rag and put it into his
pocket. The woman served his plate from the dish. The others were
already eating, silently and steadily, but the old man sat there, his
head bent over his plate, his beard working faintly. He fumbled at
the plate with a diffident, shaking hand and found a small piece of
meat and began to suck at it until the woman returned and rapped
his knuckles. He put the meat back on the plate then and Benbow
watched her cut up the food on the plate, meat, bread and all, and
then pour sorghum over it. Then Benbow quit looking. When the
meal was over, Goodwin led the old man out again. Benbow
watched the two of them pass out the door and heard them go up the
hall.[31]

As *Sanctuary* unfolds (and as our recollection of *Sartoris/Flags
in the Dust* might tell us), Benbow is fascinated in part because
he has no father, and is unable himself to play the role of dutiful
son. No matter how ancient or handicapped this father-figure
nor how criminal this common-law son, there is a sense of family
devotion and ritual at the Goodwin place. That the old man is
handicapped physically (as Tommy is mentally) but yet accepted
only underscores the sterility of Horace's lives with Narcissa and
with Belle. That the old man, moreover, resembles Popeye in
his eyes reminds us that Popeye, too, comes to the old Frenchman place to find the family he never truly had. This scene,
which manages a certain warmth despite apparently overwhelming odds, prepares us for Ruby's concern for Temple at the
decaying house and her constant concern for her baby and for
Lee in Jefferson despite the town's osctracism of her. Such natural affection passes sharp judgment on the Drakes and the Ben-

31. *Sanctuary* (New York: Random House, n.d.), 11–12.

bows, as well as on the women of Jefferson who prefer respectability to compassion and who seem oftentimes incapable of love.

This second period of Faulkner's concern with the need for family is also seen in the *menage á trois* that so fascinates and puzzles the reporter in *Pylon* (1935). Here the natural love that simulates family relationships bewilders a reporter whose chief ability is verbal, as he tried to understand, for his editor and for himself, whether they are the products of or the salvation for the postwar world as a wasteland of mechanical contrivances and despair.

> "The third guy, the horse one, is just the mechanic; he aint even a husband, let alone a flyer. Yair. Shumann and the airplane landing at Iowa or Indiana or wherever it is, and her coming out of the schoolhouse without even arranging to have her books took home, and they went off maybe with a canopener and a blanket to sleep on under the wing of the airplane when it rained hard; and then the other guy, the parachute guy, dropping in, falling the couple or three miles with his sack of flour before pulling the ripcord. They aint human, you see. No ties; no place where you were born and have to go back to it now and then even if it's just only to hate the damn place good and comfortable for a day or two. From coast to coast and Canada in summer and Mexico in winter, with one suitcase and the same canopener because three can live on one canopener as easy as one or twelve."[32]

The irony is that the reporter is tied to the mechanism of the printing press—so much so, in fact, that he cannot explain to an editor who is likewise limited just what devotion to other people and to a particular life can mean. The boy who is born and who forces Laverne to marry suggests how superficial conventional behavior can be; it is contrasted with Roger's attempt to sacrifice his life to win money for Laverne, Jack, and the child. His sacrifice catapults others: Jiggs gives up his prize boots to buy toys for the child, Jack and Laverne take little Jackie to his grandparents in Ohio where they give him up, and the reporter and Jiggs surrender their association with the stunt fliers. But in

---

32. *Pylon* (New York: Random House, n.d.), 46.

the course of events, both Jiggs *and the reporter* did not simply learn the meaning of love; they also *tacitly joined a family* and so felt themselves, for once, as members of it. It is a nice question, at the novel's close, whether the reporter as a member of that family is more or less successful when he returns to straight reportage.

Still another examination of the family, and of the need for a family, comes in *The Wild Palms* where the respectability of the marriage of Charlotte and Rat Rittenmeyer is seen as stifling and imprisoning against the liberty of romantic love such as Charlotte envisions with Harry Wilbourne. It is true that the Rittenmeyer marriage is respectable but empty of feeling and significance, as Harry learns when he visits them a second time.

> He found a modest though comfortable apartment in an irreproachable neighborhood near Audubon Park, a negro maid, two not particularly remarkable children of two and four, with her hair but otherwise looking like the father (who in another dark obviously expensive double-breasted suit made a cocktail not particularly remarkable either and insisted that Wilbourne call him Rat) and she in something he knew had been purchased as a semi-formal garment and which she wore with the same ruthless indifference as she had the garment in which he had first seen her, as if both of them were overalls. After the meal, which was considerably better than the cocktails, she went out with the older child, who had dined with them, but she returned presently to lie on the sofa smoking while Rittenmeyer continued to ask Wilbourne questions about his profession such as the president of a college fraternity might ask of a pledge from the medical school.[33]

But freedom and romanticism are delusions for people as basically conventional as Harry and Charlotte. Her attempt to be creative produces only twisted, grotesque shapes in papier-mâché, while in Wisconsin they develop

> a bourgeois standard of respectability as he watched her, barefoot, moving about the room, making those subtle alterations in the fixtures of this temporary abode as they even do in hotel rooms

33. *The Wild Palms* (New York: Random House, n.d.), 42.

rented for but one night, producing from one of the boxes which he had believed to contain only food objects from their apartment in Chicago which he not only did not know she still had but had forgotten they ever owned—the books they had acquired, a copper bowl, even the chintz cover from the ex-work bench, then from a cigarette carton which she had converted into a small receptacle, resembling a coffin, the tiny figure of the old man, the Bad Smell.[34] Little wonder that their child, an accident from Charlotte's perspective, brings about an abortion which is as fatal to her as to the child. For Harry and Charlotte form no marriage, no family in any true sense of the word; and Harry is left, in the end, only to mourn his isolation by observing a 1918 emergency ship now converted into a home where a woman does laundry and the man casts and mends nets. Harry yearns for such a normal, if paltry, family life where its naturalness or its legality does not matter and its conventionality is a thing to be prized.

Yet for Faulkner Harry's final dream is as naive as Charlotte's initial one. Between the degeneration and corruption of the aristocratic and middle-class families in Yoknapatawpha and the artificiality and routine emptiness of the prefabricated families in a present age of despair there was little choice. Yet for William Faulkner, the great-grandson of Colonel W. C. Falkner, there remained a strong belief in the family as the saving unit in society. At this point in his career, he returned once more to the Sartorises (in *The Unvanquished*, 1938), the Snopeses (beginning with *The Hamlet*, 1940), and even tried to create a new family in the several generations of the McCaslins. But none of these was able to found a vital dynasty any more than Margaret Powers was able to find with Donald Mahon. In the 1940s, Faulkner seems to enter a third period in his study of the family: he begins to focus on the family of man. Ike raises the possibility in "The Bear" and in "Delta Autumn," but it is Chick Mallison in *Intruder in the Dust* who, with Miss Habersham and Aleck Sander, is able to suggest first that compassion for the whole human race—including obedience to Uncle Gavin and the accused and ignored Lucas Beauchamp both—is the way to rees-

34. Ibid., 104–5.

tablish those verities which found their first site in family lines and family life: compassion and pity and humanity and sacrifice. The words of the Nobel Prize echo Miss Habersham rather than Gavin Stevens and they look forward to the speeches of the Corporal in *A Fable* (1954). Here the Corporal is a man with a father, the distinguished Old General, the Marshal and commander-in-chief of the Allied Forces, and half-brother to Marthe and Marya. But it is the challenge he receives from the former— temptations, really, in this relived Passion Week of the heart— and the devotion from the latter that lead the Corporal to rebell against his father, as Young Bayard rebelled against the Sartoris myth of glorious fatality, in order to preserve life. The Corporal's disciple, the maimed Runner, teaches the last remnant of the military hierarchy when he is cared for at his death by the Quartermaster General. At the burial of the Unknown Soldier in Paris, the Runner comes to protest the heroism that relies on military power and massacre while the Quartermaster General comes to observe. But the Runner learns humility (which he needs) and the Quartermaster General compassion when the Runner is attacked by the mob, to be comforted only by the man whose vocation was to supply the war machine.

> The man in the gutter opened his eyes and began to laugh, or tried to, choking at first, trying to turn his head as though to clear his mouth and throat of what he choked on, when another man thrust through the crowd and approached him—an old man, a gaunt giant of a man with a vast worn sick face with hungry and passionate eyes above a white military moustache, in a dingy black overcoat in the lapel of which were three tiny faded ribbons, who came and knelt beside him and slipped one arm under his head and shoulders and raised him and turned his head a little until he could spit out the blood and shattered teeth and speak. Or laugh rather, which is what he did first, lying in the cradle of the old man's arm, laughing up at the ring of faces enclosing him, then speaking himself in French:
> "That's right," he said: "Tremble. I'm not going to die. Never."
> "I am not laughing," the old man bending over him said. "What you see are tears."[35]

35. *A Fable* (New York: Random House, 1966), 437.

The sudden, powerful transformation startles: the Quartermaster General cradling the Corporal's disciple as if it were his child, as the Old General could not bring himself to cradle the Corporal, suggests that the family of man replaces the military machine. So long as the true verities of the heart are in active operation, Faulkner seems to be saying, there will be a sense of the greatest of all families, in which the distinctions between aristocrat and poor white, white man and black, legal and natural marriage melt away.

Faulkner never underestimated the importance of *A Fable* in his canon, as we have. But when we look at his body of work from the perspective of family we see that "the war" to Southerners, the War Between the States, was also a war of brother against brother; and it was on such bloodshed that the Sartoris myth came into being, as well as a measure of fame for the Compsons, a challenge to Sutpen, and a new economy for the McCaslins. The rituals of such families that promoted their fame and enhanced their clans rested on such bloodshed. The Armistice of the Great War in *A Fable*, however, transports us from such a narrow sense of family into the wider sense of universal brotherhood which alone assures peace, prosperity, hope, and eternal love. In *A Fable* Faulkner brings to full realization an idea he had had early in his career and had published in an early short story, "Ad Astra." There a captured German pilot who had once been a baron but who has since renounced his aristocratic position says,

> "I return home; I say to my father, in the University I haf learned it iss not good; baron I will not be. He cannot believe. He talks of Germany, the fatherland; I say to him, It iss there; so. You say fatherland; I, brotherland, I say, the word *father* iss that barbarism which will be first swept away; it iss the symbol of that hierarchy which hass stained the history of man with injustice of arbitrary instead of moral; force instead of love."[3]

36. *Collected Stories* (New York: Random House, 1977), 417. I am grateful to Bruce Kawin and his essay "*War Birds* and the Politics of Refusal," forthcoming in my *Critical Essays on William Faulkner: The Sartoris Family*, for this observation.

We have yet to learn fully what the former German baron already knows—that between the concept of family that honors the father and the one that declares all men to be brothers lies a good part of the richness that is Yoknapatawpha.

Some Yoknapatawpha Names

JAMES HINKLE

*"I knowed you wasn't Oklahomy folks. You talk queer,
kinda—that ain't no blame, you understand."
"Ever'body says words different," said Ivy. "Arkansas
says 'em different, and Oklahomy folks says 'em different.
And we seen a lady from Massachusetts, an' she said 'em
differentest of all. Couldn't hardly make out what she was
sayin'."*

STEINBECK, *The Grapes of Wrath*

I want to talk with you today about Faulkner's Yoknapatawpha
names, beginning with advice and even instruction on how to
pronounce some of them. Why you should have any confidence
in anything that I, an obvious Northerner, might say about Mississippi pronunciations calls for an explanation, because it is true
that I am enough an outsider still to react with slight shock each
time I hear your courthouse called the coat-house. So let me tell
you how it happened that I came to know some things you
probably do not know about Faulkner's names.

My path to expertise began with a TV program about ten
years ago, a not-too-good attempt at *Requiem for a Nun*. There
was an opening shot of the Oxford courthouse and then of a
bailiff convening court: "Oyez, oyez, oyez, the ahnuhbul coat of
Yock-nuh-POT-uh-fuh County is now in session." Ahnuhbul and
coat I could believe, but Yock-nuh-POT-uh-fuh? That is not how
I had imagined it. Admittedly PBS is not the last word in Faulkner scholarship, but wouldn't you think someone there would
have asked someone who really *knew* before going ahead with
the program? I remembered that earlier the same day in class I
had been uncertain how to say the name of one of Faulkner's

172

Indians. Was Issetibbeha Iss-ih-tib-BAY-uh or Iss-ih-TIB-bay-haw? Clearly if I were going to keep on teaching Faulkner these were matters I ought to get straight.

Since I wasn't going to learn what I needed to know by talking to myself in California, I bought an overcoat and went to New York for my first MLA meeting in twenty years, mainly to attend the Faulkner session and to hear from experts what was right. That year's experts knew very little more than I did. One of the talks was about Ba·y-YARD Sar-TOR-iss and another about BY-erd SAR-tor-iss. Incredibly no one seemed to care about the difference or, as far as I could tell, even to notice it. We belong to a profession which routinely patronizes anyone who in print spells Caddy as Caddie, but just talking about her is apparently another matter and it is all the same whether her parents meant Candace to be CAN-dis or CAN-duh-see.

So I decided I had better try one of these new Faulkner conferences they had started holding in the cool of August in Mississippi, and learn at the source. Already by Memphis I knew I was heading to the right place, for names curious to an outsider seemed on every sign: Shainberg, Shinault, Seesel's. In Oxford I saw a repair shop with a magnificent Faulkner name, Lice Varner. I drove on in the general direction Faulkner indicated for Frenchman's Bend, came to a hand-lettered sign which said LISSARD CREEK CHURCH (with two z's, both reversed to s's as if in mirror image of 2NOPE2 HOTEL), and finally to a river which the people who lived there all told me was the YAWK-nee but which the University's tour guide a few days later called the Yo-CONE-uh, for that is the way it is spelled—Yocona—and 150 years of oral tradition was in his case no match against logic, education, and the "modren" world.

On my car radio I heard a country preacher talking about his pool-pit. He mentioned pool-pit over and over and I figured he must be a Baptist with a new indoor church pool for total immersions. When it finally got through to me that he meant what I had been brought up to call a pulpit (and, I hasten to add, what the majority of present-day Mississippians also call a pulpit), I realized how far I would have to go before I would ever be at ease with some of the more exotic (to my ear) Southern pronunciations. Maybe Quentin and Floyd Watkins were right: you just have to be born there. Even the pleasant ritual at the end of a restaurant meal—"Y'awl come back, y'heah," and its set response, "Ah sho WEE-yul"—suggested lurking problems: if "will" becomes a two-syllable WEE-yul, then would McWillie in *The Reivers* be Mc-WEE-yul-ee, a combination requiring more phonetic virtuosity than I could imagine even mother-tongue speakers easily managing?

At the conference itself I learned much that was new and interesting, but not about how to say Faulkner's names. Miss Emily's servant, Tobe, either rhymed with robe or he was two-syllable Toby. Dilsey had an s or a z in the middle. Millard was MILL-erd or Mil-LARD. Labove rhymed with a stove or with above.

Next I tried writing to several older scholars who actually knew Faulkner, to see what they remembered. That sounds like a better idea than it turned out. They answered and were polite and tried to help, but I did not find out much that was necessarily right. As the saying goes: the palest ink is more certain than the clearest memory. One "definitely remember(ed)" that Faulkner pronounced Bayard as BY-erd ("rhymes with liar with a d," he said);[1] another "distinctly remember(ed)" him saying BARED ("rhymes with SHARED");[2] a third reported he had heard Phil Stone say the name "probably a dozen times," always as "bay-yawd, each syllable given equal stress";[3] and a fourth "thinks he remembers" hearing Faulkner say bay-YARD.[4] That is enough to give considerable pause to an earnest seeker-after-the-truth. While I am prepared to believe Faulkner may have changed his mind about some things, I doubt that he wavered so wildly in how he said his characters' names.

1. Letter from Thomas Daniel Young, September 1982.
2. Letter from Joseph Blotner, September 1982.
3. Letter from Carvel Collins, July 1983.
4. Conversation with James B. Meriwether, June 1980.

I had about run out of leads when the University of Virginia announced that it had forty-eight tapes of Faulkner reading from his work and answering questions. These were the same tapes Gwynn and Blotner had once transcribed about a quarter of for *Faulkner in the University.* I spent more than a week in Charlottesville listening to all of them. I am told by the librarian there that I am not the only one so far to have done this, but I appear to be the only one whose purpose was to record authentic Faulkner pronunciations. And thus it happens that for about forty-five potentially mis-pronouncable Yoknapatawpha names I, a Northerner, am for the moment the sole proprietor of what Calvin Brown calls hippostomatic evidence. (I will explain that one: Hippos is Greek for horse. Stoma is Greek for mouth. Hippostomatic evidence is horse's mouth evidence.) Some of Faulkner's pronunciations confirm what most readers have always assumed, some answer questions we have wondered about, and a few I think will surprise you:

Amodeus (Uncle Buddy McCaslin) = Amo-DEE-us, not Amo-DAY-us or Am-MODE-de-us.

Aunt = AINT, not ANT or AWNT or ONT.

Beauchamp = BEE-chum, not BO-champ.

Charles Bon = BAHN with the final n pronounced, like the German autobahn, not like the French bon.

Candace = CAN-dis, not CAN-DACE or CAN-duh-see.

Carothers = rhymes with another's—but his great-great-great grandson, Roth, is wroth.

Coldfield = COAL-field. As Faulkner says it there is no d in the middle, but unlike the Oxford name, Cofield, Faulkner's retains the l. COAL-field.

Compson = CAWMP-s'n. The first syllable rhymes with straw with an mp after it, not with stomp or stump. The p in the middle is distinctly pronounced by Faulkner, unlike Oxford's Thompson (TAWM-s'n) or Samson. The last syllable is s'n, said too lightly to be represented by sun. CAWMP-s'n.

De Spain = duh-SPAIN, not DEE-Spain.

Dewitt Binford (in *The Town*) = DEE-WITT, not de-WITT

(as in the North) or DEE-witt (as in Texas), but DEE-WITT, with both syllables equally accented (as Faulkner does with Estelle—ESS-STELL).

Dilsey = DIL-see, with an s, not DIL-zee.

Drusilla = usually DREW SILL-uh, with a pause after the first syllable as if Drusilla were a first and last name. Infrequently Faulkner says DREW sill-uh. He never says anything even approaching drew-SILL-uh.

Ephriam/Ephraim/Ephum (in *Intruder* and *The Reivers*) = EEF. At least that is how Faulkner says it, although he does not pronounce the full name.

Frazier (in *The Town*) = FRAY-zhee-ur, with three distinct syllables, not FRAY-zer or FRAY-zher.

Frony = rhymes with crony, not Lonnie.

Grenier = Gren-EER, the name of Faulkner's present-day Grenier County and how old Louis Grenier's name (which must have been LOO-EE Gren-YAY) is now pronounced by his heirs-at-large (except, of course, for Lonnie Grinnup).

Grier = GREER, not GRY-er.

Gowrie = rhymes with dowry, not GO-ree.

Habersham = HAB-er-shum, the last two syllables said quickly and lightly.

Hampton = HAMP-tun, with a p, not HAM-tun.

Hogganbeck = HAWG-en-beck, not hoag, not hog as a Northerner would pronounce it, not back. HAWG-en-beck.

Hub (short for the first name of Hampton and Beauchamp) = rhymes with tub, not tube, although the full name, Hubert, begins with HEW.

Ikkemotubbe = ICK-uh-mo-TUB-ee, said quickly, without internal pauses. A slow, divided ICKy-mo TUB-ee (which I have heard some readers say) has most of the sounds right but is hardly similar in effect to Faulkner's own rapid pronunciation. The last part of the name is TUB-ee, not TOOB-ee.

Issetibbeha = Ish-ee-TIB-ih-haw. The accent is on TIB and the first syllable is ish. Faulkner says his name five or six times and he always and clearly begins with ish. Apparently the Choctaw and Chickasaw sound originally transcribed as s was actually pronounced sh. In Oklahoma the county in which both tribes settled is now helpfully spelled Chickasha County (although the last syllable there is pronounced shay).

Jody = rhymes with Buffalo Bill, not with toddy (as Jody was pronounced in the movie, *The Southerner*).

Levitt (in *The Town*) = LEV-it, not LEAVE-it or luh-VITT.

McCaslin = muh-CAZ-lin, a z and not an s sound in the middle—but Cass does have an s, like gas, not jazz.

Mississippi = mis-SIP-ee, just three syllables, as Uncle Buck spells it: Missippy.

Peabody = PEE-body, not the New England PIB-uh-dee.

Quistenberry (in *The Town*) = KWISS-en-berry, with no t.

Riddell (in *The Town*) = rih-DELL, not WRY-DELL.

Rosa = ROZE-uh, a z and not an s in the middle.

Sartoris = The accent is on the first syllable. Faulkner says SAR-tor-iss most of the time, SAR-triss in two syllables at least a quarter of the time, but never sar-TOR-iss.

Shreve = SHREEVE, although Faulkner does not tell us how his full first name, Shrevlin, is pronounced.

Solon Quick = SO-lon, not SO-lun or SOL-un.

Sophonsiba = so-FON-sib-uh, not so-fon-SEE-buh. There is no trace of Sophonisba (so-fon-NIZ-buh) which Faulkner says is the source for the name.

Stovall (in "Evening Sun") = STOW-VAWL, like snowball, not STOVE-ul or STUV-ul.

Tennie = TEN-ee, not TIN-ee. While ten and tin, pen and pin are often interchangeable in much of the South and Faulkner at times takes advantage of this, for Tennie as well as for Jenny and Benjy and Quentin he settled clearly for the en sound.

Theophilus (Uncle Buck McCaslin) = Theo-FILE-us, not Thee-OFF-uh-lus. Neither Theo-FILE-us nor Amo-DEE-us is the pronunciation present Stone descendants remember for their real great-great uncles' names, but it is the way Faulkner pronounced them. A moment's thought might have told us that Theo-FILE-us had to be the way Faulkner said Buck's name, because his other nickname, Filus, has to be FILE-us, not FILL-us, since Buck would not have put up with Phyllis, the traditional romantic name for a rustic maiden. Faulkner says FILE-us as well as Theo-FILE-us several times on the tapes.

Thomas Sutpen = TAWM-us, not TOM-us or TOME-us. The last name, which Faulkner says maybe forty times, is always pronounced quickly and never with precise enunciation, never a definite SUT-PEN. I heard it usually as SUT-p'n, but other times it is more nearly SUT-f'n or SUP-'n or SUT-'n. Working by analogy from "cutpurse" and "sweetpea" (which both drop the t before the p and become "cuppurse" and "swee'pea") one would think Sut-pen after several generations of illiteracy would have become always SUP-'n, but that is not Faulkner's choice more than a tenth of the time. He usually says SUT-p'n.

Tomey's Turl = TOME-eez TURL, not TOM-eez or TAWN-eez, and not TARE-ul.

Warwick = WAW-ick (a completely r-less Southern version of the British Worrick).

Wash = pronounced with the flattest of flat a's, rhymes with a Northerner's gosh, not with squawsh or like the Midwestern worsh.

Yoknapatawpha = YAWK-nuh-puh-TAW-fuh. The first syllable rhymes with hawk, not hock. Gwynn and Blotner in their partial transcription of the tapes show the first syllable as Yock, but Faulkner clearly says YAWK. In any event, TV's Yock-nuh-POT-uh-fuh is wrong.

That is all I could learn from the Virginia tapes about how Faulkner pronounced his names. While forty-five authentic Faulkner pronunciations make a good start, there are still about seventy more in doubt. For some of these I can offer second-best evidence—how older non-Faulkner-reading citizens of Oxford say they remember the names to have been pronounced in reference to *real local people:*

Ballenbaugh (in *The Reivers* and *KG*) = BAL (rhymes with PAL)-en-baw, not BALL (rhymes with Paul)-en-baw.

Barbour (in "Uncle Willy") = barber, not bar-boor.

Sonny Barger (in "Uncle Willy") = rhymes with larger.

Beard = beerd, not bired or bared or bird.

Brother Bedenberry (in *Light in August*) = BEED-en-berry.

Matt Bowden (in *The Unvanquished*) = first syllable of last name rhymes with cow, not go.

Callicoat = first syllable rhymes with pal, not Paul, and final syllable is coat, not cut. Thus, CAL-ee-coat, not CALL-ee-cut.

Cedric Nunnery (in *The Town*) = SED-rick, not SEED-rick.

Clarence Egglestone Snopes = Clance, with only the slightest hesitation in the middle to suggest an r-less pronunciation of a two syllable name: Cla'ence. Egglestone = EGG-ul-stun, like GLAD-stun for Gladstone.

Minnie Cooper = first syllable of last name has the same vowel sound as in book.

Dupre = DEW-PREE, both syllables equally accented, ending with PREE, not PRAY.

Eustace = YOU-stiss, not you-STACE.

Ewell = YOU-el, not EE-well.

Houston = HEW-stun, not HOUSE-tun or HUS-tun.

Hule (in "Mountain Victory") = HEW-el said as one syllable: hyool.

Isom = EYE-sum, not ISS-um.

Labove = luh-BOVE, rhymes with a stove, not Iuh-BUV. (There have been several Oxford people with this name in various spellings, all pronounced luh-BOVE.)

Ludus (in *The Reivers* and *The Mansion*) = LOO-dus, not LUD-us.

McCallum = muh-CAL-um, not muh-CALL-um or muh-CULL-um.

McCarron = muh-CARE-un, not muh-CAR-un. (The Oxford spelling was McCharen.)

McWillie = Mc-WILLy, I am relieved to report.

Meloney (in *Sartoris*) = MEL-uh-nee. (The Oxford spelling was Melne.)

Odum = O-dum, not ODD-um.

Q'Milla (in *The Mansion*) = kew-MILL-uh, not Camilla or Quimilla.

Suratt = shur-RAT, not suh-RAT or SUR-rat.

Theron (in *The Town*) = THIR-un, a vowel sound like the i in hit. The final syllable is an almost mute 'n, not a clear ron. Thus, THIR-un, not THAIR-ron.

Tobe = Toby.

Vaiden (in *The Town*) = VAY-den, not VYE-den.

Vinie/Vynie (in *The Hamlet*) = VIN-ee, not VINE-ee.

Wyatt/Wyott = rhymes with BY-it or BY-ut said as one syllable.

For a remaining forty-or-so Yoknapatawpha names of doubtful pronunciation we have neither Faulkner's own testimony nor agreed-upon memories of local citizens. For most of these I have been able to find some kind of evidence. For some the evidence seems to point clearly to one pronunciation, for others it is less certain. For a few we might as well flip a coin.

Admiral Dewey Snopes = probably pronounced as anyone would expect, but Arthur Palmer Hudson discovered a man who actually bore this double first name and he was known as Ad-MIRE-al.[5]

Henry Armstid = ARM-st'd. With Southern accent that would be AHM-st'd. His first name Faulkner apparently pronounced with three syllables, HEN-er-ree, since he spelled it Henery in the typescript of "As I Lay Dying" (his working title for an early version of "Spotted Horses").

Bayard = There is no way of knowing for sure how Faulkner pronounced this name. He did not say it on the Virginia tapes. I am not about to be referee for the contradictory memories and testimony of Mr. Young, Mr. Blotner, Mr. Collins, and Mr. Meriwether. Still, we have to call Bayard something. I opt for saying his name the same way the name BAIRD is pronounced.

---

5. Arthur Palmer Hudson, "Some Curious Negro Names," *Southern Folklore Quarterly*, 2 (1938), 187.

That would be BAY-erd (or BAY-ud) compressed into almost one syllable—BAIRD. My reason for this choice is the not-entirely-satisfactory one that this is the *usual* pronounciation of Bayard by present-day Mississippians—i.e., the way most of them normally say the name in a context unrelated to Faulkner. Until someone tracks down an as-yet-unknown recording of Faulkner saying the name, I don't see how we can do any better. Thus, Bayard = (tentatively) BAIRD.

Blount = Blunt, the name of a prominent Memphis family. Faulkner at one time (in the faded manuscript of "The Golden Book") was going to have Col. Sartoris marry a Tessie Blount of Memphis.

Benbow Sartoris = Narcissa calls him Bory. That would be BO-REE, not BORRy. General Beauregard was known as Old Bory (BO-REE), from the first two syllables of his name. In Benbow Sartoris's case Bory derived apparently from the last syllable of Benbow plus Narcissa's play on her name for her earlier "child," Horry.

Caroline Compson = CAH-line, sometimes spelled less flatteringly as cowline.[6] Even if one wanted to ignore the Southern accent and say Carol-line, the last syllable would still be line, not lin.

Hence Cayley (in *KG*) = There is no problem with his first name. Hence (or Hense) is short for Henderson and has a standard pronunciation. His last name, Cayley, is probably meant to be pronounced like the Irish Kelly. The other possibility is CAY-lee, but that is unlikely in a town in which Cearly is pronounced Kelly. The Lafayette Chancery Clerk was for years a Cearly Slough, his first name pronounced Kelly. There also was a Dink Cearly in Oxford that Webb and Green and Blotner, relying on oral sources, all spell as Kelly.

Colbert = KAHL-bert. This half-French half-English pronunciation is historically accurate for the real family of part-

6. Floyd C. Watkins and Charles Herbert Watkins, *Yesterday in the Hills* (Athens: University of Georgia Press, 1973), 33.

Chickasaws who had the concession for a ferry at unreasonable price across the Tennessee River.

Crenshaw = CREN-SHAW, as one would expect. There is a town of Crenshaw about thirty-five miles west of Oxford and the residents there had never heard of another pronunciation. My reason for wondering is that Faulkner seemed drawn to names that have pronunciations conspicuously different from their spellings—Beauchamp (Beechum), Talliaferro (Tolliver), Mahon (Mann), for example. Probably the two most outrageous of these primarily Southern anomalies are Enroughty (pronounced Darby)[7] and Crenshaw (pronounced Grainger)[8]—both originally from Virginia. But there is no indication Faulkner had Grainger in mind for the minor character of Jack Crenshaw in *The Town*.

Damuddy = DAM-muddy. This Falkner family pronunciation I have on the authority of William's nephew, Jim Faulkner.

Devries (in *The Mansion*) = DEV-reez or de-VREEZ? Oxford claims not to recognize the name.

Eulalia = There are a number of possible ways to pronounce this name of Sutpen's first wife. She lived in New Orleans and was from an island in the Caribbean where we know at least the slaves spoke French. Her father was French but her mother was represented to Sutpen as Spanish. The name Eulalia is Spanish, pronounced in Spanish ay-oo-LAH-lee-uh. The French form of the name is Eulalie, pronounced in French uh-la-LEE, with the first syllable having a non-English sound close to the vowel in put. Eulalia in English is sometimes you-la-LEE-uh and sometimes you-LAY-lee-uh. The one Oxford woman with the name is you-LEE-luh. There is no way to tell which of these Faulkner had in mind.

Eupheus Hines and **Euphus Tubbs** = Their first names, however spelled, probably rhyme with Rufus, since Euphus is an Oxford name and is so pronounced. If this seems unlikely for

7. John N. Ware, "Enroughty, Darby, and General McClellan," *American Heritage* (February 1956), 120.

8. P. Burwell Rogers, "Changes in Virginia Names," *American Speech*, 31 (1956), 22.

Eupheus, remember that Odysseus also ends in eus and can be correctly pronounced as ee-us, oos, or us.

Everbe = EVER-BE, like Andy Griffith's Obie (short for Oh Be Joyful).

Forrest = Forris, rhymes with Morris throughout the South, although to a Northern ear this may sometimes sound like FAW-ris.

Gihon = GUY-hon. Faulkner has a fictional Gihon County, presumably named after a pre–Civil War Governor of Tennessee. His name was pronounced GUY-hon.

Marshal Gombault (in "Tall Men") = probably GUM-bo. If the Charleston name of Manigault is Mannigoe and Raimbault is Rambo (or even Rainbow), then Gombault is probably Gumbo.

Guster = Since this name is short for Augusta, even Northerners should pronounce it GUS-tuh. Dickens in *Bleak House* also has an Augusta, called Guster.

Horace = Calvin Brown suggests that the way this name is said would probably vary with the speaker. "The upper-class, educated, pronunciation (that of the circles in which Horace Benbow moved) would rhyme with Morris." Others might say HAW-ris, or HORSE (as in Walt Disney's Horace Horsecollar), or even HAWSE.[9] Narcissa's nickname for Horace (Horry) is OH-REE. The Benbows come from South Carolina where Horry (always pronounced OH-REE) is a prominent name. Thus Horry and Bory rhyme.

Isham = The same as Isom: EYE-sum. Isham was not usually recognized as an Oxford name, but two people said they did remember it and said it was EYE-sum. The will of Oxford's first settler, Dr. Thomas D. Isom, spells his name Isham.[10]

Jubal = JEW-bul, as in the beginning of jubilation.

Legate = usually LEG-it, not le-GATE. In Oxford the name was often spelled Leggit. There was, however, one man around 1915–1920 who called himself le-GATE.

9. Letter from Calvin Brown, July 1983.
10. I have not seen Dr. Isom's will. A member of the conference audience (whose name I failed to get) told me about it after I had presented the oral version of this paper.

Lessep = The film of *The Reivers* had it LESS-up, but Lucius Priest's grandfather lived in Bay St. Louis and that is near New Orleans where Lesseps (luh-SEPPS) is a big name. In fact a DeLesseps Morrison was mayor of New Orleans during the '40s and '50s, shortly before Faulkner wrote *The Reivers*. The evidence here seems evenly divided between LESS-up and luh-SEPP.

Louvinia = luh-VIN-ee-uh, not loo-VIN-ee-uh. In "Rose of Lebanon" Faulkner spelled the name Levinia. The pronunciation seems the same, however spelled.

McEachern = Mc-ECK-ern. One thing is sure: the accented part of the name is pronounced ECK, as in Eck Snopes. It is not EACH or EEK. This is the nearly unanimous testimony of Lafayette descendants of one of the original settlers of Abbeville whose name was then spelled McEachin but now is McEachern, as Faulkner spells it. About the ending of the name there is disagreement. Some now say Mc-ECK-ern, some Mc-ECK-run. One branch of the family changes the beginning of the name to muh-KECK-ern. We do not know Faulkner's choice, but the weight of Lafayette numbers would suggest Mc-ECK-ern. It is perhaps worth mentioning that in Scotland McEachern is usually pronounced McCann. Occasionally a Mississippian will look at the name and call it McCann, a phenomenon which puzzled me until I learned about the Scots practice.

Maclachan = Mc-LAWK-lan, the standard Scots pronunciation.

Maury = For Maury Bascomb this is almost certainly intended to be MUR-ee, the same as Faulkner's father's name, Murry. I have never heard anyone connected with Faulkner pronounce Maury Bascomb's name in this way, but the argument for it is a strong one. Both Maury and his sister are concerned that their family background be recognized as equal to the Compsons'. Maury (pronounced Murry) was among the more important names of the old coastal South. It is often given as an example of a name which in the twentieth century began to be pronounced as it was spelled, much to the irritation of the more traditional bearers of the name. Certainly Caroline and Maury would have been among the most insistent on retaining the old, more prestigious pronunciation. Maury Priest's name also is probably meant to be MUR-ee, given his many similarities to Faulkner's father.

Millard = MILL-erd or mil-LARD? In Oxford the name is pronounced MILL-erd, although it is not an Oxford name. Thomas Daniel Young says he heard Faulkner pronounce it mil-LARD. Frances Pate in her dissertation, *Names of Characters in Faulkner's Mississippi*, says MILL-erd tends to be used in rural areas, mil-LARD in cities, but she cites no authority for this statement.[11] In southern Mississippi between Picayune and Hattiesburg there is a hamlet called Millard, pronounced mil-LARD. Willard and Dillard both accent the first syllable but Milland and Piffard hit the second. In the case of Millard the evidence appears about equal for either choice. I suppose I will continue to say mil-LARD, but I have no assurance that this is how Faulkner intended it.

Moketubbe = The rhythm of the name is clear: Mock-uh-TUB-ee. The question is about the first syllable—is it mock or moke or mawk? By analogy with Oktibbeha (Ock-TIB-ih-haw) I conclude Moketubbe probably begins with MOCK, but once again there is no certainty that this was Faulkner's intention.

Hogeye Mosby (in *Intruder*) = MOZE-bee. The celebrated Confederate Colonel's name was pronounced this way and there is no reason to think Hogeye's would be different.

Odlethrop = This is a frequent corruption of Oglethorpe and is pronounced as it is spelled: O-del-throp.

Paralee (in *Intruder*) = I could discover nothing to indicate whether this is PAR-uh-lee or PAIR-uh-lee.[12] In either case, it is a nice name.

---

11. Frances Willard Pate, "Names of Characters in Faulkner's Mississippi" (Ph.D. diss., Emory University, 1967), 200.

12. Another member of the conference audience (whose name I failed to get also) told me after I had presented the oral version of this paper that he knew several Southern women with this name and that they pronounced it PAIR-uh-lee.

Parsham = PAHSH-um, actually like possum except for the sh in the middle.

Mr. Poleymus (in *The Reivers*) = Except as a shortened form of Polyphemus, no one recognizes this name at all. The pronunciation choices would seem to be po-LEE-mus or POL-ee-mus, but there are no clues to work from.

Saddie = SAD-ee, not SAYD-ee. The name is a shortened form of Saturday. She had a twin brother, Sundy, in the *Sanctuary* galleys.

Saucier = SO-SHAY, as Jubal says it. This name is not especially rare in southern Mississippi and Louisiana.

Secretary (in "Uncle Willy") = SEC-uh-teh'y, vaguely like succotash with no r's anyplace, the end rhyming with the Southern pronunciation of carry.

Semmes (in *GDM* and also the middle name of Rafe McCallum) = SIMMS. This is a standard pronunciation throughout the South.

Tomasina = If her daughter, Tomey, is TOME-ee, then Tomasina must be tome-uh-SEEN-uh.

Vidal = The Mississippi pronunciation is vih-DAL, not vih-DAHL or vee-DAHL.

Weddel = either WED-ul or wed-DELL, as the chief of "Lo" says. Like Cabell, Jarrell, and perhaps Millard, this is one of those names which allows its possessor more than one right option.

Whitfield = WHIT-field, whether it is spelled whit or white.

Except for Grierson which I will get to later, that is pretty much all I have been able to learn about pronouncing Yoknapatawpha names. I have tried to provide the sort of nuts and bolts guide someone ought to have done years ago. If anyone wants to protest that a good bit of what I have tried to set straight really has to do with accent rather than pronunciation, I won't argue. From an outsider's point of view, Mississippi accents are as much a cause for puzzlement and surprise and even awe as Mississippi pronunciations. If anyone wants to say my listings reveal my own Northern provincialism, I am sure I am guilty. I selected for comment the names I did because they were the ones whose pronunciations seemed odd to my Northern ear, or at least subject to possible mispronunciation. But if anyone thinks I have been making fun of how Mississippians talk, my message was somehow garbled in transmission. Vance Randolph, who spent a lifetime reporting the speech and folklore of the Ozarks, writes about a similar misunderstanding:

> Several educated hillmen have read this chapter in manuscript, and they didn't like it. "Everything you say is true," a small-town lawyer said, "if each sentence is considered by itself. But when you string these items together, the over-all picture is false and misleading."
>
> "What do you mean, false and misleading?" I asked.
>
> "Well, suppose some possum hunter talks for two hours and mispronounces ten words. You record the mispronunciations accurately enough, but never mention the other words that were pronounced correctly. The Goddamn Yankees who buy your book will think that the fellow only spoke ten words, and mispronounced every one of them!"[13]

For the rest of the time I have been allowed I have a different kind of report to make. This will be about eighteen Faulkner names and will be a mixed bag of miscellaneous facts, observations, and speculations—some probably sound and some not so sound, some intended seriously and some not so seriously. Much of it will be about where Faulkner got his names or what he intended them to mean. Of course I don't really *know* where he got any of them or what he intended any of them to mean. My evidence here will necessarily be circumstantial and my reasoning a series of inferences that I hope are at least sometimes plausible.

Horace Benbow = In *Ivanhoe* Captain Diccon Bend-the-Bow says "and [I] have a great name."

Michael Millgate has pointed out that Benbow is one of several seafaring names that surface in *Sanctuary:* Admiral Benbow,

13. Vance Randolph and George P. Wilson, *Down in the Holler: A Gallery of Ozark Folk Speech* (Norman: University of Oklahoma Press, 1953), 33–34.

Sir Francis Drake, Popeye the Sailor. Elsewhere in Faulkner there is an Admiral Dewey Snopes, and there was once a real British Admiral named Sartorious, famous enough to appear in encyclopedias. Millgate mentioned these more as curiosities than as parts of any consistent pattern.[14] I think I was more impressed with his sea-related associations that he was, and so I would like to add to what he reported.

There is Mississippi precedent for naval commander names: Jones County was named for Commodore John Paul Jones, Perry County for Commodore Oliver Hazard Perry, and Leflore County for Greenwood Leflore, the Greenwood part of his name being in honor of an English sea-captain. Also there is Lafayette precedent: a John Paul Jones was an early large landowner and, closer to Horace Benbow's name, a Horatio Nelson was the first Lafayette Representative to the State Legislature. He was the ineffectual dreamer who proposed in 1837 the idea of building a railroad from Pontotoc through Oxford to the Mississippi River, an idea that went nowhere.

That Faulkner had Admiral Benbow in mind when he selected his name of Benbow seems more likely when, at the end of *Sanctuary,* Horace retreats in defeat to Kinston, no more to be heard from in Yoknapatawpha history. The real Admiral Benbow also was buried in Kingston, although his Kingston was in Jamaica more than 200 years earlier.

It makes some sense that Popeye should be a bootlegger, for in the early Thimble Theatre episodes, the ones Faulkner would have been able to see at the time he started writing *Sanctuary,* Popeye got his sudden infusions of strength not from spinach but from drinking forty beers. The spinach, like Babe Ruth's stomachaches from too many hotdogs, was a later cleaning up of the act to make it suitable for youthful readers.

To the Memphis roadhouse in *Sanctuary,* in reality the Crystal Gardens, Faulkner gave the underwater name of the Grotto. There is a Ruby *Lamar,* and if we go from salt water to fresh

---

14. Michael Millgate, "Faulkner's First Trilogy: *Sartoris, Sanctuary,* and *Requiem for a Nun,*" in *Fifty Years of Yoknapatawpha,* ed. Doreen Fowler and Ann J. Abadie (Jackson: University Press of Mississippi, 1980), 97.

water, we have a Reba *Rivers*. All of this we find in a book which begins with Benbow and Popeye facing each other across a Mississippi pool and ends with Temple watching a fountain play into a Paris pool, dully listening to the crash of the waves of the music.

Faulkner said on the Virginia tapes that evil washed off Temple Drake "like water off a duck's back." At first I thought that was simply an undistinguished cliché playing with ducks and drakes, but then I realized that even after almost thirty years, Faulkner was still elaborating his water metaphor.

Percival Brownlee = It has been only in the last five-or-so years that scholars have understood that many, if not most, slaves had last names, even if their masters were unaware of them. From the whites' point of view, slaves were like dogs in the window, nameless until someone bought them and named them. From the blacks' point of view, the story was different, and it is interesting that Faulkner, with Percival Brownlee, seems to have been aware of this while academics were not.

The name of Percival Brownlee for a troublesome slave who says he "aims to be a Precher" must come from the notorious Parson Brownlow, a religiously-oriented Reconstruction Governor of Tennessee, a man difficult to admire even by his supporters. He claimed that FFV during the Civil War stood for "fleet-footed Virginians," and his policies after the war were said to "serve as an antidote to forgive and forget."[15]

Colonel Sartoris Snopes = In the manuscript of "Barn Burning" he was Gen. Forrest Snopes.

To name a child after someone complete with his title is hardly a common Southern practice, but it is not Faulkner's invention either. There was a major league baseball player in the 1930s named Colonel Buster Mills and the University of Alabama had a running back a few years ago named Major Ogilvie.

Philip Momberger wondered why Ab would have named his

15. W. T. Couch, *Culture in the South* (Chapel Hill: University of North Carolina Press, 1935), 483; Thomas B. Alexander, Introduction to W. G. Brownlow, *Sketches of the Rise, Progress, and Decline of Secession* (New York: Dacapo Press, 1968, orig. 1862), xviii.

son after Col. Sartoris. Faulkner nowhere provides a reason. Momberger suggested it might have been for revenge—so Ab could order Col. Sartoris about.[16] I suggest an opposite reason. Ab was partly responsible for the death of Rosa Millard, Col. Sartoris's mother-in-law. When Bayard and Ringo finally caught him after chasing him for three months, Ab said: "I made a mistake. I admit hit. . . . The question is, what are you fellows going to do about hit?" What the boys did was to horsewhip him and let him go. But a question remained: What was Col. Sartoris going to do about it when he got back from the war? Ab had his doubts and played safe by hiding in the hills for several years after the war. I suspect his naming a son after Col. Sartoris was Ab's attempt to placate Col. Sartoris—to send the message that he was trying to make up for a mistake he admitted he had made.

Celia Cook/Cecilia Farmer = The girl's name and the main facts of Faulkner's story in *The Unvanquished* and *Requiem for a Nun* of a Jefferson jailer's daughter and her one-day courtship and marriage to a Confederate cavalryman have their basis in Oxford history and legend. The cavalryman is said to have been the son of Gen. Forrest and the jailer's daughter is known to have been Taylor Cook. Faulkner did not give his story a title, but if he had, "Cecilia Cook's Wedding" would fit, and that immediately suggests George Washington Harris's "Sicily Burns's Wedding." The details of the story Faulkner had to tell are different from Harris's but the subject is the same and so, essentially, are the names of the protagonists. Faulkner shades Sicily to Cecilia and for Burns he gives us Cook. If Cecilia's father got his job because of his own ineptitude (as Faulkner says he did), then "cook" and "burns" amount to much the same thing.

Frenchman's Bend = Greenwood Leflore's father, Louis LeFleur, had a trading post on the Natchez Trace known as French Camp. The original name for Nashville was French Lick.

---

16. Philip Momberger, "Faulkner's 'Country' as Ideal Community," in *Individual and Community: Variations on a Theme in American Fiction*, ed. Kenneth H. Baldwin and David K. Kirby (Durham: Duke University Press, 1975), 133.

A Frenchman, William DeLay, gave his name to the nearest settlement south of the Yocona River. Just north of the river was Dutch Bend, where a Flem McCain and a Eula Coleman lived and whose chronicler for the Oxford *Eagle* in 1918–1920 was "Lonesome Willie" (no last name given). In any event, to name a hamlet after a foreigner, a Frenchman, follows local tradition, since Lafayette County obviously was so named.

And in case anyone has wondered, "the bend" always refers to the land which is *inside* the arc made by a river. The land on the opposite side is not part of "the bend."

Emily Grierson = To all the previous suggestions of sources and analogues for "A Rose for Emily" I would like to add three new ones—all of which registered with me because I was curious about the names in the story.

1. Faulkner does not pronounce Grierson on the Virginia tapes and neither his Caedmon recording nor a private tape he made for Carvel Collins includes "A Rose for Emily." I have never heard anyone even wonder if Emily's last name could be anything other than GREER-son, yet I think Faulkner intended the name to be GRY-er-son (GRY-uh-son to a Southerner). Grierson is not a Lafayette name but my argument stems from local history.

One of the belles of Lafayette County at the time of the Civil War was Miss Em Frierson of College Hill (spelled like Grierson except with an F instead of a G, and pronounced by her family's many descendants as FRY-uh-son). According to Oxford historian Maud Morrow Brown, there was a Patty Frierson, an Adeline Frierson, an Elizabeth Frierson, a Sally Dick Frierson, a Sally Wyatt Frierson, and an Em Frierson—all sisters or cousins.[17] Em is the one who is remembered because of her role in an incident which has become Lafayette legend. As Mrs. Brown tells it:

> A Yankee officer ordered Em. Frierson to sit down at the piano and sing all the southern songs she knew. Some other Yankees,

17. Mrs. Calvin Brown (Maud Morrow Brown), "Lafayette County in 1860–1865: A Narrative" (Oxford, Mississippi: typescript in the Mississippi Collection, University of Mississippi Library, 1935), 15.

hearing the strains, came angrily in and ordered her to stop but the officer protected her until she finished. She was in terror all the time because the silver was hidden in the piano.[18]

Why do I think Faulkner had this Em Frierson in mind when he named his Emily Grierson? I am struck by the coincidence in names. One of the College Hill cousins was Sally Wyatt Frierson. In "A Rose for Emily" the Griersons and the Wyatts are cousins. And in the manuscript of "A Rose for Emily" Faulkner's opening sentence was originally about an Emily Wyatt; he later crossed out Wyatt and substituted Grierson. It is playing the odds to believe that real cousins Sally Wyatt Frierson and Em Frierson from Lafayette's past had some connection in Faulkner's mind with the name of his fictional Emily Wyatt/Grierson.

I don't suppose anyone except me, on the basis of this, will start pronouncing Emily's name GRY-er-son, but that does seem to be how Faulkner must have thought of the name.

2. A New Orleans and Mobile popular historian, Harnett T. Kane, in a 1951 book, *Gentlemen, Swords and Pistols*, has a chapter with a title that should alert the antennae of any Faulkner reader: "Emily and the Baron."[19] Kane makes no mention of Faulkner and, as far as I can tell, he was not aware of "A Rose for Emily." His account is about an Emily Blount of Mobile. It begins around the Civil War and ends with her death in 1917.

Kane's Emily was from a well-to-do family, "perhaps a trifle too proud, one observer said," and with a father who was "over-haughty." Like Faulkner's Emily, Emily Blount had a problem in getting married. She had two active and competing suitors: a Henry Maury of Virginia, and a man who claimed to be Baron Henri Arnous de Rivière, a swaggering, dark, ladies' man from some place vaguely in France. Emily and her mother preferred the Baron, her father approved of neither. The Baron and Maury exchanged harsh words (Maury called the Baron "Count No-Account" and "Baron of Intellect"), a duel was fought, and the Baron, wounded, lay in bed for months in Emily's house.

18. Ibid., 33.
19. Harnett T. Kane, *Gentlemen, Swords and Pistols* (New York: William Morrow, 1951), 3–22.

Then one day Emily and her Baron disappeared. When the father discovered they had eloped, he pursued them, one step behind, all the way to Europe, where he caught up with them still unmarried. Emily's off again and on again marriage "flamed in the newspapers; for a time Emily and her Baron became names as familiar to readers as European rulers . . . *Harper's Weekly* noted that she had achieved the status of 'household word.'"

On July 4, 1865, Emily and the Baron were finally married in Paris. A few years later Emily reappeared in Mobile, unannounced, alone, and silent. She reopened the big old house, which by then was beginning to need repair and which she did nothing to fix. She dismissed the servants and closed off all but a few rooms. She did not go out. As the years went by and as the house became more and more shabby she would send out some of her jewelry or furnishings to be sold. People of Mobile took to referring to her as "Poor Emily," until eventually she faded from attention.

When she died in 1917 at age 73, only "old men and women, here and there, noted her passing." In life she had been overmatched by the romantic but unreliable Baron, and Kane says she "lost in the obituary columns, too."

Jefferson did better by its Emily. "Alive, Miss Emily had been a tradition, a duty, and a care; a sort of hereditary obligation upon the town." Dead, she received the town's collective tribute, a rose for Emily, which reaffirmed the mixture of pride and respectful affection and shame the town felt and acknowledged. Not having had the opportunity to send flowers for her wedding, the town, through its spokesman, presented at her death a rose which would not fade—which for fifty years has not faded—as if to say: "Emily is indeed one of our own—to have and to hold, for better or worse, for richer or poorer, in sickness and in health, to love and to cherish, though death us do part."

If the story of the real Emily Blount of Mobile was actually once as well-known as Kane says it was, then I think Faulkner's Emily and her Homer Barron owe at least something to the Alabama Emily and her Baron.

3. Let me tell about my third Emily-connection in the order I learned about it. When I first visited Oxford in the early 1970s, there was a house on University, since torn down, which was pointed out to visitors as the Rose for Emily house. It did have a balcony and a kind of cupola and a smattering of gingerbread, and it did need paint, but it was very tame for the decayed coquettish flamboyance I had imagined for Emily's house, and I was not happy with it.

Then one day I saw a picture—a Cofield picture which I do not believe is in the Cofield scrapbook—which showed part of a house which did seem as if it could have been Emily's. It had several small balconies, some steamboat gothic ornament, and a gasoline pump and bait shop in what had once been the front yard. I later saw a painting of the house as it was burning, called "Small Town Fire" by Oxford artist John McCrady.[20]

Faulkner's story says Emily lived on "what once had been our most select street." The house in my picture once stood across the street from the entrance to the Episcopal church on what the Oxford *Eagle* said was old Oxford's "quality row." But I could not be *sure* I had discovered the right place—that my house was really Faulkner's model for the house where Emily Grierson had kept Homer Barron for forty years—until I learned that my Emily's house was known in Oxford during Faulkner's time as the Homer Duke house. From Homer Duke to Homer Barron is not, I submit, just an after-the-fact coincidence.

(I hope it is understood, especially by the Oxford people in the audience, that my point here, as with the Friersons and the Mobile Emily, has to do only with Faulkner's *names*. I am not suggesting any connection between the real people who had those names and Emily's selective insanity in Faulkner's story. While I am sure Oxford, like any town, must have its share of skeletons in the closet, I doubt that anyone kept one in an identifiable bed for forty years. Faulkner did work from local history and local names but he also drew on his imagination, and

20. A reproduction of this painting appears in *Art Digest*, 1 July 1937.

certainly his imagination was responsible for the central event in "A Rose for Emily." I hope this is clear to everyone, since I don't want to be the cause for grandchildren of Homer Duke and Em Frierson issuing frantic denials or digging out certificates attesting to the real Homer's honorable death from natural causes.)

I. O. Snopes = To have just initials instead of a first and middle name is not exactly a Southern custom, although it seems more frequent in the South than in other parts of the country. For blacks it may have been a device to prevent whites from calling them by their first name. For some whites it could have been a carryover from the Scots tradition of being willing to reveal their last name but refusing to give their first for official records, initials being the compromise finally settled on. Or maybe there were simply a number of upwardly mobile parents who observed that successful businessmen were often known by their initials (J. P. Morgan, for example) and wanted their child to have a name that followed the same pattern.

But whatever were the usual reasons for initials instead of a first and middle name, in the case of I. O. the explanation is traceable directly to the U.S. Army. The Army assumes every man has a first, middle, and last name. If he doesn't have all of these, the details of his deficiency are spelled out at every roll call. To the Army, Robert Beauchamp Jones is Jones, Robert B. If he should happen to have no middle name or initial, he is Jones, Robert NMI (no middle initial). If his first two names are only initials (R. B. Jones) to the Army he is Jones, R(only), B(only)—which gives us the real (and famous to students of names) Ronly Bonly Jones, otherwise known as Initials Only Jones. I. O. Snopes is Initials Only Snopes.

Isaac = The operative association with this name for Faulkner was the Abraham and Isaac story. In the Bible Isaac is saved because God provided a ram to be sacrificed in his stead. For Isaac Snopes in *The Hamlet* the ram becomes a cow, slaughtered for Isaac's benefit. For Isaac McCaslin in *Go Down, Moses* the ram becomes a kid. He suspects "this time the exasperated Hand might not supply the kid." And so it doesn't, although not in the sense Isaac McCaslin meant. The "exasperated hand" turns out to be that of Isaac's wife who, exasperated at his stubbornness, uses her hand to manipulate his desire as she tries to barter her body for his promise they will move to the McCaslin plantation. The kid that is not supplied is the son Isaac doesn't get because his wife won't give him another chance to produce one. All of this makes for a version of Genesis that a preacher would find hard to recognize, but it is what Faulkner made of Isaac's name and story.

Jefferson = Looking at the name from the point of view of the fictional namers of the city: they could not choose Washington or Jackson because those names had already been taken by two other towns in Mississippi. Jefferson was the most logical next choice. Looking at it from the point of view of Faulkner, who was writing an imaginative history paralleling that of his own Lafayette County: Jefferson was the name originally given in 1836 to the county seat of the county just north of Lafayette, De Soto County. That town's name was later changed to Hernando, but there is a plaque outside the courthouse which tells about its earlier name. There is additional precedent for a Jefferson-Lafayette association: the annexation of the adjoining towns of Jefferson and Lafayette in Louisiana made up a good portion of the present city of New Orleans.[21]

Jenny = Bayard says in *The Unvanquished* that Col. Sartoris named the first locomotive on his railroad after Aunt Jenny and that the silver oil can in the cab had her name engraved on it. That is Bayard's mild joke. It is true in approximately the same way that Jefferson was named after the middle name of the mail rider, Thomas Jefferson Pettigrew. The purpose of Col. Sartoris's railroad was to give Jefferson direct access to the eastern seacoast. The Sartoris line joined the Memphis and Charleston at

---

21. To keep the number of footnotes from exceeding 100, I have not as a rule indicated my source for facts unless I have quoted exact words. But one of the other conference speakers questioned that there had ever been cities of Jefferson and Lafayette that were annexed to New Orleans, so I cite my source in this case: Collin Bradfield Hamer, Jr., "Records of the City of Jefferson (1850–1870) in the City Archives Department of New Orleans Public Library," *Louisiana History*, 17 (1976), 51, 52, 54.

Grand Junction. The Memphis and Charleston, despite its name, led to Richmond, Virginia. It was customary in early railroading days to name locomotives and even cars for their ultimate destination. Jenny Du Pre's name was really Virginia. What name, then, do you suppose Col. Sartoris gave to his locomotive and what do you suppose was engraved on the oil can? Jenny?

Judith and Henry Sutpen = Thomas Sutpen's dream changed to nightmare during (and partly because of) the Civil War. The first battle of the war was the Battle of Manassas, and the first civilian casualty of that battle was a widow by the name of Judith Henry.

That Sutpen named his children Judith and Henry could only be an anachronistic accident on his part, but the names were not accident on the part of Faulkner. He was acknowledging and extending a coincidence already entered into the script by reality. He wrote in *Absalom* that his Judith was "a widow before she even became a bride." The real Civil War Judith Henry is known to history as "the widow of Manassas." That is because there was an earlier Judith, in the Apocrypha, also known as "the widow of Manassas"—her husband, Manassas, having died before the events told in the Book of Judith took place. Thus the Biblical Apocrypha, Faulkner's apocrypha, and the facts of history touch the same bases. Art imitates life, and life imitates art.

Thomas Jefferson Pettigrew = Pettigrew is an old and proud Charleston name, one which helped produce the Charleston equivalent of the Cabot-Lowell-and-God verse about Boston:

I thank the Lord on bended knee;
I'm half Porcher and half Huger.
For other blessings thank Thee too:
My grandpa was a Pettigru.

Faulkner's reason for using the name Pettigrew seems to revolve around an odd passage in "The Courthouse" that others have commented on but have not, as far as I am aware, related to Pettigrew's name. It describes the mail rider as:

a weightless dessicated or fossil bird, not a vulture of course nor
even quite a hawk, but say a pterodactyl chick arrested just out of
the egg ten glaciers ago and so old in simple infancy as to be the
worn and weary ancestor of all subsequent life.

Faulkner is pursuing and burlesquing here the Charleston Pettigru family's pride in its ancient lineage by giving us a fanciful
version of *his* Pettigrew's pedigree. The image of a pterodactyl
chick—bony, angular, hairless—fits Faulkner's context because
pedigree was in Middle English *pedegrew*. It is from Old French
pied de grue, crane's foot, from the shape of a sign used in
showing lines of descent in genealogical charts.

This is my contribution to a campaign to shut up all those who
persist in maintaining that Faulkner could not possibly have
intended certain meanings or references because they would
require that he actually *knew* something, whereas we all know
he was just a talented natural writer with limited education.

Q'Milla = Oxford had a real Camilla with a Q in Miss Q'Milla
Collins. But someone—either Faulkner or Q'Milla's parents or
someone they listened to—knew Lyly's *Euphues*, for there we
find: "There is not far from here a gentlewoman whom I have
long time loved, the first letter of whose name is Camilla."

In *The Sound and the Fury* Faulkner might have had Q'Milla
somewhere in the back of his mind when he has Jason tell the
telegraph operator to send a wire to Caddy saying: "All Well. Q.
writing today." The Q means Quentin, but the operator is
puzzled, so Jason says: "Q. Can't you spell Q?" That is precisely
the issue Lyly raised with "the first letter of whose name is
Camilla."

Eudora Welty tells about mentioning an unusual Oxford name
to Faulkner and his reply: "Yes, I know the name well. Can
hardly wait for her to die so I can use it."[22]

Quentin = The most interesting thing I learned from listening to the Virginia tapes concerns Quentin. When Faulkner was

22. Hunter McKelva Cole, "Welty on Faulkner," *Notes on Mississippi Writers,* 9
(1976), 45.

asked a question about Quentin (which must have happened at least fifty times on the tapes) his answer would invariably include Quentin's name. But when he was asked about any of his other boys (Ike McCaslin, Bayard, Chick Mallison, Sarty—and together there must have been more of these than about Quentin) his answer would not include their name. To him they were always and only "the boy."

I think the conclusion to be drawn from this is inescapable: Faulkner thought of Quentin as a specific person with fixed and special qualities; he thought of his other boys as simply boys whose qualities could emerge or change according to whatever was useful to the story he was telling at the moment.

Also, Faulkner's memory on the tapes did not fail when the subject was Quentin, as it sometimes did with Ike and Cass and Bayard. When he said that he had invested more of himself in *The Sound and the Fury* and again to a lesser extent in *Absalom* than he had in his other work, I believe him. Quentin was real to him in a way his other boys were not—so real in fact that I don't quite accept that *The Sound and the Fury* began for him as he said it did with Caddy and muddy drawers and a tree. I would bet that it began with Quentin *watching* Caddy and muddy drawers and a tree.

Ringo = His proper name is Marengo, after Napoleon's victory over the Austrians at Marengo in 1800. Col. Sartoris had a copy of Napoleon's *Maxims* in his library; Napoleon said "My nobility dates from the day of Marengo." This all seems innocent enough as a source for a name, but actually it is not. Ringo's name, Marengo, is one of the most condescending jokes in all of Faulkner—one that I hope can be attributed to Col. Sartoris's sense of humor rather than to Faulkner's.

Ringo and Bayard were born in the same month, nursed at the same breast, and both called Rosa Millard "Granny." They were, in short, a team—mismatched but still a team. There are a number of reasons why Bayard was named Bayard: one was that Bayard was the name of a mythical horse of great swiftness, of normal size with one rider but capable of growing in length to accommodate as many as four riders. In other words, Bayard was superior to start with and could improve himself according to changing circumstances.

The other half of Col. Sartoris' newly-foaled team he named Marengo. That was after Marengo Mammoth, equally famous as an equine, although in different circles. Marengo Mammoth was antebellum Tennessee's (and thus the nation's) most celebrated jackass.

Shreve McCannon = Both his first and last name have to do with *Absalom*'s repeated image of the Mississippi River as the umbilical joining the North and the South. Captain Henry M. Shreve was the man who made Mississippi River steamboating possible. He is the one who built the first shallow draft steamboat, one that floated on the water instead of cutting through it, and he made in 1815 the first up-river trip from New Orleans—twenty-five days to Louisville. Shreve McCannon's last name seems to have been based on Captain John W. Cannon, who was captain of the Robert E. Lee when it won its famous race with the Natchez in 1870, going from New Orleans to St. Louis in less than four days.

McCannon also was the name of the murderer young Col. Falkner rescued from a mob in Ripley and whose life story he quickly wrote and sold, but I do not see that this has any connection with Shreve McCannon's name in *Absalom*.

Captain Strutterbuck = Originally in *The Mansion* this bragger-about-his-war-experiences was called Clapsaddle but Faulkner changed the name in his final revision to Strutterbuck. Montgomery Ward says about him: "He got his name from a book. I don't remember what book right now, but it was a better book than the one he got his war experiences from."

The book the name came from was any one of several by Scott. His name in Scott was Clutterbuck, a fictional retired officer who devoted himself to antiquarian interests and literary pursuits. He was supposed to be on the board for publishing the Waverley novels.

Popeye Vitelli = In *Requiem*, twenty years after *Sanctuary*, we learn that Popeye's last name is Vitelli. Why that name? I

suggest the name may be related to Popeye's strange preoccupation as he is about to be hanged:

> . . . they adjusted the rope, dragging it over Popeye's sleek, oiled
> head, breaking his hair loose. His hands were tied, so he began to
> jerk his head, flipping his hair back each time it fell forward
> again . . .
> "Fix my hair, Jack," he said.
> "Sure," the sheriff said. "I'll fix it for you"; springing the trap.

In Suetonius's *Lives of the Caesars* (where Faulkner found the
name Spintrius for Percival Brownlee as well as a number of
other details in "The Bear") we find an unusual circumstance in
the hanging of the notoriously corrupt Emperor Vitellius: after
they put the noose about his neck "his head was held back by the
hair." Vitellius-Vitelli, hanging-hanging, hair-hair. I concede this
does not amount to much as proof, but does anyone have a
better explanation for why Faulkner would give to a not-
particularly-Italian-seeming gangster based on a non-Italian
model named Pumphrey such a conspicuously Italian name as
Vitelli? As Faulkner goes on to say about Popeye in *Requiem:*
"Vitelli. What a name for him . . . a sybarite, centuries, perhaps
hemispheres before his time; in spirit and glands he was of that
age of princely despots. . . ."[23]

At one point in *Death in the Afternoon* Hemingway, after
having given maybe half an hour's worth of highly subjective
statements about honor, courage, and cowardice, talking as if he
knew what he was talking about to an old lady who had been
listening interestedly and politely, suddenly broke off:
"Madame, it may well be that we are talking horseshit." That is a
possibility which occurred to me as I was preparing the last half
of what I have been telling you about Faulkner's names. Still, we
all do what we can. And, as Mr. Millgate reminded us earlier in
the week: "Criticism believes before scholarship demonstrates."

---

23. It is axiomatic among students of names that most names are chosen for more
than one reason. "Vitalis" was registered by Bristol Myers as a trademark for a hair oil in
1930. In the typescript of *Requiem* Faulkner spelled Popeye's last name Vitalli. That he
later changed this spelling to Vitelli suggests that he perhaps had both Vitellius and
Vitalis in mind.

Faulkner's Short Stories: "And Now What's to Do"

JAMES B. CAROTHERS

For a man who confessed to a prospective publisher early in his career, "I am quite sure that I have no feeling for short stories," and who was quoted much later in that distinguished career as saying, "I never wrote a story I liked," and for a man who referred to his short stories as "pot boilers" or "trash," and to short story writing as "whoring,"[1] William Faulkner was a remarkably persistent and accomplished practitioner of the craft of short fiction. We can now count over 130 Faulkner titles that are demonstrably or arguably short stories,[2] and we can list a number of ways that short stories contributed to Faulkner's art as well as to his livelihood.

Faulkner's early experiments in short fiction apparently began in his student days at the University of Mississippi, with "Landing in Luck" and "The Hill," the first a flying story heavy in plot and irony, and the second a richly allusive "poetic" narrative.[3]

---

1. The first quotation is from a 1928 letter to Alfred Dashiell, published in *Selected Letters of William Faulkner*, ed. Joseph Blotner (New York: Random House, 1977), 42. (Hereafter cited as *SLWF*.) The second quotation is attributed to Faulkner by John K. Hutchens in a 1948 interview reprinted in *Lion in the Garden: Interviews with William Faulkner, 1926–1962*, ed. James B. Meriwether and Michael Millgate (New York: Random House, 1968), 59. Faulkner's variations of the "pot boiling" and "trash" metaphors can be seen in *SLWF*, 84, 111, 114, 121, 122, 131, and 136. The "whoring" allusion is in a 1932 letter to Harrison Smith, *SLWF*, 59.

2. The most comprehensive recent listing of Faulkner's short fiction is in Thomas E. Dasher's *William Faulkner's Characters: An Index to the Published and Unpublished Fiction* (New York and London: Garland Publishing, Inc., 1981).

3. Both stories are available in *William Faulkner: Early Prose and Poetry*, ed. Carvel Collins (Boston: Little, Brown, 1962). For extended comment on the latter story see Michel Gresset, "Faulkner's 'The Hill,'" *Southern Literary Journal*, 6 (Spring 1974), 3–18 and Philip Momberger, "A Reading of Faulkner's 'The Hill,'" *Southern Literary Journal*, 9 (Spring 1977), 16–29.

He continued to work in short prose forms during his New Orleans phase, in a series of newspaper sketches as well as in the Al Jackson letters to Sherwood Anderson.[4] Although these stories were probably less important in his artistic apprenticeship than his work in poetry, Faulkner had written at least thirty short stories and prose sketches before *Soldiers' Pay* was published in 1926. But he had published four novels and written two others before he enjoyed his first sale of a short story to a national magazine.

Faulkner eventually oversaw the publication of five short story collections: *These 13* (1931), *Doctor Martino and Other Stories* (1934), *Knight's Gambit* (1949), *Collected Stories* (1950), and *Big Woods* (1955). In addition, he saw the publication of limited editions of *Idyll in the Desert* (1931), *Miss Zilphia Gant* (1932), and *Notes on a Horsethief* (1950). Two of his novels, *The Unvanquished* (1938) and *Go Down, Moses* (1942), were treated as short story collections by some reviewers, the latter almost certainly because Random House published it as a book of stories,[5] while some critics have attempted to read *Knight's Gambit* as a novel, perhaps for balance. From 1930 on, Faulkner sold dozens of short stories to national magazines, from high-paying "slicks" such as the *Saturday Evening Post* and *Collier's*, through prestigious but lesser-paying quality magazines such as *Scribner's*, *Harper's*, the *Atlantic*, *American Mercury*, and *Story*, to a variety of other outlets, including *American Caravan*, *Contempo*, *College Life*, *Furioso*, and the *Sewanee Review*. Faulkner's stories were frequently cited in the O. Henry and O'Brien competitions, and they began to find their way into short story anthologies.

Faulkner was, of course, paid for his short stories, though

---

4. See *New Orleans Sketches*, ed. Carvel Collins (New York: Random House, 1968) and *Uncollected Stories of William Faulkner*, ed. Joseph Blotner (New York: Random House, 1979).

5. Faulkner wrote to Robert K. Haas in 1949, "Indeed, if you will permit me to say so at this late date, nobody but Random House seemed to labor under the impression that GO DOWN, MOSES should be titled 'and other stories.' I remember the shock (mild) when I saw the printed title page" (*SLWF*, 285).

rarely as well and almost never as quickly as he would have liked, and he often expressed contempt for the entire process of writing, marketing, and publishing short stories. Writing to Robert Haas in 1940, Faulkner complained

> I had planned, after finishing THE HAMLET, to try to earn enough from short stories by July 1 to carry me through the year, allow me six months to write another novel. I wrote six short stories by March 15, trying to write the sort of pot boilers which the Post pays me $1,000.00 each for, because the best I could hope for good stories is 3 or 4 hundred, and the only mag. to buy them is Harper's etc.
>
> So I wrote the six stories, but only one of them has sold yet. Actually I would have been better off now if I had written the good ones. Now I have not only wasted the mental effort and concentration which went into the trash, but the six months between November when I finished THE HAMLET, and March 15, when I finished the last story, as well as the time since March 15 which I have spent mortgaging my mares and colts one at a time to pay food and electricity and washing and such, and watching each mail train in hopes of a check.[6]

And in January of 1946 he wrote to Harold Ober: "Thank you for the Ellery Queen check. What a commentary. In France I am the father of a literary movement. In Europe I am considered the best modern American and among the first of all writers. In America I eke out a hack's motion picture wages by winning second prize in a manufactured mystery story contest."[7]

At other times and in other contexts, to be sure, Faulkner made numerous observations indicating his respect for the short story as a genre, often asserting that the short story was, after poetry, the most demanding of literary forms.[8] The evidence of his manuscripts and typescripts suggests that Faulkner's short stories were usually the result of the same painstaking and complex craftsmanship that produced his novels. Faulkner, moreover, believed that short story volumes should have novelistic structure and integration, and he accordingly exercised great

6. *SLWF*, 121–22.
7. *SLWF*, 217–18.
8. See, for example, *Lion in the Garden*, 217, 238.

care in selecting and arranging his short stories into books.[9] Several of his novels, of course, are structures of material he had previously developed in short stories, *The Unvanquished* (1938), *The Hamlet* (1940), and *Go Down Moses* (1940) being the best-known and most extensively studied examples. Too, we have Faulkner's assertion that *The Sound and the Fury* (1929) began as a short story, and there is evidence that important points in the genesis and composition of *Absalom, Absalom!* (1936) are to be found in short stories such as "The Big Shot," "Evangeline," "Dull Tale," and "Wash."[10] It is, in fact, possible to argue that elements of virtually every novel in the Faulkner canon derive in part from materials Faulkner had at hand in the short story bin of his "lumber room."

But we have been a long time in coming to the view that Faulkner's short stories deserve the same careful, systematic, and respectful attention that has been accorded to his novels, and that view is by no means common today. Though we have recently come a long way from the time when a critic could omit discussion of the short stories from his guide to Faulkner on the grounds that they "do not appreciably add to our knowledge of Faulkner's techniques and ideas,"[11] much of the recent work on the short stories continues to manifest the same critical attitudes and habits of mind that caused the vast majority of Faulkner's short stories to be ignored, denigrated, or simply misread during the earlier years.

Simplified to primer class, my thesis is that short stories were, for Faulkner, considerably more than a way to make money or a way to make novels, and that, while some significant and encouraging work has been done on the short stories in recent

9. Faulkner insisted to Malcolm Cowley that "even to a collection of short stories, form, integration, is as important as to a novel—an entity of its own, single, set for one pitch, contrapuntal in integration, toward one end, one finale." *The Faulkner-Cowley File: Letters and Memories, 1944–1962*, ed. Malcolm Cowley (New York: Viking, 1966), 15–16.

10. See Joseph Blotner's notes to these latter stories in *Uncollected Stories of William Faulkner*, 707–9.

11. Edmond L. Volpe, *A Reader's Guide to William Faulkner* (New York: Noonday, 1964), x.

years, we are going to have to question, and to modify or discard some of the prevailing notions, habits, and practices of the past if we are to deal responsibly with the short stories in the future. The time seems ripe for a reassessment of the critical, scholarly, and popular attitudes towards Faulkner's short stories, for only an individual who demands that everything be done at once and to perfection can seriously complain of the quantity and quality of attention the short stories have received in the last ten or twelve years, and we need to recognize this work if we are to discover what's to do now.

There are, first of all, more of Faulkner's short stories available for general reading and for scholarly study than at any time before. Joseph Blotner's edition of the *Uncollected Stories* and Leland H. Cox's edition of the *Sinbad in New Orleans* material[12] supplement previously published volumes to the extent that approximately 90 percent of Faulkner's short stories are now available in immediately accessible editions.[13] James B. Meriwether's 1971 bibliographical study of the short fiction continues to provide the best single overview of Faulkner's short story production,[14] while Joseph Blotner's biography and his edition of Faulkner's *Selected Letters* give us an enormous amount of data relating to individual stories.[15] The first book-length study of the subject, Hans H. Skei's *William Faulkner: The Short Story Career,* has appeared, and there have been frequent studies of a great variety of particular stories, rewarding studies of individual short story volumes, and sometimes more responsible examinations of the complex relations between Faulkner's short stories and his other texts.[16]

12. *Sinbad in New Orleans,* ed. Leland Cox (Spartanburg, S.C.: The Reprint Company, 1981).

13. In addition to the volumes edited by Blotner, Collins, and Cox (above, n. 3, 4 and 12), the essential texts are William Faulkner, *Knight's Gambit* (New York: Random House, 1949) and William Faulkner, *Collected Stories* (New York: Random House, 1950).

14. James B. Meriwether, "The Short Fiction of William Faulkner," *Proof,* 1 (1971), 293–329.

15. Joseph Blotner, *Faulkner: A Biography,* 2 vols. (New York: Random House, 1974).

16. Skei provides a useful listing of secondary materials dealing with Faulkner's short stories in *William Faulkner: The Short Story Career* (Oslo—Bergen—Tromsø: Universitetsforlaget, 1981), 143–57.

But before I suggest some of the kinds of attention that Faulkner's short stories might usefully receive in the future, I should like to list a number of things I think we should stop doing.

First, we should cease giving credence to the notion that Faulkner's short stories are not important or not artistically worthy because they were "written for money." Much has been made, both early and late, of the fact that Faulkner wrote stories for money. Faulkner's own comments in letters and in interviews have lent support to this view, and Hans H. Skei has demonstrated that Faulkner's interest in short stories diminished when he was economically free to write novels, when he was indentured to Hollywood, and when he freed himself of the financial exigencies that had driven him to boiling the pot with the *Post* and hacking in Hollywood in the earlier years. The taint of "commercialism" is, of course, standard dismissive criticism of the short story careers of many important American writers, particularly when the stories in question are apparently written for the *Saturday Evening Post*. It is also evident that Faulkner was occasionally willing to revise his stories in order to enhance their chances of publication, as in the cases of "Spotted Horses" for *Scribner's*, "That Evening Sun Go Down" for Mencken's *American Mercury*, and "Snow," "Knight's Gambit," and "Shall Not Perish" in other contexts.[17]

But the distinction between Faulkner's economic hopes and his artistic achievement in such cases must be maintained, for Faulkner's story-telling sense almost invariably led him away from the kind of fiction that would have made him a truly successful commercial writer. While it is true that the stories that Faulkner sold to the *Post* are, as a group, rather less impressive than the stories he sold to more prestigious, lower-paying magazines, it is also true that the *Post* published a number of Faulk-

---

17. For evidence of Faulkner's willingness to revise "Spotted Horses" see James B. Meriwether, "Faulkner's Correspondence with *Scribner's Magazine*," *Proof,* 3 (1973), 263–64 and Hans H. Skei, *William Faulkner: The Short Story Career,* 43–47. Skei (65–67) summarizes the textual and printing history of "That Evening Sun." Faulkner's composition of "Snow" is described by Frank Cantrell in "An Unpublished Faulkner Short Story: 'Snow,'" *Mississippi Quarterly* 26 (1973), 325–30. On "Knight's Gambit," see particularly *SLWF,* 149, and for "Shall Not Perish," see *SLWF,* 150–51.

ner's best stories, and it is also evident that the stories Faulkner published in the *Post* in the 1930s are, with few exceptions, far superior in quality to the other fiction that magazine was publishing during this period. None of this is to deny that Faulkner's stories were conceived and executed in economic desperation, for the evidence is overwhelming that this was often the case. But Faulkner was still Faulkner, even when he was writing what he self-defensively called "trash," and we must not forget that he managed on a number of occasions to erect from this "trash" fictional structures that met even his own demanding personal standards.

A second notion that must be dispensed with, I think, is that Faulkner's short stories are interesting or valuable primarily because they became elements of his novels. This notion is more respectable than the commercialism charge, and hence more difficult to refute, but it is, in its way, equally pernicious. Faulkner, of course, revised many of his short stories, often radically, in making his novels, and when he did so he usually chose not to include in his short story collections the stories he had thus revised. But to deny these short stories their autonomy and their appropriate place in the canon is to ignore a number of superb stories, stories every bit as distinguished as those that repeatedly find their way into the anthologies. "The Hound," "Fool About a Horse," "Lizards in Jamshyd's Courtyard," "Lion," and the original version of "Delta Autumn," to name only a few, are excellent stories in their own right, significantly different from the reworked materials of the novels into which they were incorporated, and in no sense "negated" or "replaced" by the novels.

In revising from one story or novel to the next, Faulkner altered both important and trivial portions of his earlier material, leading some readers to the mistaken conclusion that the last version of a particular Faulkner story somehow embodies his "final intention." But while Faulkner sometimes developed new material from the direct examination of his previously published stories or the manuscript or typescript drafts of those stories, he

JAMES B. CAROTHERS 209

also sometimes depended on his selective and imperfect memory of what he had written or published earlier, and in any case he was never loath to alter the supposed "facts" of his other fictions.

A third point that ought to be emphasized in future studies of the short stories is that makers of anthologies should be enjoined from publishing excerpts from novels in the guise of short fiction. Pioneered by Malcolm Cowley in his generation of *The Portable Faulkner*, followed on many occasions by Faulkner's publisher, and even occasionally condoned by Faulkner himself, the editorial practice of publishing as autonomous works what are in fact extracts from novels has caused more than a little confusion and misunderstanding for general readers and for presumably more sophisticated critics. The *Go Down, Moses* text of "The Bear," to take the obvious example, is a chapter from a novel, and, while there is no denying that this text conveys a moving and powerful story, it is also true that this text contains much that is simply incomprehensible outside the novel's context. Similarly, although there is a story in "An Odor of Verbena" when published by itself, that text is fully understandable only as the resolving element of the structure of *The Unvanquished.* *The Hamlet*, similarly, is a questionable source for the best texts of the stories that went into it. The original stories are no more replaced by the novels that followed them than a later Faulkner novel replaces an earlier one.

A fourth practice that needs to be questioned occurs in the work of the anthologists who persist in selecting the same stories over and over for those volumes that give potential readers of Faulkner their first and sometimes their exclusive exposure to his work. If the practice of the anthologists can be changed, perhaps we may eventually be able to call for a moratorium on the habit of critics of interpreting and reinterpreting these same stories over and over again, particularly the story about the lady who murdered the street-paving contractor and the story about the big animal that lived in the big woods. The six Faulkner stories most often reprinted, some of them excerpts from novels, are the subject of well over half of the published criticism of individual Faulkner short story titles.[18] This is not to say that these stories do not invite and reward continued close reading, but that to concentrate exclusively on them is to ignore a significant body of other excellent work, which similarly invites and may similarly reward us in our studies.

Thus, finally, we need to dispense with the notion that certain stories may be safely ignored simply because Faulkner himself seemed to ignore or belittle them. Faulkner almost always wrote better than he knew, and we know from some of his comments on his novels, particularly his self-deprecatory comments, that he was an imperfect judge of his own work. Taking their cue from Faulkner's practice and commentary, critics have tended to concentrate their attention on the stories Faulkner chose for his own story collections, and they have tended to ignore those stories Faulkner chose not to include in his collections or revise for his novels. "Thrift," for example, ought to have been especially memorable to Faulkner at the time he compiled *These 13*, for it had been published only the year before, and it was notable as the first story he had managed to sell to the *Post*. But the comic story of the Scots trickster MacWyrglinchbeath would have been radically incompatible with other World War I stories in Part I of *These 13*, as it would later be inappropriate for "The Wasteland" section of *Collected Stories* in 1950. The stories "Elmer" and *Miss Zilphia Gant* are other strong stories that Faulkner chose not to collect, perhaps implicitly accepting the judgments of the many editors who had rejected both of them. The fact that each of these three stories has been singled out for careful scholarly attention in recent years is an encouraging sign,[19] and ought to help us to focus our attention on other

18. Thomas L. McHaney's *William Faulkner: A Reference Guide* (Boston: G. K. Hall, 1976) contains 89 entries for "The Bear," 33 for "A Rose for Emily," 24 for "That Evening Sun," 11 for "Spotted Horses," 9 for "Barn Burning," and 8 for "Delta Autumn." A check of the MLA annual bibliographies since 1973 suggests that these texts continue to receive the preponderance of critical and scholarly attention, though "Pantaloon in Black"—like "The Bear," a story with problematic relations to the novel *Go Down, Moses*—has received increased attention.

19. See Hans H. Skei, "A Forgotten Faulkner Story: 'Thrift,'" *Mississippi Quarterly*, 32 (1979), 453–60; Thomas L. McHaney, "The Elmer Papers: Faulkner's Comic Portraits

worthy but neglected stories. Similarly to be commended are recent studies of Faulkner's principles of selection and arrangement of his short story volumes, though while this work has yielded eloquent and provocative interpretations and descriptions of what Arthur F. Kinney has called "the narrative poetics" of Faulkner's short story volumes,[20] it remains true that such studies should complement rather than replace our understanding of the poetics of individual Faulkner short stories.[21]

What, then, are we to do, what specific studies of Faulkner's short fiction should occupy us in the coming years, assuming that we can avoid some of the misconceptions and malpractices that have adversely affected the understanding and appreciation of Faulkner's short stories up to now? As a general procedure, I suggest that we ought to approach individual Faulkner short stories with an openness to the possibility that each of them has a coherent and discoverable narrative structure, a setting in place and time appropriate to the narrative situation, characters who are rendered with sufficient precision, solidity, and depth to stand up on their hind legs and cast shadows, and serious thematic purpose to reward close reading. We should approach each story, in other words, prepared to believe that it may have meaning and value independent of its eventual place in a Faulkner novel, a short story volume, or his income ledger.[22] To illus-

of the Artist," *Mississippi Quarterly*, 26 (1973), 281–311; and Giliane Morell, "Prisoners of the Inner World: Mother and Daughter in *Miss Zilphia Gant*," *Mississippi Quarterly*, 28 (1975), 299–305.

20. Arthur F. Kinney, "Faulkner's Narrative Poetics and *Collected Stories*," *Faulkner Studies*, 1 (1980), 58–79.

21. Stories like "An Odor of Verbena" and "Was," for example, were by-products of novels in progress, and were offered for magazine publication as autonomous short stories. They were first published, however, as chapters in *The Unvanquished* and *Go Down, Moses*, respectively. The novel chapters cannot be responsibly read as short stories, though the versions of these two texts published in *USWF* may be read autonomously. In spite of the care that Faulkner took in the arrangement of *Collected Stories*, however, no story in that collection functions primarily or exclusively as a unit in that volume.

22. See Michael Milligate's proposition that "each Faulkner text must be considered a unique, independent, and self-sufficient work of art, not only capable of being read and contemplated in isolation but actually demanding such treatment." "Faulkner's First Trilogy: *Sartoris, Sanctuary,* and *Requiem for a Nun*," in *Fifty Years of Yoknapatawpha*, ed. Doreen Fowler and Ann J. Abadie (Jackson: University Press of Mississippi, 1980), 105.

trate the possible benefits of this procedure, I should like to discuss aspects of two particular stories and one rather large group of stories, to suggest some of the sorts of study we might usefully undertake in the future.

The first story I wish to consider is the second story Faulkner attempted to publish under the title of "Once Aboard the Lugger," which he had written by late 1928, and which he failed to publish or collect. The story was discovered among the Rowan Oak papers, first published in *The Mississippi Quarterly*, and subsequently included in *Uncollected Stories*.[23] This narrative is a violent story of rum-running in the Gulf, undoubtedly a product of the experiences Faulkner liked to recount of his early days in New Orleans. It is related by common characters and setting to another story called "Once Aboard the Lugger," presumably composed about the same time, eventually published in *Contempo* magazine at Chapel Hill in 1932, but also uncollected, and—except for a brief allusion in Faulkner's 1954 "Mississippi" piece—ignored until it, too, was included in *Uncollected Stories*.[24]

The two "Lugger" stories, though they may have been intended to form parts of a novel or a cycle of stories, contrast radically in substance and mood. The first story is relatively slight of action. Four men—an unnamed narrator, the Captain of the vessel, a Negro cook, and a sullen young man named Pete—sail to an island in the Gulf uninhabited except for some wild cattle and equally wild mosquitoes, dig up some bootleg alcohol, and load it on the boat for return to the mainland. They accomplish these tasks in arduous silence, working in the dark to avoid detection by the Coast Guard. The main interest in the story, I should say, is in the contrasts among the four men, especially between Pete, who is too ill for most of the working part of the

23. See *USWF*, 359–67 and 699–700.
24. Material corresponding to "Once Aboard the Lugger" (I) is in William Faulkner, "Mississippi," in *William Faulkner: Essays, Speeches and Public Letters*, ed. James B. Meriwether (New York: Random House, 1965), 30–31.

trip to be of any use, and the unnamed narrator, who is a sensitive, literate observer, a willing participant in the action, and an articulate exponent of the experience:

> Pete and I went forward and lay again on the mattress. I heard Pete go to sleep, but for a long while I was too tired to sleep, although I could hear the nigger snoring in the galley, where he had made his bed after that infatuated conviction of his race that fresh air may be slept in only at the gravest peril. My back and arms and loins ached, and whenever I closed my eyes it seemed immediately that I was struggling through sand that shifted and shifted under me with patient derision, and that I still heard the dark high breath of the sea in the pines.
>
> Out of this sound another sound grew, mounted swiftly, and I raised my head and watched a red navigating light and that pale wing of water that seemed to have a quality of luminousness of its own, stand up and pass and fade, and I thought of Conrad's centaur, the half man, half tugboat, charging up and down river in the same higheared, myopic haste, purposeful but without destination, oblivious to all save what was immediately in its path, and to that a dire and violent menace. Then it was gone, the sound too died away, and I lay back again while my muscles jerked and twitched to the fading echo of the old striving and the Hush   Hush   of the sea in my ears.[25]

The story thus concluded, Faulkner submitted it to *Scribner's* in November, 1928, only to have it rejected by editor Alfred Dashiell. Calling the story "a nice piece of atmosphere," Dashiell nevertheless admonished Faulkner:

> The trouble with your writing, it seems to me, is that you get mostly the overtones and avoid the real core of the story. It would seem that in the attempt to avoid the obvious you have manufactured the vague. You are skirting around drama and not writing it. It might be worthwhile to attempt to tell a straightforward tale as you might narrate an incident to a friend, then all this atmosphere and all the background which you sketch in so skilfully will come right handy and make your work distinctive.[26]

25. *USWF,* 358.
26. Meriwether, "Faulkner's Correspondence with *Scribner's* Magazine," 257.

Though Faulkner did not respond in detail to this criticism, he submitted to *Scribner's* the next month the second "Lugger" story, with the following explanation: "In case you recall a mss. entitled 'Once Aboard the Lugger——' which I submitted while in New York, I have merely used this same title for the rest of the episode with which the other manuscript dealt, with the hope that the present half of the episode will suit you better."[27] "Presumably," Joseph Blotner comments, "he had taken existing material and reshaped it with Dashiell's strictures in mind about more story and less atmosphere."[28] This is a plausible general account of this episode, though it is less than clear just what form the "existing material" may have had previously,[29] but I also want to suggest that in selecting and "reshaping" the second "Lugger" story for *Scribner's* Faulkner not only sought to submit a story that complied with Dashiell's strictures, but that he did so by the expedient of adapting elements of a story by one of *Scribner's* leading authors, Ernest Hemingway.

The Hemingway story is "The Killers," first published in *Scribner's* in March 1927, and collected that same year in *Men Without Women*.[30] The two stories are remarkably similar in parallels of situation, characterization, narrative incident, and phrasing. In Faulkner's story, the four men are carrying the load of bootleg alcohol toward the mainland when they are stopped by modern pirates. The pirate with red hair and an Alabama accent immediately shoots the cook, and it is clear that the other three are in grave danger. Pete, who is belligerent with the pirates, is knocked unconscious, as is the Captain, and the unnamed narrator is quite clearly in mortal jeopardy:

> The man with the high voice was talking forward, then he came through the galley and stuck his head in the cuddy—a wop in a dirty cap and a green silk shirt without a collar. There was a diamond stud

27. *SLWF*, 41–42.
28. *Faulkner: A Biography*, 600.
29. See Skei, *William Faulkner: The Short Story Career*, 42–43.
30. Audre Hanneman, *Ernest Hemingway: A Comprehensive Bibliography* (Princeton: Princeton University Press, 1967), 20.

in the front of it, and he had an automatic in his hand. He looked at me.

"What about this one?" he said.

"Nothing," the other said. "Git on back there and git that stuff out." I fitted the pump.

"Call me a hophead, will you?" the wop said. "Who do you think you are, anyway?"

"Git on back there and git that stuff out," the other said. I could feel the wop looking at the back of my head.

"What do you think about it?" he said.

"Nothing," I said. I fitted the pump. (*USWF*, 362–63)

Pete, however, is killed by "the hophead" in a graphic passage that could hardly be said to involve "skirting around drama and not writing it":

"Call me a hophead," the wop wailed. Pete was looking at him across his shoulder. The wop jerked the pistol down and Pete ducked his head away and the wop jabbed the pistol at him and shot him in the back of the head. It was a heavy Colt's and it slammed Pete into the wall. The wall slammed him again, like he'd been hit twice, and as he fell again and banged his head on the engine, the other man jumped over him, onto the wop.

The sound of the explosion kept on, slamming back and forth between the walls. It was like the air was full of it, and every time anybody moved, they jarred some more of it down and I could smell powder and a faint scorching smell. (*USWF*, 364)

The narrator and the Captain are, however, ultimately spared, and as the story concludes, the narrator takes steps to recover from his wounds, following the Captain's instructions to clear the hold of its mortal wreckage.

There was a scuttle in the bulkhead. Pete went through easily. But the nigger, naked from the waist up, was pretty bloody, where they had dumped him in on the broken bottles and then trampled on him, beside the wound itself, which began to bleed again when I moved him. I wedged him into the scuttle and went around into the galley and hauled at him. I tried to slip my hand down and catch the waist of his pants, but he stuck again and something broke and my hand came free with the broken string on which his charm—a cloth tobacco sack containing three hard pellets—the charm which he had said would protect him from anything that came to him across water—hung, the soiled bag dangling at the end of it. But at last I got him through.

My hand was smarting again, and all at once we passed out of the island's lee and the boat began to roll a little, and I leaned against the grease-crusted stove, wondering where the soda was. I didn't see it, but I saw Pete's bottle, the one he had brought aboard with him in New Orleans. I got it and took a big drink. As soon as I swallowed I knew I was going to be sick, but I kept on swallowing. Then I stopped and I thought about trying to make it topside, but I quit thinking about anything and leaned on the stove and got pretty sick. I was sick for a good while, but afterward I took another drink and then I felt a little better. (*USWF*, 366–67)

Both "The Killers" and "Once Aboard the Lugger" (II) center on threats of violence by underworld characters, and both Hemingway's Nick Adams and Faulkner's narrator are quiet observers who prudently decline physical or verbal resistance to the intruders, in contrast to Hemingway's George and Faulkner's Pete, who are both belligerent towards the armed outsiders and earn their derision. In "The Killers" the two outsiders gradually assume control over the situation in the diner with implied threats succeeded by direct threats, while the intruders in "Lugger" establish their authority through immediate and direct violence. Both pairs are armed with sawed-off shotguns. The black character in both stories is a cook who is immediately sensitive to the situation:

> The door to the kitchen opened and the nigger came in. "What was it?" he asked. The two men at the counter took a look at him.
>
> "All right, nigger. You stand right there," Al said.
>
> Sam, the nigger, standing in his apron, looked at the two men sitting at the counter. "Yes, sir," he said.[31]

---

31. Ernest Hemingway, *The Short Stories of Ernest Hemingway* (New York: Charles Scribner's Sons, 1954), 282. Subsequent references to this story are noted in the text as *SSEH*.

Faulkner's cook speaks "in a still whisper, like the words were shaped in silence, without breath or sound. 'They got us. What I do?'" (USWF, 360).

In both stories the two outsiders quarrel with one another and employ ethnic slurs, and both are derisive of their would-be rebellious captives, as George is contemptuously called "bright boy" by Max and Al, and Pete is called "Houdini" by the Italian gunman. Both stories are set in a confined physical space, below the deck of the boat in Faulkner's story, and within Henry's lunchroom and Ole Andreason's rooming house in Hemingway's. Perhaps the most striking minute similarity is in the way Faulkner's concluding lines resemble and perhaps echo the concluding dialogue of "The Killers":

> "I'm going to get out of this town," Nick said.
> "Yes," said George. "That's a good thing to do."
> "I can't stand to think about him waiting in the room and knowing he's going to get it. It's too damned awful."
> "Well," said George, "you better not think about it." (SSEH, 289)

Faulkner's "I quit thinking about anything" (USWF, 367) seems a clear echo of the Hemingway phrasing and philosophy.

Numerous and substantial differences between the two stories, however, suggest that Faulkner was not writing a slavish imitation of the Hemingway story. "The Killers" concentrates on the unfulfilled threat of death to Ole Andreason, and is only incidentally concerned with the threat of death to Nick, George, and the cook. The threats to the three men in the diner are brief and almost casual. Only twice in "The Killers" is it suggested that Nick and his co-workers may be killed, first when George asks "What you going to do with us afterward?" and Max replies, "That'll depend. . . . That's one of those things you never know at the time" (SSEH, 284), and shortly thereafter when George puts off a potential customer, Al says that "he knew I'd blow his head off" (SSEH, 284) if he didn't. In Faulkner's story the threat of death is fulfilled immediately, the narrator, Pete, and the Captain are directly and personally threatened, and Pete's head

is actually blown off. A second major contrast can be observed in
the fact that Hemingway's characters are disturbed in their
routine of tedious and respectable activities in a small-town
diner, while Faulkner's characters are threatened in a somewhat
exotic setting, in which they are themselves already outside the
law, and are armed against the law and the underworld. A third
major contrast is in the narrative method, omniscient third-
person reportorial in "The Killers," first-person retrospective in
the "Lugger" story.

So, in calling attention to the similarity of these two stories, I
do not mean to suggest that Faulkner's story was a simple and
direct imitation of "The Killers," nor even that the Hemingway
influence is necessarily the single best explanation of the origin
of Faulkner's text. It seems likely that both "Lugger" stories
derive in part from things Faulkner observed or heard described
by others in New Orleans, references to Conrad's "Falk" in both
stories point to another possible source, and it remains possible
that the two stories were primarily, as Faulkner implied to
Dashiell, part of a projected series or novel on the whiskey
trade. But by submitting to *Scribner's* a story that so closely
resembles a well-known story by a leading *Scribner's* author,
Faulkner seems to have made a subtle and deeply ironic response to Dashiell's criticism, as though Faulkner were saying to
Dashiell, "All right, if you want action, I'll give you action. If you
want Hemingway, I can do him too, and have done, and here it
is."

The second "Lugger" story, it must be said, is not very good
imitation Hemingway, and it is far from being good Faulkner.
The story is perhaps more interesting for the way it develops or
anticipates characters and incidents from other Faulkner texts,
characters such as Pete of *Mosquitoes* or Popeye and Red of
Sanctuary, and the incident in which the narrator's first thought
after the murder of the cook is to seek baking powder for his own
burned hand evokes Quentin's reaction to the news of Nancy's
possible death in "That Evening Sun" by wondering who will do

the family's washing.[32] But Faulkner, trying to publish a story in what he might well have thought of as "Hemingway's magazine," seems to have turned naturally to a story that probably owes much to Hemingway in its basic elements and individual details. Given that Faulkner maintained a long competitive interest in Hemingway, and especially given that *Men Without Women* was a Hemingway text Faulkner recalled with approval over twenty years later, the second "Lugger" story, thus interpreted, may add some minor but intriguing possibilities to our understanding of the relations between these two writers.[33]

In examining an aspect of a somewhat better-known Faulkner story, "The Leg," I want to call attention to what seems to me to be a characteristic Faulkner practice, that of creating deliberate ambiguity regarding the facts of death. By this I mean the situation in which a Faulkner character may be dying, but the actual death is not described, and is, therefore, uncertain. The case of Nancy in "That Evening Sun" is a prime example, and similar ambiguities obtain in the situations of Sarty Snopes's father and brother in "Barn Burning," the title character of "Elly," Jubal in "Mountain Victory," the protagonist of "Carcassonne," Gail Hightower at the end of *Light in August,* and Mink Snopes at the conclusion of *The Mansion.* In these texts, Faulkner imples the possibility of death through descriptive imagery and through details of situation, but he creates ambiguity by choosing to leave the moment of death, and, therefore, the actuality of the death itself, to the imagination and conjecture of his readers.

"The Leg" may have been first written as early as 1925. Faulkner submitted it to a number of magazines without success, and

32. For another possible Faulkner echo and variant on Hemingway's "not thinking about it," see Rider's explanation of his behavior following his wife's death: "Hit look lack Ah just can't quit thinking. Look lack Ah just can't quit"; in "Pantaloon in Black," *USWF,* 255. The identical passage is in William Faulkner, *Go Down, Moses and Other Stories* (New York: Random House, 1942), 159, except that the 1942 version features Faulkner's characteristic omission of the apostrophe in the contraction.

33. See Faulkner's allusion to *Men Without Women* in a 1952 letter to Harvey Breit (*SLWF,* 333).

it remained unpublished until he chose to include it in *Doctor Martino*.[34] The distinctive feature of "The Leg" is the abnormal psychological deterioration of the narrator, Davy—always an important name for Faulkner—who begins as a pleasant, civilized, and carefree schoolboy and ends as a maimed, mad, and possibly murderous deviate. The ostensible cause of Davy's transformation is his experience in World War I, including the wound that causes him to lose his leg, and the death of his best friend, George. The central ambiguity of "The Leg" seems to reside in its conclusion, which implies that Davy has wrought some unspeakable violence upon the English girl, Everbe Corinthia Rust, even though at the time of the apparent crime Davy has an incontrovertible alibi, having been in a hospital. Yet there is apparently incontrovertible proof that Davy has lived a psychologically double life, proof in the form of a photographic postcard bearing an obscene superscription to Everbe. Everbe, apparently, was attacked by Davy, or by the ghost of Davy's amputated leg.

"The Leg" shows that stark and irreconcilable contrast between man's better and worse natures that Faulkner dramatized so often in his early fiction. It is also, at least superficially, an account of the devastating effects of the World War. It is also, I believe, a case study in sexual guilt and retribution, in which Davy's real or imagined attack on Everbe Corinthia constitutes an unconscious projection of his resentment over the fact that Everbe, as Circe, provokes "swinish" behavior in himself and in George. By several turns of the screw, Faulkner leaves his reader wondering what "really" happened to Davy, to his amputated leg, to Everbe Corinthia, and even, as I hope to show, to George. Is Davy a reliable narrator, and, if he is, are we thus given a story that involves "a case of reincarnation,"[35] or is Davy quite simply or complexly insane?

---

34. "The Leg" was subsequently included in the "Beyond" section of William Faulkner, *Collected Stories* (New York Random House, 1950), 823–42. References to this edition are noted parenthetically in the text as *CS*.

35. Most critics accept Blotner's speculation (*SLWF*, 31) that Faulkner used this phrase to describe an early version of "The Leg."

I want to focus now on the opening scene of the story, not to attempt to resolve the ambiguity of the ending, but to suggest an additional ambiguity at the beginning. As "The Leg" opens, Davy and his friend George are schoolboys taking their weekly boating holiday on the Thames, with George spouting Milton and flirting decorously with the lockkeeper's daughter, Everbe Corinthia. As a consequence of George's showing off, there is an accident.

> The skiff shot away under me; I had a fleeting picture of George still clinging with one arm around the pile, his knees drawn up to his chin and the hat in his lifted hand and of a long running shadow carrying the shadow of a boat-hook falling across the lock. Then I was too busy steering. I shot through the gates, carrying with me that picture of George, the glazed hat still gallantly aloft like the mastheaded pennant of a man-of-war, vanishing beneath the surface. Then I was floating quietly in slack water while the round eyes of two men stared quietly down at me from the yawl.
>
> "Yer've lost yer mate, sir," one of them said in a civil voice. Then they had drawn me alongside with a boat-hook and standing up in the skiff, I saw George. He was standing in the towpath now, and Simon, Everbe Corinthia's father, and another man—he was the one with the boat-hook, whose shadow I had seen across the lock—were there too. But I saw only George with his ugly crooked face and his round head now dark in the sunlight. One of the watermen was still talking. "Steady, sir. Lend 'im a 'and, Sam'l. There. 'E'll do now. Give 'im a turn, seeing 'is mate. (CS, 824–25)

What I want to suggest is that this passage describes not merely a temporary and quickly rectified embarrassment by immersion for George, but actually his death by drowning, and that Davy's madness stems from this incident, rather from his later experiences in the war, including his grief over the supposed death of George in battle and his own mutilation. To be sure, Davy recounts a conversation with George immediately following the latter's immersion and ostensible rescue, and Davy also reports seeing George once, briefly, during the war, but it is interesting to note that no one but Davy shows any reaction to anything George reportedly does or says after he falls into the lock.

In order to sustain this interpretation we must understand that Davy is, at this point in the story, limited by "that certitude of the young which so arbitrarily distinguishes between verities and allusions, establishing with such assurance that line between truth and delirium which sages knit their brows over" (CS, 833). If Davy is himself eventually delirious in the later hospital scenes in which he carries on extended conversations with George's ghost over the ghost of his own amputated leg, it seems equally possible that he is delirious following George's immersion, and appropriately so, if we are meant to understand that George actually drowns here.

The distinction to be made, then, is that while Davy is throughout the story a *plausible* narrator, he is not to be taken as a *reliable* narrator, unless we can stipulate that there may be reliable accounts of the supernatural. Other elements of the story suggest madness or the supernatural, particularly the hints that Davy and his amputated leg are susceptible to some sort of transformation under the influence of the moon, and in the otherwise unexplained transformation of Everbe Corinthia from an innocent girl to a devastated wanton. If George drowns in the Thames, this event, rather than George's reported death in the war or Davy's own wounding, is the precipitating event in Davy's delirium and eventual madness, and the remainder of "The Leg" describes Davy's sublimation and expiation of his guilt over his part in his friend's death.

Although I will not insist on this reading—it seems to me as difficult to say with certainty that George does or does not drown in the Thames as it is to say with certainty that Davy does or does not subsequently violate Everbe Corinthia in some fashion—I believe the admission of this initial ambiguity makes the beginning of "The Leg" consistent with its end, and helps to account for a number of curious details in the description of events immediately following Davy's immersion. If this was Faulkner's point, it was made too subtly, both for the editors who rejected the story in the late 1920s and early 1930s and for the readers who have puzzled briefly over the story since. But, as in his other deliberately ambiguous treatments of death—Skei calls this Faulkner's "open ending"[36]—Faulkner suggests in "The Leg" that knowledge of the possibility of death is just as existentially disturbing as the actuality.

Those who would insist on a definitive answer to the question what *really* happens to Davy or to George are asking an unanswerable question. There are three explanations of "The Leg." The first or "natural" explanation is that George is rescued from the Thames, only to be killed in the war, and these two incidents form the constituent elements of Davy's delirious fantasies after his wounding and amputation. The "natural" explanation leaves unexplained the events culminating in Everbe Corinthia's death. The second explanation is "supernatural" and centers on the supposition that Davy's double or the ghost of his amputated leg pursues and ravishes Everbe Corinthia. The reading I am suggesting here represents, I believe, a psychological middle ground between the natural and supernatural explanations, a place where a reader of "The Leg" can stand with tentative confidence, even though the narrator of the story is quite clearly "beyond."

Simultaneous or consecutive presentation of natural, psychological, and supernatural interpretations of a fictional event without the presentation of an absolute authorial choice among them is by no means unique within the American tradition. It was well-established by Hawthorne in "Young Goodman Brown" and *The Scarlet Letter* among other places, it was rather baldly followed by Hemingway in "The Short Happy Life of Francis Macomber," and it continues today in the fiction of John Barth and Thomas Pynchon. Pynchon puts the question succinctly in *Gravity's Rainbow:* "Is the baby smiling, or is it just gas? Which do you want it to be?"[37] Critics too often insist, I would suggest, that a Faulkner story be one thing or another, when Faulkner throughout his career went to a good deal of trouble to show us

---

36. *William Faulkner: The Short Story Career,* 66.
37. Thomas Pynchon, *Gravity's Rainbow* (New York: Viking, 1973), 131.

that the events and meanings of his stories are multiple and problematic, rather than reducible to some formulaic certainty.

At the risk of seeming to offer a formulaic reduction of my own, I want now to sketch a Faulkner formula that occurs repeatedly in his short fiction and his novels. As I suggested earlier, I believe that interest in the poetics of Faulkner's short story collections has sometimes led us to neglect the poetics of individual Faulkner short stories. Faulkner himself said that his stories often began with an image or picture in his mind, or with a situation or character, but always with the aim of rendering "some moving passionate moment of the human condition distilled to its absolute essence."[38] While this general formulation is useful and important, it does not help us to identify the source of the *substance* of Faulkner's fiction, and so, for a portion of that substance, I wish to call attention to a character type that occurs almost ubiquitously within the Faulkner canon, particularly in his comic and humorous fiction, and most particularly in his short stories.

The character is the trickster, by which I mean any individual who practices deceit for personal gain. In the trickster Faulkner had ready to hand a character, a situation, and a vehicle for plot development from the beginning to the end of his career. The Faulkner trickster is at once a generalized type and a very particular individual, and probably owes something to a variety of sources. His Indian and black tricksters—Ikkemotubbe and Crawford in "A Justice," Lucas Beauchamp in "A Point of Law" and "Gold Is Not Always," for example—have close affinities with clearly identifiable character types within their respective ethnic traditions, but Faulkner's knowledge of the trickster figure undoubtedly owes something to other sources, Mark Twain and the Southwestern humorists, Shakespeare, Cervantes, and the Greek drama, to name some of the most likely.

38. *Faulkner in the University: Class Conferences at the University of Virginia 1957–1958*, ed. Frederick L. Gwynn and Joseph Blotner (New York: Vintage, 1965), 202.

And the variety of possible sources is reflected in the fact that Faulkner himself added substantially to the trickster tradition.

A trickster appears in Faulkner's very first published short story, "Landing in Luck," in the person of Cadet Thompson, a thoroughly dislikable individual who seeks to represent his amazingly fortunate landing as proof of his aeronautical skill. Other early trickster figures appear in "The Liar" and "Sunset" among the New Orleans pieces, though the figures there are not rendered with particular skill or sympathy. But about this time Faulkner also began to write *Father Abraham*, in which, by creating the consummate trickster, Flem Snopes, he opened for himself a rich mine of humor that he never truly exhausted. Flem, we are told in *Father Abraham*, "had reduced all human conduct to a single workable belief: that some men are fools, but all men are no honester than the occasion requires."[39] Flem's success at foisting the untamable ponies on Frenchman's Bend while escaping legal responsibility for the havoc and destruction they wreak there derives from this precept, and the pattern is maintained consistently through the versions of this incident that were recounted in *Father Abraham*, "Spotted Horses," and *The Hamlet*. Flem functions as trickster in unloading the Old Frenchman's place in both "Lizards in Jamshyd's Courtyard" and *The Hamlet*, and Flem's trickster nature is apparent throughout the Snopes trilogy.

A number of other stories that Faulkner eventually adapted for his Snopes saga, such as "Fool About a Horse" and "The Hound," have significant trickster elements, and a large number of Faulkner's short stories develop the plot of the trickster tricked. Where Faulkner's earliest trickster stories describe characters who simply trick others, or who are simply tricked themselves, this later group shows more sophisticated development and comic reversals, as when Pap in "Fool About a

39. William Faulkner, *Father Abraham*, ed. James B. Meriwether (New York: Red Ozier Press, 1983), 19.

Horse" is gulled by Pat Stamper with a fish hook, a bicycle pump, and some shoe blacking into buying back at a dear price a horse he had traded cheaply away earlier in the day. Surratt's practical joke on Luke Provine in "A Bear Hunt" is compounded by the tricks of Uncle Ash and the Indians so that the result is not only a good scare for Provine, but a sound thrashing for Surratt as well. Ernest Cotton's murderous treachery in "The Hound" is betrayed by his own guilt and ineptitude as well as by the howling of his victim's dog. More complexly comic reversals occur in "Mule in the Yard" and in "Centaur in Brass," two excellent stories that are unusual in that they were included in *Collected Stories,* even though Faulkner already had plans for them in subsequent volumes of the Snopes trilogy.

Trickster figures and plots abound in the stories of *The Unvanquished* as well, with Granny's silver-and-mule business being the most obvious. Granny serves as a trickster also in "Ambuscade" when she saves Bayard and Ringo by hiding them under her skirts. John Sartoris proves himself to be an accomplished trickster by capturing sixty Yankees virtually without assistance and by escaping from the Yankees himself by pretending to be lame, hard-of-hearing, and dull-witted. And Granny's death at the hands of Grumby is, among other things, the result of her own overreaching as a trickster.

Faulkner also wrote trickster stories in the latter portion of his career, as evidenced by "Shingles for the Lord," "A Courtship," *Notes on a Horsethief,* "Hog Pawn," and "By the People." In several of these later stories he developed a theme that was also sounded in the later novels: that the respectable community must occasionally resort to trickery to overcome threats from within or without. This is particularly evident in a story like "By the People," when Ratliff thwarts Clarence Snopes, but it had also been demonstrated by the supposedly bumbling Gavin Stevens as early as 1932 in "Smoke."

Such variations on the trickster character, subject, and theme suggest, I hope, the incredible variety of Faulkner's short fiction. Some of his tricksters are successful, some are unsuccessful. Some trick themselves, and some are tricked by others in turn. Some of them are essentially harmless, some are dangerous, and some are even murderous. Some are subversive and some are reputable. Trickster characters and situations appear in Faulkner's apprentice fiction, in short stories that he reworked for novels, and in stories that continue to stand splendidly in their own right. I do not mean to suggest that the trickster is the essential figure in Faulkner's humor, for it is simply one of a number of elements of his humor, but I would insist that Faulkner's tricksters can be examined in extensive variety and in careful isolation within the texts of his short stories.

The same must also be said for many of the other more or less traditional topics of Faulkner studies: Faulkner's attitudes towards women or towards blacks, the Civil War, World War I, aviation, Christianity, literature, marriage, love and death, his use of point-of-view, his handling of narrative chronology, his characteristic settings in place and time, his prose style. In addition, some other possible areas for future study seem to be unique to the short stories. We need, I think, to know a good deal more than we currently do about Faulkner's reading within the short story form, both classics and contemporaries, and we would benefit particularly from more detailed knowledge of Faulkner's reading of such writers as Poe, Hawthorne, Henry James, Joyce, and Hemingway, to list some of the obvious possibilities. We need guides to the short stories as detailed and comprehensive as the various guides to his novels. And I have little doubt that these things will be accomplished, if we can cease viewing the short stories as "lesser Faulkner," or the key to the solution of some other problems. Given proper attention, Faulkner's short stories reveal of their author what Faulkner himself wrote of the autobiographical character in the story fragment from which I have taken my title: "There was a giant in him. . . ."[40]

40. William Faulkner, "And Now What's to Do," ed. James B. Meriwether, *Mississippi Quarterly*, 26 (1973), 400.

"But Damn Letters Anyway":
Letters and Fictions

JAMES G. WATSON

No sort of writing is more revealing of its author than the personal letter. Each one is a fragment of autobiography. The self revealed in a letter is a self contemplated, a studied epistolary image that the writer presents as himself to his correspondent of the moment. Whether the Sender of a letter consciously portrays himself to the Receiver or not, the interests he inclines to, the ideas and theories he expounds, and especially the everyday details of his life as he selects and arranges them into expressive forms betray him in the guises he assumes. In this sense, at least, each letter is also a fiction, one that is governed, however, by generic conventions of its own that we are still coming to understand. My concern is with three of these as they are revealed in Faulkner's personal correspondence and employed in the letters in his fictions. The conventions include, first, the letter as a self-portrayal, a reflexive fiction of the self of the writer; second, the often very personal nature of the self so portrayed in letters, as indicated by the privacy normally accorded personal correspondence; and, third, the accordant power of the personal letter to express, and in some circumstances to substitute for, the writer's actual self. Important related issues to these include the relationship between Sender and Receiver; the form of the letter, whether a personal or a formal communication, hand-written or typed; and the means of delivery.[1] My title, taken from a fragment of an undated letter to Helen Baird, partly typed and partly in script, signed "Bill," is meant to suggest that like others of his written texts, Faulkner's letters are often complex and enigmatic, charged with an intensity of feeling that is nonetheless distanced by his having written it, and suggestive for Sender and Receiver alike of the rare and frustrating relation of the man to the man writing. "I remember a sullen-jawed yellow-eyed belligerent humorless gal in a linen dress and sunburned bare legs sitting on Spratling's balcony and not thinking even a hell of a little bit of me that afternoon, maybe already decided not to," Faulkner wrote to Helen. "But damn letters anyway."[2]

William Faulkner's letters were certainly never intended for publication. He was a very private man, to begin with, who claimed to despise letters, and he wrote relatively fewer of them than many of his literary contemporaries. It is one of the clearest indications of the power and value of personal letters, however, that they are kept. Receivers are archivists. There are several hundred letters and letter fragments in the collection selected and edited by Joseph Blotner; more still are transcribed or alluded to in Blotner's *Faulkner: A Biography,* Malcolm Cowley's *The Faulkner-Cowley File,* Malcolm Franklin's *Bitterweeds,* and

---

1. A number of works have assisted my thinking about letters and fictions, including Janet Gurkin Altman, *Epistolarity: Approaches to a Form* (Columbus: Ohio State University Press, 1982); Peggy Kamuf, *Fictions of Feminine Desire: Disclosures of Heloise* (Lincoln: University of Nebraska Press, 1982); Ruth Perry, *Women, Letters, and the Novel* (New York: AMS Press, 1980); Jacques Lacan, "Seminar on 'The Purloined Letter,'" *Yale French Studies,* 48 (1972), 38–72; Jacques Derrida, "The Purveyor of Truth," *Yale French Studies,* 52 (1975), 31–113. I am grateful particularly to the work of my colleagues, Shari Benstock, "The Printed Letters in *Ulysses," James Joyce Quarterly,* 19 (Spring 1982), 415–28; Bernard Duyfhuizen, "Epistolary Narratives of Transmission and Transgression," *Comparative Literature* (forthcoming); Joseph Kestner, "The *Letters* of Jane Austen: The Writer as *Émetteur/Récepteur," Papers on Language and Literature,* 14 (1978), 249–69; and Thomas F. Staley, "Compositions of Self: Portraits of Joyce in His Early Letters," forthcoming in a volume of commemorative essays edited by Staley and Hugh Kenner (University of California Press).

2. Item 148, *William Faulkner: The William B. Wisdom Collection in the Howard-Tilton Memorial Library, Tulane University,* comp. Thomas Bonner, Jr. (New Orleans: Tulane University Libraries, 1980). The fragment of Faulkner's letter is quoted by Bonner in his "Introduction," 4.

Meta Carpenter Wilde's *A Loving Gentleman*. The several volumes of *A Comprehensive Guide to the Brodsky Collection*, now in publication, will contain hundreds more.[3] This canon reveals that from the first Faulkner was an accomplished and enthusiastic letter writer, skilled in the creation of epistolary personae and disguises. His first extended body of correspondence, consisting of letters written from Europe in the autumn of 1925, provides cogent examples. In *Selected Letters of William Faulkner* Blotner includes six postcards and twenty letters written in just over the first two months of Faulkner's four-month stay. Of these, nineteen are addressed to his mother, although they must have been written with the understanding, even the intention, that his father would read them too. Faulkner's immediate model for this correspondence was his great-grandfather, Col. W. C. Falkner, whose own travel letters were published in 1884 as *Rapid Ramblings in Europe*, but the devices and strategies were necessarily his own. As Sender he adapted quickly to his various Receivers, both those addressed and those implied. To his mother he portrayed himself as an aspiring artist, serious about experiencing Europe rather than "doing" it as a tourist, and his letters to her address her literary and painterly interests. He wrote her about Cezanne, Matisse, and Picasso, the Castle of Chillon, and a story he had written "about the Luxembourg Gardens and death" that he said was "poetry though written in prose form."[4] According to these letters he drank wine when the occasion demanded but left whiskey to the beefy-faced Scots. He was never drunk in letters to

3. Joseph Blotner, ed., *Selected Letters of William Faulkner* (New York: Random House, 1977); Joseph Blotner, *Faulkner: A Biography* (New York: Random House, 1974); Malcolm Cowley, *The Faulkner-Cowley File: Letters and Memories, 1944–1962* (New York: Viking, 1966); Malcolm Franklin, *Bitterweeds: Life with William Faulkner at Rowan Oak* (Irving, Texas: Society for the Study of Traditional Culture, 1977); Meta Carpenter Wilde and Orin Borsten, *A Loving Gentleman: The Love Story of William Faulkner and Meta Carpenter* (New York: Jove/HBJ, 1977); Louis Daniel Brodsky and Robert W. Hamblin, *Faulkner: A Comprehensive Guide to the Brodsky Collection*, vol. II (Jackson: University Press of Mississippi, 1982, 1984).

4. "To Mrs. M. C. Falkner," [postmarked 6 September 1925], in *Selected Letters of William Faulkner*, 17. Hereafter cited in my notes as *SL*.

his mother, who disliked alcohol. Like most correspondents he was concerned when he suspected that his letters were not being promptly delivered, and he asked Maud Falkner to imagine him writing to her, as he said he did, every Wednesday and Sunday, whether his letters arrived regularly or not. "I can always tell how you feel by your letters," he wrote early in September, and to help her know how he felt, and looked, he drew himself in his new beard in a postscript.[5] The long, detailed letters to his mother are in contrast to a postcard showing a mounted hunt at Chantilly that he sent his father at this period. Here the Sender addressed himself to a different Receiver who, as he well knew, would be interested in red-coated hunters, "the best-looking horses you ever saw," and barrooms "full of bow-legged cockney grooms and jockeys."[6] A second postcard from Chantilly, to his eighteen-year-old brother Dean, describes the hunt but omits the bars.[7]

In 1925 Murry Falkner still was not reconciled to his son's artistic aspirations and pretensions, and if Faulkner seldom wrote directly to him it was perhaps because he suspected that his father would not answer.[8] Yet he clearly needed his father as a Receiver, even if an implied one, for the epistolary image of himself that he was constructing. For Murry's sake as well as for Maud's, Faulkner modulated his adventures with traveling companions such as Bill Spratling in his letters home and emphasized the stable virtues of a Southern aristocrat with simple tastes. For his father, he kept close track of expenses, detailing the cost of his rooms, his dinner, his pipe tobacco, his coat, a bus tour, and a museum ticket. His letters are filled with references to austerity. In Paris in mid-August he was eating at "a restaurant

5. "To Mrs. M. C. Falkner," 2 September 1925; *SL*, 17. The drawing is reproduced in *Faulkner: A Biography*, I, 461.

6. "To Mr. M. C. Falkner," 29 September 1925; *SL*, 26.

7. "To Mr. Dean Falkner," [postmarked 30 September 1925]; *SL*, 27.

8. Faulkner's European correspondence with his mother and father is treated briefly in David Minter, *William Faulkner: His Life and Work* (Baltimore: Johns Hopkins University Press, 1980), 16, 33.

where cabmen and janitors eat."[9] "Country folks are my sort, anyway," he wrote. "So I am going to move next week. I think that I can live cheaper than $1.50 per day."[10] To his mother he spoke of writing "some travel things,"[11] and he tried them out in his letters. The artist he depicted to her no doubt owes some of his "country" ways to the fictional artist taking shape simultaneously in Faulkner's novel "Elmer," for which he was likewise the self-conscious model. On 13 August 1925, he wrote to Maud about his week in Switzerland, describing himself as a type of Tolstoy's Konstantin Levine going to the harvest fields above Lake Maggiore with his peasantry. "I was there 4 days," he wrote, "going out with them to cut grass on the mountains, for hay, eating bread and cheese and wine at noon, coming home in the evening bringing the hay on mules while bells rang from the churches all about the mountains. . . . The day I left the whole village told me goodbye."[12] A letter to his aunt, Mrs. Walter B. McLean, maintains the romantic literary tone of this report but modifies the facts. In that letter the bells are on the mules, not in the churches, "the churches all about the mountains" become "a faded shrine with a poor little bunch of flowers in it," and the communal farewell at dawn is cast as an evening meal, complete with the significant additional detail that he had been "mildly drunk" talking with "those kind quiet happy people by signs."[13] As his imagination took hold of his material, one letter became the draft for another, and his epistolary guises sometimes merged with those actual personae he had adapted for other occasions. A letter in October that sounds suspiciously like his stories of rum-running in New Orleans contains an account of working for two days hauling nets aboard a Breton fishing boat. There he tasted shark for the first time, he told his mother, and he added, "It was cold, cold! Hands raw all the time."[14]

9. "To Mrs. M. C. Falkner," Sunday 16 August 1925; SL, 12.
10. Ibid.
11. "To Mrs. M. C. Falkner," Thursday 13 [August] 192[5]; SL, 11.
12. Ibid., 10.
13. Quoted in Faulkner: A Biography, I, 449.
14. "To Mrs. M. C. Falkner," 15 October 1925; SL, 31.

Such self-characterizations exhibit Faulkner's need to verify the persona he was constructing by writing it.[15] His inventions, if inventions they altogether were, were no doubt carried forward when he returned to Oxford, where they were enhanced by his English tweeds, his beard, and the William C. Odiorne photographs of him in Paris, staring across the Luxembourg Gardens with pipe in hand. In his correspondence he continued to resort to such guises and disguises as the need arose. It was Faulkner the Southern aristocrat who told Horace Liveright in February 1927, "I envy you England. England is 'ome to me, in a way."[16] But writing in the same month to William Stanley Braithwaite about a royalty due him for *The Marble Faun* he was again the provincial country poet, appealing for fair play to the Eastern literary establishment. "It never occurred to me," he told the famous poet-anthologist, "that anyone would rob a poet. It's like robbing a whore or a child."[17] The child was then nearly thirty years old. A quarter of a century later, in a letter to Joan Williams, he adopted the same provincial persona to point up the contrast between himself and his work. Describing himself as "uneducated in every formal sense, without even very literate, let alone literary, companions," he asked, "I wonder if you have ever had that thought about the work and the country man whom you know as Bill Faulkner—what little connection there seems to be between them."[18] Far from the detached inventions of a knowing ironist, the reality for Faulkner of this and his other personae is verified by his continual reaffirmation of them in his personal letters where, of necessity, the self and the word are one.

Whether stimulated by his European correspondence or not, letters and fictions combined almost immediately, and for the first time in Faulkner's work, when he returned to Oxford in

15. Minter speculates in this regard that "the creation of a persona was, among other things, an imaginative rehearsal" for fictions; *Faulkner: His Life and Work*, 33.
16. "To Horace Liveright," 18 February 1927; *SL*, 34.
17. "To William Stanley Braithwaite," [February 1927]; *SL*, 35.
18. "To Joan Williams," Wednesday [29 April 1953]; *SL*, 348.

December of 1925. The gift-book *Mayday*, dated 27 January 1926, is a courtship letter to Helen Baird in the form of an allegorical story, hand-inscribed and hand-illustrated, with a courtly knight as persona of the Sender, and addressed "to thee/ O wise and lovely." In the tradition of courtly love, *Mayday* is self-consciously literary and the narrator-Sender is fully aware that his visionary lover is unattainable except in visions or in death.[19] By June 1926, when Helen was abroad, a second such letter-book was in preparation, this the sonnet sequence he called *Helen: A Courtship*, the poems dated from Pascagoula the previous summer and from the sites of Faulkner's own trip later that year. Like the love letters they were no doubt intended to be, several of these address Helen passionately and directly, and again sexual love is envisioned in the context of dreams. Poem X, dated "Pavia—August—1925," concludes, "So you no virgin are, my sweet unchaste:/Why, I've lain lonely nights and nights with you."[20] The writing substitutes for love-making as the poem does, in this case, for the lover. The next year parodies of love letters, whether his own or others', were written into *Flags in the Dust*, where the poetically named Byron Snopes composes ungrammatical letters to Narcissa and Horace sends her one floridly poetic one.

Given these experiments with epistolary forms, and the provocative body of his own correspondence, it is hardly surprising that the real and imagined materials of Faulkner's letters sometimes crossed generic lines to become the stuff of letters in fictions. *Mosquitoes*, for example, incorporates parts of the comic "Al Jackson Letters" Faulkner had traded with Sherwood Anderson in New Orleans two years before. Sometimes the debt

---

19. William Faulkner, *Mayday* (Notre Dame: University of Notre Dame Press, 1978), 45. For a discussion of courtly love and Faulkner's self-depiction in *Mayday* see Carvel Collins's "Introduction" and James G. Watson, "Literary Self-Criticism: Faulkner in Fiction on Fiction," *Southern Quarterly*, 20 (1981), 46–63.

20. William Faulkner, *Helen: A Courtship* in *Helen: A Courtship and Mississippi Poems* (New Orleans: Tulane University, and Oxford, Mississippi: Yoknapatawpha Press, 1981), 121.

is more personal, and more telling. In a funny, self-assured letter to Horace Liveright written in July 1927, when he was working on *Flags in the Dust,* Faulkner explained his having drawn a $200 draft on Liveright's bank as "a case of dire necessity." Piling one misfortune on another, he told his publisher that he had, in fact, lost $300 gambling in Memphis but would not have drawn even the $200 draft except that the alcohol he had buried in his garden against such emergencies had been smelled out and dug up by "one of our niggers," who had sold a little, been caught, and so lost the rest. Set upon by Chance and Circumstance, he had "turned to" Liveright only because "what with the flood last spring, southern people have no cash money for gambling debts." It was, he admitted, "quite a yarn."[21] This is Faulkner at his most confident as Novelist—so confident, in fact, that he was calling his bookish antihero with the "air of fine and delicate futility"[22] by his publisher's given name, Horace. In November, Liveright rejected *Flags in the Dust.* Faulkner's work had been deteriorating, he said; the present manuscript was too diffuse and unplotted even to be called a novel.[23] Liveright's letter rejected the Novelist's persona as well as his novel and brought to an abrupt end Faulkner's self-confident tone and easy tale-telling in their correspondence. He used a significantly epistolary image to describe the change when he wrote, in 1933, that "it suddenly seemed as if a door had clapped silently and forever to between me and all publishers' addresses and booklists and I said to myself, Now I can write. Now I can just write."[24] He retained the details of his "yarn," however, and the letterly context, to portray Jason's destruction at the hands of his own Chance and Circumstance in *The Sound and the Fury,* the novel begun immediately after *Flags.* Like Faulkner in his epistolary

21. "To Horace Liveright," [late July 1927]; *SL,* 37.
22. William Faulkner, *Flags in the Dust* (New York: Random House, 1973), 145.
23. *Faulkner: A Biography,* I, 259–60.
24. William Faulkner, "An Introduction to *The Sound and the Fury,*" in *A Faulkner Miscellany,* ed. James B. Meriwether (Jackson: University Press of Mississippi, 1974), 158–59.

relationship with Liveright, Jason is betrayed by telegrams from "one of the biggest manipulators in New York,"[25] loses the same $200 gambling when the cotton market closes forty points down (SF, 303), and blames his lack of ready cash on the same flood (SF, 292). His injuries are compounded by Uncle Maury's drawing a draft on the bank account he administers for his mother. Like Faulkner's letters, the fictional telegrams Jason sends on April 6, 1928, and the letters he receives from Caddy, Lorraine, and Uncle Maury are elements of an epistolary dialogue in which Sender and Receiver must cooperate to define themselves in terms of each other. Identity is crucially at issue in the epistolary situation, but the evidence of Jason's correspondence is of incompleteness, even anonymity. As if he were a postal clerk—a job Faulkner had and hated in 1922—Jason's letters contain messages for other people, checks made out in others' names, and baleful misaddresses such as Lorraine's "Dear daddy" (SF, 240). His telegram to Caddy is a cryptic lie; his final one to his broker in New York openly confesses the provinciality he has been trying to conceal by having a broker in the first place. "Buy," he writes. "Market just on point of blowing its head off. Occasional flurries for purposes of hooking a few more country suckers who haven't got in to the telegraph office yet. Do not be alarmed" (SF, 304–5). Because the market is closed, even this letter is undeliverable.

These are not isolated letters. In *The Sound and the Fury* alone there are seventeen of them. Ten are transcribed, including Jason's letters and telegrams, the Compson wedding announcement, and Quentin's imaginary letter to Mrs. Bland. Her unread invitation to him is untranscribed, as are his letters to Deacon and Shreve, Uncle Maury's two to Mrs. Patterson, and one that Mrs. Compson says she has written to Caddy. Quentin's letter to his father on June 2, 1910, is literally unwritten in that

25. William Faulkner, *The Sound and the Fury* (1929; rpt. New York: Modern Library, 1967), 238. Hereafter cited in my text as *SF*.

it contains only the symbolic key to his trunk of clothes and books. These letters and the delays, misdirections, and interceptions to which they are subject portray characters, move the plots of the novel, and convey the themes of failed communication and broken identity proposed by the sound and fury in the title. Sometimes what letters actually say is less significant for Sender and Receiver than what they do. In *Light in August*, for example, Joe is bound to Joanna "just as tightly by [a] small square of still undivulging paper as though it were a lock and chain."[26] If he is the abstraction of "Negro" to her, she is the image of her written word to him: as prisoner of her letters, Joe responds erotically to those "evocative of unspoken promise, of rich and unmentionable delights," then murderously to the final ones "briefer than epitaphs and more terse than commands" (*LIA*, 263). Often, too, a letter signifies merely by existing as a physical object. In the essentially epistolary relationship between the lovers in *Absalom, Absalom!*, where they meet only twice, Judith's last letter from Charles Bon proves his existence. She gives it to Grandmother Compson, she says, "just because it would have happened, be remembered even if only from passing from one hand to another, one mind to another."[27] Judith here anticipates by two decades Faulkner's statement in the "Foreword" to *The Faulkner Reader* that "he who, from the isolation of cold impersonal print, can engender this excitement, himself partakes of the immortality which he has engendered"[28]—but with this qualification, that in *Absalom, Absalom!* Bon's letter partakes less of passion than of his actual physical appearance. The letter writer whom Mr. Compson calls

26. William Faulkner, *Light in August* (1932; rpt. New York: Modern Library, 1967), 257. Hereafter cited in my text as *LIA*.

27. William Faulkner, *Absalom, Absalom!* (1936; rpt. New York: Modern Library, 1966), 127. Hereafter cited in my text as *AA*.

28. William Faulkner, "Foreword to *The Faulkner Reader*," rpt. in *Essays, Speeches, and Public Letters by William Faulkner*, ed. James B. Meriwether (New York: Random House, 1965), 182.

"shadowy, almost substanceless" (*AA*, 93) is present in his text, where Quentin sees and hears him as he reads the letter:

> the faint spidery script not like something impressed upon the paper by a once-living hand but like a shadow cast upon it which had resolved on the paper the instant before he looked at it and which might fade, vanish, at any instant while he still read: the dead tongue speaking after the four years and then after almost fifty more, gentle sardonic whimsical and incurably pessimistic, without date or salutation or signature. (*AA*, 129)

At the end of the novel Mr. Compson is similarly shadowed forth from his letter announcing the death of Rosa Coldfield by his "sloped whimsical ironic hand out of Mississippi attenuated" (*AA*, 377).

That Bon appears to Quentin across time in his letter, and Mr. Compson across space in his, implies an important corollary to the convention of letterly self-portrayal: letters are generated and correspondence is sustained by separations which the letter attempts to overcome. Handwritten letters make possible particularly close contact between Sender and Receiver: Mr. Compson's letter, for example, puts his own "sloped whimsical ironic hand" directly into Quentin's hands. The greater the power of the Sender to evoke himself in his text, the closer the contact: in the case of erotic letters, the written text temporarily substitutes for the absent lover and is cherished by the beloved accordingly. Bon's last letter to Judith is "gentle sardonic whimsical" rather than erotic—she has destroyed his love letters—and even his motive for declaring "*We have waited long enough*" (*AA*, 131) is suspect in terms of love for her. Nonetheless, by announcing an end to separation, Bon effectively announces an end to the four-year correspondence in which, for Judith, he almost exclusively exists. The lover she cherishes is the shadow in his letters, and when Henry shoots him at the Sutpen gate before he can deliver himself to her, he dooms them both—Bon to shadowhood and Judith to the anomalies of unwed wife, verifying her symbolic widowhood by sharing her lover's letter with strangers. The exigencies of this paradoxical conflux are primal in Faulkner's imagined world as they are also in the long tradition of epistolary fiction from which the modern novel arose. Ruth Perry points out in her study of the eighteenth-century letter novel that the only conclusions possible to epistolary love affairs are sex, the presumable object of love letters, and death—two elements of Faulkner's fiction that are bound inextricably together. Perry says, "These alternatives . . . make sense within the paradigm of the letter novel, for either one puts a stop to the letter writing and resolves the separation which the characters spend their fictional lives trying to overcome. . . . Where sex is the reward for those with fixed characters of the right sort, death is the just desert for those who are flawed."[29] *Absalom, Absalom!* is not *Clarissa,* but the convention holds. It holds, as well, in the two outcomes of Joanna's correspondence with Joe Christmas, and echoes in Quentin's imagining that his sister's wedding announcement is a coffin, "*a candle burning at each corner upon the envelope tied in a soiled pink garter two artificial flowers*" (*SF,* 115). And it holds, finally, in the most passionately erotic epistolary situation in Faulkner's fiction—in *Requiem for a Nun*—where Temple Drake's lover, Red, summoned to Miss Reba's by Temple's letters, is shot at the moment, as Temple says, "when all of him except just his body was already in the room with me and the door locked at last for just the two of us alone."[30] Not coincidentally, I think that phrasing is perfectly descriptive of the situation of a reader of love letters and wonderfully expressive of the intensity of erotic substitution love letters have power to achieve.

The untranscribed, misdirected, read and unread, purloined, misused, and tragic love letters of Temple Drake to Alabama Red are surely the most mysterious and enigmatic personal documents in all of Faulkner's fiction. The situation, as Temple explains it to the Governor in Act II, Scene i of *Requiem,* is this:

29. *Women, Letters, and the Novel,* 95–96.
30. William Faulkner, *Requiem for a Nun* (1951; rpt. New York: Vintage, 1975), 132. Hereafter cited in my text as *RN.*

> I wrote some letters that you would have thought that even Temple
> Drake might have been ashamed to put on paper, and then the man
> I wrote them to died, and I married another man and reformed, or
> thought I had, and bore two children and hired another reformed
> whore so that I would have somebody to talk to, and I even thought
> I had forgotton about the letters until they turned up again and then
> I found out that I not only hadn't forgot about the letters, I hadn't
> even reformed. (*RN*, 131)

We do not know what Temple Drake wrote to Red. Gavin,
Gowan, and the Governor never read his letters, Popeye according to Gavin cannot read them at all, being illiterate, and Red's
brother Pete, who does read them, returns them without reporting what they say. It is Nancy's opinion that, whatever is in the
letters, "It was already there in whoever could write the kind of
letters that even eight years afterward could still make grief and
ruin. The letters never did matter" (*RN*, 159). Again according to
Gavin, Nancy "cant read or write either" (*RN*, 103), but she may
know part of the truth, being as she is a dark image of Temple.
Temple herself says, "I met the man, how doesn't matter, and I
fell what I called in love with him and what it was or what I
called it doesn't matter either because all that matters is that I
wrote the letters" (*RN*, 127).

If we do not know what Temple wrote, what she wrote about
and how she wrote it are implicit in the way she describes her
letters. She says she knew the "right words. Though all you
would have needed probably would be an old dictionary from
back in Shakespeare's time when, so they say, people hadn't
learned how to blush at words. That is, anybody except Temple
Drake, who didn't need a dictionary, who was a fast learner and
so even just one lesson would have been enough for her" (*RN*,
130). The "right words" produce what she repeatedly calls "good
letters": obscene, of course, but shards of emotionally charged
autobiography for all of that, designedly confessional and totally
unrestrained, transcriptions truer than flesh. Written in the
aftermath of love-making with Red, and "two or three when it
would be two or three days between" (*RN*, 128), the letters

contain sentiments the more intimate in that they can never be
spoken, Popeye being always present. They are generated by
separation, fueled by isolation, and they substitute literally for
the physical image of Temple displayed in "the two-foot glass
with nobody to be disturbed even by the . . . pants, or even no
pants. Good letters—" (RN, 128). The "good" image in the letters is contradistinguished from her several other self-images:
from "Temple Drake, the foolish virgin" (RN, 113), and especially, being "good letters," from the Temple Drake who "liked
evil" (RN, 117). Faulkner apparently meant to portray the otherwise inexpressible self of her letters by such inversions, and it
may be, given his modernist fondness for literary allusion and
Temple's insistence on Shakespeare's words, that in this half-
play, half-novel of multiple mirrorings there is literary precedent for her letter writing. My candidate is *King Lear*, where
Lear's daughter Goneril, herself the alter-aspect of good Cor-
delia, writes a love letter to Edmund proposing adultery and
murder that perfectly mirrors her evil nature. "If your will want
not," she writes in Act IV, Scene vi, punning on the word *will*
(lust), "time and place will be fruitfully offered" for Edmund to
kill her husband, Albany, and bed his wife. Should Albany survive her murderous design, the sexual design will fail as well:
"Then am I the prisoner," she tells her lover, "and his bed my
jail, from the loathed warmth whereof deliver me, and supply
the place for your labor." Edmund's half-brother Edgar inter-
cepts this "post unsanctified/Of murderous lechers" and delivers
it, and the lovers, into Albany's hands. The letters at the center
of each work bring into focus both the parallels to *King Lear* and
the inversions in Faulkner's novel. Temple is, in fact, a prisoner
in Popeye's bed, delivered periodically from its "loathed
warmth" by Red, who takes Popeye's "place" and supplies his
"labor." Temple's letters likewise come into the possession of her
lover's brother, Pete, who threatens, as Edgar does, to show
them to her husband. Consistent with epistolary love affairs,
both erotic correspondences propose an end to separation in
sex, and both end ironically in deaths. But Temple is the victim

of Popeye's evil, Goneril the agent of her own and Edmund's. Temple's letters are ignored; Goneril's return to convict her. When Albany confronts the "murderous lechers" in *Lear*, Act V, Scene iii, he threatens to put Goneril's written words back into her mouth, then delivers her misdirected letter himself, not as an erotic invitation now but as Edmund's death warrant. "Shut your mouth," he orders his wife, "Or with this paper I shall stop it. Hold, sir,/Thou worse than any name, read thine own evil."

Why Temple writes letters in *Requiem for a Nun* is still another matter, one that depends on another context. Recall that in *Sanctuary* there are no love letters. In *Flags in the Dust*, it is true, Byron Snopes writes letters that Narcissa finds exciting enough to hide among her underwear, and in the story "There Was a Queen" she submits to sexual blackmail to get them back. There are other connections between the two books, and it may be that the Snopes letters in *Flags* inspired Temple's in *Requiem*. But *Sanctuary* is its closer companion text, and in *Sanctuary* the letters that move the plot of *Requiem* from blackmail to the murder of Temple's child and the execution of Nancy Mannigoe are missing. Instead of writing her erotic imaginings into letters, Temple hurls herself on Red at a roadhouse, "her mouth gaped and ugly like that of a dying fish as she writhed her loins against him."[31] Faulkner wrote *Sanctuary* in 1929, revised and published it in 1931, and by 1933 had started on a book "about a nigger woman" that he was calling "Requiem for a Nun."[32] When he returned to *Requiem* in 1949, he was deeply involved in an erotic correspondence of his own. By the time the novel was well begun he was engaged in another, and a third would follow

31. William Faulkner, *Sanctuary* (1931; rpt. New York: Vintage, 1967), 232. Hereafter cited in my text as S.

32. "To Harrison Smith," something October [1933]; *SL*, 75. Cogent commentaries on the composition of *Requiem for a Nun* are Michael Millgate, *The Achievement of William Faulkner* (New York: Random House, 1966), 221–26, and Noel Polk, *Faulkner's "Requiem for a Nun": A Critical Study* (Bloomington: Indiana University Press, 1981), 237–45. Polk's book is the fullest, and wisest, treatment of the novel and its place in the canon, and I am indebted to his insights and judgments in a number of ways. Neither Polk nor Millgate treats Temple's letters extensively, however.

in 1954. This correspondence is the second, personal, epistolary context of Temple's letters.

In a 1981 interview with Meta Carpenter Wilde, Panthea Broughton notes that her relationship with William Faulkner "was characterized more by separation than by togetherness,"[33] and Broughton's chronology of the relationship makes clear what Ms. Wilde's book, A Loving Gentleman, implies—that after 1935–1936, when Faulkner and Meta Carpenter were first together in Hollywood, their love affair was maintained largely by letter. Ms. Wilde told Professor Broughton that Faulkner revealed himself openly in his letters to her. "Thinking back," she said, "he could envision the romantic scenes we had together and out of that would come the memories that would help him put other things in writing. He really could write love letters."[34] The method she describes is the same that produces Temple's "good letters" in the aftermath of love-making with Red, and what Temple implies about hers is confirmed by the sexually explicit passages of Faulkner's in the fragments quoted in A Loving Gentleman. Author and character are writing within the same epistolary convention. Faulkner portrayed himself to Meta in what Temple calls the "right words," and he illustrated his letters with erotic drawings as he had illustrated Mayday with idealized knights and ladies for Helen Baird. Throughout, the portrayed self is designedly substitute for the man, his words for the deeds of love. He wrote, "I want to put words into your hands and into your heart both,"[35] and Meta says that she knew he loved her "by looks, by touch, by the poems and the letters, only seldom by what he said to me."[36] A fragment apparently from the early 1940s reads, "I weigh 129 pounds and I want to put it all on you and as much in you as I can can can must must will will shall."[37] Such letters were clearly physical experi-

33. Panthea Reid Broughton, "An Interview with Meta Carpenter Wilde," Southern Review, 18 (October 1982), 801.

34. Ibid., 787.

35. Quoted in A Loving Gentleman, 166.

36. A Loving Gentleman, 248.

37. Quoted in A Loving Gentleman, 264.

ences for the Receiver. "A Faulkner letter," Meta says, "made me shut myself off from everyone and allow images of our days together to cut like flung golden disks across my mind. . . . I would go to bed early, sometimes without food, and think on Bill happily, as a novitiate on her lord."[38] Another "novitiate"—the word has tempting overtones of the title *Requiem for a Nun*—to whom Faulkner was writing by 1949 was the young novice writer Joan Williams. Meta remembers that "the idealization of me as a girl far too young for him was to last for a number of years and to appear in some of his letters to me. I never protested and my acceptance of his vision of me as a maiden nourished his fantasy."[39] The same epistolary fantasy is evoked in a 1949 letter Faulkner wrote Joan, who was then a twenty-one-year-old college student. Her questions were the wrong ones to ask in letters, he said. "A woman must ask these of a man while they are lying in bed together . . . when they are lying at peace or at least quiet and maybe on the edge of sleep, so you'll have to wait, even to ask them. You may not find the answers even then; most dont. . . . I'd like to know if you ever do. Maybe you will tell me; that can be a good subject for the last letter you will need to write me."[40] The letter constitutes a veiled erotic scene repeated, in the correspondence with Joan, in several guises. On 29 September 1950, Faulkner sent her a story idea about "a young woman, senior at school, a man of fifty, famous—could be artist, soldier, whatever seems best. . . . she likes him, feels drawn to an understanding, make it wisdom, of her, of people, man, a sympathy for her in particular; maybe he will of a sudden talk of love to her."[41] He was comparing her to Renata in Hemingway's *Across the River and into the Trees,* and himself to her lover, Col. Cantwell. It is worth noting in light of his several subsequent requests that Joan help him "decide what is wrong

38. *A Loving Gentleman,* 117.
39. Ibid., 78.
40. Quoted in *Faulkner: A Biography,* II, 1299.
41. "To Joan Williams," Friday night [29 September 1950]; *SL,* 307. Blotner notes the fact that *Across the River and into the Trees* was published in the same month, 307, ln.

with Temple"[42] that in *Requiem* Temple compares herself to another of Hemingway's young women in love with an older soldier-writer, Maria in *For Whom the Bell Tolls*.

Master-student relationships and letterly situations from his own fictions may have provided materials for his letters to Joan as well. In September 1949, when he began writing to her, he was making final preparations for the publication of *Knight's Gambit*. In the title story of that collection, Gavin Stevens writes innocent love letters to his sixteen year old "betrothed," Melisandre Backus, and passionate ones to his Russian mistress. When the two correspondences are accidentally reversed, the situation of the "cloistered and nunlike maiden"[43] as Receiver is effectively the same as Joan's. As if to emphasize the letterly nature of the story, there is even a copy of *Clarissa* in Gavin's family library. As work on *Requiem* proceeded, there were other confluences. In March 1950, Faulkner wrote Joan, "I tell you again, the play is yours too. . . . I would not have thought of writing one if I hadn't known you";[44] but in a 1952 letter to Harold Ober he said he had promised it to Ruth Ford. "I have known Miss Ford a long time," he told Ober, "admire her rather terrifying determination to be an actress, and wrote this play for her to abet it."[45] There is an air of mixed pleasure and pain in these letters and the relationships behind them, suggestive of the same prohibitions that govern Gavin Stevens's betrothal to Melisandre and his later relationship, in *The Town*, to Linda Snopes. Whatever his actual relationship to Jean Stein in 1954, the then fifty-six-year-old novelist was summoning the same persona when he wrote to Saxe Commins in March about the nineteen-year-old child-woman who "came to me in St. Moritz almost exactly as Joan did in Oxford. But she has none of the emotional conventional confusion which poor Joan had. This one is so uninhibited that she frightens me a little. . . . She doesn't

---

42. Quoted in *Faulkner: A Biography*, II, 1313.

43. William Faulkner, "Knight's Gambit," in *Knight's Gambit* (New York: Random House, 1949), 145.

44. "To Joan Williams," Thursday night [2 March 1950]; *SL*, 300.

45. "To Harold Ober," [received 5 January 1952]; *SL*, 324.

want anything of me—only to love me, be in love. . . . The other affair would have hurt of course, except for this."[46]

From the changed and changing circumstances of Faulkner's life and art, this tangle of real and fictional lovers and their letters produced Temple Drake's letters in *Requiem for a Nun*. And it naturally produced a changed Temple Drake, compounded of the Temple in *Sanctuary*, of course, but of Shakespeare's Goneril and Hemingway's Maria and Renata now, as well, and of Meta Carpenter and Joan Williams and Ruth Ford and the fictions of feminine mystery he had spun from them all in the intervening twenty years since Horace Benbow became obsessed with the secret loves and sexual injuries of Temple and his step-daughter, Little Belle. Gavin's obsession with Temple's past extends this theme from *Sanctuary*, and the historical Prologues to the three acts of *Requiem* extend and expand its contexts. Still, the Temple Drake who tells Gavin and the Governor, "all that matters is that I wrote the letters," is most profoundly revealed—and concealed—by her letters, and it is of the most profound significance that no one except her lover reads them, including even readers of the novel. The self portrayed there is the contemplated, imaginatively fired Self as Word, and to breach that most intimate self, as Ruth Perry has said, "is the most reprehensible invasion of privacy and consciousness. . . . There are overtones of sexual invasion—of mind-rape—in the intercepting or 'violating' of another's words. This equivalence is suggestive for the audience as well since they are reading letters not intended for public consumption."[47] Read in her "good letters" by Red (his name is homonymous with the past tense of the verb *to read*), Temple *is* and is "good." Eight years later Pete succeeds so easily in his blackmail scheme because Temple chooses to protect her letterly image by sacrificing the socially acceptable, "reformed" one projected by her marriage to Gowan. Blackmail, as the word suggests, is a misuse of letters

46. Item 992, *A Comprehensive Guide to the Brodsky Collection*, I; transcribed 206–7.
47. *Women, Letters, and the Novel*, 130–31.

that would *blacken* the image of the Sender and Receiver, and so
Mrs. Gowan Stevens offers herself to Pete "to produce the material for another set of them" (*RN*, 131) consistent with Pete's
misreading of Temple Drake as "Baby" (*RN*, 154). "I'm trying to
tell you about one Temple Drake," she tells the Governor, "and
our Uncle Gavin is showing you another one. So already you've
got two different people begging for the same clemency; if
everybody concerned keeps on splitting up into two people, you
wont even know who to pardon, will you?" (*RN*, 135). Temple's
Temple Drake is no more evil than Caddy Compson, whose true
self Faulkner likewise concealed in a fabric of masculine obsession. More even than Cecilia Farmer's name on the jailhouse
window, Temple's letters from the prisoning confines of Miss
Reba's brothel represent her own statement, *"Listen, stranger;
this was myself: this was I"* (*RN*, 225).

Temple's appeal to her letters as the true transcriptions of an
otherwise fragmented, contradictory, and inexpressible identity
is fully consistent with her subject matter and her method, and
it suggests a final, deep-running source for her love letters and
for Faulkner's. Writing early in the twelfth century to the Abbot
of St. Gildas Abbey in Brittany, the Abbess of the convent of the
Paraclete found it equally difficult to determine whom to
address, let alone how and in what person. The Abbot was her
lover, husband, and the father of her child as well as her spiritual
superior in orders. She was writing, moreover, after a separation
of ten years, during which he had been castrated by her uncle
for seducing her and she confined to her nunnery. She addressed her letter in this fashion:

> To her master, or rather her father, husband, or rather brother; his
> handmaid, or rather his daughter, wife, or rather sister; to Abelard,
> Heloise.[48]

48. "Letter I. Heloise to Abelard," in *The Letters of Abelard and Heloise*, trans.
Betty Radice (New York: Penguin, 1974), 109. For information about Heloise and
Abelard I am indebted to Radice's "Introduction," and to Peggy Kamuf, *Fictions of
Feminine Desire: Disclosures of Heloise*, whose discussion of the letters is particularly
instructive.

Whoever else Heloise was forced by circumstance to be, in her letters she is a passionate lover. A gifted student, she had been brought to study with Abelard by her uncle, Fulbert, when she was seventeen and Abelard, then in his mid-thirties, was the justly famous Master of Cloister Schools in Paris. Master and student immediately became lovers. When Fulbert found them together, Abelard sent Heloise to his sister in Brittany disguised as a nun, and there she bore him a child. To satisfy her uncle's honor they were secretly married in Paris, but Fulbert objecting to the secrecy, Abelard again sought sanctuary for Heloise in a nunnery, this time the convent at Argenteuil. After the castration, both took religious orders, she unwillingly. Although Heloise had renounced the world at nineteen, her letters to Abelard ten years later urge him to resume contact with her, if only in writing. Their letterly intercourse, she argues, will substitute for the sexuality no longer possible between them, and she begs him, "restore your presence to me in the way you can—by writing me some word of comfort."[49] Substitute, perhaps, but never satisfy. In answer to a letter from Abelard disguising his physical disability as spiritual commitment, Heloise portrays herself as a passionate woman, despairing of her confinement, and longing for erotic release.

> In my case, the pleasures of lovers which we shared have been too sweet—they can never displease me, and can scarcely be banished from my thoughts. Wherever I turn they are always there before my eyes, bringing with them awakened longings and fantasies which will not even let me sleep. Even during the celebration of the Mass, when our prayers should be purer, lewd visions of those pleasures take such a hold upon my unhappy soul that my thoughts are on their wantonness instead of on prayers. I should be groaning over the sins I have committed, but I can only sigh for what I have lost. Everything we did and also the times and places are stamped on my heart along with your image, so that I live through it all again with you. Even in sleep I know no respite. Sometimes my thoughts are betrayed in a movement of my body, or they break out in an unguarded word. In my utter wretchedness, that cry from a suffering soul could well be mine: "Miserable creature that I am, who is there

49. "Letter I. Heloise to Abelard," *Letters of Abelard and Heloise*, 117.

to rescue me out of the body doomed to this death?" Would that in truth I could go on: "The grace of God through Jesus Christ our Lord."[50]

Moved by the same anguished longing, she tells Abelard in a famous passage from her first letter, "The name of wife may seem more sacred or more binding, but sweeter for me will always be the word mistress, or, if you will permit me, that of concubine or whore."[51]

There are suggestive correspondences between this body of love letters and Faulkner's real and fictional letter canon. In his own correspondence, and in *Requiem for a Nun* where the master-student relationship is portrayed obliquely through Gavin and Temple, Faulkner was appealing again to the tradition of courtly love that Cleanth Brooks describes in terms drawn from Denis de Rougemont's *Love in the Western World*. Brooks might be speaking for the story of Heloise and Abelard, as well as for Tristan and Iseult, when he writes that "it is not in the least necessary to suppose that Faulkner ever read Rougemont. As Rougemont makes abundantly clear, the myth of passionate love has diffused itself throughout the literature of the West and is part of the culture in which we live. Faulkner might have derived the myth from almost anywhere."[52] Rougemont also claims a place for Heloise and Abelard in that myth: the *first* place. "The earliest passionate lovers whose story has reached us," Rougemont writes, "are Abélard and Héloïse, who met for the first time in 1118!"[53] Their story shaped Gottfried's version of *Tristan*, where the marriage of Tristan and Iseult is consummated for the first time, and is therefore at the root of the courtly love tradition.[54] But it is the passionate and anguished love depicted in their letters that gained them immortality, and

50. "Letter III. Heloise to Abelard," *Letters of Abelard and Heloise*, 133.
51. "Letter I. Heloise to Abelard," *Letters of Abelard and Heloise*, 113.
52. Cleanth Brooks, *William Faulkner: The Yoknapatawpha Country* (New Haven: Yale University Press, 1963), 203–4. Thomas McHaney follows Brooks's lead to good purpose in *William Faulkner's "The Wild Palms": A Study* (Jackson: University Press of Mississippi, 1975), 51ff.
53. Denis de Rougemont, *Love in the Western World*, trans. Montgomery Belgion, rev. and aug. edition (New York: Pantheon, 1956), 74–75.
54. Ibid., 131–36.

the power of their love over the Western imagination is suggested by the fact that for the next 650 years after Heloise's death in 1164 her bones and Abelard's were frequently exhumed, examined, and from 1800 to 1817 even publicly displayed in Paris. In the eighteenth century Alexander Pope's poem, *Eloisa to Abelard* (1717), was popular enough to be translated into Italian, French, and German; and Rousseau's *La Nouvelle Heloise* (1761) crossed the Channel translated into English almost immediately after its French publication. Modern instances include George Moore's novel, *Heloise and Abelard* (1921), C. K. Moncrief's modern translation of the letters (1925), and Helen Waddell's novel, *Peter Abelard* (1933). By the time he invented Temple's letters in *Requiem*, Faulkner might have known the lovers from any of these or from the 1940 English edition of Rougemont's book. But much earlier than that he would have encountered them in his great-grandfather's travel letters. In a letter from *Rapid Ramblings* dated Paris, August 13, W. C. Falkner reported on a visit to the tomb of Heloise and Abelard where, he said, "sentimental nonsense usually culminates and falls in the shape of tears on the grave of those unfortunate lovers. The names of Abelard and Heloise have furnished the theme of song for many an amateur poet and material for many a silly novel, most of which might justly be pronounced froth."[55] For Heloise, Col. Falkner has great sympathy, for Abelard none. "He was a hypocrite, a villain, and a seducer," he wrote of the medieval priest. "At the mature age of forty, when men of virtue and integrity are supposed to be able to subdue and control their evil passions, he seduced Heloise, a beautiful maiden of eighteen, whom he had been employed to teach by her confiding uncle."[56] The Old Colonel could hardly have imagined then that eighty years later his own great-grandson would be involved in a master-student, lover-maiden relationship with

55. W. C. Falkner, *Rapid Ramblings in Europe* (Philadelphia: J. B. Lippincott, 1884), 417. I am indebted to Donald Duclos for telling me about the reference to Abelard and Heloise in *Rapid Ramblings* and for providing me with his own copy of the book.
56. Ibid., 417.

not one but two young women protégés, or that he would be "transfiguring" those personal relationships and their letterly antecedents into a novel of his own.

Faulkner's earliest Abelard may be Gail Hightower, who learns "from a book" (*LIA*, 454) to hide love letters to his wife-to-be in a hollow tree at his seminary. But Temple is far more fully drawn to the pattern of Heloise, whose story may even give the title to Faulkner's book. Both women are students abducted to the ironic sanctuary of nunneries—one a convent literally, one in the Shakespearean sense of nunnery as brothel; each is disguised as a member of her respective sisterhood, and each undergoes a sexual novitiate to which her passionate letters confess. Each set of letters depicts the letter writer to her lover in terms of her erotic fantasies, and each text, insufficiently substituting for the woman herself, constitutes an artifact of her, what Peggy Kamuf calls "the residue of woman's excessive desire."[57] The seducers, in each case, are unmanned. The priest, Abelard, is castrated by Heloise's uncle, Fulbert, and Popeye, the "black man" of *Santuary* (*S*, 47), is impotent according to "our Uncle Gavin," who imagines his incapacity extending to an inability even to read about love. The "eunuch slaves" (*RN*, 126) that he further imagines reading to Popeye recall the unmanned lovers in *Flags in the Dust* and *Sanctuary:* bookish Horace with "his air of fine and delicate futility," and Lee Goodwin, accused of raping Temple, who is castrated by a mob. All of these men betray their women in ways that reveal the women truly. In one letter to Heloise Abelard resolves the paradox of the unmanned lover rhetorically by arguing from Scripture that her lust is the coarse outer garment of her loving heart as her body is of her soul. His illustration compares her to King Solomon's Ethiopian concubine in *Song of Songs* who says, "I am black but lovely, daughters of Jerusalem; therefore the king has loved me and brought me into his chamber."[58] Heloise had expressed in her

57. *Fictions of Feminine Desire*, xiv.
58. "Letter IV. Abelard to Heloise," *Letters of Abelard and Heloise*, 138ff.

first letter her wish to be Abelard's "concubine or whore," and he answers in this letter by turning her desire against her: in her nun's habit she is the Bride of Christ he calls her, outwardly "black" but inwardly "lovely," the sexually forbidden spiritual counterpart of a physical wife. In fact, Heloise knows herself to be the reverse of this—outwardly a nun but inwardly wanton. The tension between the two Heloises is what generates her letters of self-depiction. Recalling Abelard's analogy in the context of *Requiem for a Nun* explains one symbolic function of Nancy Mannigoe. The "ex-dope-fiend nigger whore" (*RN*, 136) who urges Temple to "believe" (*RN*, 243) ironically combines the concubine and the nun in the way that Abelard means. And like Heloise, Temple is the reverse of that "reformed" image. The tension between Nancy and Temple is brought about by the "good letters," and Nancy's death frees Temple to be the image of her written words. So it is that, according to Gavin, Nancy's name, Mannigoe, once was Maingault and her heritage "runs Norman blood" (*RN*, 103). Gavin's own name and Gowan's suggest the same medieval era as does the setting of Temple's rape at the Old Frenchman's Place. Heloise's name is the feminine of God's, Elohim, and Temple's is the name of His sanctuary. The last Receiver of Temple's letters is not Peter Abelard but simply Pete, a character Faulkner invented for the letterly plot of *Requiem for a Nun*.

As yet I have found but one named reference in Faulkner's writing to Heloise and Abelard—in Poem XXXII of *A Green Bough*[59]—although it seems to me the sort of reference one might expect to occur more broadly, especially in the context of so many otherwise accidental echoes of their story. But letters abound. Like other written texts, letters signify within a tradition and according to conventions and forms of expression unique to them, and Faulkner drew on these for *Requiem* as he did on the forms of drama. Letterly modes, including the very personal, even passionate fictions of self that substitute for the

59. William Faulkner, *A Green Bough*, in *The Marble Faun and A Green Bough* (New York: Random House, 1965), 55. I am grateful to Panthea Reid Broughton for bringing the reference to my attention.

self of the letter writer, are everywhere to be found in Faulkner's writing—not only in his personal correspondence but in his books, and, indeed, in his discussions of his books in two letterly prefaces. In the 1932 "Introduction" to *Sanctuary,* he divided himself into two personae, the village handyman—carpenter, house painter—who narrates the piece, and the writer he addresses as "Faulkner": "So I told Faulkner, 'You're damned. You'll have to work now and then for the rest of your life.' "[60] Addressing himself to his reader, he concluded that he had made a "fair job" of revising *Sanctuary,* "and I hope you will buy it and tell your friends and I hope they will buy it too."[61] In the "Foreword" to *The Faulkner Reader* in 1954, he introduced himself through his family's library, again mentioning *Clarissa,* before settling on Sienkiewicz to illustrate his point that writers write "to uplift men's hearts."[62] As he had when he portrayed his physical vitality in love letters, he chose sexual terms to describe the force of feeling in his books that he said would give him immortality. He had written "while the blood and glands and flesh still remained strong and potent."[63] Engendered in "cold impersonal print," those passions were invulnerable, capable in their turn of "engendering still the old deathless excitement in hearts and glands whose owners and custodians are generations from even the air he breathed and anguished in . . . capable and potent skill."[64] By this figurative letter he was delivering his words into the hands and hearts of readers of *The Faulkner Reader.* This context of the "Foreword" reminds us that Yoknapatawpha County is not only a literary world but a lettered one. The history of Yoknapatawpha, recorded in the Prologues of *Requiem for a Nun,* reminds us of the foundation of that world in letters, for Jefferson, we are told there, is named for a letter carrier.

60. William Faulkner, "Introduction to the Modern Library Edition of *Sanctuary,*" rpt. in *Essays, Speeches, and Public Letters by William Faulkner,* ed. James B. Meriwether (New York: Random House, 1965), 177.
    61. "Introduction to the Modern Library Edition of *Sanctuary,*" 178.
    62. "Foreword to *The Faulkner Reader,*" 180.
    63. Ibid.
    64. Ibid., 182.

On the Road to the Mullen Holdings:
A Faulkner Collector's Odyssey

LOUIS DANIEL BRODSKY

Thursday, December 9, 1982

Ostensibly, this trip was not markedly different from myriad others I had taken south.

Slogging through the empty, early-morning downtown whose orange mercury-vapor street lamps were still humming through the fog, I knew only two things for certain: a seven-hour drive lay before me, and I was heading first toward Oxford instead of West Helena; this reversal in routine made me feel a little like Faulkner's Luster at the conclusion of *The Sound and the Fury* hauling his idiot load, Benjy, in a fated wagon around the "sinister" side of the monument on the Square. But the Chancellor of the University of Mississippi, Porter Fortune, had made a special effort to divert his extensive fund-raising campaign long enough to make himself available to me for a 4:00 meeting in his office on this afternoon. I could hardly refuse!

A decade earlier, I had proclaimed myself "Manager of Outlet Stores." Prior to 1972, I had been in charge of one factory outlet store through which I channeled many of the imperfects and overstocks that the clothing company for which I worked generated in the normal course of its manufacturing. As the company continued to expand its growth, and one factory outlet after another was opened, I became a nomad, a wandering rag-man, a silhouetted Chaplinesque figure not cakewalking into endless sunsets so much as seated behind the wheel of a tumbling, rolling, pitching station wagon loaded with goods to be sold in desolate thieves' markets and emporiums at bargain

prices; a picaro transporting the world's leftovers from one spe-
cious situation to the next. But, for all the traveling my self-
appointed position entailed, it presented a refuge of a kind:
while driving, I could concoct my strategies on how I was going
to corner the market on William Faulkner memorabilia, and I
could also fashion from silence my poetry, a special technique for
which I mastered by teaching myself to write into a ledger book
positioned at my side atop an attaché case without having to look
away from the road before me.

On this particular morning, December 9, 1982, as I coursed
over Highway 32, meandering easterly toward the great north-
south Highway 55, I sensed an approach-avoidance conflict con-
verging on me from Oxford, a sounding that seemed to be
emanating from the Chancellor's office.

I had made my intentions known on a few unofficial occasions,
had actually expressed to this kind man once before in private
session that I would be proud to have my Faulkner collection
placed someday at his institution: it seemed more than appropriate in light of my belief that I was a mere custodian for a very
public trust. Oxford, including the University of Mississippi,
located there, was at the source of William Faulkner's spirit. My
more than twenty years of work with Faulkner memorabilia
could have no more lasting and significant memorial to its accomplishment than to find the collection on permanent display
in the sanctum sanctorum, the heart of the heart of Yoknapatawpha itself.

But lately I had been experiencing not second thoughts, not
doubts about the ultimate rightness of my determination, but
uneasiness about my timing. I was, in short, not at all sure that
my psyche could handle such an abrupt jettisoning of its ballast
as the University had led me to believe it was prepared to effect.
I had contrived numerous stringent stipulations and provisos,
devised elaborate schemes for delayed payments on what I had
thought would be more than a generous remuneration for the
entire collection, certain that although desirable, these impedi-
ments would cause those responsible for making decisions of this

caliber to back off, at least temporarily. Instead, what I had found was an absolutely unequivocal willingness on their part to acquiesce to my every demand.

The problem was I still loved the damn stuff too much; felt too close to the inscribed books, letters, manuscripts—even all the ephemeral, minimal pieces. And I realized that by 4:00 on this afternoon, I would have to make a declaration!

As I moved ahead toward West Memphis, approaching the Highway 40 turnoff, still a few miles south, my mind reiterated some of the wonderful place names prominently billboarded on the green state signs I had passed the last few hours. To my tongue's delight, I repeated aloud: Bragadoccio, Luxora, Victoria, Lepanto, Joiner, Osceola, Tyronza, Jericho. Ah, what a glorious road poetry my mere proclaiming had fashioned from Arkansas's Burma Shave verse! At least one of those wonderful Arkansas place names, Osceola, did more than weave in and down and out off my tongue's fricative slide without remark. In fact, my antennae had for the last hour picked up a significant, if distant, ululation, a distant kind of vague baying, and were now directing me to the source of the positive distraction. Not more than thirty minutes south of Blytheville was the town of Osceola.

As I passed the sign announcing its otherwise unobtrusive exit, I repeated to myself the brilliant insight which, no doubt, had not varied either in its lack of elaboration or neglect to think it into existence before now: "Indian Name—Phil Mullen!" I wondered to myself whether Phil Mullen were still living . . . living here still in Osceola, Arkansas. And what a weird place this seemed, so out in the middle of nowhere. I had passed here at least half a hundred times, passed again equally that many on my returns from West Helena and from Oxford over the past seven years; and never once stopped, unmotivated each time I passed by that same isolated fact that Phil Mullen lived here. Never before this moment had I actually sensed palpably the possibility of meeting the man whom I knew from my studies had been, along with his father, associate editor of *The Oxford*

(Mississippi) *Eagle* from 1933 until 1951, and who certainly knew William Faulkner on a first-hand basis.

As I drove through the amoeba-like desolations of squalid and shabby downtown Memphis, I vowed repeatedly that I would not let one more trip go by without making an effort to contact Mr. Phil Mullen. Already, I realized, I had most likely squandered one of those precious contacts which almost alone afford the serious collector of Faulkner memorabilia a chance to get at the real plums, those artifacts which have remained in the possession of family, close friends, and associates; gifts and tokens of friendship which the author was frequently disposed to give persons he loved and trusted and respected. No doubt, Mr. Phil Mullen was deceased. My God, I reasoned, at a minimum, he would have to be in his seventies; Faulkner would be eighty-six were he living today. Then again, I had nothing to lose, since I had been permitting the loss to go unchecked all these years without even realizing it for what it was not: a definitive, positive chance to make an important contact. And it had been there, right under my antennae, all these trips without calling attention to itself. This time, I asserted, I wouldn't let the opportunity slip away.

For the next hour and a half I could not unfocus Mr. Phil Mullen from my inner vision. In fact, as I drove, I was madly pulling file drawers from my storeroom of arcane Faulkneriana, reviewing yellowed memories and interbrain memos, trying to resurrect from forgetting anything and everything I could on the former editor of *The Oxford Eagle*, probably one of the most celebrated small-town weeklies in the universe.

I did retrieve a few items which held my attention all the way to Oxford. One was a very vague recollection of an eight-page Faulkner memorial which had appeared in, of all places, *The Osceola Times*, sometime in 1966. I recalled its consisting of a rather lengthy series of anecdotes relating to William Faulkner written by Phil Mullen, the current editor of the paper, accompanied by numerous photographs of Faulkner and his environs.

I had two copies in the collection. One had originally come from a book dealer. The second copy I was more familiar with in terms of its provenance, if not its content. It had come as part of an impressive group of memorabilia which James W. Silver, former head of the Ole Miss history department, and a very good friend of both Mullen and Faulkner, had allowed me to acquire a few years earlier. This copy was still in its original mailing envelope from Mullen to Silver, accompanied by a full set of the photographs which appeared in the Supplement along with a very interesting letter to Silver explaining the contents and the Who's Who of the sender.

More than this, I could not recall. All I knew as I entered Oxford, was that tomorrow morning, just as soon as I arrived in West Helena, I would call Osceola information and inquire whether they showed a listing for a Mr. Phillip Mullen. Just now, I had fifteen minutes to freshen up before I was to meet the Chancellor in his office in the restored Lyceum building, a monument, indeed, to the stalwartness and perdurability of the Old South.

By the time the Chancellor arrived, the day had dissolved into wet darkness. I felt exhausted, yet relieved at the conclusion of our meeting: namely, to place a moratorium on making any decision until I felt the timing better satisfied my present misgivings. The Chancellor understood my need to have more time with the materials, that my work included publication of a seven-volume series on the Brodsky Faulkner Collection. My relief was at once enormous and liberating. I had given myself a reprieve to continue not only indulging my fantasies as a collector of world-class reputation, but nurturing my obsession with making contributions to scholarship almost exclusively from documents in my own collection.

Friday, December 10, 1982

When I arrived the next day at my West Helena store, I immediately excused myself from the store's needs and dialed 1-501-555-1212. To my surprise, I discovered that Osceola, Arkansas, did indeed have a telephone listing for Mr. Phillip E. Mullen. Without deliberating, I dialed, waited, and immediately began to introduce myself to the voice that soon materialized.

"Hello, Mr. Mullen. I know you don't know me, and I beg you in advance for the intrusion, but . . ." and I didn't wait for a courteous rejoinder. "But, I am a Faulkner collector and scholar, and I am right now in West Helena, and I have passed Osceola at least forty times, and it would be a great privilege for me to meet you, if possibly you are going to be home tomorrow morning. I am returning tomorrow and could be there by 9:30, if you thought that might be O.K." I barely realized that the assaulted ear on the other end of the line had yet to listen to its own voice answer back. Mine was an urgency formed of nervousness and anxiety, of not wanting to be denied, let down, disappointed too abruptly by the simplest severance of a disgruntled "No!" or "Sorry, but I won't be home," or "Please, I've been bothered enough by all that Faulkner crap!" Suddenly I felt my ears get red, and I knew the sign all too well. I had not only showed my trump card, but laid the whole damn hand down on the table face up without noticing I'd done so until too late.

"Sure! Come on. Come right on. I'm here by myself. My wife died in '74. You just come right on ahead."

The mummy who had risen from last night's sarcophagus and stuttered around in a half-daze all morning now threw off all its wrappings. I sensed that timing was in motion, good timing, the best. Phil Mullen was not only alive and well, but accessible. Whether he still retained anything from his Oxford days, specifically his Faulkner relationship, was in the balance. I never really allowed myself to assume that his dealings with Faulkner would have been strictly casual, without surviving artifacts. It was not unreasonable to assume that, since, during a period of almost two decades, he had helped edit that paper, and because I knew, for fact, that Faulkner had submitted more than a few pieces for public dissemination in the *Eagle,* Phil Mullen would have saved at least some of those precious scraps: typescripts, letters to the editor, public notices, broadsides, reminiscences.

I was so high that my excitement refused me the necessary concentration on store matters; dashing away before the hour of 2:00 P.M., I was, once again back on the road, heading due east toward Oxford.

Saturday, December 11, 1982

Dawn couldn't come fast enough! By 8:30, I was on the north edge of West Memphis, having cleared the big green bridge spanning the Mississippi River, connecting Tennessee with Arkansas; and, sensing that I might be too early, since I suspected Osceola couldn't be more than twenty minutes or so north, I stopped for coffee. By degrees the caffeine dissolved the webs which had strung themselves out through the past two days of traveling. My eyes retraced the hand-drawn map I had doodled while on the phone with Phil Mullen yesterday as though it were a kind of sacred scroll or diagram of the secret corridors in the pyramid of Cheops. And as I pondered its all-too-brief legend, I thought back over all the many contacts I had made during the past seven years; the homes in which I had visited and slept while selling myself, trying to prove myself worthy, polishing my credentials to a finely-finished authenticity, rendering myself in all but a few cases a credible and deserving pretender to the throne. There had been Mrs. Dorothy B. Commins, in Princeton, New Jersey, wife of Faulkner's long-time editor at Random House; James W. Silver, in Dunedin, Florida; Calvin S. Brown; Malcolm Cowley; Mrs. Emily W. Stone of Montgomery, Alabama, widow of Faulkner's early mentor, lawyer, and friend, Phil Stone; Victoria Fielden Johnson, in Cape Coral, Florida, Faulkner's step-granddaughter; Jane Withers, of White Sulphur Springs, West Virginia, daughter of Myrtle Ramey, one of Faulkner's grade and high school sweethearts; Ben Wasson of Greenville, Mississippi; and Vance Carter Broach of Tulsa, Oklahoma, nephew, like Faulkner, of their beloved Aunt 'Bama McLean.

And now that old excitement of making contact, encountering

a strange, but strangely related individual by virtue of our mutual interest in William Faulkner, was pressing out centrifugally against all my veins and arteries. The problem, I quickly realized, as I knocked on the door of the modest home on the outskirts of Osceola, just four miles east of Highway 55, was how to contain myself. Immediately I was put at ease by a rather short, dishevelled man in stocking feet and loose-fitting dress shirt who admitted me with an enthusiastic hand shake and invited me to take off my coat, then sport coat, and settle in. How would I take my coffee, he asked, as I sat down on the sofa in his living room and glanced at the table before me, strewn with photographs and papers of all sorts, among which, I could tell without concentrating, were typescripts signed "Bill." There was only one BILL in the entire world!

In our brief conversation the day before, Phil Mullen had asked me whether I had ever seen his "Supplement" on William Faulkner. I had responded positively, apologizing for the fact that it had been some years, however, since I had read it. Now, as he shuffled into the kitchen, he handed me a newspaper which was, he told me, a recently reset version of the original December 1966 edition; this one was dated Thursday, December 25, 1980, and bore the masthead of *The Osceola Times*. Little did I realize that I held in my hand the entire recorded history of Phil Mullen's association with William Faulkner, spanning almost thirty years of reminiscences. If only I had been able to read this eight-page Supplement before my arrival, surely I would have been both more adept in probing him for insights, and far less taken by surprise. As it was, I had only three or four minutes in which to peruse uninterrupted the newspaper.

In that interlude, compounded by the distraction of the typed letters on the crowded coffee table, which I had declined to read out of courtesy (after all, I was a complete stranger in this man's sacred precincts), I scanned the tight columns without assimilating anything. The only thing my eyes absorbed was one absurdly disturbing fragment of a single paragraph which seemed to scream out at me from below a bold-typed transcription of a letter from Faulkner to Phil Mullen. Why I had to isolate this passage I shall never know. It read:

> "Never before have I printed all of these letters (not many) that William Faulkner wrote me. I have declined to sell them and will not sell them.
>
> And, insofar as Cowley published his Faulkner letters, why not me?"

As I glossed the photographs included in this Supplement— Faulkner in his sailboat, standing behind a podium recreating his University High School graduation speech for the Ford Omnibus television series of Writers in America, Faulkner posed with Mac Reed in his drug store, with Phil Stone in his law office, with his hunting cronies, consulting with the director and photographer of the Omnibus television crew—I surmised that this man sitting across from me, his myopic eyes staring at me, had been in close touch with William Faulkner. I knew he was an authentic source, a disciple, one of those who had considered himself fortunate to have made the acquaintance of the gifted writer.

Other than for family members, I had met only three kinds of persons in this regard: those who had never known the man, yet now referred to him as "Bill"; those who admitted they had not had contact with him either from reticence, out of deference, or studied disinterest, but wished they had; finally, there were those who had considered it a great privilege just to have been included in his confidences. Phil Mullen was of this last group. The Supplement which I held in my hand as Phil began to relate anecdote after anecdote, almost as if it were a recording, had as its bold-faced streamer the title: "WILLIAM FAULKNER, GREAT NOVELIST, ALSO a GREAT and GENTLE MAN." The first paragraph read: "In 47 years of newspaper work, my friendship with William Faulkner was my only close contact with true greatness." The second brief paragraph began: "Let me tell you about him." Phil spoke for the next half hour as though not questioning either his role as racanteur or mine as novitiate.

What I had come to know from having spent time with so many persons who had been friends of William Faulkner was that each of them had engendered from his or her experience certain key memories, insights about the man and his behavior; that each thought he had a "complete" picture, rather than a piece of the whole. I knew from my travels and work with Faulkner bibliography and biography that what each had was a fragment which, when united with other fragments, formed a composite. Frequently, in situations like this one, I was reminded of the fable in which seven blind Indian wise men encounter an elephant for the first time, each grabbing a separate part of the enigmatic creature: trunk, tail, leg, eartip, skin, tusk, toenail; each proclaiming with absolute certainty that he knows what the group has encountered, offering respectively a definitive determination. The wise man holding the trunk knows they are all in the presence of a boa constrictor; he with the tail has one end of a long hemp rope; the next is positive the leg is a banyon tree; he with the eartip has hold of a banana leaf; to another the skin suggests the group has approached the entrance flap of a thieves' market tent; the one with the tusk has discovered a great curved Bengal lance; and the man rubbing the toenail concludes that the presence in their presence is a smooth oversized sapphire of untold value.

I do not mean to imply by this extended allusion that Phil and all the others whom I had met had arrogated to themselves with immodesty the body of all knowledge; rather, that they had determined through their experiences a body subsumed within the Body of Knowledge about Faulkner, the man, the writer, the friend, the genius they all believed him to be. But, unlike the conclusions drawn by the characters in the fable, the truth each had fashioned for himself bore definite, if limited, relationship to the object of his observations. As I sat listening, I couldn't contain my admiration for this man, so isolated now in his ill-health, his solitude, his memories; admiration and respect for the fact that he had been an integral part of the events that had changed not only the face of Oxford, but the world (at least, to some modest degree, changed the way people perceived the world) as a result of William Faulkner's presence.

As he stood up with difficulty and went into the kitchen to pour two cups of coffee, he motioned to me to have a look at the materials he had spread out on the table in anticipation of my arrival. One by one I picked up five letters, each encased in plastic jackets, three typed, two handwritten in that characteristically illegible, miniscule printing; these were the letters which he had twice stated in print he would never sell. Their content was truly extraordinary in terms of depicting Faulkner's obsessive determination to guard his privacy in a world fast learning to disregard completely every man's right to remain unmolested, undissected.

The ritual of serving coffee somehow signaled a break in our meeting. Now it was my turn to share with him what had brought me to him. I drew from my attaché a set of unstitched gatherings from my newest book, *Faulkner: A Comprehensive Guide to the Brodsky Collection: Volume I: The Biobibliography,* which was to be published imminently by the University Press of Mississippi as the first in a seven-volume series. I handed it to him.

What followed was a low-keyed, high-pressure sales pitch; one that I honestly and earnestly believed was well-intentioned. Sure, I realized the letters were valuable in the collector's market, and that inscribed books, if he had any, would be of high value, too . . . but, this was not my thrust, since already the collection had more than 110 Faulkner letters, in excess of 100 inscribed books. Rather, it was my sincere hope that this man would allow me to memorialize him, in a sense, and to expand the collection's depth by including these Phil Mullen items. After all, he had played an important role in the Oxford drama; he had been editor of *The Oxford Eagle,* and more—so much more he himself had documented for posterity by writing his 1966 Supplement.

To my amazement, he not only agreed enthusiastically to my suggestion, but encouraged me to comb his book shelves. I assured him that his reading copies, with his signature, were as important to me as any he might have inscribed from Faulkner. As it happened, there was only one of the latter, a first edition, unjacketed, "seventh printing" of *Collected Stories of William Faulkner.* He noted that he had not solicited the inscription in this book. Nor would he ever have, he added, even had he dreamed back then that Bill would become so famous. "We just never would have dreamed it," he repeated, almost gleefully.

We had not talked price or value. When I inscribed for him and handed over a copy of the most recent issue of *The Faulkner Newsletter and Yoknapatawpha Review,* which had focused on the Brodsky Collection, he perused it, and looking up, told me that he had known of me before my arrival, had known of my work.

I was flattered that he knew of my scholarship; more than that, I knew in my heart that not I, but my work, the collection itself, had done the necessary persuasion, helped him determine to place his cherished artifacts in the collection for posterity. Suddenly, I realized that it was 11:30. I knew I had a 2:00 meeting with my wife in Cape Girardeau that I could not afford to miss.

I felt as though Phil and I had become friends in Faulkner, secret sharers of a kind. What an incredible privilege this was for me. And, I realized this all the more within the ten minutes prior to my apologizing for needing to leave, recognized that I had been unusually negligent in paying attention to the materials at hand for my near-total befriending of Phil Mullen. I had been conscious enough to beg Phil to sign the few reading copies of Faulkner's books which were not already signatured, but I had missed one thing completely which he brought to my attention.

"The speech?" he questioned. "What do you think about the speech?"

My heart hit an air pocket, dropped 2,000 feet before leveling off. I had no idea what he might be referring to; only that I was aware that very few Faulkner speeches had been composed and delivered, and that those few, eloquent and universal in their appreciation, were not only elusive, but virtually impossible to acquire other than in printed format. Speech? I thought. What in hell was he talking about? I had seen only five plastic packets, read five letters through their clear faces. Immediately, he worked himself from his chair, grabbed the letters, and with assurance, selected one of the packets and drew from behind the letter it protected three additional sheets of typescript which he proudly handed to me.

"I've had this for thirty years; it was in the bank until a few weeks ago. This Bill gave me that day at the high school after he delivered it to Jill's graduation class. I had gone up onto the stage to inform Bill that I wanted to print it in the morning's edition of the *Eagle*. He said, 'Keep it, Phil.' To this day I cherish the words, the thoughts . . . the gift."

If I might be forgiven a strained pun, I was speechless as I held this celebrated speech in my hand. I gazed at Faulkner's typographical errors, his blue-ink corrections on this eloquent exhortation which he had read on May 28, 1951. I was shocked and delighted merely to be holding this extraordinary document, the very sheets which Faulkner had held, read from, then handed to his friend to publish in his newspaper. That friend was now, in turn, handing the document over to me.

And as I felt then, I am certain now that Phil Mullen had no misgivings that he might not be entrusting these items to a person who would cherish them as he had, and who, more, would do other than bequeath them with respect to the future. As I began to slide into my sport coat, Phil abruptly excused himself, retired to the room at the back end of the hall, and returned with a picture frame containing something which he determinedly handed to me intact, suggesting I might want to take it from its frame, keep it with the other things; for having almost forgotten it, he apologized. I was stunned. The frame contained his most cherished letter from Faulkner; it had hung, he said, in his bedroom for many years, serving as a reminder not merely of his proximity to greatness, in the form of Faulkner the writer and friend, but of his own profession. I read the letter to myself, then dismantled the frame and carefully placed the letter in a folder with the other ones. It read:

Wednesday
Dear Phil:

I haven't seen the LIFE thing yet, and wont. I have found that my mother is furious over it, seems to consider it inferentially lies, cancelled her subscription.

I tried for years to prevent it, refused always, asked them to let me alone. It's too bad the individual in this country has no protection from journalism, I suppose they call it. But apparently he hasn't. There seems to be in this the same spirit which permits strangers to drive into my yard and pick up books or pipes I left in the chair where I had been sitting, as souvenirs.

What a commentary. Sweden gave me the Nobel Prize. France gave me the Legion d'Honneur. All my native land did for me was to invade my privacy over my protest and my plea. No wonder people in the rest of the world dont like us, since we seem to have neither taste nor courtesy, and know and believe in nothing but money and it doesn't much matter how you get it.

Yours,
Bill

This time I wasn't even consulted, didn't even know it was being done, nor did my mother. She knew she was being photographed and specifically asked the photographer not to print the picture anywhere.

This seems to me to be a pretty sorry return for a man who has only tried to be an artist and bring what honor that implies to the land of his birth.[1]

All too briefly we said goodbyes. I knew that we had met on common grounds. He had a generous check for the group of items. He knew that I was the proper person to distinguish his priceless mementos; no money could have wrested them from him. The exchange had been made by mutual consent based on mutual respect and trust. In the silence of our parting, we both

---

1. This letter appears in *Faulkner: A Comprehensive Guide to the Brodsky Collection: Volume II: The Letters,* by Louis Daniel Brodsky and Robert W. Hamblin (Jackson: University Press of Mississippi, 1984). I wish to extend my continuing appreciation to Jill Faulkner Summers for allowing me to make available this and all items in my Faulkner collection through publication of the *Comprehensive Guide* and, by extension, intervening scholarly publications which call attention to the multi-volume *Guide.*

knew that those qualities could not be and had not been mea-
sured by material standards.

Address to the Graduating Class
University High School

Years ago, before any of you were born, a wise Frenchman said, 'If
youth knew; if age could.' We all know what he meant: that when
you are young, you have the power to do anything, but you dont
know what to do. Then, when you have got old and experience and
observation have taught you [what to do, *del.*] ⟨answers,⟩ you are
tired, frightened; you dont care, you want to be left alone as long as
you yourself are safe; you no longer have the capacity or the will to
grieve over any wrongs but your own.

So you young men and women in this room tonight, and in [a *del.*]
thousands of other rooms like this one about the earth today, have
the power to change the world, rid it forever of war and injustice and
suffering, provided you know how, know what to do. And so, according to the old Frenchman, since you cant know what to do because
you are young, then anyone standing here with a head full of white
hair, should be able to tell you.

But maybe this one is not as old and white as his white hairs pretend
or claim. Because he cant give you a glib answer or pattern either.
But he [cann *del.*] ⟨can⟩ tell you this, because he believes this. What
threatens us today is fear. Not the atom bomb, nor even fear of [the
atom bomb *del.*] it, because if the bomb fell on Oxford tonight, all it
could do would be to kill us, which is nothing, since in doing that, it
will have robbed itself of its only power over us: which is fear of it,
the being afraid of it. Our danger is not that. Our danger is the
forces in the world today which are trying to use man's fear to rob
him of his individuality, his soul, trying to reduce him to an unthink-
ing mass by fear and bribery—giving him free food which he has not
earned, easy and valueless money which he has not worked for;—
the [tyrants *del.*] economies or ideologies or political [parties, *del.*]
⟨systems,⟩ communist or socialist or democratic, whatever they wish
to call themselves, the tyrants and the politicians, American or
European or Asiatic, whatever they call themselves, who would
reduce man to one obedient mass for their own aggrandisement and
power, or because they themselves are baffled and afraid, afraid of,
or incapable of, believing in man's capacity for courage ⟨and endur-
ance⟩ and [honor and compassion *del.*] and sacrifice.

That is what we must resist, if we are to change the world [and save man. *del.*] ⟨for man's peace and security.⟩ It is not [the mass *del.*] men in the mass who can and will save Man. It is Man himself, created in the image of God so that he shall have the power and the will to choose right from wrong and so be able to save himself because he is [worthy *del.*] ⟨worth⟩ saving;—Man, the individual, men and women, who will refuse always to be tricked or frightened or bribed into surrendering, not just the right but the duty too, to choose between justice and injustice, courage and cowardice, sacrifice and greed, pity and self;—who will believe always not only in the right of man to be free of injustice and rapacity and deception, but the duty and responsibility of man to see that justice and truth and pity and compassion are done.

So, never be afraid. Never be afraid to raise your voice for honesty and truth and compassion, against injustice and lying and greed. If you, not just you in this room tonight, but in all the thousands of other rooms like this one about the world today and tomorrow and next week, will do this, not as a class or classes, but as individuals, men and women, you will change the earth. In one generation all the Napoleons and Hitlers and [Alexand *del.*] Caesars and Mussolinis and Stalins and all the other tyrants who want power and aggrandisement, [or *del.*] ⟨and⟩ the simple politicians and time-servers who themselves are merely baffled or ignorant or afraid, who have used, or are using, or [will *del.*] hope to use, man's fear and greed for man's enslavement, will have vanished from the face of it.[2]

2. The internally collated text transcribed above, generally referred to as Faulkner's "Never Be Afraid" speech, to appear in a projected volume of the *Comprehensive Guide*, is also published by permission of Jill Faulkner Summers. To render a more complete textual transcription of this speech, I have resorted to placing square brackets around material followed by the phrase "*del.*" to denote punctuation, words, and phrases that were deleted in the revisionary process to which Faulkner subjected his text prior to its delivery. Angle brackets have been designated to denote interlineal words and phrases: these mainly occur in blue ink where Faulkner was merely replacing one word or words above one or others which he had struck through either by pen or typewriter.

Faulkner's View of Literature

P. V. PALIEVSKY

The subject I will consider in this essay is the relationship between Faulkner's literary views and his own writings. It is quite
uncommon. In the opinions of some, there are many prominent
writers of the twentieth century whose critical work surpasses
their own fiction. In some cases this is obvious, and the idea has
even been given approval by T. S. Eliot with his idea of the
"critical age." There are, on the other hand, writers whose artistic achievement is on the same level as their critical works; they
do both with equal pleasure and success, as, for instance, Bernard Shaw. One may find, lastly, the writers who do not need
any critical explanation at all. They write no criticism themselves and simply exist in the heart of the reader, as Jaroslav
Hasek with his "Shweik"; they are children of luck—in the artistic sense, of course.

William Faulkner does not conform to any of these patterns.
His critical endeavors are an integral part of his work. One
cannot even say that Faulkner's well-known interviews or his
university seminars are part of his literary heritage. Rather, they
are an extension of what he had always done—another way of
achieving his main goal—and in some cases the most successful
way.

How unusual Faulkner's comments on the artistic process
look when compared with traditional treatments of literature!
Faulkner's comments are not remote from the subject of the
discussion—the art; there is no distance between the work of art
and the position of the observer, as is usual in critical studies.
Faulkner's literary criticism is not an assessment in the strict

sense of the word, that is, you cannot see the difference between the critic and what he is criticizing. Rather Faulkner's discussion of art is another explosion of all his forces towards his ideal, another call for others to follow.

Very often Faulkner's literary criticism reaches the heights he attempted; in these instances the critical appraisal becomes the final and most persuasive expression of his intimate thoughts. In my opinion, these instances all occur in Faulkner's last years, especially after he was awarded the Nobel Prize, when his critical activity flourished. Faulkner's literary criticism can be compared to a dark mountain which grows and suddenly reaches snowy heights. Here it is, not so warm as the fiction, and certainly one misses the richness of life; but you can observe the whole region in one glimpse, and get an impression of the general plan. This new style of address to the reader offered new possibilities, which were used brilliantly by Faulkner.

First of all, Faulkner succeeded in preserving the values of art in critical thinking. He brought them "above," without abandoning that common feature of the ordinary human mind despised by the academic scholars—the living, moving, uniting image. He tries to argue and to convince, as usual, not with logic, but with his heart. On the other hand, his excessive, uncontrolled, and sometimes obtrusive style, which met no resistance in the form of a novel, was obliged in this form to take a more responsible attitude. It was necessary to speak directly, briefly, and always to take into account the interests of the listener. In other words, the genre compelled Faulkner to conform to accepted forms of communication—a limitation which was very useful for Faulkner, who was doomed for years to struggle along with the creations of his own imagination. Thus arose an order, not imposed on the chaotic material from above, but an order which grew from within under the pressure of new circumstances.

The result was very impressive, and it looks even more impressive today, thirty or more years later. One could suggest various causes for Faulkner's turn to explicit literary statements. Possibly he was becoming disillusioned with fiction, which seemed to have failed to attain its goal, and turned now to public speeches. But the fact is that Faulkner's art had moved thus to a new stage. His ideas became clear and convincing without losing the fullness of life; they found a balanced form of coexistence and coalesced in one image; all he wanted to say throughout his life was squeezed into a small sentence. And this last attempt produced a new kind of literature: a unique piece of successful Faulknerian art. It is needless to quote here examples—the Nobel Prize speech or the beautiful description of his artistic creed in his interview with Jean Stein—because they are known everywhere and the specialists and scholars know them almost by heart. Let us ask, however, why they appear in one book after another, article after article? The answer is simple. They are really the best that can be said about the meaning of Faulkner's art.

I would like to stress that these eruptions of his (for a long time hidden) views are not a simple explanation of his works. It is true, of course, that Faulkner proved to be the best critic of his own novels, especially because of his merciless and nonhypocritical assessments of their failures. His interpretations are very often the only possibility to break through our own critical inventions and scientific approaches. But to acknowledge this still does not fully explain their meaning. The significance of Faulkner's discussion of art becomes perhaps more vivid if we try to regard Faulkner's statements about art not as mere supplements to the fiction, but as an integral part of it—an opportunity to distill the essence or to hear the proverbial last word. One should not forget that such a "last word" does exist, in its real meaning, if we know the "first." Even the technical explanations given by Faulkner could appear then in a new light, in the "light in August" of his world. I would venture to say, for instance, that his famous account of his failure to finish *The Sound and the Fury,* after attempting to tell the story through the voices of Benjy, Quentin, Jason, and himself, this description of the origin of the work is the real end of the novel, the last point he strived to attain. After this there is nothing to say. The story with all its intricate complications has conveyed its meaning and is finished.

I do not mean to say, however, that Faulkner's literary views, his critical remarks, do not have any general meaning that could reach subjects beyond his works. They, of course, have such meaning. In fact, they impart some strategically important ideas of general interest for modern literature, even if occasionally Faulkner seems to be joking or talking rubbish. An example follows.

Professor Blotner in his well-known biography of Faulkner—held in high esteem by critics and scholars in my country—says, that Faulkner used to escape from puzzling questions by answering: "I'm not a literary man, I'm a farmer." No doubt, it is true. But if we look at Faulkner's words in the context of modern literature and its problems, we may see that Faulkner was right in another way too. There is a very important truth in this statement—a truth which concerns Faulkner's position in the literary world and his attitude towards the status of writing. It is interesting to note that, using almost the same words as Faulkner, Tolstoy said once: "Pushkin, Gogol, Goncharov are literary men; I'm not, neither is Lermontov." Tolstoy's words reflected his desire not to be a professional writer, but to write only when it was necessary to say something of extreme importance, to discuss with the people a major and urgent problem. In a way, he, like Faulkner, was a farmer, calling himself "an attorney for a hundred million farmers."

Faulkner's wish not to associate himself with professional literature reflects, one may suppose, a similar view. His remarks about style, about the choice between an ardent wish to pursue the truth and a concern for the form of expression, the exactness of language, derive from this same source. When we observe the panorama of modern literary development, we may agree that Faulkner's stance has refreshing significance. The abundance of successful writers who use their literary skill to prove anything they like (or almost anything) for a while and then change subjects—this ability to be convincing instead of discovering for the people the entire truth and making it evident for them as the only way to advance civilization—this great literary industry becomes dangerous and not only to aesthetics. A well-calculated combination of ends and means, of the goal and the device, deprives the literary image of what has always been its strongest asset—of the presence of reality with its never exhausted meaning. And at best it is replaced in such fiction by familiar ambiguity. Faulkner's revolt against the self-sufficient style has in this context profound meaning. One can certainly understand his desire to stand apart as a "farmer."

In addition, Faulkner's reluctance to be connected with the literary establishment relates to another important aspect of his work. I came to this conference straight from a distant village in the northern part of Russia, where I was the guest of our novelist and storyteller Vassily Belov. He is one of the representatives of the so-called "village prose" school of writers; I say "so-called" because only the subject of this fiction, and nothing else about it, is accurately characterized by the word "village." The themes, the ideas, and the general views of this fiction are much broader; the fiction is concerned primarily with the meaning of existence and the fundamental values of the human heart. The problem is how to preserve and to develop these values under present conditions, to sustain not only physical but also spiritual gravitation between the sputniks and the earth.

This particular writer, Belov, a man of modern education and peasant origin, permanently resides among his friends and neighbors; he knows everyone in the district for about twenty miles around, and everyone knows him personally. He is one of them. Thus, it is possible for him to see every problem in the context of a small universe, that is, not to impose the problem on the people, to find a brilliant (sometimes) but one-sided solution, but to understand its human sense and its necessary, inevitable ties with the whole range of human history. His most recent book on the farmers' way of life, entitled *Lud*, which might be translated as "Coordination" or "The Order" ("Lud" is an old native word), is currently receiving much attention by critics and the public.

I mention this to provide an example of what might be considered a growing tendency of modern literature. Faulkner's artistic decision to write about his "small postage stamp of native soil" is now widely acknowledged by writers around the world. One should confess that it was astonishing to hear something of this kind from industrialized America. In fact, Faulkner's voice was unique here, or seemed to be unique to us outside this country, because the most representative writers of this country were developing another kind of literature. This literature was concerned with technical innovation, the problems of generations, contemporary social struggles, the demons of the subconscious, sexual freedom, and other similar themes. Of course, Faulkner was not altogether alien to all this, but, at the core, the essence of his work lay in his discovery of his "native soil." One could even say that among the prominent Western writers of the twentieth century he was the first to turn to "patria minor"—the first to attempt to preserve human dignity and to support the creative mind. Here the decisive step was made. When we ask, for example, how could it happen that a writer of the extreme left in Austrian literature, a visiting writer in Paris, Peter Handke, suddenly changed his views, went home and wrote a play, *Über die Dörfer* (In the Countryside), which confronted his Austrian audience with an entirely new vision of man ("he is no longer the disgusting and hopeless beast whom we used to see on the stage, but a dignified human being," wrote one critic); when we see such a figure as John Gardner making an unexpected call for moral values, we can say that this was done by Faulkner long ago. It was Faulkner who broke through the wall of intellectual prejudices; it was he who really initiated this current of thought in Western literature of our time. We should all be grateful to him for this courageous breakthrough.

As for Russians, one can note, Faulkner's major concerns correspond with our lasting aspirations and efforts. This is, no

doubt, one of the reasons why Faulkner was received so enthusiastically in the Soviet Union. I mentioned Vassily Belov as an
example of a Soviet writer whose attitude towards literature and
life is reminiscent of Faulkner. But the most appropriate figure
of comparison would certainly be Mikhail Sholokhov. In our
literature he represents the Russian South, the Cossacks' Don;
he reveals through his piece of "native soil" universal truth;
throughout his life he has professed and defended the strongest
belief, proclaimed in America by Faulkner, that "man will endure." I think this very similarity is a sign of hope and a testimony to the belief in endurance.

Some critics assert, and these opinions are still influential
today, that an attachment to one's "native soil" is a sign of back-
wardness and thus an obstacle to progress. It is difficult to give
credence to this view. Progress moves like a chain—an individual, a family, a native land, a society, a universal truth—and
every member of this chain changes according to history; but if
you remove one member, the chain is broken and all that is left
is a blind confrontation with its links. The sole problem which
remains then is—who is stronger?—the question which is so
prevalent in the contemporary world. Faulkner's defense of his
"native soil" and his capacity to reproduce it in a living image
accessible to and comprehensible by the people of any other
"soil" is an outstanding achievement in maintaining his chain, in
reconstructing life. Recent current events prove that this capacity creates an opportunity in a very complex matter—in the
relationships among the peoples of the world. I can assure you,
and it is probably not so evident to you within this country, that
Faulkner's remote corner of life in Mississippi has helped us
very much in our country to break through the well-known
clichés about America: and these clichés, as you know, are powerful and are spread almost everywhere because they reflect
their own reality, too. Bluntly speaking, we find in Faulkner a
sincere, living, real man, concerned about everything human: in
short, a man that we may trust. At any rate, Faulkner's concern
with "his own postage stamp of native soil" is now winning sup-

porters among the most serious representatives of modern literature; this practice arises spontaneously even if its practitioners know nothing of their predecessor. Such art is not designed to solve all problems, nor is it the only way to authentic art. But in the present world it has found force anew and is gaining international recognition.

What is even more striking in this regard is Faulkner's sense of history, which permeates his entire conception of literature. To a European eye such a historical perspective is a somewhat unexpected feature to find in a writer from such a young country as America, where the pioneers, the Puritans, and the persecuted people were all united by one desire—to start life anew and to discard the past. Faulkner represents a necessary corrective to this view. Faulkner does not merely return to the past; rather his main concern is to reconstruct the ties of the new with the whole movement, to locate the rightful place of the new in the vast entirety of the universe.

And this concern leads him to a great number of extremely complex problems. With remarkable boldness and resolution he does not evade any of them. According to "his own theory of time" (which is, of course, not his own theory, but it sounds fresh and is animated by Faulkner's personal involvement), there is "no such thing as *was*, only *is*." Thus, he tries to put "everything" in his fiction. Without a thoroughly elaborated and mature image this kind of attempt could produce only another "splendid failure," and it virtually did. But the direction, the way, taken here was noble and right. Up to now there has been no great literature without historic consciousness. That Faulkner confronted American literature with this task, and with all his strength tried along to solve it, is to his great enduring credit. One can be sure, in this endeavor Faulkner will not remain without followers; it is only a matter of time.

This proves once again, if one needs proof, that Faulkner was an American patriot. Major problems of national development he experienced as his own problems, within his own vocation. Faulkner's literary opinions and statements reveal his perma-

nent concern with such considerations. How skillfully, for instance, he defended Walt Whitman against the rather shrewd
remarks of Thomas Carlyle. Carlyle wrote: "Walt Whitman
thinks, because he lives in a big country, he's a big man." To this
Faulkner responds: "Well, I would say that Carlyle's and Whitman's definition of a big man were completely different. Carlyle's an islander, a small country. His idea of a big man is a big
individual man. I should think that Whitman's idea of a big man
is one that is lucky enough to belong to a race of giants, if he's
one too. I wonder if Whitman believed that he was a bigger man
than anybody else in America?"[1]

But Faulkner never shut his eyes to "everything" that could
exist in his country, and he regarded his country's shortcomings
as a personal burden he should attempt to overcome however
difficult it might be. Such a position can evoke in a foreign
reader only deep respect. It is a pity that he was unable to
complete his book about the "American dream." All that remains
of his remarks on this topic is characterized by the same sense of
broad historic responsibility. He was here very direct and frank,
and, as usual, "not afraid of mistakes." Let me remind you of
Faulkner's words (preserved for us by Faulkner collector Carl
Petersen) on the subject of the American national character.
Addressing a Japanese audience, Faulkner explains: "The Japanese culture, for instance, is a culture of the intellect, just as the
French culture is a culture of rationality and the British culture
one of insularity. That is, each one makes its culture its national
character. Thus our American culture is not just success, but
generosity with success—a culture of successful generosity. We
desire and we work to be successful in order to be generous with
the fruits of that success. We get as much spiritual pleasure out
of giving as we do out of gaining. All of these cultures are important, and in a way, they are interdependent."[2]

    1. *Faulkner in the University*, ed. Frederick L. Gwynn and Joseph L. Blotner
(Charlottesville: University of Virginia Press, 1959), 138.
    2. Carl Petersen, *Each in Its Ordered Place: A Faulkner Collector's Notebook* (Ann
Arbor: Ardis, 1975), 164.

I shall not go in detail, nor have I any intention of criticizing Faulkner's definitions of various national characters, although every foreigner has his own opinion on such matters. In general, it is a doubtful practice to attribute such distinguishing qualities to separate peoples. But look how attentively and carefully Faulkner tries to detach the national ideal or national habit from possible charges of egoism. Clearly aware of this kind of criticism, expressed, for instance, by Tocqueville or Dickens, he does not simply reject it, but takes it into account and says: yes, Americans do pursue success, but success with generosity. Faulkner wants to see an American as a member of a vast human family, where everything is "interdependent."

Although he could not succeed in every individual case, Faulkner understood very well that literature needs a living person, an individual, in whose life you believe as in the life of your neighbor or relative. If such a person does not exist in the story, or in the novel, all the writer's efforts are in vain, and every technical sophistication of style is only boring. It was for this reason that Faulkner refused to be preoccupied with the problems of language: in his opinion, the real language of a writer was a living character, an individual, the human heart. The behavior of such a person, each of his steps, is the form of a writer's thought. To understand this fact is not as easy as it may seem at first. To many modern critics the imminent surface of the work, the language, obscured the essence of literature instead of clarifying it; the human face and soul were regarded as merely the subjects of description. But how can you describe them, if they never existed? One should create them first, and this creation is the only worthy endeavor of art. Here lies the way of attaining the meaning the artist intends to reveal. If the creations, the characters, are dead and artificial, the sense is dead too, and language cannot save it.

Faulkner's defense of life was consequently connected with a defense of this creative ability. He criticized modern fiction for forgetting these fundamental qualities of art. Modern characters, he said, "do not function, live, breathe, struggle, in that moil and seethe of simple humanity as did those of our predecessors who were the masters from whom we learned our craft."[3] These words were addressed to young writers. One should appreciate Faulkner's attempt to be convincing for his young colleagues—stressing the point to which they were especially sensitive: freedom. Faulkner has shown that if the writer loses the ability to put life into his images freedom vanishes from art. The characters of the writer, he said, are doomed then to function "not in individuality but in isolation, not to pursue in myriad company the anguishes and hopes of all human hearts in a world of a few simple comprehensible truths and moral principles, but to exist alone inside a vacuum of facts which he did not choose and cannot cope with and cannot escape from like a fly inside an inverted tumbler."[4]

Isolation, mentioned in the quoted passage, is probably the quality most detested by Faulkner. For Faulkner, isolation is the chief enemy of life and literature. Isolation means death, death of every sort: moral, spiritual, physical. Faulkner's art, on the other hand, strives always for a complete presence of all possible ties with his subject.

What deserves special attention here is the subtle distinction Faulkner makes between seemingly similar notions. For example, he says: "not in individuality, but in isolation." On the surface, nothing is more isolated than "individuality"; the very essence of individuality is to be unique, without resemblance, to emerge only once in life—never before and never after; individuality is an island of privacy. But for Faulkner it is also a unique concentration of remote and contradictory forces of the world. Individuality can bring these forces together, advance, and conquer isolation. In Faulkner's universe "individuality" recalls its original meaning: *individuus,* that is, something that cannot be divided, something that contains everything in itself. As long as it lives, it has a moving center, and is an active

3. *Faulkner in the University,* 243.
4. Ibid., 244.

participant in the universal "moil and seethe." To keep in touch with individuality, according to Faulkner, is the primary duty of a writer.

One can reproach Faulkner, as some critics do, for retreating from this ideal in his writings. It is true that in Faulkner's fiction sometimes this individual truth is diluted in many additional and occasionally unnecessary explanations. In these instances, Faulkner would enumerate all the possible connections with his subject, one after another, instead of giving us a single feature which could unite them all without further explanation; Faulkner was inclined sometimes to symbols and allegories, apparently forgetting that a living character, one of "flesh and blood," as he himself called it, does not need such literary devices. In connection with this, I'd like to bring to your attention a kind of kinship that exists between certain rationalistic trends of art in the eighteenth century and in twentieth-century modernism: not unlike the painters of the eighteenth century who could not do without such extraneous symbols as doves and lambs symbolizing virtue, the modernists of our age resort to mythological techniques to conceal the inner inadequacy of their imagery. Faulkner was not totally impervious to such influences. But he never ceased to pursue his goal—to find an individual expression for hundreds of ideas at once. When he could find it, it was a marvelous revelation for the reader, as for the author himself. Just recollect with what pleasure he repeated the answer of Lena Grove to Byron Bunch. Each such example of "individuality" was, no doubt, an important contribution to the struggle against isolation.

Faulkner's wide-ranging look at art in his last years helped him to understand better his native American literature. One needs only to recall his changed attitude towards Mark Twain, whom Faulkner regarded, at first, as a writer without proper artistic structure and order, only to reverse himself later when, full of admiration, Faulkner was ready to place Twain at the top of American fiction. Faulkner's humanistic approach also became clearer and more confident, and his investigation of human vice developed into an open offensive. The contrast between Faulkner's new revelations and his former writings was so strong that he was suspected of arriving at these new conclusions at the last moment in an effort to justify his previous missteps. Thus, for example, in his later years Faulkner was asked whether he really believed that *The Sound and the Fury* fostered the impression that "man will prevail." Questions like this one intimated that Faulkner could (or should) rewrite everything once again, as he had done many times before.

But Faulkner did not need to rewrite his novels. The hidden force that always moved his fantasies and had proudly met every challenge, the force which before had been sometimes lost from view, at last, in his statements about art, became clearly visible. Although perhaps Faulkner did not realize it himself, his discussions of literature illuminated the whole picture of his literary career and put it in the ultimate frame. And this is the victory of his art.

Word and Idea
in *The Sound and the Fury*

SERGEI CHAKOVSKY

This work deals with the relationship between "artistry" ("word")
and ideology ("idea") which of course are inseparable because
any "ideologizing," that is, conveying some new, human meaning while depicting it, *is* artistry. Yet, as we all know, in critical
practice these notions are all too often separated, the results
ranging from arbitrariness to vulgarization. This tendency, fear,
is enhanced by the intellectual passing winds of our highly spe-
cialized age. The data obtained, for instance, by specialists in
poetics and stylistics tend to be optional, if not totally irrelevant,
for literary historians and "practical critics." Research in the
ideological sphere of art and research pertaining to "style" are
more likely to communicate with the "adjacent" humanitarian
sciences (history, sociology, psychology, on the one hand; lin-
guistics, semiotics, on the other) than with each other. The
rationale behind this is the perception of a work of art not as a
product but as a *sum* of various properties which fall under the
jurisdiction of various social sciences, the subject of literary
scholarship proper being extremely vague. The unity of a field of
learning, we surmise, is inconceivable without the unity of its
object. A work of art possessing a certain undeniable integrity is
at the same time many things to many people. The specific
province of literary scholarship would seem to be the study of
the combination and the interaction of those "things," the
mutual functional conditionality of various elements which comprise a work of literature and its relationship to the outer world.
The aim of such analysis is the reconstruction of a hierarchy of

"ends and means" which reflect and embody in objectively perceivable categories the author's artistic intention.

Since a serious work of literature (poetry and prose alike, although the degree may vary) is a system oriented towards a certain general effect, it would be wrong to ascribe the nature of any *one* of its elements (however seemingly important) to any one extraneous factor. This is the aspect with which I am particularly concerned. An element is always a part of an artistic-ideological whole, and the meaning attributed to it is often conditioned not only and not as much by what the author "wants" or "thinks" as by what the text "wants" (in order to be able to fulfil its general artistic function). It is common knowledge that sometimes an element of reality brought into the context of a work of art acquires meaning which may contradict the author's personal views. The work of art through its inner logic "teaches" the author, often challenging his political, ideological, and moral preconceptions. Statements to this effect have been made by writers from Balzac through Chekhov to Faulkner. Faulkner, for example, described the process of artistic creation as "listening" to the story-to-be, trying to understand how it "wants to be told." So it is only natural for the scholar of literature to try to understand why the novel or the short story "wanted" to be told in this particular way and not otherwise, to assess the artistic meaningfulness and the expediency with which the action is presented.

I would not have expanded on these generalities if I did not feel that they are of special importance to understanding William Faulkner and the book he had "the most tenderness for"[1]— *The Sound and the Fury*.

As has been pointed out on more than one occasion, Faulkner's artistic evolution (at least in the first half of his creative career) was "less directly influenced by the extraneous factors of American life than that of the other writers of his generation."[2]

---

1. *Faulkner at Nagano*, ed. Robert A. Jelliffe (Tokyo: Kenkyusha Ltd., 1956), 105.
2. N. A. Anastasiev, Preface to *Absalom, Absalom!* (Moscow, 1982), 4.

The whole structural tendency of Faulkner's work is "not outwards but inwards, not centrifugal but centripetal,"[3] remarked Michael Millgate in his important study. The principal role in Faulkner's development as a writer was played by the "inner" work of his artistic consciousness, by the successive attempts of the author to understand the will of his material, to reconcile it with the imperatives of his lyrical persona, of his ideology and imagination, in the agonizing search for artistic truth. It is this devotion to the inner truth of the work of art which has always instilled in Faulkner, in the words of P. Palievsky, "the indomitable desire to rewrite everything from the beginning, cutting short the thought yet scarcely outlined."[4]

According to his well-known account in the introduction to *The Sound and the Fury*, Faulkner wrote "the same story four times" and it "failed four times."[5] I will return to this statement to note that it may be just as misleading as it is revealing. For the moment I will simply point out that he has tried to "rewrite" the novel on at least two other occasions. The first rewrite is the famous Appendix added at Cowley's request some fifteen years later; the second and, perhaps, most important is *The Sound and the Fury* itself, which as a whole is a "rewrite" of his unhappy novel of the previous year—*Flags in the Dust* (which became known in the editorially "rewritten" version as *Sartoris*). It is the Appendix that makes it possible to treat *Sartoris* and *The Sound and the Fury*, however outwardly dissimilar they may seem, as realizations, variants, of the same intention.

The Appendix is of particular interest because it contains the plan of *The Sound and the Fury* as it could have been written (to the satisfaction of the more conservative critics of the 1930s and perhaps of the '80s as well) but luckily never was: following in a straightforward way the fate of the Compsons in the course of two and a half centuries—including a sequence of legendary

3. Michael Millgate, *The Achievement of William Faulkner* (New York: Random House, 1966), 286.

4. P. V. Palievsky, "Folkner i Camu," in *Literatura i teoriya* (Moscow, 1978), 223.

5. *Faulkner at Nagano*, 103–5.

warriors, profiteers, adventurers, dreamers—up to their modern descendants who are lost in the intricate destinies of their family and their land. Actually *Sartoris* was such a novel—the first draft of a "tragedy of fate" which found a splendid incarnation in *The Sound and the Fury* and its "sequel" *Absalom! Absalom!* But let us concentrate on the thematic relationship between the former two novels. *Sartoris,* according to the narrator's famous summation, is "a game outmoded and played with pawns shaped too late and to an old dead pattern, and of which the Player Himself is a little wearied. For there is death in the sound of it, and a glamorous fatality, like silver pennons downrushing at sunset."[6]

This theme is reiterated in *The Sound and the Fury:* "It used to be," Quentin remembers, "I thought of death as a man something like Grandfather a friend of his a kind of private and particular friend like we used to think of Grandfather's desk not to touch it not even to talk loud in the room where it was I always thought of them as being together somewhere all the time waiting for old Colonel Sartoris to come down and sit with them."[7] So why then should the final text "choose for itself" a form so unusual, so drastically different both from its conceptual plan—the Appendix—and from the preceding novel? To answer this question (however incompletely) we have to analyze the ideological and aesthetic implications of the narrative structure of *The Sound and the Fury.*

If the narrative form of *The Sound and the Fury* is abstracted from deceptive external analogies (which caused so much critical confusion) and is approached from the point of view of its artistic meaningfulness, then it can be understood in terms of the author's instinctive desire to overcome the ideological-artistic contradictions of the previous novel. Essentially Faulkner was an empirical (and, therefore, a very "authentic") artist; to this, to a

---

6. William Faulkner, *Sartoris* (New York: A Signet Classic, 1964), 303.
7. William Faulkner, *The Sound and the Fury* (New York: Vintage Books, 1964), 218. Further references to this work will appear in the text.

considerable extent, his remarkable artistic insights were due as well as his no less remarkable failures.

In the words of Calvin S. Brown, "Novelists like Zola and Thomas Mann did extensive reading and note-taking, and called on experts for help in fields where they were not so sure of themselves. Faulkner never did this. . . . He did not look in a library. There is a great deal of history in his work but he was probably telling the truth when he said that he had read little history. He had picked it up from family traditions, reminiscences of Confederate soldiers and other oral sources."[8]

The narrative form used in *Sartoris* (the "objective," omniscient narrator) was clearly uncongenial to the expression of Faulkner's "emotional" rather than "intellectual" knowledge of history. The plot was romantically tendentious; the narrator failed to sustain the indispensable (given the role he had assumed) objectivity at every stage. He did "not know," or knew but could not bring himself to accept the fact, that it was not a mysterious and noble "doom," but history with its sufficiently unrefined social laws, which condemned the Sartorises to extinction.

"As regards any specific book," wrote Faulkner to Cowley, "I'm trying primarily to tell the story in the most effective way I can think of, the most moving, the most exhaustive."[9] Clearly, the way *Sartoris* was told (as well as Faulkner's two previous novels) was *not* effective. So Faulkner makes a turnabout. He starts to "tell the story" again but with a radical change of face; transforming an "imposing" narrator, claiming omniscience and intellectual aloofness, into a miserable idiot, who "sees what's happening but cannot understand why." The substitution of a different narrator, even if perhaps an absolutely spontaneous act, was far from accidental and resulted in a radical restructuring of the novel as a whole: a changed relationship between

8. *A Glossary of Faulkner's South* (New Haven: Yale University Press, 1976), 4.
9. Quoted in *The Achievement of William Faulkner*, 286.

author, character, word, event, and, accordingly, their functions in the novel. It is very important to try to understand how this system works, to describe at least some of its aesthetic and ideological implications. In *Sartoris*, Faulkner discovered his material. In *The Sound and the Fury*, he found his true artistic self—that central principle of perception of World and Man on which the originality of his artistic system wholly depends. It may of course be obscured in the novel by the rhetoric which many critics regarded as offensively complicated. But the rhetoric conveys meaning far beyond the illustration of the inner workings of the imbecile consciousness (about which Faulkner knew little and cared, I believe, even less).

As compared with *Sartoris*, the structure of *The Sound and the Fury* is inverted. A complete change of roles occurs as the character takes the author's place and, relying on the power of words, tries to change the course of events of which he is part. This, as I will try to demonstrate, is the principle that is sustained throughout the novel, the principle on which the novel's style and composition are largely dependent. It is artistically "formulated" for the first time in Benjy's section: " 'He know lot more than folks thinks,' Roskus said. 'He knowed they time was coming, like that pointer done. He could tell you when hisn coming, *if he could talk*' " (38). " 'What is it. What are you trying to *tell* Caddy' " (italics mine) (5).

Benjy's "story" is among other things the dramatization of the torment of dumbness. Hence the magical attitude toward the word. The underlying assumption that life can be reconstructed the way a sentence can determines the structure of the character's "speech" and constitutes the inner motivation of a sometimes capricious style.

Take, for example, the opening scene of *The Sound and the Fury*:

> Through the fence, between the curling flower spaces, I could see them hitting. They were coming toward where the flag was and I went along the fence. Luster was hunting in the grass by the flower tree. They took the flag out, and they were hitting. Then they put

the flag back and they went to the table, and he hit and the other hit. Then they went on, and I went along the fence. Luster came away from the flower tree and we went along the fence and they stopped and we stopped and I looked through the fence while Luster was hunting in the grass. (1)

As can be seen even in the first sentence, Benjy's phrasing is a rhythmically well-balanced and "lucid." Although the narrator fails to keep up the originally planned meter for any length of time (such sentences do not occur often) it is important that the reader be fully conscious of its "standardness," since all deviations are psychologically significant. Benjy (an "innocent," to use Faulkner's term) is incompetent in mundane matters and he uses language (with which he is equally incompetent) to conceal it. The reader cannot help sensing the artificiality and implausibility of his naive pretense.

The very first sentence of the novel captures the reader's attention with its lexical and rhythmical heterogeneity. On the one hand, there is the conventionally poetic "curling flower spaces"; on the other, the energetic "carnal" and also ambiguous "hitting." This more or less palpable ambiguity is the semantic realization of a certain stylistic "conflict" discernible in the beginning of the sentence. This conflict consists of using as homogeneous parts (separated by means of a comma) the two adverbial modifiers—of place and mode of action—which possess entirely different connotations: "Through the fence, between the curling flower spaces . . . ." Using the word "fence" in such a prominent stylistic situation—the beginning of the novel, the beginning of the phrase—has, so it would seem, quite a definite stylistic connotation—the limitation of freedom, i.e., captivity. An altogether different attitude and "persona" is associated with the metaphorical word combination, "curling flower spaces." This conflict, which at first manifests itself at the level of stylistic connotation, is then "suppressed" as the sentence continues, and finally develops into flagrant ambiguity— "them hitting," which in the absence of an object may mean anything. This principle of developing the conflict from latent to overt dramatic form, from the level of the stylistics of speech to the level of event, is consistently sustained throughout the narrative. The development of the novel, we may say, is predicated on the stylistic "mistake" of the narrator, which by gradual accumulation leads to catastrophic consequences.

Benjy's mistake in this case consists of his trying subconsciously to reconcile two unreconcilable elements—the symbolism of flowers (i.e., of childhood, Caddy) and the symbolism of the "iron age," which had deprived him of Caddy and put a fence around his favorite pasture. The conflict develops "vertically" and is realized on the surface of the plot. The incomprehensible actions of the golf players frighten the character-narrator. When they hit the ball he apprehends it as a blow on his own body.

The "microexplosion" of the conflict takes place in the paragraph that follows. One of the players calls for the boy and pronounces the sacred combination of sounds: "'Here, caddie.' He hit. They went across the pasture. I held to the fence and watched them going away" (1). Contrasted with the preceding paragraph and the drawn-out rambling phrase which concludes it, this phrasing is strikingly compact and meaningful. Particularly noteworthy is the second sentence, which emphasizes by means of its jerky rhythm the now unequivocal hostility of the verb "to hit." It is at this moment that Luster's remark is made, confirming and qualifying the reader's conjectures concerning the identity of the character-narrator and revealing the futility of his attempts to feign calm and aloofness.

> "Listen at you, now." Luster said. "Ain't you something, thirty-three years old, going on that way. After I done went all the way to town to buy you that cake. Hush up that moaning. Ain't you going to help me find that quarter so I can go to the show tonight." (1)

Luster's remark suppresses the conflict between Benjy and the golfers, or rather gives it a new dimension. On the one hand, the reader, who sees the character from within, cannot fail to understand the inadequacy of Luster's common sense "version" of

Benjy. At the same time he is conscious of the necessity and inevitability of Luster's words.

An "inner dialogue," an implicit argument, begins between the characters. It is expressed, on the one hand, in Luster's remarks and, on the other, in Benjy's oblique answers which show that he is trying not to "take notice" of those of Luster's words that are not to his liking, that his mind is set on something else. It takes time for Luster to persuade Benjy that the players have gone and will not come back: "'Come on,' Luster said. 'We done looked there. They aint no more coming right now. Lets go down to the branch and find that quarter before them niggers finds it'" (2). Benjy obviously likes the respectful "we" Luster uses, thus changing the patronizing tone of his previous remarks. Benjy wanted to "identify" with him from the outset, trying in vain to incorporate Luster's strange occupation ("hunting in the grass") into his milieu so that he could call on him as an ally against the players ("we went along the fence and they stopped and we stopped"). Now he seizes the opportunity to draw Luster over to his side (he measures up his shadow against Luster's, remarking with renewed self-assurance that "my shadow was higher than Luster's on the fence" [2]). The reader understands that nothing can possibly develop from this identification because their interests (for Luster—to find the coin so that he can go to the show; for Benjy—to bring back a lost harmony) are incompatible. That's why Benjy's next phrase, "We came to the broken place and went through it" (2), is apprehended as another attempt on his part to reconcile the irreconcilable, as an illusion of the character which is doomed to vanish sooner or later. It vanishes at once: "'Wait a minute,' Luster said. 'You snagged on that nail again. Cant you never crawl through here without snagging on that nail'" (3).

Availing herself of an associative pretext, *real* Caddy rushes into Benjy's world. If in the context of the preceding scene the pronunciation of the word "caddy" is apprehended as a blow ("hit"), here it is striking how easily and organically it forms part of the phonetic sequence. This effect is achieved by saturating Luster's remark and Benjy's "reply" with vowels as well as by a clearly marked k alliteration: "*C*ant you never *cra*wl through here without snagging on that nail."

Caddy uncaught me and we crawled through. (3)

Here for the first time Faulkner uses italics. Their function as we see it is to render the bewilderment of the character-narrator at this encounter with the *real* theme which he laboriously tries to avoid in his intense desire to gain control over it.[10] No other function can be consistently attributed to this device, which serves the same purpose throughout the novel despite the change of narrators.

The appearance of Caddy is the first of a series of "substitutions" which the hero instinctively commits in order to avoid the undesirable conflict. It becomes clear that in the beginning Benjy was trying to substitute Luster for Caddy (by artificially combining his name with the symbolism of the "flower tree"). Between them the unavoidable contradictions arise. Benjy starts looking for a new savior. But now that the real Caddy appears the reader apprehends the extraneous analogy of which the hero is unaware. Like Luster in the opening scene, Caddy is introduced unexpectedly but, on the other hand, as something "given" (in the syntactic sense of the word). The obvious parallel evokes in the reader anticipation of the repetition of the collision. The author does not fail to satisfy these expectations: the relations between Benjy and Caddy follow at first the same pattern as the ones with Luster and then lead to a far more severe crisis.

Benjy is happy to have Caddy near him. "*We stooped over and crossed the garden where the flowers rasped and rattled against us*" (3). His impulse is to "freeze" this moment of happiness, to

---

10. Admitting to the absence of a definite plan in using italics, Faulkner wrote to Ben Wasson: "I think italics are necessary to establish for the reader Benjy's confusion; that unbroken surfaced confusion of an idiot which is outwardly a dynamic and logical coherence." *Selected Letters of William Faulkner*, ed. Joseph Blotner (New York: Random House, 1977), 44.

shut off Caddy and himself from the entire world. Yet she belongs to that other world—the real world of their alcoholic Uncle
Maury, whose errand she is commissioned to run, the world of
their lamenting mother, of their cruel brother Jason. "'You're
not a poor baby. Are you. You've got your Caddy. Haven't you
got your Caddy'" (8).

This we may call the moment of ultimate truth and ultimate
falsehood of their relationship. Because even as she pronounces
those words she cannot help thinking of the intriguing errand on
which her uncle sends her—to pass his love letter to the wife of
their neighbor Mrs. Patterson. The predominant impulse of
Benjy's "speech" is to subdue the conflict between what Caddy
actually says and what he wants her to say. And when he fails to
do so, he steps back and starts to "tell the story all over again."
That is why the episode, the action "proper," which would
hardly take more than a page and a half, runs into fifteen pages,
resembling in its "vertical" structure (just as the novel as a
whole) Faulkner's famous later "long sentence." At the end of
the episode the sometimes vague stylistic undercurrent
translates itself into dynamic action; "words" become "deeds."
Caddy abandons Benjy, leaving him face to face with a now
openly hostile world:

> *You, idiot, . . . I told him never to send you alone again. Give it to*
> *me. Quick. Mr Patterson came fast, with the hoe. Mrs Patterson*
> *leaned across the fence, reaching her hand. She was trying to climb*
> *the fence. Give it to me, she said. Give it to me. Mr Patterson climbed*
> *the fence. He took the letter. Mrs Patterson's dress was caught on the*
> *fence. I saw her eyes again and I ran down the hill.* (14–15)

The definitions often applied to the narrative form of *The Sound
and the Fury*—"the stream of consciousness novel" or "the novel
of inner monologue"—are to a considerable extent misleading.
"Stream of consciousness" is just one of the narrative forms employed in the novel, a transition or rather a lapse which is always
an artistically-psychologically meaningful deviation from the
form of an orderly narration. The term "inner monologue" can
be regarded as correct only in so far as it presupposes the artistic

conditionality of a speech act; at the same time the most characteristic trait of the narrator's speech in a Faulkner novel (*The Sound and the Fury* being a prototypical if a somewhat paradoxical example) is its inner "dialogism," to use the notion, which Mikhail Boechtin introduced in his analysis of Dostoevsky's work, or "polylogism," to be precise. Faulkner's narrator addresses not only the reader, thus challenging the traditional "author-reader pact," but some unnamed opponent *within* the novel and "itself." The situation of a multisided argument (because the narrator is always arguing with himself as well) is a typically "Faulknerian" speech situation which is clearly evident in *The Sound and the Fury*. In the beginning—in Benjy's section—the argument is oblique, then it becomes clearly manifest—in Quentin's and Jason's sections; but it always remains the unifying and the style-determining element of the novel.

Benjy "argues" with Luster, Mother, Uncle Maury, Caddy; Quentin, with the "abductors" of Caddy—Dalton Ames, Herbert Head—and with Father and Caddy; Jason argues with Caddy, Quentin, "the man with a red tie," with Dilsey and with Father's memory; they all argue with one another, and with their destiny.

Disappearing from the "stage," the author leaves his word with the character (this is quite obvious in Benjy's case). The character tries to put the word to "work," but he does not quite know how to use it; the word remains *strange* to him (those "in the know" are the author and the reader who are brought closer together through this common knowledge). This to a great extent holds true in regard to Quentin and Jason. They also speak a language that is not entirely their own. Quentin unconsciously uses Father's language, trying to use the worldly wisdom embodied in it as a shield against the tormenting recollections of Caddy's "betrayal." Jason speaks in the markedly vulgar manner of a country shopkeeper in order to alienate himself from his disintegrating, despite its "aristocracy of the spirit," family. The word, the text as a whole having been "left" to the character, becomes for him a temptation and a trial. "Things and deeds"

SERGEI CHAKOVSKY   295

refuse to submit to words, hence the use of language at the
limits of its capacity, the burning desire to "bend" it to one's
needs, and hence also that special meaningfulness of all the
"formal" elements of the text. Faulkner's character-narrator is in
constant need of more words, more punctuation marks, more
types of print so that he can preserve the crumbling unity of his
story, make the real unreal and vice versa, and prolong the
desired event and "erase" the unwanted one. The character does
his utmost to suppress the conflict which inevitably arises from
the encounter with reality, with real people and events that will
not conform to his illusionary scheme. At such moments the
rhythm of the narration breaks down and the narrator's orderly
speech may "slip" into stream of consciousness. The conflict
suppressed on one level inevitably reappears on another, thus
constituting the answer of reality to the arbitrariness of human
will, a kind of "retribution" of the text for the abuse of the power
of the word.

In *The Sound and the Fury* the "event" and the "character-
narrator" are antagonistic elements. By the time the story begins
all major events have already taken place. These events are
compulsory whereas the character, aspiring to the position of the
"author," is more or less "accidental" (being a chance victim of
the curse which haunts his family and his class). From the beginning, events tend to force the characters out: they "act," flowing
from one section of the novel into another, while the characters
"happen." This struggle between the character and the events
constitutes the plot.

The three character-narrators *do not want* to tell "Caddy's
story." That is why all the most important events are reported as
though by accident, out of the narrator's "negligence," rather
than his intent. The real story as it were "tells itself" despite the
resistance of the narrator for whom "the plot" is his own life and
the act of telling it is not a form of communication but rather a
form of personal "salvation."

The characters of *The Sound and the Fury* are sources of
various *centrifugal* impulses (the strongest expression of which

is Caddy's threat "to run away and never come back"). The *centripetal* impulses come from the corpus of events that constitute the plot of the novel and which develops spirally, according to the principle of "repetition with increment," in the same "vicious circle." All the chronological "disorderliness" and the outward "incoherence" of the novel turn out to be the backdrop which brings out the absolute coherence in the development of Caddy's story: in the first section the reader learns about Caddy's childhood and adolescence; in the second about her marriage and the destiny of her daughter, Quentin, her structural substitute in the latter sections.

With respect to the character-narrators Caddy acts as a predominant power, which to a great extent levels their differences. Benjy's latent suffering finds a more articulate expression in Quentin; their unhappy love for the unconsciously "insidious" Caddy (love-hate) turns into open hostility on the part of Jason who becomes the most obvious victim of her "insidiousness." In relation to the heroine these three "different" characters act more or less as one. Since these characters are narrators as well, the text, in spite of their desperate attempts to underscore their individuality through action as well as through speech, assumes the "unplanned for" unity, an extremely high degree of inner *isomorphism.* The structure of the novel with its ironic analogies, the relentlessness of the central conflict and the almost fatal predestination of events emphasizes the drama of the character-narrator's predicament. The structure of the novel reinforces Father's bitter wisdom which Quentin then failed to understand or accept: "but you are still blind to what is in yourself to that part of general truth the sequence of natural events and their causes which shadows every mans brow even benjys" (220). Of no less importance is another of his cryptic phrases: "On the instant when we come to realize that tragedy is second-hand" (143). In this phrase, quite unexpectedly, the principle of the artistic effect of the novel is formulated: it is based on making the reader aware of the precedent, of the analogies which the character cannot perceive. It is "on the instant" when the reader realizes that Quentin's tragedy has already been experienced by Benjy and that Jason's dilemma is not new either, that the breakthrough towards the general artistic and human meaning of the novel takes place.

It is worth mentioning that it would be hardly correct to oppose radically Jason Compson to all the other characters of the novel. Following Faulkner's devastating references to Jason ("the most vicious character . . . I ever thought of")[11] quite a few Faulkner critics would not only condemn Jason on the grounds of everyday morality which is, of course, quite justifiable, but virtually exclude him from the world of the novel. The two latter parts of *The Sound and the Fury* are quite often referred to as nothing short of being "another novel."

In Jason the conflict between the centrifugal and the centripetal impulses of novel is aggravated to the last extreme. On the one hand, he longs to dissociate himself from everything "Compsonian." Unlike Benjy and Quentin, Jason always (or almost always) exists in time. Time is money for him; the striking of a clock not a reminder of the fatal predestination of human existence, but a signal that he must rush to the post office in order not to miss the latest stock-market exchange report. His only problem is that he has not only more "warm blood" in him than Caddy or Dilsey would admit but also than he himself would like to have. Even in his endeavors to be grotesquely "bad," Jason is not original. Quentin was dreaming of doing something horrible enough to "isolate [Caddy] out of the loud world so that it would have to flee us of necessity" (220). He smashes and coldbloodedly "dissects" his grandfather's watch, thus commiting a no less sacrilegious act against the family tradition than Jason with all his philippics. Jason's petty utilitarianism is no less a family trait and "virtue" than Quentin's idealism (after all it is to the enterprise of their great-grandfather Jason Lycurgus, who cheated Ikkemotubbe out of his strip of land,

11. William Faulkner, *Lion in the Garden: Interviews with William Faulkner 1926–1962*, ed. James B. Meriwether and Michael Millgate (New York: Random House, 1968), 146.

that the Compson family owes its rise to eminence). ("Watching pennies has healed more scars than Jesus" [221], says Father to Quentin.)

Jason's pathetic attempt to make a "killing" at the cotton market (like Benjy's and Quentin's maniacal obsession with their sister's honor) is just another manifestation of the hopeless, and hence all the more desperate, desire to reverse time, to regain the former power of his family. Despite all Jason's talent for fending off and holding his own with Compsons (about which the author tells us in the Appendix) his narrative, like Benjy's and Quentin's, fails to become a "different story." There appear a host of "unexpected" parallels and analogies between Jason, Quentin, and Benjy (they all hate artificial odors, be it perfume, whiskey, or gasoline; hate Caddy's beaus; and try to strike a personal deal with their common fate). Events fail to conform to the personal will of the character-narrator despite or, in the context of the novel, due to the attempts of the character to exercise a rigid control over them.

Like Benjy and more than Quentin, Jason *does not want* to talk about Caddy. He tries to screen himself from her not only with harsh words, but on the "plot level" as well—with intrigue and blackmail. In his life, Caddy's place—the object of the sublime adoration of Benjy and Quentin—is occupied by an "honest whore"—Lorraine. Yet Jason cannot help coming back to Caddy again and again in his story—she is not only his guilty conscience, but the secret object of his envy and admiration. Even in terms of enterprise Caddy by far surpasses Jason. She never fails to astound him with her resolve and impudence and with her absolute contempt for Compsonian mores, of which he himself is incapable.

Thus, the chief narrative device of the novel is valid in Jason's section as in his brothers' sections. Like Benjy and Quentin, Jason seeks to erect a shield of words (corroborated by deeds) between himself and the real world. When this shield is torn down, the rigidly cerebral narrative of the "first sane Compson since Culloden" gives way to the barely controlled "stream of consciousness." This and the ironic reversal of the opposition between sanity and insanity once again underscore the unity of the novel:

> And there I was, without any hat, looking like I was crazy too. Like a man would naturally think, one of them is crazy and another one drowned himself and the other one was turned out into the street by her husband, what's the reason the rest of them are not crazy too. All the time I could see them watching me like a hawk, waiting for a chance to say Well I'm not surprised I expected it all the time the whole family's crazy. Selling land to send him to Harvard and paying taxes to support a state University all the time that I never saw except twice at a baseball game and not letting her daughter's name be spoken on the place until after a while Father wouldn't even come down town anymore but just sat there all day with the de- canter I could see the bottom of his night-shirt and his bare legs and hear the decanter clinking until finally T. P. had to pour it for him and she says You have no respect for your Father's memory and I says I dont know why not it sure is preserved well enough to last only if I'm crazy too God knows what I'll do about it just to look at water makes me sick and I'd just as soon swallow gasoline as a glass of whiskey and Lorraine telling them. . . ." (290–91)

Interpreting *The Sound and the Fury* as an artistic whole makes it possible to draw some general conclusions and to sug- gest some formulations which could be applied to the study of Faulkner's artistic evolution as well as to various comparative- typological studies.

Defined in a nutshell, the essence of the poetic originality of *The Sound and the Fury,* is that in this novel (in comparison to more "traditional," "standard" works of fiction) we deal with a different relationship between *word* and *action.* In a "tradi- tional" work of fiction the word and the text, despite all their influence on the perception of the described events, in the final analysis are reduced in the mind of the reader to the subservient status of a somewhat transparent *cover* for the action. The word remains subject to the more or less conventional logic of a coher- ent narrative while the action is determined by the more or less unconditional logic of life. Depending on the type of narrator, these sequences may approach one another, but the dichotomy between "word" and "deed," "narration" and "action" always remains (this holds true in regard to "Ich-erzahlung" as well as to various forms of "skaz"—a stylized, "colorful" narration in the first person). A narrator cannot be a character, an "actor," while he is a narrator. In *The Sound and the Fury* this rule is broken; the dichotomy between action and narration is abolished. The narrator becomes a character and his word becomes a *factor of the plot.* The word appears to lose its conditional, information-conveying function and becomes an *act* to which the plot, as if lending an attentive ear to what the character-narrator says, reacts. In his turn the narrator struggles with the plot, trying to set the logic of speech against the logic of life. Outside of these assumptions the text of *The Sound and the Fury* is incoherent.

The one methodological implication I would like to mention is that it would be particularly detrimental to one's understanding of the novel to try to "look through" the word and to define its idea exclusively on the basis of what the heroes "do." On the other hand, the acceptance of "word" as *action* makes it possible to interpret the novel in ideological terms.

Thus, the theme of "curse" or "doom," which in *Sartoris* was just "talked about," became artistically meaningful in *The Sound and the Fury* and was filled with profound moral and social content. The author of *The Sound and the Fury* no longer sees "glamor" in "fatality." In *Sartoris* the characters are resigned to their fate; in *The Sound and the Fury* they try, however ineffectively, to overcome or to "deceive" it. They do not want to be "dolls stuffed with sawdust swept up from the trash heaps where all previous dolls had been thrown away." Furiously and ineptly they defend their right to primogeniture from the claims of the powerful tradition which threatens to turn them into the "shadows" (the "key-word" of the novel) of their legendary ancestors. They are fully resolved to prove the *reality* of their existence at any cost—even suicide.

Faulkner was quite sincere when he said that what interested him most were "people, not ideas." At the same time there is at least some truth in the notion that "Faulkner is an artist of a special kind, he deals not with an individual proper (Quentin as well as his other characters are not so much real people with their individual traits as a portrayal of the epoch) but with a collective psychology of a whole class of people."[12] Faulkner's hero, in the words of P. Palievsky, is always "the continuation of something distant." Nevertheless, the dignity of Faulkner's character always lies in his attempt to maintain his individuality, to demonstrate his independence from the "idea" or "type" which pretends faithfully to represent him. And it is this struggle for individuality which infuses Faulkner's realism with its personal lyrical quality.

Despite its outwardly whimsical, "subjective" form, in *The Sound and the Fury* Faulkner made a definite step towards artistic objectivity. The clash of illusion and reality, personal will and the objective will of events, which Faulkner outlined in this novel, to a great extent conditioned the imagery, meaning, and poetics of his fictional world.

12. N. A. Anastasiev, "Put' Folknera k Derevushke," *Voprosi literaturi*, 11 (1970), 125.

Faulkner's Narrative Discourse:
Mediation and Mimesis

SONJA BAŠIĆ

The critical-theoretical discipline sometimes called narratology
has developed from an interest in narrative.[1] Narrative, a word
that seems to have replaced the term "fiction," is nowadays used
much too widely and indiscriminately—it has in fact become just
another passe-partout term encompassing nearly every aspect of
the novel: its style and structure, its use of metaphor and irony,
its reliance on symbol and myth. Perhaps this is as it should be.
Perhaps this is the natural fate of all terms. And, certainly, there
is no harm in using the word narrative synonymously with the
term fiction as an alternative generic name for novels and short
stories. Speaking of narrative we should, however, be aware that
the term itself indicates a basic shift in critical interest. Dealing
with the novel as fiction, we show an interest in what makes it
different from life and from our notion of it which we call reality.
In the first half of the twentieth century critics focused especially on whatever made a novel unique and autonomous as a
literary artifact, what made it an art form. Brooks and Warren,
Kaiser and Spitzer, Eichenbaum and Shklovsky accordingly concentrated on problems of style—another passe-partout term
which has been conspicuously absent in some critical jargons of

1. In the course of 1980 and 1981 *Poetics Today*, one of the leading magazines
dedicated to critical theory, had three issues subtitled *Narratology I—Poetics of Fiction,
Narratology II—The Fictional Text and the Reader*, and *Narratology III—Narrators and
Voices in Fiction*. In them the term "narratology" is applied rather loosely to more recent
work in narrative theory, primarily in the field of structuralist, formalist, and reader-
oriented criticism. (See Introduction to *Narratology I*.) The works by Gérard Genette,
Roland Barthes, and Tzvetan Todorov discussed below can also be considered as dealing
with problems of "narratology."

our time.[2] Interest in style focused on ways of recognizing and defining heightening of effect. Some key terms used were imagery, irony, ambiguity, along with terms coined in Russia or Czechoslovakia in the twenties and thirties, and becoming current in Anglo-American criticism considerably later: Shklovsky's defamiliarization or making strange and Mukařovski's actualization or foregrounding[3]—both terms closely linked to the idea of heightening or distortion which in their view distinguishes a poetic text from the discursive, nonartistic one.

Speaking of a novel as narrative, on the other hand, we are not primarily interested in what makes it different from life, but what makes it different from other literary modes, what determines the novel as a genre. As a genre, narrative is thus distinguished from drama, which imitates speech and actions, and from lyric, which expresses something while formally at least ignoring a listener or reader, and defined as a set of real or fictive events arranged in time and narrated or told.[4] Differing from the notion of a novel as autonomous artifact, or something passing only between a narrator (author) and the story, the notion of narrative has also introduced into criticism a renewed and complex awareness of the various relations between the narrating source or instance (narrator, author)—the narrative—and the reader.[5] This shift has naturally stressed the importance of narrative transmission or mediation as the generically defining and constitutive property of the act of telling.

2. Instructive in this regard is the index to *Narrative Discourse: An Essay in Method* (Ithaca: Cornell University Press, 1979) by Gérard Genette. It does not list the term style, while listing terms like code, speech, scene, story, along with a host of more "technical" terms applied, redefined, or invented by Genette.

3. In recent English criticism these terms are discussed in David Lodge, *Modes of Modern Writing* (London: Edward Arnold, 1977).

4. Gerald Prince's definition of narrative is perhaps deceptively simple: "Narrative is the representation of real and fictive events in a time sequence" (*Narratology* [Spring 1980], 49). It does, however, reduce the importance of fictionality, dumping it in together with nonfictionality, stressing representation and time-sequence. The Introduction to the same issue of *Poetics Today* stresses the shift of interest in modern critical theory from poetry to prose. Narratology, it says, has become as central to the study of literature as the concept "language of poetry" was to an earlier generation.

5. See, for example, Susan Suleiman and Inge Crossman, eds., *The Reader in the Text* (Princeton: Princeton University Press, 1980).

Structuralism and formalism have relied heavily on linguistic analogies, and it is therefore quite natural that much structuralist and formalist oriented fiction theory has concentrated on the analogy of narration in fiction with the grammatical categories of direct and indirect speech. Dialogue and internal monologue have thus come to be seen as analogues of direct or unmediated speech, while the other more typical ways of telling (first and third person narration) have been related to indirect speech which is mediated by definition and should be considered the norm of all narrative discourse.[6]

Reading a number of critics of formalist-structuralist orientation—Roland Barthes (especially in his earlier work), Tzvetan Todorov, or Gérard Genette,[7] one notices that they tend to relate the question of narrative transmission to the definition of mimesis and the uses of realism, and it is this relation, as manifested in the work of William Faulkner, that I propose to explore in the following pages.

Placing narrative mediation in relation to mimesis and realism, one should perhaps start by reminding oneself that in its initial insistence on "objective" social, material, and also psychological documentation realism naturally tended to avoid all poetic or rhetorical devices which obscured its "main issues."[8] Classic realistic narrative strategies were accordingly marked not only by a movement away from the ideal and the imaginary but, more significantly for the present argument, they were also marked by a movement away from the conventions of narrative poetics and rhetoric. Underlying these efforts was the notion, attacked by Barthes and Todorov in particular, that literature

6. For major presentation of these issues see Gérard Genette, *Narrative Discourse*, and Seymour Chatman, *Story and Discourse* (Ithaca: Cornell University Press, 1980).

7. In this paper I refer specifically to Roland Barthes, "To Write: An Intransitive Verb?" in *The Structuralist Controversy*, ed. Richard Macksey and Eugenio Donato (Baltimore: Johns Hopkins, 1972); Tzvetan Todorov, *The Poetics of Prose* (Ithaca: Cornell University Press, 1980); and Gérard Genette, *Narrative Discourse: An Essay in Method.*

8. See George J. Becker, ed., *Documents of Modern Literary Realism* (Princeton: Princeton University Press, 1963), 28.

could, and in fact should, strive to become a transparent medium, a glass through which we could see the world. The eyes of the realists were focused with particular attention on the outside world, but—and this seems crucial at this point—we know that their gaze began to include more and more of the inner world as well. It is the effort to *imitate* the processes of mind-function—a mimetic strategy—which in fact led to the device called stream of consciousness, usually considered to be the prime prerogative of modernism—a movement with a strong antimimetic bias. Contrary to many approaches which deal with stream of consciousness as a preeminently poetic, subjective device (and in one perspective this approach is certainly absolutely valid) it is notable that in its mimetic aspect stream of consciousness is for example recorded—and branded—by Roland Barthes as a realistic device. Barthes criticizes literature which pretends to be the "transparent expression" of "either objective calendar time of or psychological subjectivity," because in his opinion such literature rests on a "totalitarian ideology of the referent," or, more commonly speaking, on realistic, mimetic assumptions.[9] In the introduction to *Documents of Modern Literary Realism* George Becker also lists "unstructured interior monologue" as a realistic device.[10] In her excellent *Transparent Minds: Narrative Modes for Presenting Consciousness in Fiction,* Dorrit Cohn goes as far as to indicate that stream of consciousness *must* rely on the mimetic principle both in its content and form.[11] Viewed formally, then, the initial impulse of realism, either when expressing "objective calendar time" or "psychological subjectivity," was to reject or reduce everything that veiled its transparence. This resulted, in theory at least, in a demand for simplicity of vocabulary and syntax. In this regard

9. See Barthes as quoted by Lodge, 60.
10. Becker, 29.
11. Princeton University Press, 1978. "Since interior monologue purports to *render a real psychological process, the mimetic norms that apply to its content apply equally to its form:* like the language a character speaks to others, the language he speaks to himself will appear valid only if it is in character" (88–89; italics mine).

David Lodge has defined realism as "the representation of experience in a manner which approximates closely to descriptions of similar experience in nonliterary texts of the same culture."[12]

This trend also resulted, however, in the simplification of narrative devices, especially in a reduction of the role of the narrator and the entire apparatus of narrative transmission. The story sounded more objective, more "natural," if the narrator and the process of narration were not given too much prominence. Realism, therefore, also attempted to disguise the machinery of telling, which tends to destroy realistic illusion.[13] Suppressing one set of devices, realism, especially in its later development, introduced and perfected others. It should be stressed, however, that these devices tended to be of a different order—more discreet, less glaringly "artificial." Whenever heightening was used, it was used, as a rule, to enhance the illusion of reality in the reader, to involve him in it.

It is inevitable at this point to remind ourselves of Henry James's distinction between telling and showing. It can never be sufficiently stressed, I think, that showing for James meant achieving the maximum of realistic illusion.[14] By dramatizing an action in the mind so as "to make it tell all its story itself,"[15] James reduced the presence of the narrator in the text, pretending that he is not telling. It is sometimes not realized, I think, that insisting on this particular device, James acted as the quintessential realist, at least in theory. (His practice is very complex and cannot be discussed here. The fact that, following these theories, James in the end forsook realism is a paradox which must also this time remain unexplored.) In James's opinion the visible and direct telling of narrator or author is not conducive to

12. Lodge, 25.

13. Here I refer particularly to realism as it developed in France with Gustave Flaubert and Emile Zola and which, strictly speaking, did not include most of the Victorian novelists who did very little to suppress their personal comments and voices. See Becker's Introduction in *Documents of Modern Literary Realism*.

14. See my article "From James's Figures to Genette's *Figures*: Point of View and Narratology," *Revue française d'etudes américaines*, 17 (1983).

15. James E. Miller, ed., *Theory of Fiction: Henry James* (Lincoln: University of Nebraska Press 1972), 181.

the creation of realistic illusion based on mimesis. Mimesis is served best when the story pretends it is "telling itself." It is in this that Gérard Genette disagrees most with James, and especially with some of his rather dogmatic disciples such as Percy Lubbock or Joseph Warren Beach. Genette affirms categorically that in narrative fiction which, following Plato, he calls diegesis, there can be no mimesis. The notion of showing in narrative is, therefore, an illusion. Words are signifiers bearing meanings, they cannot imitate actions, the only things they can imitate are other words.[16] Therefore, the only mimetic form of narrative is imitation of speech: dialogue and interior monologue or stream of consciousness—unmediated inner speech which Genette prefers to call *immediate speech.* Genette's narrowing down of the role of mimesis is quite in keeping with the antimimetic bias of the critics under discussion. It also illustrates the shift of critical interest from the fictionality of fiction to its definition as narrative. Instead of measuring the difference between a novel and life (this difference is posited as an axiom anyway, and is taken for granted), the critic studies how a novel functions in literary space as a set of relations analogous, among others, to the structures of language. In a sense, critical interest in narrative is the result of these critics' rejection not so much of realism itself as of its pretension of picturing life, showing it directly, creating the illusion. Insofar as they are "antimimeticists," these critics are, therefore, also champions of telling—a device underlying the very notion of narrative discourse as expounded by Todorov and Genette.[17] The realists had discarded the artificial narrative strategies of Cervantes, of Fielding and Diderot as antimimetic

16. "The idea of showing, like that of imitation or narrative representation . . . is completely illusory: in contrast to dramatic representation no narrative can show or imitate the story it tells" because "narration, oral or written, is a fact of language, and language signifies without imitating—mimesis in words can only be mimesis of words" (Genette, 163–64). After making this point—stressing that mimesis in narrative must be restricted to imitation of words—he does, however, allow for the existence of "referential illusions" and "connotators of mimesis" (165) facilitating our task and also supplying us with the necessary terminology!

17. Cf. Todorov, in particular "Language and Literature," 19–28 and Genette, "Les frontières du récit," *Figures II* (Paris: Seuil, 1969).

and detrimental to the creation of realistic illusion. For this very reason Genette and Todorov reinstate telling as the lawful narrative mode, which was only temporarily dethroned by realism. It is no wonder, therefore, that stream of consciousness—which in its imitative tendencies (coexisting with nonimitative ones) can be seen as the extreme outcome of reality-seeming artifice—should not be in great favor with Genette,[18] who in his *Narrative Discourse* has erected a monument of praise to the narrative of Marcel Proust—more discursive, moralistic, philosophic, and also more frankly *told*.[19]

In this way overt telling comes to be seen as the conventional generic property of narrative, reaffirming its status as artifice, a structure of words, and undermining the notion of showing as an aberration perpetrated by realistic "illusionism." The notion of showing, on the other hand, comes to be seen as an outcrop of mimetic illusion. If mimesis is limited to imitation of speech, however, it becomes formally possible only in dialogue and interior monologue. It follows that *mimesis is in inverse ratio with the presence of the narrator in the text.* In this perspective, certainly not the only one, but a legitimate one, I believe, *dialogue and interior monologue (stream of consciousness) can be seen as the most mimetic because least mediated forms of narrative transmission, and in that sense closest to the demands of realistic illusion.*

At this point we should begin to grasp the implications of this

---

18. "Nothing is more foreign to Proustian psychology than *the utopia of an authentic interior monologue* whose inchoateness *supposedly guarantees transparency* and faithfulness to the deepest eddies of the 'stream of consciousness'—or of unconsciousness." Genette, 180, italics mine.

19. In the light of these arguments it is interesting to cast a glance upon the American critical scene and note, for instance, that Robert Scholes, one of the authors of the influential book significantly entitled *The Nature of Narrative* (New York: Oxford University Press, 1966) is also the author of one of the two best-known expositions of structuralism in the United States, *Structuralism in Literature: An Introduction* (New Haven: Yale University Press, 1974). No wonder, therefore, that in *Nature of Narrative* great stress is laid on more traditional types of prerealistic narrative and no wonder again that in another of his works, *The Fabulators* (New York: Oxford University Press, 1969), dealing with contemporary novelists, Scholes singles out for inspection those among them who openly tell their stories and stress the artificiality of narrative by variously departing from the conventions of realism.

line of critical thinking for a novel like *The Sound and the Fury*—a novel quintessentially shown (unmediated)—and contrasted to a novel like *Absalom, Absalom!*—preeminently told (mediated) through a string of highly idiosyncratic voices and points of view.

Before continuing, however, one should perhaps consider another Jamesian term, both different from and closely related to showing—the notion of rendering. ("Don't state, render," James said.) Rendering is related to showing, it is in fact one of its natural outcomes. We know that showing excluded outside descriptions of inner events, the device James somewhat patronizingly called "analysis." The author, therefore, must rely more and more heavily on recreating these events through ellipsis and indirection. Indeed, how else?

This, of course, was one of the lessons of Gustave Flaubert that James had learned quite well, although perhaps only in theory. When Maupassant read *Madame Bovary*, he praised it because reading it he forgot that it was a novel. Instead, "it was life itself making an appearance."[20] From its context we gather that Maupassant's remark was primarily referring to the sobriety and discipline that made this novel an objective study of life, a truthful document, a representation that did not embellish or distort. We know, however, that Flaubert—that objective and impersonal, seemingly cold writer—was obsessed by questions of both craft and art, and relied for his effects on the use of images and symbols. And it is in this inevitable, yet paradoxical marriage of documentary objectivity and symbolist indirectness that *Madame Bovary* has to be regarded as the matrix of the modernist novel. We must not forget, furthermore, that the suppression of all visible signs of narrative transmission, of which we have spoken above, was also axiomatic for the narrative strategy of *Bovary*.

The realist's need to document the life which exists "out there" was from the very beginning mixed with the need to

20. Quoted in Becker, 89.

render its existence by other than discursive, descriptive means, the need to show it as experienced, lived, felt. Inherent in this need, however, is the very paradox of Flaubert's—and James's—aesthetic, which points to the subsequent mutations of realism (impressionism, for instance), and its final metamorphosis or absorption into modernism.[21]

James spoke of the novelist's need to paint a vivid picture of life by conveying its "sense and taste." This certainly implied another related indirectness: the accidents seen in the field "rather of their second than their first exhibition"[22]—in other words, as we are well aware, accidents seen as reflected in the mind. The need to convey the "sense and taste" of this reflection brings us back to the concreteness and indirection of Flaubert which, owing to its sensory, materialistic basis Tzvetan Todorov has called his "sensationalism."[23] It also clearly points forward to whatever Ezra Pound meant by "presenting" and perhaps also Eliot by the objective correlative: a way of using images and situations—elliptic, indirect, metaphoric, yet still aimed at enhancing the illusion of life. A paradoxical development: clearly an extension of basic realistic premises, and yet leading in other

21. I am using here the term most commonly used to denote the generation of Joyce, Eliot, Pound, and Faulkner, fully aware of the problems it raises. Moreover, I am relating this term to other terms used to denote movements and trends in art and literature after 1850: realism, impressionism, symbolism, cubism. Edmund Wilson has stressed the symbolist legacy of modernism; René Wellek wants us to call it the symbolist period. Faulkner's impressionism has been discussed by Albert J. Guerard, *The Triumph of the Novel: Dickens, Dostoevsky, Faulkner* (New York: Oxford University Press, 1976) and Arthur F. Kinney, *Faulkner's Narrative Poetics* (Amherst: University of Massachusetts Press, 1978), among others. Panthea Reid Broughton has offered an exposition of the "cubist" novel and exemplified it in her analysis of Faulkner in two essays in *"A Cosmos of My Own": Faulkner and Yoknapatawpha, 1980* (Jackson: The University Press of Mississippi, 1981). This proliferation of terms and definitions, offered by the most eminent scholars, indicates the urgent need for more precise definition and redefinition as regards both the period and its writers.

22. See note 15.

23. Todorov compares a "direct" description by Victor Hugo with another kind of description from *Madame Bovary:* "She noticed his nails, which were longer than was usual in Yonville. The clerk spent a great deal of time caring for them: he kept a special penknife in his desk for the purpose" (*The Poetics of Prose,* 151). Todorov says that this is an example of Flaubert's "sensationalism (or antiessentialism)," one way in which James also expressed his need for "indirect vision." Flaubert does not describe the clerk directly—by saying that he was vain, for instance—but indirectly, through an image, in this case a synechdoche.

directions—for example in the direction of impressionism. Impressionism must be regarded as an extension of realism insofar as it is rooted in the sensory perception of the outside world. In literature, however, this trend has always meant the avoidance of concepts and discursive shortcuts and the reliance on concrete and indirect presentation. As such presentation necessarily involves the use of images, it has also led to "poetic," "lyrical" expression in the novel. Furthermore, the impressionist bias for the rendering of sensuous experience in language used as "experiential activity"[24] has also been subtly and treacherously mixed up with the indirectness of symbolism, which tended to be non-referential, nonrepresentational and was therefore clearly non-realistic.

An aside seems appropriate at this point: the Jamesian aim to render the sense and taste of experience, so superbly achieved by Faulkner in *The Sound and the Fury,* had already reached one of its peaks in the quintessential modernist novel *Ulysses.* In certain passages in "Lestrygonians," for instance, where Joyce recreates Bloom's sensations while eating and drinking, longing for love, or remembering his first encounter with Molly, language seems to try to penetrate experience, recreate it both from the inside and the outside, even stand for it, replace it. One of the great illusions is that literature can forget it is literature and capture, incapsule, become life. (Perhaps the supreme referential illusion, the attempt to break the barrier between word and thing and have word become thing, is not so different after all from its *symboliste* counterpart—the liberated word breaking its links with things and assuming independence!)

In the stream of consciousness technique, language used as experiential activity further relies on another basically realistic trait: psychological motivation and verisimilitude and, more often than not, the attempt to imitate, to approximate the idiom

24. "Literary impressionism is, not surprisingly, a matter of linguistic techniques, the attempt to make language the act of perception rather than analysis of the act, to make language *experiential activity* rather than a description of activity" (italics mine). *Modernism,* ed. Malcolm Bradbury and James McFarlane (Harmondsworth, Middlesex: Penguin, 1976), 222.

and speech of the character in order to achieve at least some degree of reader involvement with the characters and their predicament.[25]

Concluding this part of my argument, which centers on notions of narrative mediation as related to realistic illusion, I wish to propose that *in the light of recent fiction theory the two Jamesian terms, showing and rendering, although firmly rooted in realist assumptions and practices, also reveal themselves as distinctive modernist devices adopted and adapted by both Joyce and Faulkner.* The notion of showing rests on realistic assumptions and has at some point been seen by Genette and Barthes as a subterfuge, an escape from telling, the legitimate narrative mode. The notion of rendering (which, insofar as it involves dealing with imagery and "style" is rather neglected by these critics), as a means of enhancing the illusion of felt life, is inextricably intertwined with the notion of showing. However, by avoiding discursive statement through indirection, it leads inevitably from a reflection of life to its re-creation, and from there perhaps also to *symboliste* suggestiveness and self-reflexiveness, which of course are always at odds with realistic aims. These two notions have brought us to the crossroads which had confused so many travellers—the crossroads leading from realism to modernism. The solution of the dilemma, however, does not lie in choosing one road and excluding all the others, but in realizing that several roads are possible, depending on the panorama we wish to contemplate.

To illustrate some possibilities, different but in no way mutually exclusive, let us digress briefly by comparing Hemingway's "The Killers" and Faulkner's *The Sound and the Fury*. In several perspectives they can, and should, be considered as opposites. "The Killers" is quite objective in its behaviorist insistence on appearances; *The Sound and the Fury*, steeped in inwardness and subjectivity. "The Killers," in its reliance on dialogue, seems

25. For some of the theoretical background of this paper and my approach to *Ulysses* see my article "Joyce's Fire and Ice: The Reader of *Ulysses* between Involvement and Distanciation," *Studia Romanica et Anglica Zagrabiensia*, 26:1–2 (1981), 367–96.

to be moving away from narrative into drama while *The Sound
and the Fury* relies on patterns of imagery and rhythmic repetition and through them strains to be "poetic."[26] And yet, travelling the road of narratology, in the lane of narrative transmission
in particular, we can reach a point at which these two works
converge. Far away from whatever began in France 150 years
ago, and seemingly far away from each other, Hemingway's "The
Killers" and the stream of consciousness chapters in Faulkner's
The Sound and the Fury could legitimately be taken to represent the final, paradoxically related twin outcomes of one and
the same realistic tendency: the tendency to enhance the illusion, in this case by playing down the artifice of telling, the
function of narrative mediation.

The Sound and the Fury in fact illustrates both outcomes,
although it is more justly famous for the latter: the unmediated
internal monologues of the first three sections. The fourth section, however, approaches the illusion of objectivity by completely avoiding omniscience and also by avoiding the distanciating narrative intricacies of overt telling. (In this fourth section
we do not get one single glimpse into the thoughts of any of the
characters, and such glimpses, as we know, are the basic prerequisites of omniscience. True, we get much more indirect help
from Faulkner than from Hemingway. Basically, however, we
are expected to judge about the characters only from their outward appearance and their reactions.) In this sense *all* of *The
Sound and the Fury* is minimally mediated, minimally told.

Studying carefully the text of this novel we realize that it is in
several ways more transparent than *Absalom, Absalom!* for example. Much of the first, third, and fourth sections, even parts
of Quentin's section, are less opaque than anything in *Ulysses*
after Calypso. As in Hemingway, presentation is often objective
(in Benjy's section, for instance), although the selection of the
material remains highly subjective. Yet these transparencies are

---

26. In this they might represent another tendency of the novel of our century: to
escape the rules of its genre (narration being one of them), and reach towards drama,
poetry, or the essay.

glazed over with various degrees and types of opacity derived from images, symbols, patterns of motifs, sentence-rhythm (most richly orchestrated in Quentin's section), or sheer absence of reference (the principal difficulty of Benjy's section, on first reading especially). In spite of intense use of defamiliarizing devices and a great degree of artifice, the narrative remains psychologically and stylistically consistent with character motivation. The artifice is predominantly (although by no means exclusively) used to involve the reader with the characters and their story, to render, as James would have put it, the sense and taste of their life. It remains in the service of illusion.

In this *The Sound and the Fury* is analogous to the earlier chapters of Joyce's *Ulysses*. Both are minimally narrated, minimally mediated (in pure stream-of-consciousness segments technically unmediated, in fact), and consist of a certain amount of objective, third-person narration counterbalanced by a massive body of more or less unstructured interior monologue. In both of these narrative modes the writing extends from transparence to the greatest opacity, heightened by the use of elliptic, indirect, metaphoric, "sensationalist," and poetic devices. Both modes are supremely shown and supremely rendered at the same time.

While the narration in *The Sound and the Fury* thus still rests on certain mimetic premises, *Absalom, Absalom!* comes much closer to Genette's notion of diegesis. *Absalom* is both much more and much more openly told, and in this its narrative is both more traditional and more innovative (fabulistic) than the "illusionist" narrative of *The Sound and the Fury*. In this it is also, I believe, more typical of Faulkner's work as a whole.

To prove this, however, is not simple. The similarities between these two novels are so numerous, and they occur on so many different levels, that they tend to confuse the critic. Let us review some of the more important similarities—not the historical, regional, thematic, ideological ones, which are obvious and have received much critical attention in the past, but rather the

similarities which are more closely related to the topic of this
paper. Both novels are, for instance, supreme examples of rendering: the "summer of wistaria," the "mote-palpitant sunlight,"
Quentin's feverish shaking on his bed at Harvard, his "I don't
hate it . . . I dont. I dont! I dont hate it! I dont hate it!"—all
these and many more examples show Faulkner recreating experience, getting under its skin, being both sensationalist and illusionist if you like, following the rules of psychological motivation in the best traditions of realism-cum-impressionism. It is in
their impressionism, as a matter of fact, that the two novels have
been emphatically thrown together by the authors of one of the
best recent presentations of American literature, the anthology
American Literature: The Makers and the Making. The authors
say, unfortunately only in passing, in a footnote to a discussion of
Stephen Crane and Joseph Conrad as impressionists: "In American literature the most important examples of impressionism are
William Faulkner's *The Sound and the Fury* and *Absalom, Absalom!*"[27] True, the thrust of their discussion of impressionism is
different from mine in this paper, but it is still related to it. In its
focus on psychological fragmentation it also, incidentally, indicates the extent to which *Absalom, Absalom!* is a novel that
shows—this is, dramatizes—the mind in James's sense. There
exists an additional similarity between these two novels which
complicates even further my wish to define it as a novel of
telling, one that transpires from a comparison made between
The Red Badge of Courage and *Lord Jim* in the same anthology:

> In *Lord Jim*, Conrad wrote something close to the ultimate in im-
> pressionist fiction; that is a fiction in which the author works in
> terms not of a fixed and objectively conceived reality, but of a
> character's (or characters') "impressions" of what is taken to be real-
> ity. In *Lord Jim* we have the series of "impressions" of Jim filtered
> through Marlowe's mind, and we have Marlowe's sorting out of the

---

27. Cleanth Brooks, R. W. B. Lewis, Robert Penn Warren, eds., *American Literature: The Makers and the Making*, 2 vols. (New York: St. Martin's Press, 1973), 2: 1643.

various views; then, in the end, what is offered by Marlowe is re-sorted by the author, who, however, declines to give a definitive statement.[28]

In a certain sense, this is also an accurate description of Quentin as far as he is the narrator of Sutpen's story, as far as he is Marlowe. This aspect of Quentin has, of course, also been firmly established already in the critical canon of *Absalom.*

It has been stressed by critics, however, that apart from see-ing reality differently, impressionism also shifted the artist's at-tention to the *process* of seeing, the process of artistic or literary composition. This stress on the process is antirealist by definition. It does not involve us with the illusion, but distan-ciates us from it. Instead of pretending to have no devices (pre-tending not to tell, for instance), or using only devices that strengthen the illusion of "reality," the artist "bares his device," shows his tools, destroys the illusion. Impressionism thus also led to a formalist aesthetic, a solipsistic contemplation of its own processes.[29] Among the devices "bared" in *Absalom* one looms especially large: the device of telling. One of the narrative strategies—a strategy of mediation or transmission—finally brings us to the point when we can speak of the differences that divide *Absalom* from *The Sound and the Fury.*

Before doing this, however, let me return again for a moment to my standard-setter of modernism, Joyce's *Ulysses.* In most modernist narratives, along with devices serving realist illu-sion—and we have just dwelt on some of them—there is present a countercurrent, a counterthrust, leading us in the opposite direction. In *Ulysses* this countercurrent becomes dominant in the second part of the novel where the reader is distanciated through irony, parody, deliberate and calculated or crazy lan-guage play, and visibly imposed yet often arbitrary grids: mythic, symbolic, literary. After gaining very convincing realistic credibility, moving against the dense specification of

28. Ibid.
29. Cf. Scott.

street, city, politics, and creed, and spurred by the closely observed biology, psychology, and intellectual effort of Bloom and Stephen (very often as they are refracted in their minds—in their second rather than first exhibition—as James would say), Joyce seems to abandon reality-seeming artifice, moving his characters from Irish into literary space. The realistic illusion is drowned in stylistic exercises: words are used as musical notes, names disintegrate into nonsense (Poldy the Rixdix Doldy!), the characters are inflated by the gigantism of "Cyclops," deflated by the verbal tour de force of "Ithaca," deformed out of existence in "Circe," touching base only at the very end in Molly's chapter.

In emphatic contrast to *The Sound and the Fury*, the Faulkner of *Absalom, Absalom!* shares Joyce's visibly contrived, mannerist bent (their mannerisms differ, but they are mannerisms nevertheless!). The sentence of *Absalom, Absalom!* meanders and shimmers before us both like a mimetic analogue of sense and sensibility—the type which prevails in *The Sound and the Fury*—and as a monster in literary space, a mannerist monster. Doing this, it mysteriously travels to and from the reader, involving and distanciating him in turn. Quentin's panting in the iron New England cold involves us with the illusion as does his panting with grief and honeysuckle in *The Sound and the Fury*. There are many more sentences in *Absalom, Absalom!*, however, which pant with artifice and create "screens of language" obscuring rather than revealing the world beyond.[30]

Differing from *Ulysses*, which has no narrator (except intermittently in "Cyclops"), narrative transmission becomes an outstanding device of distanciation in *Absalom, Absalom!* The story of Sutpen is filtered through and created by the directly and indirectly transmitted discourses of the various narrators. These discourses are often not imitative, but rather mannered, outsize, meandering, heavily marked by the devices of the author's telling, which all work against the illusion.

The Sutpen story is, for instance, verbatim compared by

30. Hugh Kenner, *Joyce's Voices* (London: Faber & Faber, 1978), 41.

Faulkner to a dream, the persons to ogres, and more significantly, their legend is compared to words on a printed page, a comparison unthinkable within the narrative convention of *The Sound and the Fury*. *Absalom* is a novel about a legend, a dream, a myth, the vampire of history, the Southern fever with which Quentin is shaking on his Harvard bed. We all know that, of course. Further, as many critics have noted, it is also a story about how a story comes into existence out of scraps of evidence, mysterious alchemies in the chamber of consciousness, out of despair and the wildest conjecturing. What I should like to stress, however, is that this process of making a story is not only shown and recreated—as the story of the Compsons is recreated by each of the three brothers in *The Sound and the Fury*, but that it is also, and primarily, told, narrated, mediated, as the story of *The Sound and the Fury* is not.

Let me say it again: in spite of its modernity, its high degree of defamiliarization, *The Sound and the Fury* relies on verisimilitude and referentiality to an extraordinary degree: the characters are "true to life," or appear to be so, in both their actions and their speech (their stream of consciousness is highly individualized, mimetic). Not so in *Absalom*, where they are often openly confessed and professed to be inventions, constructions, distorted by the various narrators and also—if I may coin a word—"denaturalized" through language. True, there is the unsurpassed imitative ring of Wash's summons to Miss Rosa after Henry "done shot that durn French feller. Kilt him dead as a beef."[31] But such examples are extremely rare in *Absalom*. In this novel the characters speak a language that people have never spoken and will never speak. Judith talking to herself, for instance: "If happy I can be I will, if suffer I must I can."[32] And Bon's letter, the only remaining written document in Quentin's hands! Letters are a written form, they also have their conventions, but Faulkner flouts them all. In its impenetrable

---

31. William Faulkner, *Absalom, Absalom!* (New York: Random House, 1936), 133.
32. Ibid., 121.

artificiality this letter is not a contribution to convincing characterization, but rather an exercise in Southern rhetoric. Whose rhetoric, we are tempted to ask: Bon's, Quentin's, Faulkner's? This question is wrong, however; it should not even be asked because this letter does not aim at an imitative effect, it is not supposed to sound like Bon's letter at all. It is an exercise in rhetoric, just as "Oxen of the Sun" is an exercise in parody, and as Miss Rosa's style perhaps often is, too.

Also, coming even closer to the question of narrative transmission, we should note that the text of *Absalom* abounds in interpolations and asides, comments and correctives, afterthoughts and qualifiers reminding us constantly that they are, after all, only words on a page. Typical in this respect is Quentin's recapitulation in chapter 1 of Miss Rosa's version of the Sutpen saga.

> *It seems that this demon—his name was Sutpen—(Colonel Sutpen)—Colonel Sutpen. Who came out of nowhere and without warning upon the land with a band of strange niggers and built a plantation—(Tore violently a plantation, Miss Rosa Coldfield says)—tore violently. And married her sister Ellen and begot a son and a daughter which—(Without gentleness begot, Miss Rosa Coldfield says)—without gentleness. Which should have been the jewels of his pride and the shield and comfort of his old age, only—(Only they destroyed him or something or he destroyed them or something. And died)—and died. Without regret, Miss Rosa Coldfield says—(Save by her) Yes, save by her. (And by Quentin Compson) Yes. And by Quentin Compson.*[33]

This passage is printed in italics as stream of consciousness as in other Faulkner novels. It is not imitative, however. The mere repetition of "Miss Rosa Coldfield says" with full name and surname repeated three times within this short paragraph, along with all the dashes and brackets, would establish it as artificially structured, written, nonimitative telling. Another example is the special little language games—such as the game of ambiguous pronouns—and games are always destroyers of realistic illu-

33. Ibid., 9.

sion—e.g., "it (the wedding)" to be distinguished within the same sentence from "it (the rain)."

In stream of consciousness the convention has the mind racing back and forth between points in time, arguments and images, without syntactic ordering or preparation. More conventional narration usually relies more strongly on chronology, while stream of consciousness ignores it on purpose. In *Absalom* we have a strange mixture of the two. The novel builds an immensely complex pattern of jumbled points in time,[34] refracted through numerous points of view, and spoken in several (rarely mimetic!) voices. There are references to what a character saw and said or imagined, or remembered having seen or said. Much of this is, however, insistently and formally mediated, leading to a perhaps unprecedented agglomeration of literal notations of "saying" and "thinking" and "guessing," along with adverbs indicating when this was done (much of it "afterwards" just as in James's *The Wings of the Dove*). Much of the telling is laced with auctorial commentary and rhetorical periods and repetitions, different from the more fluid surges and falls of Quentin's style in *The Sound and the Fury*.

> . . . because our father knew who his father was in Tennessee and who his grandfather had been in Virginia and our neighbours and the people we lived among knew that we knew and we knew they knew we knew and we knew that they would have believed us about whom and where he came from even if we had lied, just as anyone could have looked at him once and known that he would be lying about who and where and why he came from. . . .[35]

These are only some of the rhetorical effects and technical devices used to underline narrative transmission, which realism had tried to reduce, and stream of consciousness had completely abolished, now back again with a vengeance to become the for-

34. The complexity of the time scheme has been discussed by several critics and also in a work on Faulkner's narrative, Joseph W. Reed, Jr., *Faulkner's Narrative* (New Haven: Yale University Press, 1973). In the chapter on *Absalom* the author, however, concentrates on Faulkner's use of metaphor in this novel.

35. *Absalom, Absalom!*, 16–17.

mal features of Faulkner's narrative in this novel, as well as in many subsequent ones.

The distinction between showing and telling as interpreted by narratology, and especially as related to the creation of realist illusion, allows us to see *The Sound and the Fury* and *Absalom, Absalom!* as antipodes emblematic of one of the contradictions inherent in modernism. With his dual and paradoxical allegiance to the belief in language as experiential activity and unmediated narration on one hand, and the distanciation of mannerist and therefore antirealist artifice, stressing that of open and involuted telling on the other, Faulkner has created in these two separate novels modes analogous to those encompassed in the summa of modernism, Joyce's *Ulysses*. The involvement created by the illusionism of *The Sound and the Fury* relies on the same devices appropriated by Joyce in the stream of consciousness chapters of *Ulysses*. The final effect of distanciation achieved by different, though related, means allows us to place the artifice of *Absalom, Absalom!* alongside that of "Circe," "Ithaca," or "Cyclops." In his full and glorious embodiment of this important and perhaps central formal paradox of modernism, Faulkner is equal to Joyce and second to none.

An Amazing Gift:
The Early Essays
and Faulkner's Apprenticeship
in Aesthetics and Criticism

PANTHEA REID BROUGHTON

Writing to Joan Williams in 1953, Faulkner looked back upon his life's work incredulously; he wrote:

> . . . I realize for the first time what an amazing gift I had: uneducated in every formal sense, without even very literate, let alone literary, companions, yet to have made the things I made. I dont know where it came from. I dont know why God or gods or whoever it was, selected me to be the vessel. Believe me, this is not humility, false modesty: it is simply amazement. I wonder if you have ever had that thought about the work and the country man whom you know as Bill Faulkner—what little connection there seems to be between them. . . .[1]

That statement acknowledges the grandeur of the achievement but denigrates the thoroughness of the training, as well as the literateness of the friends. We now recognize the "country man whom [Joan] knew as Bill Faulkner" as another of Faulkner's romantic poses. We recognize that the actual William Faulkner, though "uneducated in every formal sense," was indeed a well (if somewhat unevenly) educated man. Everything we can learn about that education enhances our understanding of the ways genius works to transform experience and knowledge into art. In this essay I shall trace that transformation process through Faulkner's early forays into aesthetics and literary criticism.

1. Joseph L. Blotner, ed., *Selected Letters of William Faulkner* (New York: Random House, 1977), 348. The final ellipses are the editor's.

In Faulkner's unfinished 1925 novel "Elmer," the would-be painter Elmer Hodge takes "Clive Bell" and "Elie Faure's *Outline of Art*"[2] to study on board a boat bound for Paris. Writing "Elmer" in Paris, Faulkner misremembers the title of Faure's *History of Art*, probably because, unlike Elmer, he had not brought Bell and Faure to Paris with him. Nevertheless, he did know these books. Stone's copy of Bell's *Art*, now in the Brodsky collection, carries the "penciled underlinings throughout"[3] which testify to Stone's serious attention. Brodsky and Hamblin explain: "According to Emily Stone, this book and Willard Huntingdon Wright's *The Creative Will: Studies in the Philosophy and the Syntax of Aesthetics* were the two most influential books upon Stone's aesthetic theory and the sources of much of the advice Stone communicated to Faulkner."[4] Mick Gidley and Martin Kreiswirth have already written about Wright's influence upon Faulkner.[5] I am concerned with Faulkner's readings in Bell and Faure and other theorists between 1920 and 1925.

Phil Stone dated his copy of Bell's *Art* March 8, 1917.[6] He ordered Faure's *History of Art* in March 1922,[7] when Faure's first two volumes, in translation from the French, were available in America.[8] We have no first-hand testimony from Stone or anyone else about Faure's impact on Faulkner, perhaps because,

2. Thomas L. McHaney, "The Elmer Papers: Faulkner's Comic Portraits of the Artist," in *A Faulkner Miscellany*, James B. Meriwether, ed. (Jackson: University Press of Mississippi, 1974), 48–49.

3. Robert W. Hamblin and Louis Daniel Brodsky, eds. *Selections from the William Faulkner Collection of Louis Daniel Brodsky: A Descriptive Catalogue* (Charlottesville: The University Press of Virginia, 1979), 20.

4. Ibid., 20–21.

5. See Mick Gidley's "William Faulkner and Willard Huntington Wright's *The Creative Will*," *Canadian Review of American Studies*, 9 (Fall 1978), 169–77 and Martin Kreiswirth's "The Will to Create: Faulkner's Apprenticeship and Willard Huntington Wright," *Arizona Quarterly*, 37 (Summer 1981), 149–65.

6. Hamblin and Brodsky, 20.

7. See the Appendix, compiled by James B. Meriwether, to *William Faulkner's Library: A Catalogue*, Compiled, with an Introduction, by Joseph Blotner (Charlottesville: The University Press of Virginia, 1964), 124.

8. Harper and Brothers published in both New York and London the English translation of Volume I in 1921, II in 1922, III in 1923, and IV in 1924. See the *National Union Catalogue*.

toward the mid-1920s, Faulkner kept his reading to himself. Probably too Faure's appreciative survey appealed less to Stone than did the abstract argument of Bell. But whether or not Stone or Faulkner or anyone else talked about Faure, we can be reasonably sure that Faulkner had read some of Faure by late 1922 and had internalized a great deal by 1925.

One might argue that if Bell and Faure and other theorists were so important to Faulkner, he should have referred to them as he did to Shakespeare, Dickens, Melville, Conrad, and other major writers. Instead, Faulkner did not mention the other theorists he read in this period at all and only mentioned Bell and Faure in the unfinished "Elmer." Furthermore, recasting the Elmer materials as "Portrait of Elmer," a satirical story he tried unsuccessfully to sell in the 1930s, Faulkner deleted the Bell/Faure reference altogether.[9]

Perhaps he did so because he recognized the absurdity of having a painter learn painting by studying these two theorists. A typically abstract Bell statement is "art is the creation of significant form, and simplification is the liberating of what is significant from what is not."[10] Under the influence of G. E. Moore, Bell speaks of art as a "direct means to good" (Bell, 115). While Bell can be irritatingly abstract, Faure can be tediously concrete; of a Roman landscape vase he says it is "less stylized, doubtless, but more moving and sensual than the Greek setting. One hears the crunch of the vintagers' feet on the grapes, the oak offers armfuls of firm acorns and black leaves, the ears of wheat loaded with grain group themselves into thick sheaves, we smell the floating perfume of green boughs and the odor of the plowed soil."[11] Faure's rhapsodies about blood in bodies,

9. See "Portrait of Elmer" in *Uncollected Stories of William Faulkner,* Joseph Blotner, ed. (New York: Random House, 1979), 610–41.
10. Clive Bell, *Art* (London: Chatto and Windus, 1914), 220. Hereafter cited parenthetically in the text as Bell.
11. Elie Faure, *History of Art,* vol. I, *Ancient Art,* Walter Pach, trans. (New York: Harper & Brothers, 1921), 282. Hereafter cited parenthetically as Faure, I. Volume II, *Medieval Art,* Walter Pach, trans. (New York: Harper & Brothers, 1922) is cited as Faure, II.

milk in breasts, sap in trees would help a painter about as much as Bell's notion of significant form. But if Faulkner had recognized that fact he might better have left the references in his ironic "Portrait"; for they would further expose the absurdity of Elmer's abstract attempt to be an artist.

Perhaps instead Faulkner deleted these references because he did not wish to associate the pretentious Elmer of the story with two theorists important to himself. Perhaps he deleted them, as he avoided references to Joyce and Eliot, to cover his tracks. Perhaps by the 1930s Bell and Faure seemed dated references. Perhaps Faulkner preferred to acknowledge debts to artists rather than to theoreticians. Or perhaps, as Thomas McHaney has suggested to me, he simply deleted references to Bell and Faure because they were too esoteric for a story he hoped to sell to a popular magazine.[12] At any rate, though explicit references to these aestheticians exist only in "Elmer," the early nonfiction prose establishes a genuine debt to Bell, Faure, and other literary and aesthetic theorists.

The uneven quality of Faulkner's early critical essays has made—and does make—them difficult to discuss. No one, since George Garrett in 1959,[13] has studied these essays in their own right partly because, I suspect, they seem too confusing to bother with. For example, in the first of these essays, a review of William Alexander Percy's *In April Once*, Faulkner imagines Percy "as a violinist who became blind about the time Mozart died, it would seem that the last thing he saw with his subjective intellect was Browning standing in naive admiration before his own mediocrity, of which Mr. Percy's 'Epistle from Corinth' is the fruit."[14] Why Faulkner wishes to characterize Percy as a blind violinist is unclear except as it illustrates Faulkner's knowl-

12. McHaney also says "I suppose Faulkner took out the reference to Bell and Faure in part because he omitted the sea journey and its (Bergsonian?) associations for Elmer." Thomas McHaney to the author, July 28, 1983.

13. George Garrett, "Faulkner's Early Literary Criticism," *Texas Studies in Literature and Language*, 1 (1959–60), 3–10.

14. William Faulkner, *Early Prose and Poetry*, Compilation and Introduction by Carvel Collins (Boston: Little, Brown and Company, 1962), 72. Hereafter cited parenthetically as *EPP*.

edge and imaginativeness. Nor is it clear how Percy's "Epistle" derives from Browning's mediocrity; or does it derive from Browning's self-admiration? I cannot tell since Faulkner's "which" has no clear antecedent. (Later Faulkner would make the vague pronoun reference a source of suggestive ambiguity; here it is a source of confusion.) More confusion follows when, after apparently associating Percy's "Epistle" with mediocrity, Faulkner says that this poem is "far and away the best thing in the book, and would have been better except for the fact that Mr. Percy, like every man who has ever lived, is the victim of his age" (*EPP*, 72). How this poem is both best and mediocre and how it could have been better if Percy weren't a victim of his age, since all men are victims of their ages, remains unclear.

Similarly unclear in a review of Edna St. Vincent Millay's *Aria da Capo* is Faulkner's discussion of Millay's language. He writes: "the choice of words, with one exception—a speech of Pierrot's which I do not remember contains a word of inexcusable crudeness—is sound" (*EPP*, 85). A possible paraphrase of that statement is that Millay's language is sound except for one speech which, lacking inexcusable crudeness, is not sound; but then Faulkner would be equating "inexcusable" crudeness with "sound" theatrical language. More probably, Pierrot's speech, which Faulkner does not remember, does contain one word of inexcusable crudeness, while the rest of Millay's language is sound. Nevertheless, the unclear references, clauses within clauses, and the sequence of negatives make the contradictory and illogical reading at least a possibility. Given such confusions, those of us who have taught English composition might guess why Faulkner made a *D* in English at Ole Miss; the essays are filled with illogical constructions, undefended assertions, mixed metaphors, and self-projection. No wonder most critics have passed over them in embarrassed silence.

I must hasten to say that the essays can be insightful and witty, as well as arrogant and confused. And they become increasingly accomplished. Certainly, the very fact that Faulkner reviewed regularly over a roughly five-year period—as he did at no other time in his life—signifies that between 1920 and 1925 he was formulating his own aesthetic values. The essays chart his critical reading and suggest the part it played in a crucial aesthetic and personal drama. They suggest that before 1920 contemporary aesthetic theory had not been on Faulkner's reading program, though it definitely had been on Stone's program for Faulkner. Perhaps before 1920 Faulkner thought of theory as abstract, irrelevant, or effete; at any rate, he does not seem to have paid any attention to it. Instead he paid attention to ancient and modern literary classics. His brother John tells the now familiar story of the Stone's "big old Studebaker touring car" being loaded with books and turned over to Faulkner who, beginning around 1914, would drive out to the country and read all day. John Faulkner explains: "What Phil picked for Bill to read was pretty much what [Maud Faulkner] would have chosen. Bill read Plato, Socrates, the Greek poets, all the good Romans and Shakespeare. He also read the other good English writers and the French and German classics." With her son on a self-directed great books course far more rigorous than any offered by the public schools, no wonder Miss Maud "didn't object any more than she did over Bill's quitting school."[15]

Faulkner claimed to have been educated by omnivorous and undirected reading.[16] The evidence suggests that his reading was omnivorous, but not undirected. He directed himself, first, to absorb nearly the entire literary tradition of the West. And Phil Stone pointed him, not so much in the direction John Faulkner suggests, but rather toward what Joseph Blotner calls the more "avant-garde"[17] works of the late nineteenth and early twentieth centuries. According to Emily Stone, "Phil fired the younger

15. John Faulkner, *My Brother Bill: An Affectionate Reminiscence* (New York: Trident, 1963), 130.
16. Writing this essay in England, at some distance from most of my notes, I have been unable to locate the source for this statement.
17. See Joseph Blotner, *Faulkner: A Biography* (New York: Random House, 1974), 170 for a discussion of Faulkner's reading. Also see Calvin S. Brown, "From Jefferson to the World," in *Faulkner: International Perspectives*, ed. Doreen Fowler and Ann J. Abadie (Jackson: University Press of Mississippi, 1984).

boy with talk about the perfection of Swinburne's technique, the beautiful sound of Verlaine's poetry, the simple lucidity of Housman's. 'Try writing in somebody else's style,' Phil advised him. 'Then compare yours with his and see how much better he does it.' "[18]

That imitative method had many advantages, but one disadvantage was dependence. Faulkner's omnivorous ingesting of his models—of Verlaine, Mallarmé, Swinburne, Housman, and others—also tended to use them up and to keep Faulkner always on the lookout for new models. (Perhaps he registered at the University here in 1919 in French, Spanish, and a survey of English literature because he was searching for literary models beyond those that his mother and friend could provide.) At any rate, Faulkner's early reading and writing suggest a curious mix of inner direction (self-education) and outer-direction (derivative writing). Overstating, one might hypothesize that Faulkner knew how to read but not yet how to write on his own.

Apparently Faulkner accepted the need for poetic models but wrote his first critical review—about the time he withdrew from the University—without models. This—the Percy review—appeared in the campus paper *The Mississippian* on November 20, 1920. The twenty-three-year-old Faulkner begins his review rather mechanically with a paragraph of information about William Alexander Percy and then continues with a personal protest: "Mr. Percy—like alas! how many of us—suffered the misfortune of having been born out of his time" (*EPP*, 71). Faulkner shows that he has read Swinburne, Browning, and the decadents who make "beauty almost like physical pain" (*EPP*, 72). Referring to Percy's retreat from modernity to "the colorful romantic pageantry of the middle ages" (*EPP*, 72), Faulkner seems to be connecting the Mississippi poet with the Pre-Raphaelites. The review displays familiarity with a wide range of late nineteenth-century poetry but is based on only one critical prin-

18. Emily Whitehurst Stone, "How a Writer Finds His Material," *Harper's Magazine* (November 1965), 158.

ciple: distrust of the artificial. We see that principle in Faulkner's contempt for war poems in which "nightingales wear
swords and Red Cross brassards" and in his conclusion that there
is "too much music" in Percy's poetry (*EPP,* 73). Faulkner both
praises and blames Percy but concludes "he is a difficult person
to whom to render justice" (*EPP,* 73). The difficulty seems to be,
not Percy's variety or complexity, but Faulkner's ignorance of
critical theory.

Apparently, he recognized the problem and began to read
theory. In his review of Conrad Aiken's *Turns and Movies,* published just over three months later, on February 19, 1921, Faulkner alludes to, as his poetry had echoed, the Greeks and the
French symbolists. He also mentions approvingly John
Masefield whose works Stone would give to Katrina Carter and
order for himself.[19] Apparently, Stone was championing
Masefield before he made the book orders which are documented, and Faulkner mentions "bits of soft sonority that
Masefield might have formed" (*EPP,* 76) in deference to Stone's
opinion.

But in addition to such familiar or traceable references, Faulkner for the first time uses a set of concepts borrowed from Willard Huntington Wright and especially from Clive Bell. Both
Bell and Wright conceive of aesthetics as a science (Bell, vi).[20]
Reviewing Aiken, Faulkner says that many contemporary
versifiers "have realized that aesthetics is as much a science as
chemistry, that there are certain definite scientific rules which,
when properly applied, will produce great art as surely as certain chemical elements, combined in the proper proportions,
will produce certain reactions; yet Mr. Aiken alone has made any
effort to discover them and apply them intelligently" (*EPP,* 74).
Given the order date for Bell's *Art* listed in the appendix to
Faulkner's Library: A Catalogue and the inscription in the copy

19. See Hamblin and Brodsky, 21–23 and *Faulkner's Library,* 125.
20. Stone often insisted upon Wright's influence. See Mick Gidley, cited above, and
James B. Meriwether, ed., "Early Notices of Faulkner by Phil Stone and Louis Cochran," *Mississippi Quarterly,* 17 (Summer 1964), 141. Stone however was not always
consistent; see note 21.

of Wright's *The Creative Will* (now in the Boozer collection),[21] Stone might have been proselytizing for Bell and Wright for some three years. Faulkner, however, seems to have paid attention only after he realized that his one book review, lacking a theoretical foundation, was a very shaky structure. He listened then when he needed to.

And so, Faulkner founded his second review upon the theories of Clive Bell. In this review Faulkner follows Bell who asks, "Before we feel an aesthetic emotion for a combination of forms, do we not perceive intellectually the rightness and necessity of the combination?" (Bell, 26). Faulkner's version of that theory is praise for Conrad Aiken's avoidance of the accidental (*EPP*, 75) and the haphazard (*EPP*, 76). Bell laments, "Since Zola, every novelist has known that nothing gives so imposing an air of reality as a mass of irrelevant facts, and very few have cared to give much else. Detail is the heart of realism, and the fatty degeneration of Art" (Bell, 222). Faulkner accepts Bell's program of trimming the fat out of art and praises Aiken for "most happily escap[ing] our national curse of filling each and every space" (*EPP*, 75). Faulkner's use of words like "space," "three dimensional," and "plastic" (*EPP*, 75 and 76) assumes, with Bell, an analogy between the visual and verbal arts. And his praise of Aiken's "impersonally sincere poems" (*EPP*, 76) follows the emphasis on impersonality we find in such passages from Bell as "art transports from a world of man's activity to a world of aesthetic exaltation" (Bell, 25) and, in a phrase that anticipates new criticism, "to appreciate a man's art I need know nothing whatever about the artist" (Bell, 99).

Bell argues for the similarity of aesthetic responses to all the

21. William Boozer now owns the 1916 edition of *The Creative Will* which bears the inscription "From Phil to Bill on his birthday. 9/25/17." Thirty-six years later Stone added the following explanation: "I gave this book to Bill and I don't think he ever read any of it. My copy was burned when our old house burned January 10, 1942. I was down at Bill's house one day and asked him to give this copy back to me and he did. I make this note for Philip and Araminta. Oxford, Miss. Christmas Eve Night. 1953." I wish to thank William Boozer for providing me with this information.

arts. He knows that when he properly appreciates music he hears it, as he views a painting, in terms of form: as "pure musical form, as sounds combined according to the laws of a mysterious necessity" (Bell, 185). Faulkner, who a few months earlier had condemned Percy for too much music, praises Aiken's experiments "with an abstract three dimensional verse patterned on polyphonic music form" (*EPP*, 76).

Of course, with the exception of the statement about aesthetics being a science, none of these comments is explicitly lifted from Bell; nevertheless, that Faulkner echoes Bell's aesthetic values and terminology when a few months before he had only one value and no terminology suggests that Faulkner had indeed buttressed his newly erected critical house with Clive Bell's aesthetics.

It was nearly a year before Faulkner wrote another review. But his treatment of Edna St. Vincent Millay's *Aria da Capo*, appearing in the January 13, 1922, *Mississippian*, still testifies to Bell's influence. Faulkner's pleasure in Millay's "idea so simple" (*EPP*, 84) reminds us of Bell's "simplification is the conversion of irrelevant detail into significant form" (Bell, 185). But Faulkner shows some uncertainty in this review about one Bell-associated idea: the need for an ideal conception of the work of art. Faulkner acknowledges that "though an idea alone does not make or mar a piece of writing, it is something" (*EPP*, 85). Faulkner has recognized that a work of art must be judged on execution, not conception. Perhaps he has begun to wonder just how an ideal conception of "combinations of lines and colours" can be counted upon to "provoke aesthetic emotion" (Bell, 12).

Certainly Faulkner was thinking about aesthetics as he had not been when he wrote the Percy review, and perhaps also he had been reading Rebecca West's *Henry James*. Stone dated his copy of West's overview of James 1/15/17—not quite two months before the date in Bell's *Art*.[22] West is contemptuous of "books

22. Hamblin and Brodsky, 20.

about ideas," and she criticizes James as a man "who wanted to live wholly without violence even of the emotions."[23] Lacking a full range of emotions, James created, she feels, "people [who] are not even human."[24]

We do not know whether or not Faulkner read West on James, but the "numerous underlinings and annotations by Stone, primarily in sections relating to narrative theory"[25] suggest that Stone probably pushed West on his friend. Reading West might have heightened Faulkner's empathy for James whose inauspicious beginnings, West says, confirmed his "tutors' opinion that he was an inarticulate mediocrity who would never be able to take a hand in the business of life," so that in defiance of such a judgment James "set to work to become a writer."[26] But if Faulkner empathized with James's sense of inferiority, he had no empathy for one to whom the "profound truth that an artist should feel passion for his subject was naturally distasteful." West concludes that James's prose achieves a "beauty of its own; but it is no longer the beauty of a living thing."[27] West might have influenced Faulkner's opinion of James, or she may only have confirmed his presuppositions; at any rate, Faulkner agreed with her. Half a lifetime after he may first have read Rebecca West on Henry James, Faulkner called James a "prig"[28] who was too "detached from life"[29] to write about it. West may have offered Faulkner an opinion about James; she certainly provided him with a theory of literary values.

If Faulkner read Bell and West together or in the order in which I think we see their impact on him—first Bell, then West—they must have engaged him in a curious dialectic. Bell

23. Rebecca West, *Henry James* (London: Nisbet & Co., 1916), 53 and 52.
24. Ibid., 113.
25. Hamblin and Brodsky, 20.
26. West, 21.
27. Ibid., 52 and 116.
28. Frederick L. Gwynn and Joseph L. Blotner, eds., *Faulkner in the University: Class Conferences at the University of Virginia 1957–58* (Charlottesville: The University of Virginia Press, 1959), 16.
29. Ibid., 169.

ranks art according to its detachment, West according to its engagement. To Bell, the world of art is "a world with an intense and peculiar significance of its own; that significance is unrelated to the significance of life. In this world the emotions of life find no place" (Bell, 26–27). But West values literature, at least in part, by the artist's "passion for his subject."[30] The two critics epitomize a dialectic between formal and naturalistic values or between, in terms I have used elsewhere, the abstract and the actual.

Reading and writing poetry, Faulkner had formed the habit of absorbing his models. Reading and writing criticism, he again absorbed his models, but he discovered a problem. Imitating poetry was valuable because it taught him different approaches; imitating criticism was troublesome because it led him to contradict himself. Faulkner had originally turned to aesthetic theory—especially Bell—for standards to use in passing aesthetic judgment. He read on in writers like Rebecca West and discovered a diametrically opposed standard of judgment. His imaginative writing at the time suggests he was testing the value of artifice (as in *Marionettes*) and of realism (as in "Adolescence").

Apparently, he continued reading theory in hopes of discovering what art should be. He begins his next review, a discussion of Eugene O'Neill's dramas, by saying "Some one has said—a Frenchman, probably; they have said everything—that art is preeminently provincial" (*EPP*, 86). Here Faulkner is covering his tracks;[31] the "Frenchman" he had in mind turns out to be the Irishman George Moore. In *Ave*, the first volume of the

30. West, 52.
31. That Faulkner was capable of such techniques is, I think, suggested by his references to Thomas Beer who, Faulkner said, "influenced me a lot" (see *Faulkner in the University*, 20 and 23–24). In *Sherwood Anderson and Other Famous Creoles* the caption under the drawing of Lyle Saxon is "The Mauve Decade in Saint Peter Street." Since William Spratling tells us that Faulkner wrote these captions (see his "Chronicle of a Friendship: William Faulkner in New Orleans," *Texas Quarterly*, 9 [Spring 1966], 34–40), we know that Faulkner knew Beer's *The Mauve Decade*; but it seems to me that the most he might have learned from it was a flippant technique of exposing tastelessness, prudery, and amorality; thus when he says "I got quite a lot from [Beer]" one suspects him of laying a false scent.

Hail and Farewell trilogy, Moore remembers arguing with Edward Martyn about "nationality in art."[32] Moore wonders "if it were true that whoever cast off tradition is like a tree transplanted into uncongenial soil."[33] Then Moore remembers that he himself—he does not say where—has written "that art must be parochial in the beginning to become cosmopolitan in the end."[34] Thinking with Moore about the value of the Irish tradition, Faulkner asserts that "Synge is provincial, smacking of the soil from which he sprang as no other modern does" (*EPP*, 87). Moore's thinking about an Irish national language is echoed in Faulkner's thinking about the American language. Mencken too, as Mick Gidley and others have pointed out, seems to lie behind Faulkner's discussion of the American language.

Another theorist Faulkner seems to have tapped for the O'Neill review was William Stanley Braithwaite. We know Faulkner read Braithwaite's introduction to his *Anthology of Magazine Verse for 1920 and Year Book of American Poetry* because, in the copy Ben Wasson gave him on January 5, 1921, Faulkner wrote what Joseph Blotner calls "one of his extremely rare marginal comments." Drawing an arrow to Braithwaite's comment that "no one who matters actually thinks that a national literature can be founded on such alien bases [as Indian and Negro folklore],"[35] Faulkner writes "Good God." The full text from Braithwaite reads:

> Indian and negro materials, however, are in our poetry still hardly better than aspects of the exotic. No one who matters actually thinks that a national literature can be founded on such alien bases. Where, then, are our poets to find some such stout tap-root of memory and knowledge as Thomas Hardy follows deep down to the primal rock of England? The answer is that for the present we are not to find it. We possess no such commodity. Out literature for generations, per-

    32. George Moore, *Ave*, I of *Hail and Farewell!* (London: William Heinemann, 1911), 8.
    33. Ibid., 9.
    34. Ibid., 9–10.
    35. Blotner, *Faulkner: A Biography*, 300.

haps centuries, will have to be symbolized by the melting pot, not by the tap-root. Our geographical is also our spiritual destiny.[36]

In the O'Neill review Faulkner writes: "A national literature cannot spring from folk lore—though heaven knows, such a forcing has been tried often enough—for America is too big and there are too many folk lores: Southern negroes, Spanish and French strains, the old west, for these always will remain colloquial" (*EPP*, 89). And Faulkner also assumes the "fact that America has no drama or literature worth the name, and hence no tradition" (*EPP*, 87). Since he is virtually paraphrasing Braithwaite, we can assume that, for the time at least, Faulkner agreed with him. Perhaps then Faulkner's marginal "Good God" was a reaction to the snobbish "no one who matters"; or perhaps it was an expression of delight as Braithwaite offered Faulkner the very idea he needed. Faulkner's use of Bell, West, Moore, Mencken, and Braithwaite all in one review suggests that he was reading like a vacuum cleaner: sucking up ideas as he needed them.

The O'Neill review shows Faulkner absorbing various literary opinions, but it also shows him seriously trying to think through an aesthetic premise and its implications. He finds Conrad and O'Neill exceptions to the premise "that art is preeminently provincial" (*EPP*, 86). He wonders if "the Fates have indeed played a scurvy trick upon him [O'Neill, but Faulkner must have been thinking of himself as well] in casting into twentieth century America a man who might go to astounding lengths in a land possessing traditions" (*EPP*, 87). Here Faulkner projects his own malaise onto O'Neill as he had earlier done with Percy; this time, however, his meaning is clear. He grapples with the question of how much great art is simply a matter of that "incalculable, indefinable quantity genius"—which he calls a "horrible word" (*EPP*, 87)—and how much it is a matter of tradition.

Like Bell (see Bell, 91), Faulkner endorses a sort of artistic

---

36. William Stanley Braithewaite, "Tap-Root or Melting-Pot," in *Anthology of Magazine Verse for 1920 and Year Book of American Poetry* (Boston, 1920), xi.

ruthlessness (*EPP*, 87). And he praises O'Neill's "clarity and simplicity of plot and language" (*EPP*, 88), criteria which relate back to Bell. But he also praises O'Neill's development from a Bell-like "detached observation of his people" towards a West-like "more personal regard for their joys and hopes, their sufferings and despairs" (*EPP*, 88). Here Faulkner is still caught on the horns of an aesthetic dilemma: should art be, in Bell's terms, the "contemplation of pure form [which] leads to a state of extraordinary exaltation and complete detachment from the concerns or life" (Bell, 68); or should it, as West infers, further engage us in the human community?

In his next published piece of prose, the short sketch "The Hill," Faulkner seems to have tried to explore in fiction the Clive Bell aesthetic of distance. The author is distanced from his nameless, unspecified protagonist, and that character is distanced from the landscape, so that from "the hilltop the valley was a motionless mosaic of tree and house" (*EPP*, 91). From this distance, the "tieless casual" (*EPP*, 92)—that is as close as Faulkner gets to a specific description of him—sees only abstract, dehumanized patterning: "There was no suggestion of striving, or whipped vanities, of ambition and lusts, of the drying spittle of religious controversy; he could not see that the sonorous simplicity of the court house columns was discolored and stained with casual tobacco" (*EPP*, 91). So distanced, the man senses the "devastating unimportance of his destiny" (*EPP*, 92).

"The Hill" is almost an unresolved aesthetic argument. Distanced from the valley, the man can see pattern as in a Cézanne landscape. Distanced, he also is divorced from the messy confusion of the human community. But such distance dehumanizes him as well as the landscape. Presumably when he descends the hill at the end of the sketch he will reenter the human community but lose the clear vision of a patterned mosaic. Thus the sketch seems to say: achieve the pattern and lose the humanity, or gain the humanity and lose the pattern; you cannot have both.

On March 17, 1922, one week after publishing "The Hill," *The Mississippian* carried an essay entitled "American Drama:

Inhibitions" and signed "W. F." In this essay, on the one hand, Faulkner denounces America as being "aesthetically impossible"; on the other, he concludes that it offers "an inexhaustible fund of dramatic material." But then, as if recalling Clive Bell, he writes: "Sound art, however, does not depend on the quality or quantity of available material: a man with real ability finds sufficient what he has to hand. Material does aid that person who does not possess quite enough driving force to create living figures out of his own brain; wealth of material does enable him to build better than he otherwise could" (*EPP*, 94). Similarly, Bell says, "Every sacrifice made to representation is something stolen from art" (Bell, 44) and claims that representation is often "a sign of weakness in an artist. A painter too feeble to create forms that provoke more than a little aesthetic emotion will try to eke that little out by suggesting the emotions of life" (Bell, 28). Of course, Bell is criticizing painting which elicits an emotional response to the subject—a beautiful woman, a pastoral scene, a great battle, perhaps a mythological figure—rather than to the formal values of the painting itself. And Faulkner knows that poorly written fiction too can depend on an emotionally charged subject matter for its impact. But he does wonder why, if aesthetic value is independent of subject matter, all writing does not become a simple matter of following the rules for pure form: "It does not always follow that a play built according to sound rules—i. e. simplicity and strength of language, thorough knowledge of material, and clarity of plot—will be a good play as a result; else playwriting would become a comparatively simple process" (*EPP*, 95). Caught on the horns of the dilemma between art and realism, formalism and naturalism, Faulkner begs the question in this essay on "American Drama." He changes the subject, rather as he had done in the O'Neill essay, and announces that American English—the "lustiest language of modern times" (*EPP*, 96)—will be the salvation of the American drama. That he shows himself aware of two contradictory approaches to art and then avoids resolving the contradiction suggests that Faulkner still lacked a unified aesthetic sense.

Elie Faure's *History of Art*[37] and Percy Lubbock's *The Craft of Fiction* were ordered by Stone in March of 1922.[38] Faulkner seems not to have read them when he wrote "The Hill" or his essay on American Drama; but he does seem to have known Lubbock and the two volumes of Faure then in translation before writing his next critical essay. This review of three novels by Joseph Hergesheimer appeared in the December 15, 1922, *Mississippian*. The review is peculiar because, first of all, Faulkner's critique of Hergesheimer's *Linda Condon* describes Faulkner's own *Marionettes* better than it does *Linda Condon*. Hergesheimer's characters are said to be "like puppets assuming graceful but meaningless postures in answer to the author's compulsions" (*EPP*, 101). Faulkner says that Hergesheimer's "people are never actuated from within" (*EPP*, 101). He seems to be comparing Hergesheimer's art to Golden Age Greek sculpture whose figures, Faure says, obey "inner forces in order to reveal their meaning to us." According to Faure, the "artist of today is afraid of words, when he does not fall victim to them" (Faure, I, xxxvii–xxxix). Faulkner says Hergesheimer is "enslaved by words" (*EPP*, 101) and compares his fiction to the sort of Byzantine frieze he may have been reading about in Faure.

Essentially, Faulkner attacks Hergesheimer, as West had attacked James, for being "afraid of living" (*EPP*, 101) and hence unable to create human characters. He dismisses the novel *Cythera* completely, calling it "the apostle James making an obscene gesture. Rather the apostle James trying to carry off a top hat and a morning coat" (*EPP*, 102). Presumably, his point is that Hergesheimer is writing an obscene imitation of the apostle Henry James, trying to apply an idealist technique to a story of "morbid men and obscene women" (*EPP*, 102).

Another possible influence here is Percy Lubbock's *The Craft of Fiction*, which calls for the novel to be first of all a "picture of

---

37. See the Appendix to *Faulkner's Library*, 125.
38. Ibid.

life."[39] Lubbock acknowledges that the novel must have "form, design, composition,"[40] but he wonders: "Does the fact that a novel is well designed, well proportioned, really make a very great difference in its power to please?"[41] Despite his title, then, Lubbock would have seemed to Faulkner to have sided with West and against Bell for human, not formal values.

Faulkner's own treatment of Hergesheimer shows him trying to work through those two conflicting value systems. He says that Hergesheimer's *Linda Condon* is too stylized to contain life, while in the other two novels "Hergesheimer has tried to enter life, with disastrous results; Sinclair Lewis and the New York Times have corrupted him" (*EPP,* 103). Hergesheimer's "ability to write flawless prose [is] tortured by his unfortunate reactions to the apish imbecilities of the human race" (*EPP,* 103). The Faulkner who wrote *Marionettes* and the poems which would form *The Marble Faun,* then, criticizes one Hergesheimer novel for presenting "puppets assuming graceful but meaningless postures." But that same Faulkner attacks the other two Hergesheimer novels for displaying their author's distaste for the "apish imbecilities of the human race." This is the Faulkner who "cured" himself, according to Carvel Collins in a masterpiece of euphemism, of an infatuation with a young woman, "by deliberately developing mental pictures of that otherwise idealized person engaged in the least romantic regularly repeated acts of our species."[42] Given such information about Faulkner, we might conclude that he projects his own idealism and revulsion onto Hergesheimer. As he condemns one Hergesheimer novel for being too artificial, the other two for being too naturalistic, Faulkner shows himself still unable to decide what art should be.

39. Percy Lubbock, *The Craft of Fiction* (London: Jonathan Cape, 1921; rpt., 1926), 9.

40. Ibid.

41. Ibid.

42. Carvel Collins, Introduction to *Mayday* by William Faulkner (Notre Dame: University of Notre Dame Press, 1976), 18.

In late 1924, Faulkner began for the first time to write extensively in prose. Apparently, as Leland Cox suggests in his dissertation—an edition of the *New Orleans Sketches* entitled "Sinbad in New Orleans"—Faulkner began this writing in 1924 in hopes of placing it when he got to New Orleans.[43] He must have brought with him two pieces of nonfiction prose and have written three more during his first three and a half months in New Orleans. The most chronologically puzzling of these essays is the brief "Literature and War" which Michael Millgate says "presumably dates, like other manuscripts in the Berg group, from late 1924 or the first half of 1925."[44] Since Faulkner refers to R. H. Mottram's 1924 *Spanish Farm,* the essay could not have been written before 1924; yet it carries a puzzling similarity to Faulkner's earlier work. In the essay he refers to Siegfried Sassoon, Henry Barbusse, Rupert Brooke, and Stephen Crane, as well as Mottram. He praises all but Brooke for fidelity to grim, unidealistic details of war like rain, mud, and stench. He ends with a startling metaphor: "Mankind's emotional gamut is like his auricular gamut; there are some things which he cannot feel, as there are sounds he cannot hear. And war, taken as a whole, is one of these things."[45] Such "smart cynicism" (the phrase is Millgate's)[46] begs the question: is Faulkner saying that though war itself cannot be felt, naturalistic language can be? or is he ignoring a fundamental contradiction between what he says about war and what he says about the literature of war?

I cannot be sure how that statement applies to literature, but I am sure that, in this five-paragraph, 300-word essay, Faulkner values the literature of war exclusively by its fidelity to actual experience, as he had in the William Alexander Percy review.

43. Lenard H. Cox, Jr., *Sinbad in New Orleans: Early Short Fiction by William Faulkner—An Annotated Edition* (Ann Arbor: University Microfilms International, 1977), vi and xx.

44. Michael Millgate, "Faulkner on the Literature of the First World War," in *A Faulkner Miscellany,* James B. Meriwether, ed. (Jackson: University Press of Mississippi, 1974), 98.

45. Ibid., 99.

46. Ibid., 104.

He regresses into a fantasy of himself as battle-weary soldier, as "one who had himself slogged up Arras or its corresponding objective, who has trod duck-boards and heard and felt them sqush [sic] and suck in the mud, who has seen the casual dead rotting beneath dissolving Flemish skies, who has smelt that dreadful smell of war."[47] Perhaps war was never a topic about which Faulkner could think in personally honest or critically sophisticated terms, but this piece would fit a coherent scheme of Faulkner's development if it had been written about the time of the Percy review when Faulkner was (1) thinking about the literature of war; (2) maintaining a fantasy of himself as wounded war hero; and (3) unaware of—or at least silent about—any literary value except verisimilitude. Since it could not have been written before 1924, however, we have to consider it a psychological and critical regression.[48]

Other essays do fit a coherent scheme. A carbon typescript of "Verse Old and Nascent: A Pilgrimage" bears the date October 1924,[49] though the essay was not published until April 1925, in the *Double Dealer*. Faulkner's review of John Cowper Powys's *Ducdame* must have been written in early 1925 since both American and English editions were 1925 publications and Faulkner's review was published in the *Times-Picayune* on March 22, 1925; he may have been given an advance copy and so could have written the review any time between mid-January and mid-March. The January–February issue of *The Double Dealer* published Faulkner's essay "On Criticism" along with his sketches entitled "New Orleans,"[50] and his poem "Dying Gladiator." Though the first of these essays to be published, "On Criticism" was written at least three months after "Verse Old and

47. Ibid., 99.
48. Another possibility is that Faulkner did write a rough draft of the essay earlier and revise it in 1924 adding the reference to Mottram. I have not yet been able to examine the manuscript to determine if there is any evidence to support such a hypothesis.
49. Hamblin and Brodsky, 39.
50. Cox argues, from manuscript evidence, that several of these sketches were completed before Faulkner's arrival in New Orleans. Cox, xx.

Nascent" and in roughly the same period as the Powys review. The fifth essay in this group, Faulkner's essay on Sherwood Anderson for the *Dallas Morning News,* was written between mid-March and mid-April of 1925 and is therefore clearly the last of this group.

Knowing that "Verse Old and Nascent" was written in October 1924, about the time when his ill-fated career as a postmaster was ending, when he was waiting for his first book of poems to appear, and when he was preparing to leave Mississippi for Europe, we better understand the essay's subtitle: "A Pilgrimage." "Verse Old and Nascent" is an autobiographical essay which essentially says good-bye to childish things and exhibits a new self-possession and self-confidence. In the manner of George Moore's *Confessions of a Young Man,* a book Faulkner refers to by name in his essay on Anderson,[51] this essay charts a series of awakenings in literary taste. But before Faulkner considers his serious involvement with verse, he spends more than two pages discussing his early and apparently insincere absorption in Swinburne. He couches the story of his discovery of Swinburne in terms that could also apply to the various theorists he had been reading for the last four years: "I found him nothing but a flexible vessel into which I might put my own vague emotional shapes without breaking them" (*EPP,* 114). Explaining the effect of his captivation by Swinburne, Faulkner draws a somewhat fuzzy conclusion: "Therefore, I believe I came as near as possible to approaching poetry with an unprejudiced mind" (*EPP,* 116). Faulkner then seems to turn to the aesthetic opinions which he had been trying on like new coats over the past four years; for he says, "I had no opinions at that time, the opinions I later formed were all factitious and were discarded" (*EPP,* 116). But he may at about this time have consulted one writer whose opinion of art he would never discard. That writer was Elie Faure.

51. Faulkner refers to Moore in "Portrait of Elmer" and in "Sherwood Anderson," *The Dallas Morning News* (April 26, 1925), III, 7; rpt. *The Princeton University Library Chronicle,* 18 (Spring 1957), James B. Meriwether, ed., 93.

In his preface to the New Edition of Volume I of his *History of Art,* Faure acknowledges that he has been reproached for writing "not a history of art but a poem of the history" (Faure, I, xxxviii–xxxix). Faure may have deserved that reproach since he offers more rhetoric than information; nevertheless, it seems to have been the rhetoric that Faulkner needed. Faure believes that the true artist "permits the divine voices to sing within him" (Faure, I, xviii); to him "art is the appeal to the instinct of communion in men" (Faure, I, xx); thus it links the divine and the mortal. Faure, who describes himself as a " 'self-taught' " man (Faure, I, xxxvii), sees the artist's role in terms which must have been gratifying to Faulkner. Faure explains that the artist "suffers, his tyrannical disquietude often makes those around him suffer. But around him, and fifty centuries after him, he consoles millions of men" (Faure, I, xxvi). In terms that Faulkner would echo nearly a decade later in his introductions to *The Sound and the Fury,* Faure sees the artist's canon as a single effort: "In reality each writer writes only one book, each painter paints only one picture. Every new work is destined, in the mind of its author, to correct the preceding one, to complete the thought— which will not be completed" (Faure, I, xxxv).

Faure's treatment of Greek art, which he calls a "thing of living change" (Faure, I, 166), must have been both informative and affecting. Faure tells us that the Doric form was inspired by the male torso, the Ionic by the female, and that Ulysses compared Nausicaa to the stem of a palm tree (Faure, I, 247). He finds Doric art crude, Ionic more sophisticated and tender (Faure, I, 137). He suggests a distinction that sounds Faulknerian to us: man through the ages has been idealistic, while "woman, on the contrary, has before her only the near and present reality." Thus she is described, in those prefeminist days, as the "first workman" (Faure, I, 7). Yet she carried a nearly opposed significance: Faure tells us that, especially in the work of Praxiteles, the feminine body was equated with "unconquerable idealism" (Faure, I, 196–97).

Sampling Faure, we hear phrases and concepts that sound

Faulknerian. Faure describes the beginning of Greek art thusly: "In the sculpture of Olympia there is an enchaining of causes and effects which has its perfect logic, but which is still intoxicated with the discovery of itself. The mind of the artist prolongs it unbroken so that he may gather up into himself its tumult and passion. One moment more and Phidias transforms it into spiritual harmonies which mark the expansion of the intelligence into the fullness of love" (Faure, I, 162). (We remember the "overpass to love" in *Absalom, Absalom!*)

To Faure, the Fates on the tympanum of the Parthenon are "torsos mounting with the power and tumult of a wave" (Faure, I, 170). He sees in Greek art a "motionless balance" (Faure, I, 180), a "melody. Man's action is fused with his thought" (Faure, I, 184). He speaks of "Passion" and says "the Greek knew it so well that he deified it" (Faure, I, 261). He tells us that the Jews misunderstood Christ, but "the Greeks were far better prepared to understand him" (Faure, I, 266). Faure's description of Athenian vases sounds familiar. On them "nature is no longer a world of immutable and separate forms, but a moving world, constantly combining and disuniting itself." Furthermore, the vase has "the form of fruits, of the mother's belly, and of plants. The sphere is the matrix and the tomb of forms. Everything comes out of it. Everything returns to it" (Faure, I, 259). Faulkner made the image more mundane—the front door and the back door—but the concept is the same.

In volume II, *Medieval Art*, Faure begins his chapter on "Christianity and the Commune" by saying "the Semitic spirit, at the decline of the old world, tried to conquer Europe through the apostles of Christ" (Faure, II, 261). Faulkner says that the Jews gave "a fairy tale that has conquered the whole Western earth."[52] Speaking of the Italy of St. Francis, Faure explains that there "death has the attraction and the mystery of love" (Faure, II, 381). The associations of death and love pervade Faulkner's

---

52. William Faulkner, *New Orleans Sketches*, Introduction by Carvel Collins (New Brunswick, N.J.: Rutgers University Press, 1958), 54.

canon, but it is worth remembering that, according to William Spratling, when they were in Italy together, "Faulkner would [constantly] be discoursing to the effect that for him there were only two basic compulsions on earth, i.e. love and death."[53] Obviously, the association was not initiated just by reading Faure, but apparently reading him focused a death/love connection that was already congenial to Faulkner.

Faulkner's interest in St. Francis might have derived from a number of sources, but Faure is a most probable one. Faure tells us that "Francis of Assisi was transported by love as other men were by the frenzy of killing" (Faure, II, 398). He sees St. Francis's pantheism as a protest against Christian dualism and tells us that "dying, [Francis of Assisi] repented of having practiced aestheticism, of having 'offended his brother the body'" (Faure, II, 398). Faure repeats St. Francis's prayer which sees the sun and fire as brothers, the moon and water as sisters (Faure, II, 401–2). Faure compares Pisan architecture in words that we might associate with "Carcassone": the Pisan style is "like the dying poetry of the stained glass with which a sick people irritates its fever, after the living poetry that had resounded in stone and bronze with the voices of strong men" (Faure, II, 426). Admittedly, such language would not have taught Elmer Hodge how to paint, but I think it did teach William Faulkner how to think and speak about art. As evidence, I ask you to place the following phrases: "vibrant silence," "implacable portraits," "arrested life," "feverish concentration," "silent music," "immutable order of the mind," "cosmic equilibrium." They come not from "Carcassone," or from *Absalom, Absalom!*, or from *A Fable,* or from *Requiem for a Nun,* but from Faure's *History of Art* (I, 154, 248, 249, 250; II, 275, 304, 316). Of course, Faure did not hold patent on words such as "immutable" and "implacable," but Faure did use this language to solve the very aesthetic dilemmas Faulkner faced: a conflict between formal and mimetic values and a conflict between valuing and disvaluing art.

53. Spratling, (cited in note 31), 38.

Faure's specific influence upon Faulkner can be seen in the revision of "The Hill" as "Nympholepsy," a prose sketch which James B. Meriwether says "Faulkner apparently wrote early in 1925, within the first month or two of his arrival in New Orleans."[54] You will remember that in "The Hill" the man "could not see that the sonorous simplicity of the court house columns was discolored and stained with casual tobacco" (*EPP*, 91). In "Nympholepsy," the equivalent passage reads: "From here the court house was a dream dreamed by Thucydides: You could not see that pale Ionic columns were stained with casual tobacco."[55] (You will also remember that Faure says Ionic columns are female.) Language in "Nympholepsy" too is Faure-like. A few examples are the pine trees "half iron and half bronze, sculptured into a symbol of eternal quiet" which form a "green cathedral"[56] and are "calm and uncaring as Gods."[57]

In "Verse Old and Nascent" itself Faure's influence is less a matter of language than of an attitude toward art. One of Faulkner's early problems as a writer had surely been his contempt for art and the artist. That contempt surfaces in Faulkner's first piece of published nonfiction, which was not one of the essays I have been speaking about, but rather a 1920 reply to someone who had printed parodies, in the *Mississippian*, of Faulkner's translations from Verlaine. Faulkner's retort is interesting principally because of the self-contempt it exhibits; for he not only attacks his parodist but attacks the very act of imitating. He says, "The first poem submitted by [the parodist] was stupid, for my own poem was stupid. One sees at a glance then, the utter valuelessness of an imitation of an imitation" (*EPP*, 9). For a poet to denounce his own poem as "stupid" is perverse; but for him who learned by imitating to denounce all imitation is odd indeed. Following Plato, Faulkner attacks the parodist who has imitated Faulkner who has imitated Verlaine; and the acknowledgment of stupidity seems to imply that Faulkner too was

54. James B. Meriwether, *A Faulkner Miscellany*, 149.
55. Ibid., 150.
56. Ibid., 151.
57. Ibid., 152.

merely writing an imitation of an imitation, that is, Faulkner imitated Verlaine who imitated life. In this pattern of regression, art can never be more than a pale copy of life, an inadequate substitute chosen by those who have failed at life itself. Given these assumptions, a would-be artist like Faulkner could hardly respect his art or himself.

The twenty-three-year-old Faulkner characterized the artist as a person who turned to art after failing at life. Faulkner was never wholly free of the spectre of the artist as one who has failed at life. That notion appears in *Mosquitoes* and, most explicitly, in *The Unvanquished* when Bayard Sartoris says, "those who can, do, those who cannot and suffer enough because they can't, write about it."[58] Before 1925 Faulkner wrote of the writer's inadequacy as a specifically sexual inadequacy. In the Aiken review he writes of "mental puberty" (*EPP*, 74) and "aesthetic sterility" (*EPP*, 76). In the Millay review he again uses the phrase "mental puberty" (*EPP*, 84) and speaks of the "sterile clashing of ideas" (*EPP*, 85) among "modern playwrights and versifiers" (*EPP*, 84), but he uses a sexually positive image only in describing the work of a female writer; in Millay he finds a "lusty tenuous simplicity" (*EPP*, 85). Later the images are more frequently positive. In "American Drama: Inhibitions" he characterizes American English as "the lustiest language of modern times" (*EPP*, 96). Later he attacks Hergesheimer ambiguously for "sex crucifixion turned backward upon itself" (*EPP*, 101), but in that same review he also distinguishes between a healthy "masculine emotional curiosity" and "deliberate pandering to the emotions" (*EPP*, 101). Though he characterizes artifice and, by inference, poetry as emasculate (*EPP*, 103), he associates the successful novel with motion, meaning, and masculinity. (Perhaps at this point Faulkner found one of the ideas of Willard Huntington Wright convenient; for, as Mick Gidley explains, Wright saw poetry as adolescent and feminine.)[59] If Faulkner feared that all art might be an emasculate imitation of life, in the Hergesheimer review he at least tests the theory that, though

58. William Faulkner, *The Unvanquished* (New York: Random House, 1938), 262.
59. Gidley, 171.

poetry (and lifeless artifice) might be effeminate, fiction (at least the successful novel) could be masculine. In "Verse Old and Nascent" he further explores (and gives a muddled personal account of) the connection he saw between sex and art. Instead of seeing art (especially verse) as evidence of an incapacity for life (and sex), he depicts verse as an "emotional counterpart" (*EPP*, 115) to sex. Furthermore, he allows for verse, at least Keats's verse, to be associated with "entrails, masculinity" (*EPP*, 117).

In "Verse Old and Nascent" Faulkner's thinking about art and sex is muddled; his posing, at the age of twenty-seven, as a jaded man-of-the-world is absurd. He claims that he formerly used verse to seduce women, but now "my concupiscence waning,[60] I turned inevitably to verse, finding therein an emotional counterpart far more satisfactory for two reasons: (1) No partner was required (2) It was so much simpler just to close a book, and take a walk" (*EPP*, 115). However muddled, absurd, and unfortunate such assertions are, they do suggest that by late 1924 Faulkner was trying to work through various misconceptions about sex and art, particularly the notion that art was sterile and emasculate. Perhaps reading Elie Faure—who insists upon the sexuality, especially the virility, of art—provoked this reconsideration. References to the "virile harmony" or "virile tenderness" or "virile power" of art so pervade Faure's *History* that they cannot be isolated, but Faure's perspective is at least suggested by his insisting, "We must, however, in our hours of virility, have as imperious a need of artistic creation as of food and love" (Faure, II, xvii). Of course, we cannot know whether reading Faure was determinative or even affective, but we can assume that Faure's repeated insistence upon the masculinity of art and the artist was one of the factors that began to give Faulkner a new confidence in art and in himself.

A review-essay which we know definitely he wrote in early

---

60. The carbon typescript, dated October 1924, reads "my interest in fornication" rather than "my concupiscence"; the other differences between the typescript and the published version are all minor. See Hamblin and Brodsky, 38–39.

1925 displays some of that confidence. Faulkner's review of John Cowper Powys's *Ducdame* appeared in the *Times-Picayune* on March 22, 1925, and was reprinted in the *Mississippi Quarterly*'s 1975 special Faulkner issue. The review provides a minimum of information about Powys's novel; instead it is largely a Faulknerian paraphrase of Clive Bell's theory that "every sacrifice made to representation is something stolen from art" (Bell, 44). Faulkner writes, "Material and aesthetic significance are not the same, but material importance can destroy artistic importance, in spite of what we would like to believe."[61] But if this essay seems, at first glance, to represent another swing of the pendulum away from representation towards artifice, it also makes a subtle alteration in Bell's aesthetic criteria. Faulkner does borrow Bell's concept of significant form and use it as a Faulknerian yardstick, but he reconceptualizes Bell's notion of significance. He finds Powys's characters commit deeds which are "not significant." He expects a successful novel to have "completeness of form: that is the people in it do the things which you would do if you were, one by one, these people. We are all fools probably; and most of us know it: but it is unbearable to believe that the things we do are not significant."[62] That statement verges on a romantic, larger-than-life notion of significance, but it is nevertheless a human, not a formal, notion.

That ability to combine formal and humane values was a genuine aesthetic breakthrough for Faulkner which seems to have been provoked by his borrowing, reading, and keeping an anthology of critical and aesthetic theories entitled *A Modern Book of Criticism.* My guess is that reading this volume encouraged the reconceptualization of Bell's formal criteria in the Powys review and catalyzed Faulkner into writing the other piece of nonfiction which dates from this period. Faulkner titled that essay "On Criticism," and the *Double Dealer* printed it in what was virtually a Faulkner issue, the January-February 1925 num-

---

61. William Faulkner, "Review of *Ducdame,*" rpt. *Mississippi Quarterly,* 28 (Summer 1975), 343. *Ducdame* was printed in New York by Doubleday, Page, & Co. and in London by Grant Richards; both copyrights are for 1925.
62. Ibid., 346.

ber, which apparently did not appear until late February 1925.[63] In this essay Faulkner shows considerable control of style, metaphor, and humor. He says, "Surely, if there are two professions in which there should be no professional jealousy, they are prostitution and literature" (*EPP*, 112). And, in a line memorable to all of us critics who have come here to listen to each other, he wonders if critics "enjoy reading each other" and concludes "one can as easily imagine barbers shaving each other for fun" (*EPP*, 110).

If Faulkner in this essay has better control of his sentences, he also has better control of his understandings. Earlier he had complained rather vaguely that America had "no traditions"; now he had a specific complaint against American critics, some of whom have no viable standard of judgment, others of whom keep their standards a secret. He queries, "what have the periodicals and lecturers done to create either great audiences or great writers of us? Do these Sybils take the neophyte gently in hand and instruct him in the fundamentals of taste?" (*EPP*, 109). Writing what was either his ninth or his tenth critical essay, Faulkner protests that the principles of criticism and aesthetics have been kept "mysteries" (*EPP*, 109) from would-be writers and theorists like himself. In the Millay review some three years earlier he had understood that a writer learns his or her craft and subject from reading. He spoke of a "depth of experience, either mental or physical . . . acquired without conscious effort by every young writer, from the reading done during the period of his mental development, either from choice or compulsion" (*EPP*, 85). How reading could be "from choice" but "without conscious effort" is unclear, but what is clear is that Faulkner had accepted with equanimity the tutelage of other writers. "On Criticism" is remarkable because it expresses no equanimity— only outrage. Faulkner accuses critics of having a "pleasant pas-

63. Leland Cox found February 20 to be the accession date of Tulane Library's copy, Cox, xxv. In *Faulkner: A Biography* (390) Blotner says that the January-February *Double Dealer* printed its "first and longest" note on Faulkner. That note's statement that "to date [Faulkner's] literary interest has been chiefly in poetry" (*Double Dealer,* 7 [January-February 1925], iii) suggests that Faulkner had told the editors that his literary interests were shifting.

time changing [the writer's] opinion from one fallacy to another" (*EPP*, 109–10). Faulkner is outraged by critics who dogmatically assert a whole range of aesthetic standards, and he also seems to feel betrayed by his own willingness to absorb first one standard, then another, only to discover later that they were fallacious or inconsistent.

As I have said, from the time of his second review, Faulkner naively mouthed concepts from Bell, Wright, Moore, Mencken, Braithwaite, Faure, and others, but in "On Criticism" he recognizes that none of these critics have helped him distill and synthesize. He finds American criticism characterized by slick phrases like "aesthetic boy scout" (*EPP*, 111) which mean nothing. (We remember Faulkner's own "the apostle James making an obscene gesture" [*EPP*, 102] and wonder if Faulkner refers to his own glibness.) Feeling betrayed by his critical reading, Faulkner seems to have experienced a sort of aesthetic epiphany: a discovery that aesthetic and criticial works should and could guide writer and reader into a holistic understanding of art. I suspect that at last Faulkner was working out such an understanding and that at last he had books and friends to help him.

When Faulkner died he had in his library at Rowan Oak a copy of *A Modern Book of Criticism*, edited, with an introduction, by Ludwig Lewisohn. This 1919 edition bears two autographs: Hamilton Basso's and William Faulkner's.[64] Apparently, Faulkner got to know Basso early in 1925 in New Orleans through Elizabeth Anderson. Basso, then a student at Tulane, remembers that Faulkner had "been reading enormously on his own. What we talked about were the far-off places vessels tied up at the wharves brought to mind; our recent forays into the world of books (Faulkner had got past Verlaine, Eliot, Pound, and Joyce, while I was just stumbling on Conrad and Melville); and, inevitably, the South."[65] Whether or not they talked about *A Modern Book*, Faulkner got the book from Basso. The pres-

64. *Faulkner's Library*, 116.
65. Hamilton Basso, "William Faulkner: Man and Writer," *The Saturday Review* (July 28, 1962), 11.

ence of Basso's book in Faulkner's library after nearly forty years suggests, as Mick Gidley tactfully remarks, that the book left Basso's hands "due to some voluntary act of Faulkner's part—he 'borrowed' it, bought it, or accepted it as a gift."[66] However he got the book, Faulkner held on to it, perhaps because it provoked the sort of aesthetic epiphany which I have described. As a reaction to *A Modern Book*, "On Criticism" says essentially "why didn't someone tell me?"

I have no time here to précis all the essays collected in *A Modern Book of Criticism*, but I can say generally that they argue that the subjectivity of all art and all criticism is a strength and not a weakness. Lewisohn's introduction insists upon the vitality of art. He is horrified by the "staggering assumption that literature is but an elegant diversion"; instead he argues "literature is a thing of blood and tears."[67] Anatole France speaks of "the eternal verities" (*AMB*, 14)[68] and the inevitable subjectivity of art, for "one never gets out of oneself" (*AMB*, 1). Jules Lemaître argues that the true beauty of a book "cannot be hurt even by breaches of the rules of rhetoric or of convention" (*AMB*, 16)—an argument that must have been gratifying to Faulkner; Lemaître finds the value of the work of art in "the transformation or even the distortion of reality through a mind" (*AMB*, 19). In an essay entitled "The Self and the World," Remy de Gourmont says that art completes men by giving them "the treasure of an immortal idea" (*AMB*, 27). He also insists that the artist "must create his own aesthetic" (*AMB*, 29). Another excerpt from de Gourmont begins "there are two kinds of style; they correspond to the two great classes of men—the visuals and

66. Mick Gidley, "One Continuous Force: Notes on Faulkner's Extra-Literary Reading," *Mississippi Quarterly*, 23 (Summer 1970), 306.

67. Ludwig Lewisohn, ed., *A Modern Book of Criticism* (New York: Boni and Liveright, 1919), ii. Hereafter cited parenthetically as *AMB*.

68. The phrase was also used by J. W. Friend in "Joseph Conrad: An Appreciation," *The Double Dealer*, 7 (October 1924), 34. See Richard P. Adams, "The Apprenticeship of William Faulkner," in *William Faulkner: Four Decades of Criticism*, Linda W. Wagner, ed. (East Lansing: Michigan State University Press, 1973), 20.

the emotionals" (*AMB*, 31); a writer like Flaubert who belongs to both classes can be, as Faulkner hoped to be, "master of the whole art of writing" (*AMB*, 32). John Cowper Powys, whose novel Faulkner would review in March of 1925 (or at least that is when the review would be printed), speaks of the value of reading for pleasure "with real unscrupulousness" (*AMB*, 140)—a now-familiar Faulknerian notion. Hugo Von Hofmannstal asserts that all literature "derives from the few great books of the world" and, in a comment that must have startled Faulkner, he insists that "there is no meaning in making a cheap antithesis and contrasting books with real life" (*AMB*, 71). Robert Mueller-Freienfels speaks of literature and all the arts as a "necessary completion of the practical life" (*AMB*, 75).

Other writers anthologized in *A Modern Book* are less abstract and more censorious. W. L. George protests that "our literary characters are lopsided because their ordinary traits are fully portrayed, analyzed with extraordinary minuteness, while their sex life is cloaked, minimised or left out" so that characters in most fiction are "megacephalous and emasculate" (*AMB*, 132). H. L. Mencken attacks the American public that "can never imagine any work of the imagination as wholly devoid of moral content" (*AMB*, 172). Van Wyck Brooks finds literature in a "state of arrested development" (*AMB*, 194) and wonders "how can our literature be anything but impotent?" (*AMB*, 198).

Such criticism would have confirmed Faulkner's sense of the inadequacies of much of the art around him, but the book's overall emphasis upon art as expression of the poet's soul, as in Joel Spingarn's essays, must have validated Faulkner's desire to write passionately and truly by tapping his emotions and his understandings. That ideal appears in many guises in *A Modern Book*, but perhaps most explicitly in an essay by John Cowper Powys. Powys says "the real art of criticism only begins when we shake ourselves free of all books and win access to that locked and sealed and uncut volume which is the book of our own feelings" (*AMB*, 139). If the best criticism is subjective, so is the best literature. In Anatole France's words, "every novel, rightly understood, is an autobiography" (*AMB*, 1). The debt Faulkner owed to the understanding of the self and art he found in Powys, France, de Gourmont, Spingarn, and other critics anthologized in *A Modern Book* is at least suggested by the paraphrase of de Gourmont he made to Malcolm Cowley some nineteen years later, "I am telling the same story over and over, which is myself and the world."[69] Faulkner came to understand that art must mediate between the self and the world, the artist and his material, artifice and representation, formal and naturalistic standards. Such mediation is not always cordial. Faulkner's most graphic metaphor for it occurs in one of the introductions for *The Sound and the Fury* he wrote in 1933. There he says the Southern writer "has figuratively speaking taken the artist in him in one hand and his milieu in the other and thrust the one into the other like a clawing and spitting cat into a croker sack."[70] But however incompatible the artist and the milieu may seem, powerful art requires their union.

A great many things made 1924–25 an important transition period for Faulkner: he published his first collection of poems; he arrived in New Orleans with what must have been a portfolio of fiction, poetry, and exposition; the *Double Dealer* published "New Orleans," "On Criticism," and "The Dying Gladiator" before Faulkner had been in the Crescent City for two months; the *Times-Picayune* published his series of prose sketches and paid him for them; New Orleans freed him from various small town prejudices about art, sex, work, and whisky; important friends like Elizabeth and Sherwood Anderson valued his company; he learned to be easy in his own flesh; he wrote his first novel.[71] And somehow he transcended the aesthetic dilemma that had plagued him for four years. His first critical readings had set up

69. Malcolm Cowley, *The Faulkner-Cowley File: Letters and Memories, 1944–1962* (New York: The Viking Press, 1966), 14.

70. *A Faulkner Miscellany*, 158.

71. I develop these ideas further in the essay "Faulkner's Cubist Novels," given three years ago at this conference. See *"A Cosmos of My Own": Faulkner and Yoknapatawpha 1980*, Doreen Fowler and Ann J. Abadie, eds. (Jackson: University of Mississippi Press, 1981), 59–94.

that dilemma; his latest seem to have liberated him from it. Until 1925 he had listened to other writers. Elie Faure told him to listen to the voices. *A Modern Book of Criticism* told him to listen to himself not by projecting his frustrations but by delving deep within his psyche where he would find the forms which were at once aesthetically and humanly satisfying.

Believing these critics, he seems to have made a quantum leap beyond imitation and beyond division. His later writings are filled with references both to literary and to nonliterary sources. But they are no longer imitations but allusions. The difference between those terms is not a simple one, but Faulkner's own comments about his reading may help to clarify it. In the other introduction to *The Sound and the Fury* he describes his reading process as devouring and forgetting:

> I discovered then [when he had finished *The Sound and the Fury*] that I had gone through all that I had ever read, from Henry James through Henty to newspaper murders, without making any distinction or digesting any of it, as a moth or a goat might. After The Sound and The Fury and without needing to open another book and in a series of delayed repercussions like summer thunder, I discovered the Flauberts and Dostoievskys and Conrads whose books I had read ten years ago. With The Sound and The Fury I learned to read and quit reading, since I have read nothing since.[72]

Faulkner is speaking of literary readings, and he exaggerates, but the metaphor of omnivorous, unselected ingesting of various often incompatible materials which nourish only when he forgets them occurs often enough in Faulkner's comments about himself for us to grant the metaphor some measure of validity. Certainly Faulkner devoured (and regurgitated if I may pursue

72. William Faulkner, "An Introduction to *The Sound and The Fury*," James B. Meriwether, ed., *The Southern Review*, ns. 8 (Summer 1972), 708.

73. "Sherwood Anderson," 89.

74. Ibid., 89, 90, and 91.

75. Ibid., 89.

76. Ibid., 90.

77. Ibid., 93.

the metaphor) various critical and aesthetic readings with a goat-like lack of selectivity. Before 1924/5 he lifted ideas and glibly repeated them, but after this crucial turning point, he remained indebted to Bell, Faure, and the various writers in *A Modern Book*, but he no longer merely echoed them. Instead, he transmuted his now-forgotten sources into his own aesthetic.

The last critical piece Faulkner wrote in the crucial New Orleans period was entitled "Sherwood Anderson," and printed in *The Dallas Morning News* on April 26, 1925. In that essay Faulkner offers a synthesis of concepts from Bell (simplicity and brevity),[73] appreciations from Faure (lustiness, masculinity, and pride in the body) and language from Faure ("youthful pagan desire"),[74] and understandings, derived from *A Modern Book*, of the necessary subjectivity of art. For instance, in the second paragraph Faulkner refers to "that belief, necessary to a writer, that his own emotions are important."[75] He speaks of Anderson's "ability to pry into the souls of these people" and to maintain "sympathy for them."[76] And he finally attributes Anderson's failures "to the fact that Mr. Anderson is interested in his relations to other people, and very little in himself. That is, he has not enough active ego to write successfully of himself."[77] Former contradictions now seem resolved in Faulkner's conviction that a strong art of commanding form can only emerge from an intensely subjective vision.

The dichotomy Faulkner had at first seen between standards of form and standards of realism had been a false dichotomy. What Faulkner discovered, with the help of the essayists in *A Modern Book*, was that if the artist could delve into the deepest level of his or her own psyche then form and content would be inseparable. Faulkner's gift was, first, an ability to take traditions, as we have seen here with critical and aesthetic writings, to absorb and perhaps forget them, and finally to transmute them. It was, second, an ability to trust in his own talent to tell stories of human consequence in fresh experimental forms. And finally, it was an ability to trust to what we might call inspiration or, as both Faulkner and Faure put it, to listen to the voices. It was an amazing gift, but the country man was not a mere passive receptacle or flexible vessel for it.

Faulkner's early essays reveal him on a diligent and conscientious quest for principles upon which to found his art. His fiction reveals the fruit of that quest. With the *New Orleans Sketches* and *Soldiers' Pay* he structured tales about believable characters into what Thomas McHaney has called "post-Impressionist"[78] forms. In *Mosquitoes* he continued to work out theories about aesthetics and the artist's role. In *Flags in the Dust* he crafted an elaborate method of foiling the distorted romanticisms of Horace and Bayard while engaging his reader in a passionate and compelling narrative. And of course with *The Sound and the Fury* he offered an elaborate contrapuntal structure which can be appreciated as pure form (as Kenneth Haxton's symphony patterned after the novel's four movements testified to us on the opening day of the conference), but which also engages our hearts' concerns. The unique achievement of the major work through *Go Down, Moses* was couching humanly compelling stories in startling, nonlinear narrative structures, an achievement Faulkner managed, at least in part, by working his way through theory that at first suggested an inevitable choice and then offered a liberating synthesis.

78. McHaney, 53 and 63. "Post-impressionist" may be preferable to "cubist," the term I used three years ago to describe nonlinear structures, because, though it is less precise, it is more encompassing.

The Art of Ending

Judith Bryant Wittenberg

It is a truth universally acknowledged that a story of respectable pretensions must be in want of an ending. Henry James, who has provided us with so much valuable, if occasionally circumlocutory, commentary on the art of fiction, said about the relationship of a narrative to its ending, "The prime effect of so sustained a system, so prepared a surface, is to lead on and on; while the fascination of following resides, by the same token, in the presumability *somewhere* of a convenient, of a visibly appointed stopping-place."[1] Another novelist, Joyce Cary, viewed the importance of the ending as residing in the fact that "the separate forms [in the novel] do not possess their whole content until the work is complete."[2] Edgar Allan Poe similarly saw the ending as providing a sort of *raison d'être* for the work, saying "it is only with the *dénouement* constantly in view that we can give a plot its indispensable air of consequence, of causation, by making the incidents and especially the tone at all points, tend to the development of the intention."[3]

Just as writers have felt compelled to attempt to articulate their concepts of the relationship of the ending to the whole, some critics have declared themselves theoreticians of closure. Frank Kermode is perhaps the best-known of these; in his 1967 book, *The Sense of an Ending,* Kermode related issues of closure to larger problems of existence, saying that "we live in the mood

---

1. Henry James, Preface to *Roderick Hudson* (Boston: Houghton Mifflin, 1917), vii.
2. Joyce Cary, *Art and Reality* (Cambridge: Cambridge University Press, 1958), 103.
3. Edgar Allan Poe, "The Philosophy of Composition," in *Selected Writings* (Boston: Houghton Mifflin, 1956), 453.

of end-dominated crisis," in a time of eschatological pressures.[4] Because men are born and die *in mediis rebus,* in order to make sense of their span they need fictive concords with origins and ends, such as give meaning to lives and to poems.[5] Clearly, admits Kermode, there are "problems created by the divergence of comfortable story and the non-narrative contingencies of modern reality," but it is nonetheless difficult for even the contemporary novelist to resist what Iris Murdoch has called "the consolations of form."[6] While Kermode's stress in his discussion of endings is thus on the complex and often complementary relationship between art and life—art, as Henry James said, being "all discrimination and selection" while life is "all inclusion and confusion"—other critics have concerned themselves more exclusively with intratextual issues. Marianna Torgovnik, whose recent work is informed by Euclidean metaphors, tells us that "ends enable an informed definition of a work's 'geometry' and set into motion the process of retrospective rather than speculative thinking necessary to discern it—the process of 'retrospective patterning.'"[7] D. A. Miller has described the novel as moving from the "narratable," "the instances of disequilibrium, suspense and general insufficiency from which a given narrative appears to arise," to the "nonnarratable," the "state of quiescence supposedly recovered by a novel at the end." Hence the ending justifies the cessation of narrative and completes the meaning of what has gone before.[8]

Obviously there are some problems inherent in attempting to define such concepts as closure, in discussing the relationship of the ending to the text, indeed even in focusing on such a topic. Henry James derogatorily dismissed what he saw as the overly

4. Frank Kermode, *The Sense of an Ending* (New York: Oxford University Press, 1967), 98.
5. Ibid., 7.
6. Ibid., 128, 130.
7. Marianna Torgovnik, *Closure in the Novel* (Princeton: Princeton University Press, 1981), 5.
8. D. A. Miller, *Narrative and Its Discontents: Problems of Closure in the Traditional Novel* (Princeton: Princeton University Press, 1981), ix, xi.

tidy conclusions to popular novels, calling them "a distribution at the last of prizes, pensions, husbands, wives, babies, millions, appended paragraphs, and cheerful remarks."[9] Subsequently, critics of modernist bias have made it difficult to use such terms as "closed" and "open" to define the endings of novels, for "closed" has become linked with unadventurousness and narrow didacticism, while "open" has come to be a term of approbation, similar to the concept "writerly" which Roland Barthes applies to the contemporary work and contrasts with the traditional or "readerly" narrative. Moreover, J. Hillis Miller has warned us of the impossibility of ever demonstrating whether a given narrative is closed or open, because such seemingly summary endings as marriage or death imply the possibility of subsequent stories about difficulties inherent in a new way of life or about the problems of survivorship; Miller also says that even the traditional ending is both a tying up, a neat knotting leaving no loose threads, and an untying, a combing out of the tangled narrative threads.[10] Obviously Hillis Miller's metaphor offers more of an apparent than an actual paradox, but D. A. Miller also warns us not to enshrine the ending as an all-embracing cause in which the elements of a narrative find their ultimate justification, but instead to consider possible contradictions and ambiguities within closure itself.[11] Marianna Torgovnik offers what is perhaps a deceptively simple test of closure's effectiveness, the honesty and appropriateness of the ending's relationship to the beginning and middle of the text, not the degree of finality or resolution it achieves.[12]

Having thus enunciated the various warning signs marking the brink of the great swamp of closure, I will now proceed to wade in and attempt to navigate my way toward and around Faulkner and his endings, both the endings of exemplary works

9. Henry James, "The Art of Fiction," in *Theory of Fiction*, ed. James E. Miller, Jr. (Lincoln: University of Nebraska Press, 1972), 32.

10. J. Hillis Miller, "The Problematic of Ending in Narrative," *Nineteenth Century Fiction*, 33 (June 1978), 3–7.

11. D. A. Miller, *Narrative and Its Discontents*, xiii.

12. Torgovnik, *Closure in the Novel*, 6.

during his thirty-six year career as a novelist and the ending of that career itself in the final novel, *The Reivers*. Because Faulkner's oeuvre has similarities to that of nineteenth-century "traditional" novelists such as Trollope and Balzac, critical commentary about the endings of such writers is relevant to this discussion. J. Hillis Miller notes that Trollope's work offers an example of the way in which apparently closed novels can always be reopened, because Trollope reintroduces in later novels characters whose lives seemingly have been entirely closed in earlier works[13]—Quentin Compson provides the most obvious comparison here, as the life which draws to a painful close in *The Sound and the Fury* begins again in *Absalom, Absalom!*, and Faulkner of course "resurrected" other of his characters on noteworthy occasions. D. A. Miller writes of Balzac, "Each novel in *La comedie humaine* had a traditional enough ending, but what is left over is demonstrably capable of producing further narrative."[14] Faulkner's novels almost always have something "left over" in the Balzacian sense; even the work which is in some ways both the most traditional and the most "closed," *The Reivers*, provides some provocative—one is tempted to say toothsome, in keeping with one of the motifs of the novel—leftovers which could have provided material for additional narratives.

Despite his affinities with such traditional novelists, Faulkner, as Professor McHaney eloquently demonstrated, was obviously a modernist writer in many significant respects, and his endings offer notable instances of the rather "open" quality of his narratives. A number of Faulkner critics have discussed the implications of the endings of specific novels, and Walter Slatoff treated the question extensively in his critical study of the oxymoronic quality of Faulkner's "polar imagination," which almost inevitably focused on the nature of Faulkner's "last words." Slatoff saw the novels as "striking" in the "extent to which impulse or

---

13. J. Hillis Miller, "The Problematic of Ending in Narrative," 4.
14. D. A. Miller, *Narrative and Its Discontents*, 273.

tension is not released, to which conflict remains unresolved," and as frequently characterized by a state of "deadlock" in which "opposed entities . . . can neither be separated nor reconciled."[15] In Slatoff's view, Faulkner's works rarely progress in the direction of closure; "Instead of moving toward synthesis and resolution, his presentation often provides a suspension of varied or opposed suggestions."[16]

The last pages of *The Sound and the Fury* provide what is perhaps the most noteworthy example of the irresolution or deadlocked quality of Faulkner's endings. Quentin is dead, Caddy is gone, and Jason is obsessed with his pursuit of Miss Quentin; the affirmations of Dilsey's responses to the Easter service and her efforts to nurture and comfort Benjy are succeeded by Luster's petty tortures. He reduces Benjy to a state of anguished moaning first by whispering Caddy's name over and over and next by driving the wrong way around the town square. Jason restores order, so that things "flowed smoothly once more from left to right," each element "in its ordered place," but he does so with his usual peremptory threats and violent behavior. Nothing has been resolved; as Slatoff says, "the ending seems designed not to interpret or to integrate but to leave the various elements of the story in much the same suspension in which they were offered."[17] André Bleikasten agrees, asserting that "no dramatic resolution, whether tragic or comic, is provided; the tensions built up in the course of the narration are left undiminished, and the novel's complexities and ambiguities are as baffling as ever." But Professor Bleikasten disagrees with Slatoff's reduction of the end to a "neutral balancing of contrary views," saying that as part of the quest for order, the writing process, temporarily concluded with the end of the novel, creates an order of its own.[18]

15. Walter J. Slatoff, *Quest for Failure* (Ithaca: Cornell University Press, 1960), 53, 83.

16. Ibid., 143–44.

17. Ibid., 158.

18. André Bleikasten, *The Most Splendid Failure* (Bloomington: Indiana University Press, 1976), 186, 204–5.

Bleikasten also points out that the ending of *The Sound and the Fury* in many ways recapitulates the opening; both depict Benjy with his guardian Luster moaning and whimpering in his prearticulate efforts to express his grief at the loss of his sister Caddy. This tendency toward recapitulation, toward an implicit circular movement back to the initial exposition, characterizes a number of other Faulkner texts, most notably *Light in August*, which shows us Lena Grove back on the road, still expressing her amazement at how far she has progressed in the relatively short time she has been traveling. Of course by the end of the novel, she has progressed in a number of overt ways, acquiring a baby and having replaced its reluctant father, the absent Lucas Burch, with the ardently devoted Byron Bunch. At the same time, Lena has made no significant moral or psychological progress, evincing the same bovine unreflectiveness and subtly manipulative passive-aggressiveness that she did at the outset of the novel, and the somewhat cheering quality of her status at the end of the work as earth mother and desired companion is offset by the grim horror of Joe Christmas's death and castration and the rather ambiguous nature of Hightower's final recognition, which may have occurred just at the point of his death. These recapitulatory endings are all too familiar to the reader of Faulkner and in some sense need no elaboration; others are more difficult to discern, such as the elements present at the ending of *The Mansion* which, Noel Polk has proposed in a recent essay, bring us full circle, thematically and narratively, back to the beginning, not of the novel itself, but of the Snopes trilogy as a whole, thus implying that there is no resolution.[19] Such circularity serves to make the texts in which it is evident self-referential, offering us the vision of a self-contained world; in this respect, closure becomes enclosure as much as finality or disclosure.

Other Faulkner novels, which offer more seemingly traditional forms of closure, often prove, upon closer examination, to

---

19. Noel Polk, "Idealism in *The Mansion*," *Faulkner and Idealism*, ed. Michael Gresset and Patrick Samway, S. J. (Jackson: University Press of Mississippi, 1983), 124.

be at best ambiguous, their apparent resolutions undermined either by the reader's memory of what has gone before or by the subtle problematics of the resolution itself. A case in point is *As I Lay Dying*, which brings to an end the epic journey of the Bundrens and sees Addie at last committed to her desired resting place; at the same time Anse has acquired new teeth and a new wife, the increasingly deranged Darl has been dispatched to an institution, and Cash has apparently replaced his rigidity of outlook with a more mature, flexible vision. Despite the seeming affirmativeness of this ending, however, problems remain; the defiant glare of the new Mrs. Bundren augurs poorly for family dynamics, Dewey Dell's pregnancy will soon become obvious, causing difficulties for herself and her family, and the necessity of Darl's incarceration is called into question by Cash's rather facile efforts to rationalize it. Other endings Faulkner explicitly rendered ambiguous by providing elements that offset more affirmative aspects of the text. The best known of these is the double ending of *The Wild Palms*, in which Harry Wilbourne affirms his need to stay alive and thus to memorialize both his passion for Charlotte Rittenmeyer and Charlotte herself with his eloquent testimony that ends with what is perhaps the best-known of Faulkner's lines, "Between grief and nothing, I will take grief." Wilbourne's affirmation is undermined, however, by the tall convict's bitter memories of the woman who betrayed him and his final coarse and comprehensive rejection of womankind, "Women, s——!"

Other endings are significant not only for their contrapuntal or polyvocal quality, but for the way in which they provide indices to the problems of arriving at an artistic vision that is at once cohesive and psychologically sustaining; even as they comment on the narrative which has preceded them, such endings point out challenges in the process of making art and complexities in its relationship to the artist's life. The sculptor Gordon of *Mosquitoes* achieves an artistic triumph in moving from the abstract and essentially nonhuman vision represented by the marble torso of his "ideal woman" to the "savage verisimilitude" of his mask of Mrs. Maurier that captures the pathos and failures of an actual human life, but he follows his achievement with a trip to a bordello, an act which suggests how little succor the triumphant artifact may provide to one's psycho-sexual life. Similarly, the problems undergone by the reporter in *Pylon* as he attempts to find *les mots justes* for his experience with the doomed and glamorous aviators are represented by his two versions of Roger Shumann's death. The first is heightened and lyrical, describing Shumann as having "lost" to the "competitor . . . Death," but this he discards as inadequate, replacing it with a harsher, more factual version of the event. Despite his recognition of the challenges posed by the double vision almost inevitably engendered in a sensitive observer, the reporter finds no solace in it and angrily departs for a drinking spree.

Another depiction of this problem is provided by the storytelling aspects of the conclusions to *Light in August* and *Absalom, Absalom!* The whole final chapter of the 1932 novel is occupied by the furniture dealer's version of his encounter with, and transportation of, Lena and Byron and her baby. It offers some fine and gentle comedy in its depiction of Byron's dogged attendance on the woman who has awakened his passionate devotion and of his tentative and unsuccessful efforts to attain her bed; moreover, it is in some way about storytelling itself, about the importance, for the teller, of being aware of his audience's needs and perceiving the way in which any tale has potential links to, and implications for, his own life; at the same time it implies that the very act of creating narrative is healthful and order-giving.[20] However, the furniture dealer's portraits of Lena and Byron border on the ridiculous—Lena's excessive concern with propriety seems inappropriate if not bizarre and Byron appears utterly hangdog, evincing the look of a man about to be executed and an extreme timidity. It is a view through the wrong end of a telescope; both Byron's selfless loyalty and Lena's tenacious consistency are seen, reductively, as ludicrous. The end of

20. See Torgovnik, *Closure in the Novel*, 168–75, for a discussion of this.

Absalom, Absalom!, too, raises some of these same issues. Shreve has functioned throughout, via his commentary, as a salutary force for irony and deflation, serving as an anodyne to the demon-ridden vision of Miss Rosa, the heroically tragic conception of Mr. Compson, and the desperately projective account offered by Quentin, in which many of the events become "doubles" of his own haunting experiences. Yet Shreve's dismissive comment on the various narratives and their implications—"The South. Jesus. No wonder you folks all outlive yourself by years and years and years"—which culminates with the ridiculous judgment that the Jim Bonds will conquer the whole western hemisphere is as exaggerated and inadequate as any of the other versions. It obviously, like Quentin and Shreve's joint efforts to reconstruct the story of the Sutpen males, offers little solace to Quentin, who bursts out with his anguished and ambivalent defense of his native region, "I dont. I dont! *I dont hate it! I dont hate it!*"

There is perhaps no particular point in pursuing these issues further, since so many of Faulkner's "last words" are intensely familiar and other critics have explored the implications of many of them. Nor have I time to consider the poetic or rhetorical conclusions which Faulkner used in so many of his texts, especially early in his career. I'd like instead to turn now to *The Reivers* to consider not only the specific ending of the novel but the way in which the work itself closes Faulkner's career. There are some obvious problems with this approach, since while Faulkner was responsible for the ending of the novel, we have no idea whether he in fact saw the work as the last of his oeuvre—indeed, there are things that suggest otherwise, including his announced intention of creating a Golden Book or Doomsday Book which James B. Meriwether has assured us was to be a work quite different from *The Reivers*,[21] and perhaps also Faulkner's awareness of the tragic turmoil brewing in Oxford in

21. James B. Meriwether, "The Novel Faulkner Never Wrote: His *Golden Book* or *Doomsday Book*," *American Literature*, 42 (March 1970), 93–96.

the summer of 1962 which might have impelled him to a serious consideration of racial issues in the vein of *Go Down, Moses*. Still, because *The Reivers* did in fact close Faulkner's career and because, viewed as a final work, it raises some interesting questions, I want to discuss the novel in its totality as an instance of Faulknerian closure.

Rather surprisingly, some few critics, perhaps troubled by the light comedy of *The Reivers*, have treated it as a sort of unimportant postscript to Faulkner's career. When the book first appeared, a reviewer expressed the not uncommon sentiment that it revealed "Faulkner . . . fleeing from the tensions he once faced into a never-never land which is pleasant but unreal,"[22] and even a recent study of Faulkner's Yoknapatawpha comedy omits *The Reivers* from its discussion because the author finds it merely "an engaging and altogether charming 'Afterword.' . . . *The Reivers* remains a kind of coda, a late-blooming comic sport . . . Faulkner wrote it with a new and different pencil—one with a softer lead."[23] Happily, other critics have carefully delineated the novel's close links to Faulkner's previous fiction, showing us, as James Carothers said in his 1980 paper here, that it is "neither a sentimental afterthought, a commercial contradiction, nor a pusillanimous retraction of his great early work, but rather . . . a fully realized articulation of themes and techniques employed throughout his developing career."[24] The road to *The Reivers*, Professor Carothers tells us, was carefully paved by the author.

Considered both in terms of its ending and as a final work, the novel exhibits in intriguing ways elements of that circularity which marked some of Faulkner's previous fiction. Even its

22. Irving Malin, *"The Reivers," Wisconsin Studies in Contemporary Literature*, 3 (Autumn 1962), 250–55.

23. Lyall H. Powers, *Faulkner's Yoknapatawpha Comedy* (Ann Arbor: University of Michigan Press, 1980), 6.

24. James B. Carothers, "The Road to *The Reivers*," in *"A Cosmos of My Own": Faulkner and Yoknapatawpha 1980*, ed. Doreen Fowler and Ann J. Abadie (Jackson: University Press of Mississippi, 1981), 95–124; Elizabeth M. Kerr, *"The Reivers*: The Golden Book of Yoknapatawpha County," *Modern Fiction Studies*, 13 (Spring 1967), 95–113; and Edwin Moses, "Faulkner's *The Reivers*: The Art of Acceptance," *Mississippi Quarterly*, 27 (Summer 1974), 307–18, also discuss the relation of the novel to Faulkner's previous fiction.

highly allusive quality is a manifestation of what one might call literary circularity. Ever since the appearance of Richard P. Adams's 1963 article on "The Apprenticeship of William Faulkner," we have been aware of how highly indebted Faulkner was to a wide variety of literary predecessors, and *The Reivers* is one of his most overtly referential works. Not only does the text itself invoke writers such as Shakespeare and Julius Caesar and works such as the *Faust* of Marlowe or Goethe and Wordsworth's poem "My Heart Leaps Up," it more subtly recalls other works such as *Clarissa*;[25] moreover, critics have delineated its parallels to still other works, including *Huck Finn*, *The Tempest*, Sherwood Anderson's story "I Want to Know Why," and even Melville's *Pierre*. Yet another predecessor with some striking similarities to *The Reivers*, and one of particular importance because it harks back to the period when the novel as a genre was being born and, in embryonic ways, being theorized about, is Fielding's *Tom Jones*. Faulkner owned two copies of *Tom Jones*, one of them a 1931 Modern Library edition which he inscribed in December of that year, the other one also from the Modern Library and published in 1950.[26] In the latter edition, the introduction by George Sherburn makes reference to Fielding's declaration that he intended to give a picture of "the plain simple workings of honest nature," drawn from "the vast authentic doomsday book of nature" (viii). Although James Meriwether has pointed out that Faulkner's reference to his "doomsday" book in his 1956 interview with Jean Stein most likely referred to the Domesday book, the survey of England prepared for William the Conqueror and completed in 1086,[27] it is also possible that Faulkner had assimilated the term from his reading of the Sherburn preface to *Tom Jones*. Whether or not that is the case, it is worth thinking about the Fielding novel in relationship to *The Reivers*, not only because of their many specific similarities but also be-

25. Both the name and the actions of Butch Lovemaiden are similar to those of Richardson's villain.
26. *William Faulkner's Library: A Catalogue*, comp. Joseph Blotner (Charlottesville: University Press of Virginia, 1964), 66.
27. James B. Meriwether, "The Novel Faulkner Never Wrote," 93–96.

cause in them the authors were attempting to achieve some of the same goals. I am of course aware that both writers were indebted to *Don Quixote,* but it is some of the more specific connections between the novels that I want to consider.

In both the 1749 and the 1962 novel the mode is mock-heroic, that especially neo-classical genre which was appropriate to the eighteenth-century idea, as Martin Price has pointed out, that man is both a glory and a jest, the mock form being a fine means of achieving a double perspective, of playing off a pure heroic view against the more pedestrian reality;[28] the genre is, as Austin Warren has put it, "not mockery of the epic but elegantly affectionate homage, offered by a writer who finds it irrelevant to his age."[29] Fielding made use of the mock-heroic in works such as *Joseph Andrews* and *Tom Jones,* filling them with many of the elaborate similes, the energetic battles, and the high rhetoric of epic, all made comic by their application to the struggles of lusty young men and ripe wenches in farmyards or on English highways. In a newspaper article which appeared just a few years before Faulkner began work on *The Reivers,* Kingsley Amis declared that Fielding's humor was closer to that of contemporary writers than that of any writer before the twentieth century, saying contemporary novelists are comparable to Fielding in their attempt to combine the grotesque and the romantic, the farcical and the horrific, within a single novel.[30] Yet what distinguishes Fielding's works from those of many of the contemporary writers that presumably Amis had in mind—and this is also, significantly, true of Faulkner in *The Reivers*—is the double perspective, the combination of a naive hero with a sophisticated narrator who provides us with both distance from and commentary on the experiences of the hero.

Although there are significant differences between the novels, most notably in their protagonists, the one an innocent eleven-

28. Martin Price, *To the Palace of Wisdom* (Garden City: Doubleday-Anchor, 1964), 250–51.
29. Austin Warren, *Rage for Order* (Ann Arbor: University of Michigan Press, 1948), 40.
30. Kingsley Amis, "Laughter to be Taken Seriously," *New York Times Book Review* (July 7, 1957), 1, 13.

year-old boy, the other a sexually active young man who procreates almost as vigorously as he fights, there are parallels in character types, major themes, and narrative method. Fielding was often criticized by his contemporaries for his sympathetic treatment of lowlife—a treatment he shared with the painter Hogarth, to whom he often refers—and his depiction of servants, sexually frank gamekeepers' daughters, and illegitimate sons of the gentry who have obvious parallels in Faulkner's 1962 novel, as they do in much Faulkner fiction. The actual gentleman, Lucius Priest, like the innately gentlemanly Tom Jones, is surrounded by figures who are socially, if not morally, "low," spending most of his time in the novel in a brothel or at a racetrack. Although the protagonists differ in their age and their sexual awareness, not to mention their sexual activity, they are alike in their unworldliness and their basic good nature. Both also embody the essence of knightliness in their chivalrous attitudes toward women; Tom's rescue of Molly from her churchyard battle, like his courageous saving of Sophia when she falls from her horse, has its counterpart in Lucius's brave defense of the honor of Everbe Corinthia, and both males sustain arm or hand wounds which serve as badges of their chivalry. Blifil, who is both Tom's nasty opponent and a sort of evil alter ego, has an obvious parallel in the malignant Otis of *The Reivers*, and their maleficent influence is at least partially offset by the more positive contributions of a series of surrogate fathers; in Tom's case, these are Squire Allworthy and the schoolmaster Partridge, while for Lucius they include, in differing ways, Boon Hogganbeck, Ned McCaslin, Uncle Parsham Hood, and Boss Priest. Both protagonists come through their various trials successfully, and their triumphs are rewarded not only with personal gain but also with a beneficent effect on others around them who experience either remorse or reform.

Among the major themes common to both novels is the necessity of right action, which is expressed in *Tom Jones* not only through the story line but by the repeated discussions of "charity" or "benevolence," while in *The Reivers* one sees it in

Lucius's decent behavior and also in the recurrent references to "responsibility" and "gentlemanliness." Related to this is the concept of tolerance, of the need to accept human nature in all its manifestations: Fielding says that "men of true wisdom and goodness are contented to take persons and things as they are," that "the finest composition of human nature, as well as the finest china, may have a flaw in it" (67–68),[31] while Lucius expresses his inclusive sympathy for "the poor frail victims of being alive" (174)[32] and acknowledges the fact that flaws are an inevitable part of being human. Finally there is the thematic contrast between the city, a place of complexity and sometimes evil, and the country, where things are simpler if not necessarily better; both novels portray a journey to the city and back again, a circular physical movement accompanied by a linear development in the protagonists as they acquire greater knowledge of the world and of human vagaries.

The works also have points of similarity in their method. The double perspective, in which the naiveté of the hero is overlaid with the rhetorical and emotional sophistication of the narrator, as mentioned above, allows us to view the story with both sympathy and ironic detachment. At the same time as the author provides us with a dual vision, he directly involves his audience in the story; Fielding constantly addresses his reader, prefaces to each section reveal the narrator's awareness of ways in which he may be testing the reader's patience—he ends one by saying "as the reader's curiosity (if he hath any) must be now awake, and hungry, we shall provide to feed it as fast as we can" (691)—and he precedes the conclusion with the comment that he and the reader are "like fellow-travellers in a stage-coach, who have passed several days in the company of each other" (819). Faulkner's narrator makes a number of direct addresses to his putative listeners, the young grandchildren to whom he is telling his tale set fifty-six years before, which take the form of parenthetical

---

31. Page references are to the 1950 Modern Library edition.
32. Page references are to William Faulkner, *The Reivers* (New York: Random House, 1962).

explanations or commentary, serving both to reveal his irascibility and garrulousness and to give the storytelling process a certain immediacy. Similarly, Fielding warns his readers early in the narrative, "I intend to digress . . . as often as I see occasion" (5), while the grandfather of *The Reivers* simply digresses without warning, offering histories of Ballenbaugh's or the hunting camp and generic discussions of the automobile or the mule.

You will doubtless have recognized long before now all the marks of a Fieldingesque digression in my own paper. And I confess that I have to some extent developed the comparison for its own sake, as an aspect of the novel that has not thus far been much considered. But I want also to argue, to suggest as a partial answer to one of the questions Professor Millgate raised at this conference, that Faulkner's choice of the Fieldingesque form may supply some indication that he was indeed consciously and deliberately projecting *The Reivers* as a final statement or gesture of some substantial kind. The choice of a journey as structure and motif[33] gave him comfortable license to retraverse the world of earlier novels, encountering on the way a considerable number of Yoknapatawpha characters who had not seen the light of print for many years. The double narrative perspective enabled him to juxtapose songs of innocence with songs of experience, to develop a fairly simplistic and wholly positive fable of right action even at the same time as he shared with the reader—over the heads, so to speak, of his central character and

33. It is tempting to speculate whether Faulkner read another "road" novel whose publication shortly preceded his composition of *The Reivers*, Jack Kerouac's 1957 work, *On the Road*. It deals, like both Fielding's and Faulkner's novels, with "low" life, uses the journey away from home and back again as both a structural and thematic element, makes the developing emotional relationship of the protagonist to his companion[s] a central issue, focuses on the motif of the father both in its literal implications and in its relevance to the need to accept responsibility, and employs, albeit to a lesser degree than its counterparts, a double perspective, as the viewpoint of the protagonist in the moment is contrasted with the more mature vision provided by retrospect. More specific elements in the Kerouac that have parallels in Faulkner's 1962 novel are a trip to a whorehouse and the stress on specific cars, including a Hudson and a Cadillac, the latter of which gets stuck in a ditch and has to be hauled out by a farmer at a cost of $5 which the protagonist can ill afford, in an incident much like that at Hell Creek. However, as we have no record of Faulkner's familiarity with the Kerouac work, this is all pure speculation.

of the grandchildren who are the technical recipients of the narrative as a whole—an older, more mature recognition of the darker aspects of his own created world and of the world at large.

The sense of deliberately sought circularity in *The Reivers* is strengthened further by the way in which the novel refers back not only to *Sanctuary*—itself an offshoot of one of Faulkner's earliest conceptions—but also to *Flags in the Dust*, Yoknapatawpha's founding text. There can at any rate be no doubt that Faulkner's final work, in its referentiality to the novel which initiates his career as the chronicler of Yoknapatawpha, provides a close to his career which structurally recapitulates many of his specific endings.

Although the moods of the two works are quite different, the one gloomy and desperate, the other cheerful and exuberant, the likenesses between Faulkner's first Yoknapatawpha novel and his last one are numerous. In some ways, *The Reivers* almost seems to be a lighthearted reconsideration—reconstruction, if you will—of many of the somber events of *Flags in the Dust*. At the most obvious level, modes of transportation, the automobile and the horse, are central to the works in striking ways; young Bayard Sartoris's destructive fascination with powerful horses and fast cars is reincarnated in a more positive way in Lucius Priest's experience with his grandfather's car and the racehorse Lightning/Coppermine, the one becoming a vehicle bearing him toward the city and a knowledge of the adult world, the other providing a worthy test of his stalwartness and tenacity which he passes with flying colors. In the two works Faulkner also pairs a multigenerational white family with a black one, a device he also employs in works such as *The Sound and the Fury* and *Go Down, Moses;* many of the problems in coping with the past and with change one sees in the Sartoris family are recapitulated in the three generations of Strothers, even as the benevolent paternalism of the Priests finds its parallel in the Hoods, a parallel which Lucius finds comforting in a trying moment. The family myths and all those ghosts in Confederate

uniforms and fighter planes which give young Bayard so much
difficulty reappear in comic fashion in the "family legend" of the
racing mule which Grandfather recounts and in the "ghost" of
Mr. Binford which seems to reign in the brothel even after he
has been banished for gambling at the racetrack (120, 133). Miss
Jenny and Miss Reba play comparable roles in the novels in
which they appear, offering summary comments on and frequently deflating some of the excessive behavior and high
rhetoric of the males around them; their salty statements provide both comedy and a necessary ironic perspective.

To be sure, the parallels between such characterological and
thematic elements are not only apparent to anyone who reads
one work with the other in mind but hardly unique to the two
novels in question; the same might be said about similarities in
aspects of Faulkner's method in the two works, yet their reap-
pearance in the last Yoknapatawpha novel suggests that some
overt recapitulation was intended. In *Flags in the Dust*, for example, one sees Faulkner making use of the comic allusion to
heroic material in the Thanksgiving scene when Simon over-
looks the dining room as "Caesar must have stood looking down
into Gaul, once he had it well in hand, or the Lord God Himself
when he looked down upon His latest chemical experiment and
said It is well" (281);[34] such allusions are frequent in the 1962
novel and increase its humorous effect. Parodic elements in
Flags in the Dust both amplify our sense of the protagonists'
plight—I am thinking here of elements such as the impotent
lechery of Byron Snopes that echoes and exaggerates some of
the frustrations of Horace Benbow and Bayard Sartoris—and
serve somehow to distance us from it, while parody and its
milder counterpart, mimicry, are both explicit and subtle aspects of the method of *The Reivers*. Miss Reba makes sarcastic
reference to Corrie's desire that her nephew learn to "ape" the
good manners of Lucius (102), yet those manners themselves

---

34. Page references are to William Faulkner, *Flags in the Dust* (New York: Random
House, 1973).

seem so out of place in the brothel as to parody the "gentleman's" dedication to decorum regardless of context. Boon is like a parodic version of the mythic hero, a man of mysterious antecedents and awesome strength like his epic predecessors but without the attendant nobility and vision, while Lucius is a caricature of Faust, obsessed with damnation without having committed any serious sin. In *The Reivers*, Faulkner seems to use such elements in part as he did in *Flags in the Dust*, to make aspects of the text interact, but more often to make fun of serious literary forms; he even at points parodies his own technique. His early description of the fleeing Ludus as "still in the frozen attitude of running or frozen in the attitude of running or in the attitude of frozen running, whichever is right" (14), like his description of Sunday in the brothel as "Saturday night's fading tide rip in one last spumy upfling against the arduous humdrum of day-by-day for mere bread and shelter" (139), caricatures his own high rhetoric.

Another aspect of Faulkner's novelistic approach in the 1962 work which echoes that in *Flags in the Dust* is its concern with the storytelling process itself, with the effort to reconstruct events. Characters in both works stress the importance of "lies"; Horace Benbow talks about "lying" as "puny man's . . . struggle for survival" (189), while Lucius asserts that the poet and child are alike in that they "lie for pleasure rather than profit" (53). Lucius later discovers the headiness of not only lying but of being believed when he has successfully prevaricated his way to the brink of imminent departure for Memphis, saying "I had already told more lies than I had believed myself capable of inventing, and had had them believed or at least accepted with a consistency which had left me spellbound if not already appalled" (62). A number of the characters in *Flags* tell "stories" to themselves and others—Miss Jenny, old man Falls, and young Bayard among them—but the power of those narratives to provide meaning to their lives is frequently limited either by their excessive emotional involvement or by the fact that they are entrapped in some sort of repetitive iteration which becomes

almost compulsive. Lucius Priest's telling of the extended narrative which is *The Reivers* is healthier, because he sees it clearly
and sees it whole. He is certain about the nature and meaning of
his material, as evinced in the confident quality of the opening
sentence, "This is the kind of man Boon Hogganbeck was" (3),
but he is also aware of the challenges of making narrative, as he
makes clear in his presentation of the background to Boon's
effort to shoot Ludus, "as reconstructed from Boon and Mr Bal-
lott and John Powell and a little from Ludus himself" (10). He
knows that material must be gleaned from other sources outside
himself, and this awareness, along with the ironic distance from
his own story provided by time and maturity, allows him to
fashion a coherent and valid narrative. At the end of the novel,
Lucius makes a pronouncement which reveals the same
confidence as does his opening statement, even as it recapitulates the theme of lying and ironically links it with his discovery
about what it means to be a gentleman; "a gentleman always
sticks to his lie whether he told it or not" (304).

Although Lucius's narrative is both more coherent and more
objective than those of the various "storytellers" of *Flags in the
Dust*, it is like theirs in being essentially a projective creation.
The story line is pervasively concerned with the use and abuse
of patriarchal authority and the gentleman's code; in this it reveals itself as the product of a man in his mid-sixties who is
implicitly preoccupied both with interrogating and perpetuating
the values by which he was nurtured and to which he has obviously devoted his life. In the opening pages he presents a whole
series of patriarchal figures, including not only the appropriately
nicknamed grandfather, "Boss" Priest, but also Lucius's father,
Judge Stevens, and Sheriff Hampton. Their various "gentleman's" assumptions manage to keep things running smoothly
and the tendency of most of them to assume responsibility for
less able members of the community, such as Dan Grinnup and
Boon Hogganbeck, is admittedly impressive. Yet the portents
for the abrogation or misuse of such authority are evident from
the first; Boon readily collapses the "whole edifice of *entendre-*

de-noblesse" when he steals John Powell's gun, and the arbitrary imposition of the "mutual double-action bonds" by a collusion between Lucius's father and Judge Stevens is faintly troubling, as is Colonel Sartoris's arbitrary anticar decree. Subsequent events reveal more serious abuses of authority, such as the Napoleonic Mr. Binford's rigid decrees about proper Sunday behavior in the brothel whose violation results in a fine and the law officer Butch Lovemaiden's exploitation of his position to secure sexual favors from Corrie. By the end of the novel, however, order has been restored in all respects; the introduction of additional positive paternal figures such as Uncle Parsham Hood and the constable Poleymus do much to offset Lucius's distressing encounters with abusive authorities, while his own incipient Boss-hood, evident from the first in his intelligent ability to take charge of difficult situations, finds its culmination in his acceptance of responsibility for the fates of those who have been in some way dependent on him. He has become a priest indeed, at once a mediator and an important authority figure. The resolution of the novel, so reassuring in these ways, is also triumphantly masculine; it celebrates both the ascendancy of a patriarchal code in which "a gentleman accepts the responsibility of his actions and bears the burden of their consequences" (302) and the arrival of a youth at moral manhood by having met and overcome a series of traditional male challenges. One can imagine that the grandchildren being addressed are male as well, for women are not only a separate society in this work, their values seem almost entirely irrelevant; it is about the assertion, interrogation, and reassertion of an essentially masculine code.

If *The Reivers* elaborates fully on the concept of the projective quality of narrative Faulkner first adumbrated in *Flags in the Dust,* their endings are also strikingly similar; both conclude with the birth of a baby whose ambiguous heritage raises poignant questions about its future. Benbow Sartoris's prospects seem questionable at best, and even Lucius Priest Hogganbeck, whose name represents the ultimate tribute to the triumphs of his namesake, may well face a struggle between his biological

inheritance and his moral heritage, much like that undergone by
Colonel Sartoris Snopes of "Barn Burning." The baby is perhaps
the most striking instance of what is "left over" at the end of *The
Reivers* in the manner of Balzac, providing potential material for
a subsequent text, but it is worth thinking about additional ambiguities before considering the way in which the novel otherwise provides an appropriate finale to Faulkner's oeuvre. One
can imagine Corrie's difficulties living in Jefferson, with the
truths about her background likely to come to light and to en-
rage the good Baptist ladies; the experiences of Ruby Lamar and
Eula Varner provide a useful gloss on this potentiality. The narrator is obviously soon to die, as portended by the death of a
grandfather which sets the central action of the novel into motion, as Professor Kinney has noted.[35] This will perhaps cause, as
Hillis Miller says, problems for the survivors. And one wonders
about the usefulness of the story's moral to the listening grandchildren, soon to confront the racial and political turbulence of
the 1960s. For the values central to *The Reivers* are conservative; the grandchildren may find them as ill-suited to deal with a
world marked by change and upheaval as young Bayard Sartoris
discovered his own figurative inheritance to be.

The ambiguities still in evidence at the close of *The Reivers*
are certainly Faulknerian and undoubtedly appropriate—
"appropriateness" being, in Marianna Torgovnik's terms, the
only fair test of the effectiveness of an ending. While perhaps
traditional in many ways and thus vulnerable to the criticism of a
Jamesian for its distribution at the last of prizes, wives, babies,
and cheerful remarks, the ending of *The Reivers* does not offer
the sort of closure that would preclude any subsequent exploration of its implications; there are adequate "left-overs" for future
novels or short stories, had Faulkner lived to work on them. At
the same time, the novel as a whole provides a fitting conclusion
to Faulkner's career, recapitulating, in circular manner, themes

---

35. Arthur F. Kinney, *Faulkner's Narrative Poetics* (Amherst: University of Massachusetts Press, 1978), 74.

and patterns from his earlier work but essentially recasting them. Fieldingesque in its humor, tolerance, and method, *The Reivers* presents a world characterized by plenitude, harmony, and the possibility of moral growth. If previous Faulkner works were bleak and centrifugal, *The Reivers* is comic and centripetal; in its continuity with and departure from earlier novels, it is thus both a valedictory and, potentially, a commencement.

Contributors

Sonja Bašić is Associate Professor of English at Zagreb University, Yugoslavia. She has published articles on a wide variety of American authors, including Poe, James, Barth, Whitman, Fitzgerald, and Plath. She has also translated American plays for performances in Yugoslavia. In 1983 she was a visiting professor of English at New York University.

André Bleikasten is Professor of English at the University of Strasbourg, France. He has published numerous works on Faulkner in French and in English. Among the latter are *Faulkner's "As I Lay Dying," The Most Splendid Failure: Faulkner's "The Sound and the Fury," William Faulkner's "The Sound and the Fury": A Critical Casebook,* and an essay in *Faulkner and Idealism: Perspectives from Paris.* Professor Bleikasten is, along with François Pitavy, in charge of the continuation of the French edition of Faulkner in the Gallimard Pléiade series.

Louis Daniel Brodsky has published poetry in *Harper's, Texas Quarterly, Southern Review, American Scholar,* and other journals. His twelfth book of poems, *Mississippi Vistas,* and *Faulkner: A Comprehensive Guide to the Brodsky Collection, Volume I: The Biobibliography,* and *Volume II: The Letters,* with Robert W. Hamblin, were recently published by the University Press of Mississippi.

Panthea Reid Broughton is the author of *William Faulkner: The Abstract and the Actual,* coauthor of *Literature,* and editor of *Walker Percy: Stratagems for Being.* She has also published numerous articles about Faulkner and reviewed Faulkner studies for several issues of *American Literary Scholarship: An Annual.* She is Professor of English at Louisiana State University.

James B. Carothers is Professor of English at the University of Kansas, where he also serves as fiction editor of *The Cotton-*

wood Review. At the 1980 Faulkner and Yoknapatawpha Conference he presented two lectures, "The Road to *The Reivers*" and "The Myriad Heart: The Evolution of the Faulkner Hero." His *William Faulkner's Short Stories* is to be published as part of the Studies in Modern Literature Series.

Sergei Chakovsky is a research fellow at the A. M. Gorky Institute of World Literature in Moscow. He specializes in Faulkner studies as well as literary theory and the depiction of blacks in American literature. At last year's conference he lectured on "William Faulkner in Soviet Literary Criticism" and participated in planning meetings for a joint USA-USSR Faulkner project.

James Hinkle, Professor of English at San Diego State University, is a seven-year veteran of the Faulkner and Yoknapatawpha Conference. He has published extensively on Hemingway, whose work is his other chief interest besides that in Faulkner.

Arthur F. Kinney is Professor of English at the University of Massachusetts, Amherst. He has lectured and published widely on Faulkner here and abroad during the past two decades. He is author of *Faulkner's Narrative Poetics: Style As Vision*, editor of *Critical Essays on William Faulkner: The Compson Family,* and coeditor of *Bear, Man, and God: Seven Approaches to William Faulkner's "The Bear."*

Ilse Dusoir Lind is Professor of English at New York University. She has presented numerous papers and published several articles on Faulkner's works, including "The Teachable Faulkner," "The Design and Meaning of *Absalom, Absalom!*," "Faulkner and Racism," and "Faulkner's *Mosquitoes:* A New Reading." For several years Professor Lind has chaired the Special Faulkner Session at the Modern Language Association national meeting.

Thomas L. McHaney is Professor of English at Georgia State University. His publications include *William Faulkner's "The Wild Palms": A Critical Study* and *William Faulkner: A Reference Guide.* He has also published numerous articles about

Faulkner and other figures in American literature and more than a dozen short stories.

Michael Millgate, Professor of English at the University of Toronto, is author of *The Achievement of William Faulkner* and coeditor of *Lion in the Garden: Interviews with William Faulkner 1926–1962*. Among other distinguished books he has written are *American Social Fiction* and *Thomas Hardy: His Career as a Novelist.*

Berndt Ostendorf, Professor of American Cultural History at the University of Munich, has a distinguished record of teaching and publishing in both Germany and the United States. Universities in this country at which he has taught include the University of Pennsylvania, the University of Massachusetts at Amherst, and Harvard University. Among his publications are *Der Mythos in der Modernen Welt: Eine Untersuchung des amerikanischen Myth Cricitism* and *Black Literature in White America.*

P. V. Palievsky is a well-known Soviet specialist in the fields of theory of literature and foreign literature. He is author of *Literature and Theory* and many articles on William Faulkner and other American and European authors. His influential "Faulkner's Road to Realism" was translated and published in *Soviet Criticism of American Literature in the Sixties: An Anthology.* Professor Palievsky is Deputy Director of the A. M. Gorky Institute of World Literature.

Noel Polk is author of *Faulkner's "Requiem for a Nun": A Critical Study* and editor of *William Faulkner: "The Marionettes," "Requiem for a Nun": A Concordance to the Novel,* and *"Sanctuary": The Original Text.* He has written many articles on Faulkner and other Southern writers and is coeditor of *An Anthology of Mississippi Writers.* Professor Polk teaches at the University of Southern Mississippi.

James G. Watson is the author of *The Snopes Dilemma: Faulkner's Trilogy* and numerous articles about Faulkner and other American writers. He has chaired panels on Faulkner at national meetings of the Modern Language Association and is now working on a book about Faulkner's short stories. He is Professor of English at the University of Tulsa.

Judith Bryant Wittenberg is Assistant Professor of English at Simmons College in Boston. She is the author of *Faulkner: The Transfiguration of Biography* and "William Faulkner: A Feminist Consideration" in *American Novelists Revisited: Essays in Feminist Criticism.* She has also published numerous articles and book reviews.

Index

Inner monologue, 304, 305, 307, 308, 313
Intruder in the Dust (Faulkner), 3, 22, 26, 28, 121, 137, 168
Isaac, facts about the name, 195–96
Isham, pronunciation of, 183
Isom, pronunciation of, 179
Issetibbeha, pronunciation of, 176–77

Jefferson, facts about the city, 196
Jenny, facts about the name, 196–97
Jews, 119–42; agrarian anti-Semitism, 132–33; anti-Semitism in Faulkner, 120–25, 130–33; anti-Semitism in literature, 120; Friedmans of Oxford, 126–30, 133–36; Holocaust, 138–39, 140; pro-Jewish characterizations *(The Mansion)*, 140–42; in the South, 125–30; stereotypes in Faulkner, 121; in *The Town*, 135–39; in Yoknapatawpha, 135–42
Jody, pronunciation of, 177
Jubal, pronunciation of, 183
Judicial system, in *Sanctuary*, 77
"Justice, A," (Faulkner), 156, 224

"Killers, The," (Hemingway), 214–18, 312–13
Knight's Gambit (Faulkner), 26, 28, 121, 140, 156, 203, 207
Kohl, Barton, 141
Kohl, Linda Snopes, 141
Kutzik, Alfred J., 120–21, 136

Labove, pronunciation of, 179
Lamar, Ruby, 75
"Landing in Luck," (Faulkner), 202, 225
Legate, pronunciation of, 183
"Leg, The," 219–23
Lessep, pronunciation of, 184
Letters, 228–53; Abelard/Heloise letters, 248–51; "Al Jackson's Letters," 234; collection of, 229–30; Faulkner's to his father, 231–32; Faulkner's to his mother, 230–31; from Europe, 231–32; *Helen: A Courtship*, 234; in *Absalom, Absalom!*, 237–39; in *Light in August*, 237; in *Requiem for a Nun*, 239–42, 252; to Joan Williams, 244–45; *Mayday*, 234, 243; to Meta Carpenter, 243–44; real and fictional lovers and, 246–52; self-characterization in, 233; in *The Sound and the Fury*, 235–37; Temple Drake's letters, 240–43, 246–47, 251
Lettres persanes effect, 104–05
Levitt, pronunciation of, 177
"L'Homme," Ikkemotubbe, 156

"Liar, The," (Faulkner), 58, 225
Light in August (Faulkner), 13, 23, 28, 29, 30, 33, 35, 36, 41, 44, 83, 86–93, 164, 237, 363, 365
"Lion," (Faulkner), 156, 208
Literary views, 270–82; Faulkner's later views, 271–72, 281–82; Faulkner's literary criticism, 271; Faulkner's sense of history and, 277–78; human person in fiction, 279; individuality versus isolation, 280; national character and, 278–79; "native soil," perspective, 274–77; nonliterary position of Faulkner, 273–74; view of modern fiction, 279–80
"Literature and War," (Faulkner), 340–41
Little Belle, 68, 76
Little Sister Death, 79
Liveright, Horace, 233, 235
"Lizards in Jamshyd's Courtyard," (Faulkner), 208, 225
Louvinia, pronunciation of, 184
Loving Gentleman, A (Wilde), 230, 243
Ludus, pronunciation of, 179
Lycurgus, Jason, 157

MacCallum family, 146
Maclachan, pronunciation of, 184
Maclachan, Quentin, 156
Mahon, Donald, 153
Mallison, Chick, 135–37, 168
Mannigoe, Nancy, 26, 252
Mansion, The (Faulkner), 22, 25, 26, 27, 28, 121, 138, 139–42, 156
Marble Faun, The (Faulkner), 20, 339
Marionettes, The (Faulkner), 338, 339
Maurier, Mrs., 153
Maury, pronunciation of, 185
Mayday (Faulkner), 234, 243
Mayes, Will, 82
McCallum, pronunciation of, 179
McCannon, Shreve, facts about the name, 200
McCarron, pronunciation of, 179
McCaslin family, 144–45, 161–62; pronunciation of name, 177
McEachern, Mrs., 88, 89, 91
McEachern, pronunciation of, 184
McEachern, Simon, 85, 88, 89
McKnight, Son, 160–61
McWillie, pronunciation of, 179
Meloney, pronunciation of, 179
Memorabilia, collecting Faulkner, 254–69
Men Working (J. Faulkner), 59
Meriwether, James B., 206
Millard, pronunciation of, 185

/813.52F263YFW>C1/